OPINION AND REFORM IN HUME'S

POLITICAL PHILOSOPHY

OPINION AND REFORM IN HUME'S POLITICAL PHILOSOPHY

John B. Stewart

PRINCETON UNIVERSITY PRESS

PRINCETON, NEW JERSEY

LIBRARY OF CONGRESS CATALOGING-IN-PUBLICATION DATA

STEWART, JOHN B. (JOHN BENJAMIN), 1924–

OPINION AND REFORM IN HUME'S POLITICAL PHILOSOPHY/ JOHN B.
STEWART.

P. CM.

INCLUDES BIBLIOGRAPHICAL REFERENCES AND INDEX.

ISBN 0-691-08626-5

1. HUME, DAVID, 1711–1776—CONTRIBUTIONS IN POLITICAL SCIENCE.

2. HUME, DAVID, 1711–1776—CONTRIBUTIONS IN POLITICAL ETHICS.

I. TITLE.

JC176.H9S74 1992 320'.01–DC20 91-35909

THIS BOOK HAS BEEN COMPOSED IN LINOTRON SABON

PRINCETON UNIVERSITY PRESS BOOKS ARE
PRINTED ON ACID-FREE PAPER, AND MEET THE GUIDELINES
FOR PERMANENCE AND DURABILITY OF THE COMMITTEE
ON PRODUCTION GUIDELINES FOR BOOK LONGEVITY
OF THE COUNCIL ON LIBRARY RESOURCES

PRINTED IN THE UNITED STATES OF AMERICA

1 3 5 7 9 10 8 6 4 2

CONTENTS

PREFACE

W HEN I BEGAN reading Hume in the 1950s, few studies of his moral and political philosophy were available; at that time scholarly work was focused almost exclusively on his episte-mology. Since then, however, not only has Book I of the *Treatise* retained its place as a work of fundamental importance in philosophy, but scholars have gone forward to study Hume's views on "moral subjects"—eco-nomics, government, and history. In writing the chapters here presented, I have benefited greatly from books and articles by that large company of scholars who now study eighteenth-century British moral philosophy.

It is a polite, industrious company. To acknowledge here all the obli-gations I have incurred among its members would be impossible. Suffice it to say that I have profited from many works, perhaps learning more from authors with whom I disagreed—for example, those prominently mentioned in this book—than from many of those with whom I agreed. However, certain scholars must be singled out for thanks—and to do so is a great pleasure—because they participated directly in the writing of this book. Professor M. M. Goldsmith, then of Exeter University, En-gland, and now of Victoria University, Wellington, New Zealand, made perceptive observations on chapters 2, 5, and 6. Professor Russell Hardin, of the University of Chicago, commented constructively on the entire manuscript; he was especially helpful in showing me how best to marshal my argument that Hume was not a conservative. I owe most to Professor David Fate Norton of McGill University. He read the entire manuscript at two stages of its development; on both occasions he proposed some major and many minor changes. I am grateful to these scholars: they prompted important improvements; yet they were content to let me write my own book.

In 1979–1980 when, as a member of the faculty of St. Francis Xavier University, Antigonish, Nova Scotia, I was beginning the research that produced this book, I was assisted by a sabbatical leave award from the Humanities and Social Science Research Council of Canada. With plea-sure I record my gratitude.

BIBLIOGRAPHIC NOTE

Editions of Hume's works used:

A Treatise of Human Nature. Edited by L. A. Selby-Bigge. Second edition by P. H. Nidditch (Oxford: Clarendon Press, 1978). Cited as *Treatise* and, for page references in the text, as *T*.

Enquiries concerning Human Understanding and concerning the Principles of Morals. The 1777 edition, edited by L. A. Selby-Bigge. Third edition by P. H. Nidditch (Oxford: Clarendon Press, 1975). *An Enquiry concerning the Principles of Morals* is cited in the footnotes as *Enquiry* II and, for page references in the text, as *E*.

The History of Great Britain: The Reigns of James I and Charles I. First edition. Republished with an introduction by Duncan Forbes (Harmondsworth: Penguin Books Ltd., 1970). Cited as *History of Great Britain*.

The History of England from the Invasion of Julius Caesar to The Revolution in 1688, 6 vols. Reprint of the 1778 edition with a foreword by W. B. Todd (Indianapolis: Liberty Fund Inc., 1983). Cited as *History of England* and, for page references in the text, as *H*.

Essays: Moral, Political, and Literary. Reprint of the 1777 edition (with an apparatus of variant readings from the 1889 edition by T. H. Green and T. H. Grose) with a foreword and editorial additions by E. F. Miller (Indianapolis: Liberty Fund Inc., 1985). Cited as *Essays*.

The Natural History of Religion and Dialogues concerning Natural Religion, the former edited by A. W. Colver, the latter by J. V. Price (Oxford: Clarendon Press, 1976).

The Letters of David Hume, 2 vols. Edited by J.Y.T. Greig (Oxford: Clarendon Press, 1932). Cited as *Letters*.

New Letters of David Hume. Edited by Raymond Klibansky and E. C. Mossner (Oxford: Clarendon Press, 1954). Cited as *New Hume Letters*.

OPINION AND REFORM IN HUME'S

POLITICAL PHILOSOPHY

INTRODUCTION

ABOUT ten years ago I began to write a few chapters on the politics of Adam Smith. Almost immediately I saw that to prepare
myself I would have to revive, and perhaps correct, my knowledge of Hume, on whose moral and political philosophy I had published
a book in 1963. Soon my plan changed so that what I had in prospect
was two short volumes: one on Hume, the other on Smith. I had in mind
an account that showed these two North Britons analyzing the needs of
their times and prescribing for them; it was to be lucid and uncompli-
cated, the kind of account that would help the ordinary reader. Parts of
chapters 3, 4, and 6 of the present book were written on that plan; with
what success each reader will decide.

First and foremost, Hume was a moral and political philosopher. Having shown in Book I of the *Treatise* that the "moral subjects" deal with
beliefs about facts and values and with the results of those beliefs, Hume
proceeded in his later writings to examine the origins and reliability of
moral and political beliefs. Immediately a question arises: what effect did
the prominence of belief in Hume's epistemology have on his politics? In
1981 David Miller published *Philosophy and Ideology in Hume's Political Thought*.[1] There is much to be praised about that book, but it is misleading in one fundamental respect: while finding that Hume was a revolutionary in philosophy, it holds that Hume's political theory is basically
conservative, that his theory is an establishment ideology. Miller contends that Hume accepted and defended the social status quo; he married
a revolutionary philosophy to an establishment ideology "to yield what
is probably the best example we have of a secular and sceptical conservative political theory" (p. 2). Then, in 1984, came Donald W. Livingston's work, *Hume's Philosophy of Common Life*, which praises Hume
as the originator of the only true political philosophy, conservatism.[2] In
the following year, Frederick G. Whelan published *Order and Artifice in
Hume's Political Philosophy*.[3] Although finding elements of liberalism in
Hume's writings, he too presents Hume as a conservative. Hume's theory,
he says, lacks "the common liberal confidence in reason as the source or
foundation of the social order" (p. 363). Major differences of approach
appear in these three books; however all share, with variations, the nine-
teenth-century view that Hume's epistemology led him to conservatism.

[1] Oxford: Clarendon Press, 1981.
[2] Chicago: The University of Chicago Press, 1984.
[3] Princeton: Princeton University Press, 1985.

That view was stated by J. S. Mill: "This [Hume's] absolute scepticism in speculation very naturally brought him round to Toryism in practice; for if no faith can be had in the operations of human intellect, and one side of every question is about as likely as another to be true, a man will commonly be inclined to prefer that order of things which, being no more wrong than every other, he has hitherto found compatible with his private comforts."[4] In reaction to these works, I draw together, in chapters 5 and 6, what I hope is a more accurate analysis of Hume's politics. I agree that there is a connection between his epistemology and his politics; my submission, however, is that Hume is liberal, not conservative, in politics.

Hume sought to put moral subjects on "a new footing"; he sought, as the title of the *Treatise* announces, to introduce "the experimental Method of Reasoning into Moral Subjects." In a famous footnote to the introduction of the *Treatise*, he names some of the writers whom he regarded as pioneers of the new approach. In 1980 J. L. Mackie began his book *Hume's Moral Theory* with a chapter dealing with most of those writers, and also with Clarke and Wollaston, exponents of the approach rejected by Hume.[5] That chapter serves admirably to introduce the reader to the philosophical war into which Hume plunged when he published the *Treatise*. Impressed by that chapter, I undertook to make my own examination of major precursors. I concluded that Grotius and Pufendorf had to be included; without them the need for a "new footing" might not be understood. Although Hume cites Grotius only once in his works and Pufendorf not at all—both are mentioned in an early letter—the content of his political science is much like theirs on many questions; however, as stated, Hume thought that Shaftesbury, Mandeville, and the others were wise to turn to human nature as the basis of moral subjects. Why? What was wrong with the natural-jurisprudence approach? In chapters 1 and 2 of this book, I undertake, first, to show why attempts to derive systems of natural morality from supernatural sources were unsuccessful and, second, to show the nature and promise of the approach taken by Shaftesbury, Mandeville, and so on. These writers, in turn, had their own predecessors, many of them French or classical; however, it is not my business to report on the findings of scholars now hard at work discovering the more remote sources of Hume's famous "new Scene of Thought." Relying on the reader's knowledge of Hobbes and Locke, I make only passing references to those writers, important though they were.

In addition, in those two chapters I call attention to some of the leading

[4] John Stuart Mill, "Bentham" in *Essays on Ethics, Religion and Society*, ed. J. M. Robson, in *Collected Works of John Stuart Mill* (Toronto: University of Toronto Press, 1969), 10:80.

[5] *Hume's Moral Theory* (London: Routledge & Kegan Paul, 1980).

topics in public morality dealt with by Grotius, Pufendorf, Shaftesbury, Mandeville, and others and explain briefly the positions those writers took on them. Here we find antecedents of Hume's discussions of the origin and nature of sovereign power, the limits of allegiance, private property, commerce, luxurious living, and the management of religion. We see, for example, that Hume's analysis of justice as a negative virtue was not new. We see, also, that certain concepts—humanity, avarice and ambition, benevolence, sympathy, the impartial observer, the "wise and virtuous man"—had been defined and given currency long before Hume (and Adam Smith) employed them. We will understand better what Hume wrote on moral subjects if we see him as a bold, new combatant in an old war and know something of how that war stood when he ventured upon the field.

In 1975 the civic humanist tradition was given new prominence by J.G.A. Pocock in *The Machiavellian Moment.*[6] Since then much ink has been spread in an effort to show that this tradition was pervasive in British and American thought during the eighteenth century; writer after writer, including Hume and Smith, has been assayed for civic humanism. I doubt that it is possible to unravel the political discourse of the eighteenth century so that party spokesmen confidently can be labeled as belonging to one tradition and as opposed to another; there will be points of agreement and overlapping. What we find, after investigation, is that although Hume based the principles of civil society on a natural, not a supernatural, foundation, the content of his political theory is far closer to natural-law theory than to civic humanism.

That Hume, although a man of the enlightenment, was antirationalist is a dogma of orthodox intellectual history. But was he? Shaftesbury and Hutcheson, for different reasons, had sought a natural basis for morals; they had turned away from both the contemporary versions of natural law, for both, the rationalist and the voluntarist alike, taught, not natural law, but supernatural law. Both versions sought to derive the content and the obligation of natural law from God, from either His reason or His will. Hume followed Shaftesbury and Hutcheson. When we say that Hume was antirationalist, do we mean that he was opposed to the rationalist version of theological morality or to the voluntarist version of theological morality? Or both? And is it antirationalist to be opposed to theological morality in either version, or both?

Having found both theological versions of natural law defective, Hutcheson contended that the ends human beings seek are appointed by the passions; however, he never said that reason is unimportant in the

---

[6] *The Machiavellian Moment: Florentine Political Thought and the Atlantic Republican Tradition* (Princeton: Princeton University Press, 1975).

selection of the means by which those ends are to be sought; indeed, he attributes the differences in morality around the world to differences in the advance of reason. Again, Hume follows Hutcheson; but he differs from him in that he emphasizes the importance of reason far more strongly. Reason, which distinguishes human beings from beasts, is the cause of civilization. Is this antirationalism? Moreover, Hume is quite ready to uphold natural law and natural rights—insisting, obviously, on naturalistic, not theological, definitions. He believed that the opinion that there are natural laws and thus natural rights is well founded. Notwithstanding that its constitutional lawyers may announce that a government has absolute power, and that its priests may teach that it has such power by divine right, no government ought to ignore, or to be permitted to ignore, those natural laws and rights. Certain articles of Magna Carta, we are told in the *History of England*, provide for "the equal distribution of justice, and free enjoyment of property; the great objects for which political society was at first founded by men, which the people have a perpetual and unalienable right to recal, and which no time, nor precedent, nor statute, nor positive institution, ought to deter them from keeping ever uppermost in their thoughts and attention" (*H.*, 1:445). Again, in *An Enquiry concerning the Principles of Morals*, we are told, "Where a civil law is so perverse as to cross all the interests of society, it loses all its authority, and men judge by the ideas of natural justice, which are conformable to those interests" (*E.*, 197n).

Was Hume a conservative or a liberal? As he himself warns, there is nothing to be gained by mere verbal disputes: the words "conservative" and "liberal" do not have metaphysical meanings. Nor are the political parties that call themselves Conservative and Liberal vested with authority to define those words conclusively: parties took those names because the words already had achieved public meanings. When writers such as Miller, Livingston, and Whelan state that Hume was a conservative, we know immediately fairly well what they are saying; although each uses the term "conservative" in his own way, which he makes clear, all are in basic agreement. My submission is that Hume was not what they call conservative; I call him a liberal. I use the word broadly, to refer to those who thought that major reforms were highly desirable in the United Kingdom in the late-eighteenth and early-nineteenth centuries, and I have certain economic and political reforms—not socialist, Marxist, or neoliberal reforms—in mind. When I say that Hume's political principles are liberal, I trust that nobody will take me to mean that he was an advocate of democratic government as practiced in the United Kingdom, or the United States of America, over two centuries after his death.

Clearly, Livingston is correct in asserting that Hume denies the autonomy of reason, and that Hume requires that those who would be true philosophers try to understand the status quo. But Livingston does not stop there; he attributes to Hume a far more specific position, a truly conservative position. For Hume, he says, the status quo is legitimate. Hume shares "the conviction that established order has a sacred character and that this sacred character constitutes part of the authority of that order" (p. 330). We are to respect "the sacred character of common life" (p. 334). Improvements in the established order are possible, but given the subservience of reason, they can be made only pragmatically, only within "the narrative order." Where Livingston uses the expression "a narrative order" in explaining that for Hume the social and political order—of England, for example—is historical or temporal, not logical like a geometric figure, Whelan writes of "order and artifice" to make much the same point. Experience "in the form of history and tradition . . . is authoritative as a source of moral and political values. Just as mental habits unify experience into orderly cognitive patterns, rendering it a reasonable guide to the future, so also does social custom, embodying collective convictions of right, underlie the artificial rules and other continuities that constitute order in our social experience" (p. 322).

The Hume I read is far bolder. He has confidence in the philosopher's ability to discover the basic principles of economics and politics. True, he delights in pulling the props out from under the projects of those who, dreaming of antiquity, would reshape England as a patriotic republic. But, what is more revealing, he is far from reluctant to denounce contemporary laws and policies as bad—witness, his essay "Of Public Credit." He is ready to denounce as "vulgar" and "barbarous" certain maxims of those set in authority, sparing neither kings nor prime ministers. He is ready to attack entailed landed estates, the historic rights in Parliament of both the spiritual and the temporal lords, and the historic rights of electors. This hardly shows Burkean reverence for the established order.

It is my submission that Hume was out to reform moral subjects, not only in theory, but in practice. The *Treatise* is indeed "an attempt to introduce the experimental method of reasoning into moral subjects." He would have philosophers turn from "airy sciences" and apply themselves diligently to "the proper province of human reason." If they would but do this, no longer would they be dismissed as noisy "metaphysicians"; rather, they would be seen as persons useful in the business of life. Hume's great purpose was to advance moral subjects—not simply to gratify curiosity, but, carrying them nearer their perfection, to render them subservient to the genuine interests of society. To be successful, his attempt required two major advances in thought. First, the fact had to be established that reasoning has to do, not with the good (ends), but with the true (knowledge of causes, both permanent and temporary). Second, the correct method to achieve knowledge in the moral subjects had to be adopted. Knowledge about physical and moral subjects alike, acquired through either experience or education, he calls "belief," thus recognizing that, unlike fictions of the imagination, such knowledge deals with probabilities and can be either true or false, and also that, unlike mathematical knowledge, it is not demonstrable. Hume holds that we all rely on beliefs, for example, that when launched a well-built ship will not sink, that the end of international trade is the accumulation of gold, that good government requires that all governors be elected. Many of our beliefs (or opinions) are incorrect. Consequently, what is needed is a way to improve our beliefs; what is needed is the experimental method of reasoning, which combines adequate *experience* and careful *reflection*. Thereby we can test old beliefs for accuracy and acquire accurate new beliefs.

The picture of Hume clinging timidly to a raft of custom and artifice because, poor skeptic, he had no alternative, is wrong. He was confident that by experience and reflection philosophers can achieve true principles. He must not be understood as asserting that radical criticism of what exists is impossible. He opposes, not just one, but two mistaken views. The first of these exalts reason above the feelings; it holds that reason can discover immutable moral laws, laws comparable to theorems in geometry, and thus can prescribe how people ought to live and how societies ought to be organized. The other wrong view is that since the pretenses of reason are false, we have no choice but to rely on our unexamined beliefs, on beliefs produced perhaps by inadequate experience, faulty education, false analogy. We should recognize, Hume argues, that some of our beliefs are more dubious, far less reliable, than others. We need to improve our beliefs by deliberate resort to extensive experience and by engaging in profound reflection. This is the experimental method of reasoning; by using it we can liberate ourselves from an inheritance of false opinion. While Hume insists that moral subjects cannot be modeled on mathematics, he never states that we cannot improve and correct our beliefs (opinions) about moral subjects. The achievement of sounder opinion is the essential first step in the reform of laws, policies, and constitutions, for all these are based on opinion.

To say this is not to say that civil society can be reordered fancifully. The reformer must understand the reality he would reshape; he must discover the causes, some constant, some historical, which combined to create the present order. Some of those causes are natural facts; for example, the soil and insular location of England. Some are based on human passions; for example, the desire of the common man to improve his condition. Some are historical; for example, at different times the populace was highly patriotic, highly superstitious, indolent, industrious. Some are beliefs originated by particular interests; for example, the beliefs concerning the wool trade, nonconformity to the established religion, the taxation of colonies. Some of the causal factors are beyond human control. Some can be resisted, but only by violence. Others can be changed. The purpose of introducing the experimental method of reasoning into moral subjects is to bring about reform, change for the better, not simply minor improvements made incrementally by drudging empiric practitioners, but major improvements based on scientifically known principles.

To say that Hume held that there are principles that if followed will make society better—the rules of property, the sanctity of contracts, the free operation of domestic and international markets, the rule of law, religious toleration, and so on—is not to deny the assertion made by some writers that Hume would have denounced the disorder and violence of the French Revolution. He was fully aware of the danger of making radical changes too rapidly, so rapidly that the whole structure of the society is put in jeopardy. It is one thing to say that we must rely on historic beliefs and ways because there are no principles; it is another to say that the realization of the principles of civilized society requires skill and patience. It is not Burke's condemnation of the excesses of the French Revolution which makes him a conservative; rather, it is his insistence that we must rely on prejudices, inherited rights, custom, religious authorities, and the presumption that men of great property are wise and virtuous. In sharp contrast, Hume finds no evidence pointing to the conclusion that in politics whatever is established is best. In any case, Hume was focusing on the economic and political situation in Great Britain in his own day; he provides remarkably little analysis of the social and political situation of contemporary France.

When I began to write this book, I shared the view—the common view, I think—that Hume was neutral in terms of the party divisions of his age. I now doubt that this is accurate. Clearly, he accepted the mythology of neither English party and believed that both liberty (the Whig principle) and authority (the Tory principle) are essential to good government. In terms of Scottish politics, he was not a Jacobite, although many of his friends were: he accepted the Union of 1707 as progressive and argued fervently against allegiance to the Stuart line. Nor was he a Tory—he said that for historical reasons, there were no true Tories in Scotland. In other words, Hume was a Scots Whig. But what kind of Scots Whig? Writing in 1747 on behalf of his friend, Archibald Stewart, Provost of Edinburgh, 1744–1746, who had been charged with failing to defend the city against the Young Pretender, Hume observed that there is a vast difference between "political Whigs" and "religious Whigs." He praised the former; he decried the latter. Thus he revealed that he was neither unable nor unwilling to distinguish publicly between good and bad Whigs. Those whom he denounced were members of the *Squadrone Volante*, a Country interest composed of intermarried Lowland families, staunchly pro-

Union, fiercely anti-Jacobite, with fundamentalist presbyterian roots. Those whom he praised were their rivals, the Argathelians, members of the interest led after 1743 by Robert Walpole's close friend, Archibald Campbell, the third Duke of Argyll.[7] Moreover, it appears that Hume's friends knew where he stood, at least after he had explained and then corrected his essay on Walpole—written perhaps under the influence of James Oswald, William Mure, and Archibald Stewart, supporters from 1740 to 1742 of the second Duke of Argyll, who had broken with Walpole—and were prepared to recommend and support him for private and public posts, although his views on some matters were scandalous. This interpretation helps explain Hume's attitude to Patriots.

If one did not denounce the Hanoverian kings as usurpers, how could one justify opposition to their governments? From 1726 Robert Walpole's Whig rivals found their answer in Patriotism. They resorted to civic humanism: England's balanced constitution was fundamental to virtue and liberty; by places and money (with the standing army in reserve), a faction, headed by Walpole, had enslaved the country; the Patriotic task was to end robinarchy, reestablish the constitution, heal all partition, revive virtue. As the prophet of Patriotism, Bolingbroke had two great problems: first, to persuade Country Whigs and Court-at-heart Tories to cooperate year after year as an organized, industrious opposition to Walpole; second, to find true believers in the Patriotic cause, as distinct from politicians whose Patriotism fell away as they kissed hands. Very early

---

[7] The Argathelian interest had had its origins among the supporters of the Junto (or Court Whigs) during the reign of Queen Anne. It was the party of John Campbell, second Duke of Argyll, and his brother, Archibald Campbell, Earl of Islay. After 1721, when Robert Walpole returned to office, as First Lord of the Treasury, the Argathelians supported him with cooperative peers in the House of Lords and loyal members in the House of Commons; in return, he strengthened them by accepting their nominees for places and pensions, at the expense of the other Whig faction, the *Squadrone Volante*. The *Squadrone* had been formed in 1704 as an interest independent of the Court Whigs; the Tories named them "the Flying Squad" because of what the Tories saw as their unpredictable, opportunistic maneuvers in that early period. From 1725 until 1761, the Argathelians ordinarily were the dominant interest in Scottish politics. In 1739, the second Duke broke with Walpole; this contributed greatly to Walpole's fall in 1742. In 1743 the second Duke died and Islay succeeded his brother. From 1742 to 1746, the *Squadrone* was dominant. In 1746, after the *Squadrone* had demonstrated its inability to prevent and then to cope with the Rebellion of 1745, Argathelian influence was reestablished at Westminster, but at a lower level and less exclusively than when Walpole was the minister. The third Duke of Argyll (Islay) died in 1761. See Eric Cregeen, "The Changing Role of the House of Argyll in the Scottish Highlands," and J. M. Simpson, "Who Steered the Gravy Train, 1707–1766?" both in *Scotland in the Age of Improvement*, eds. N. T. Phillipson and Rosalind Mitchison (Edinburgh: Edinburgh University Press, 1970), pp. 5–23 and 47–72. Also, Alexander Murdoch, *'The People Above': Politics and Administration in Mid-Eighteenth-Century Scotland* (Edinburgh: John Donald Publishers Ltd., 1980) and J. S. Shaw, *The Management of Scottish Society 1707–1764* (Edinburgh: John Donald Publishers Ltd., 1983).

Hume began to express scorn for those who proclaimed themselves Patriots.[8]

Hume must be read as a man of his own country and times. Both his praise of political Whigs and his denunciation of religious Whigs are significant. In 1707, only four years before his birth, Scotland finally, after centuries of disorder and poverty, so he insisted, had set itself on the road to becoming a genuine civil society. The nature and value of such a society—based on justice, the rule of law, and obedience to the established government—had to be driven home to all who longed for "the good, old days." That was one item on his agenda. Another related to false religion. The pernicious effects of superstition and enthusiasm show that "the corruption of the best things produce the worst." The Reformation had shattered the monolithic authority of Rome, but that beneficial result did not show that Protestantism *per se* was a force for civilization. Indeed, some of its extreme versions were at least as bad as Roman Catholicism at its worst. For example, covenanting Calvinism, the fount of religious Whiggery in Scotland, with its special blend of enthusiasm and superstition, had contributed greatly to the political barbarism under which the Scottish people had suffered before 1707. Nor was it dead, as Francis Hutcheson and his liberal colleagues at Glasgow knew.

It was no accident that Hume came to speak well of Robert Walpole. Hume saw the need for authority, but he was no Tory; divine-right kings and bishops and the old order in society were things of the unlamented past. Nor was Hume a Patriot: the Patriotic indictment of Walpole was

[8] In his chapter, "Pitt and Patriotism," John Brewer writes, "Throughout the Hanoverian period oppositions sought to clothe their attacks on administration in patriot garb. By the 1720s the term 'patriot' had become virtually synonymous with that of 'member of the opposition'. During the 1730s, patriotism, in the hands of Lord Bolingbroke, became not only one of the chief means of legitimating opposition, but also a programme if it should win power." *Party Ideology and Popular Politics at the Accession of George III* (Cambridge: Cambridge University Press, 1976), p. 99. Both the Patriotic indictment of Walpole and the defence made by Walpole and his propagandists—the background of the essays on political subjects published by Hume in 1741—are analyzed by Isaac Kramnick in *Bolingbroke and His Circle: The Politics of Nostalgia in the Age of Walpole* (Cambridge: Harvard University Press, 1968), pp. 111–87. Hume proposed—in the preface (p. iv) to the first edition of his *Essays*—to stand above the battle: "[T]he Reader may condemn my Abilities, but must approve of my Moderation and Impartiality in my Method of handling POLITICAL SUBJECTS. . . . Public Spirit, methinks, should engage us to love the Public, and to bear an equal Affection to all our Country-Men; not to hate one Half of them, under Pretext of loving the Whole." For a more cynical interpretation of Bolingbroke's purpose than that given by Kramnick, see Quentin Skinner, "The Principles and Practice of Opposition: the Case of Bolingbroke versus Walpole," in *Historical Perspectives: Studies in English Thought and Society in Honour of J. H. Plumb*, ed. Neil McKendrick (London: Europa Publications, 1974), pp. 93–128. A general survey of the period is to be found in B. W. Hill, *The Growth of Parliamentary Parties 1689–1742* (London: George Allen & Unwin Ltd., 1976), pp. 189–226.

based on bad history, a wrong appreciation of the constitution, a false concept of virtue; moreover, the extremism of most of the Patriotic attacks on Walpole, especially those fortified with religious Whiggery, bespoke much of folly, cant, and knavery, and little or nothing of moderation, wisdom, and honesty.

1

THE ARGUMENT BEFORE HUME:

THE LEGALISTS' DILEMMA

DURING David Hume's formative years, Scotland was making a troubled new beginning. The union with England, from which so much had been hoped, seemed to have paid off badly. Scotland had given up her independence. What had she gained in return? Besides, by uniting with England, Scotland had accepted the Act of Settlement, enacted by the English Parliament in 1701, appointing the Hanoverians as Anne's successors. Did not the ancient Scottish royal family, the Stuarts, have rights not lightly to be set aside? Yet another cause of division was religion. In 1690 the Scottish Parliament had sought to end the religious turmoil which had ravaged the country for generations by determining that the Church of Scotland would be presbyterian, not episcopalian. That decision closed the fighting phase of one religious controversy; now another controversy came to the fore. Would the Church of Scotland remain true to fundamentalist Calvinism? Could the inroads of rationalist theology be stopped? In 1696 Thomas Aikenhead had been convicted of blasphemy; although he was the last person put to death in Scotland on account of religion, the defence of the old doctrines was not neglected during Hume's lifetime. From 1714 until 1729, John Simpson, professor of theology at Glasgow, was harassed for heresy. Archibald Campbell, professor of church history at St. Andrews, author of *A Discourse Proving that the Apostles were no Enthusiasts*, was charged with heresy in 1736, as was Francis Hutcheson in 1738 and William Leechman, professor of divinity at Glasgow, in 1744. Hume himself was to be charged in 1756. And there were other questions, more mundane but still important—questions relating to the economy and foreign policy. By the union, Scotland had accepted England's trade laws, England's colonial ambitions, England's continental policy. She had committed herself to provide men, and money too, for the struggle against the evil kingdom, France—represented by religious Whigs as an imperialist slave state—on the continent, in North America, in India. Were the trade, colonial, and foreign policies of the government at London, now Scotland's government, sound and wise, or ill founded and foolish?

By the time he was thirty, Hume was deep into moral philosophy. He had worked out both his theory of ends (the good) and his theory of means (the true). In addition, he had made up his mind on politics and had made a beginning in economics. New prospects were being opened up in those fields: the discoveries made by the natural philosophers had revealed that much could be learned about nature by experimentation; their successes seemed to promise comparable results from the application of the experimental method to the moral sciences. Moreover, no longer did young Scots have to go abroad to study the theory of society and government: Gerschom Carmichael at Glasgow was teaching from and writing on Pufendorf's magisterial works. Down in London, Bernard Mandeville had mounted a rousing attack on conventional wisdom, arguing that England would prosper and grow rich even if all her people did not strive for the good of the nation, or rather, especially if they did not do so. From the Molesworth circle at Dublin the liberal ideas of Molesworth's friend, the third Earl of Shaftesbury, were carried into Scotland by Francis Hutcheson, who proceeded to develop and to teach, with far-reaching consequences, a theory of morals based on neither religion nor reason. The shift to a theory of morality based on human nature was confirmed and advanced by no less a figure than the Right Reverend Joseph Butler.

Aside from sermons and books expounding Holy Writ, much of what had been written about the moral sciences in the century before Hume's birth had been the work of writers on natural jurisprudence. This line of endeavor had a long history, but it had been given a new start in Protestant Europe by Grotius. Its goal was to develop a science of society—property, government, law, trade, international relations, and so on—which depended as little as possible on divine revelation. But the authority of natural law was still in dispute. While there was agreement on many specific teachings, the nature of the authority behind those teachings was hotly disputed. Why do we, why should we, feel obliged to heed natural law? The cardinal principles had not been settled. For Hume the challenge was irresistible. He would, first, put the moral sciences on their proper basis. He would then proceed to establish the fundamental principles. Hume's first work, *A Treatise of Human Nature*—Books I and II published in 1739 and Book III in 1740—is subtitled, "An Attempt to introduce the experimental Method of Reasoning into Moral Subjects." Another subtitle, especially apt for Book I, might have been, "A Study of how the Truth may be discovered and made to serve the Good." Such a subtitle would have served to remind us that not only does the *Treatise* explain the correct method by which to advance knowledge, but it applies that method to the moral sciences.

The fact that the *Treatise* was not greeted with acclaim did not lead Hume to abandon his enterprise. His great work had failed, he reassured himself, not because the project was ill conceived, but because he had gone to the press too soon, while the book still was flawed by youthful gaucheries, defects far more of presentation than of substance. In 1741 he brought out another book, and in 1742 yet another. His concern still is moral subjects. The presentation now, however, is very different: he writes lucid, succinct essays. Presented in this way, the science of politics would not, he hoped, prove too demanding for the rulers of Britain. Thus was launched his career as a politician, an economist, an historian—a career which was to help make a revolution in the moral sciences.

Hugo Grotius

My purpose in this chapter is to indicate the main strands of the argument into which Hume plunged when he began to write *A Treatise of Human Nature*. My focus is on the warp, the continuing strands, not the woof added by writers dealing with matters to the fore at particular times and places. I begin with Grotius because, first, he introduced natural-law thinking into Protestant Europe, and, second, because his works, especially *De Iure Belli ac Pacis* (1625), exerted a powerful influence on moral and political thought in western Europe, and beyond, for many generations.[1] It could be said that Grotius set up the loom at which Hume's predecessors, and then Hume himself, were to work. Thomistic natural-law theory was based on the concept of the just (righteous) society. It asked what structures, relationships, and acts are just (or right); that is, just (or right) for rational beings living in society. The ends or goals of certain activities and institutions were regarded as self-evidently reasonable. They were required by reason—by practical reason, not theoretical reason—and were goods to be sought and promoted by all the members of the society, both severally and collectively. Every member of a society was seen as obliged to work for those goods—obliged in a way analogous to the way a subject is obliged to obey the laws of a legitimate ruler. He was obliged, it was said, to obey the "laws of nature." This term, "the laws of nature" (or "natural law"), was used to distinguish this body of

---

[1] Grotius used concepts developed over centuries and brought together by writers such as Molina and Suárez. On the precursors of "modern natural law," see Quentin Skinner, *The Foundations of Modern Political Thought* (Cambridge: Cambridge University Press, 1978) 2:113–78. One factor that gave Grotius his great influence was the fact that though writing primarily for Protestants, who took God's commands as promulgated in the Bible as their chief guide, he drew upon scholastic and classical sources. Thus he achieved relevance in a religiously divided Europe. The view that Grotius inaugurated modern natural-law philosophy was introduced by Jean Barbeyrac in his prefatory discourse on the history of the science of morality, prefixed to his translation into French of Pufendorf's *The Law of Nature and Nations*. Grotius was given the credit for founding their discipline by both Adam Smith and Thomas Reid.

law from Christian divine law, the will of God made known to His own people by particular revelation at various times after Creation, as by the Ten Commandments and the Sermon on the Mount. Also, it was called "natural"—following the Stoics—to distinguish it both from the civil law, made by the rulers of particular cities and nations, and from conventional rules, known as "laws of nations," creatures of time and custom, adopted for the conduct of trade, treaties, and the like, between neighboring nations. Since the ends or goals of natural law were set by human nature, that is, were based on what is good for human beings, they were valid in every nation. For St. Thomas Aquinas, natural law was the moral constitution of all humankind. All laws made by human governors were subordinate to it. Only so far as such laws were consistent with natural law were they valid; if *ultra vires* in either form or content, they were nullities.

Given the ambiguities of the terms "natural" and "law," it was easy for some writers to think of natural law as basic principles shared by all animals, rational and brute alike. Grotius, in contrast, insists that "natural law" applies only to rational, self-disciplined beings. It was easy also for others to think of natural law as the principles of the primitive or "natural" state, principles that continue to be valid and fundamental, but which, like the bedrock shared by a cluster of towering buildings, have been left far below and behind by the creators of advanced civilizations; thus the rude state of nature could be compared unfavorably with the glories of polite society. Grotius, in contrast, contends that highly developed cultures are certain to have a far better understanding of natural law than primitive peoples.

Like St. Thomas Aquinas, Grotius builds on Aristotelian principles. First, contrary to Carneades, man by his nature is a social animal. Among the traits that distinguish man from all other animals "is an impelling desire for society, that is, for the social life—not of any and every sort, but peaceful, and organized according to the measure of his intelligence, with those who are of his own kind; this social trend the Stoics called 'sociableness'. Stated as a universal truth, therefore, the assertion that every animal is impelled by nature to seek only its own good cannot be conceded."[2] Second, while other animals show gregarious instincts, mature men are able to act for the good of their society under the guidance of reason. Among animals, man alone has the ability to speak. "He has also been endowed with the faculty of knowing and of acting in accor-

---

[2] Hugo Grotius, *On the Law of War and Peace*, translated by Francis W. Kelsey for the Carnegie Endowment for International Peace (Oxford: Clarendon Press, 1925; reprinted Indianapolis: The Bobbs-Merrill Company, Inc., n.d.), p. 11. When Hume was completing the *Treatise* a notable English translation of *De Iure Belli ac Pacis* was published: *The Rights of War and Peace* (with Barbeyrac's notes), translated by Basil Kennet (London: for W. Innys and R. Manby, J. and P. Knapton, O. Brown, T. Osborn, and E. Wicksteed, 1738).

dance with general principles." Here, then, is the great natural end: the preservation, not of mere society, but of high-quality society, of society at the level that fosters human life of the highest quality. Here also is the special means: well-framed judgments as to what is necessary for such a society. Whatever is contrary to what is judged necessary as the best means to the end is understood to be "contrary also to the law of nature, that is, to the nature of man."[3] The law of nature prescribes the characteristics of just, righteous, or lawful society. On this view, society is essential to the good life. Human beings need to associate with others. The just man is the man who in those of his activities that involve others does not violate, by either commission or omission, the rules of justice (righteousness). Those rules are the basic constitution of society. Where those rules are badly neglected there is little or no genuine society. Grotius accepts this Aristotelian-Thomistic position. However, it is crucial to notice that what he uses most in showing what is right and wrong in war and peace is not the concept of righteous society within and among nations, but the concept of rights. Instead of moving from just (right) society to the roles and stations of the participants in such society, he proceeds from roles or stations, from the basic or natural rights of the participants. Clearly, his assumption is that when the rights of all the participants have been integrated, the result will be a just (right) society. However, from an Aristotelian-Thomistic viewpoint, the peril of proceeding thus is that the natural rights of the participants may be so defined that a genuine society will be difficult, perhaps even impossible: if societies are thought of in terms of an organic analogy, as they were in that tradition, to define the rights of the several members of a projected society abstractly, without taking their different roles into account, might produce a badly deformed, perhaps a fatally deformed, society.

Grotius's chief concern is with the basic rules that ought to be followed by sovereign states—persons, in international law—in their relations with one another, but since those rules have much in common with the rules that ought to be applied between private persons, he finds that he must begin by explaining all the main aspects of moral relationships, that is, the origin and status of private property, the various standard relationships among persons, the origin of government, the nature of sovereignty, and so forth. As a result, De Iure Belli ac Pacis is a general treatise on moral and political theory.

Grotius opens by explaining his title. Is it ever right to resort to violence (war) between individuals or states; if so, when? Are there rules as to when and how war may be waged lawfully (rightfully)? Only Christians are subject to Christian divine law. The laws of nations do not pretend to

---

[3] On the Law of War and Peace, pp. 12–13.

be more than agreed-upon practices adopted for the sake of convenience. Well then, setting aside both divine law and the laws of nations, is it still possible to say that some acts of violence are wrong, while others are right? Is resort to war ever lawful? Grotius's answer is affirmative: there are laws of natural justice, based on the requirements of society; those rules are to be upheld and defended against those who act unlawfully (unjustly). "For law," says Grotius, "in our use of the term here means nothing else than what is just, and that, too, rather in a negative than in an affirmative sense, that being lawful which is not unjust. Now that is unjust which is in conflict with the nature of society of beings endowed with reason."[4]

What then is essential to rational society? First, there are certain standard relationships, such as those of parent and child, master and servant, brother and brother, citizen and citizen: acts consistent with those relationships are right; discordant acts are wrong. Second, there are the rights of persons. The term "rights" here refers to what a person may justly claim in society either as an *aptitude* or as a *power*. An aptitude right is based on suitability or worthiness, that is, merit. Aptitudes, says Grotius, are the subject of "attributive justice"—what Aristotle called distributive justice. Aptitude rights are *imperfect*; they are claims to good works to be done by others. In contrast, a faculty right is a power. Rights of this kind are the subject of "expletive justice"—or what Aristotle called commutative justice—and are *perfect*. While Grotius does not dismiss distributive justice as unimportant, it is powers—that is, perfect rights or rights properly so called—that he emphasizes.

> A legal right (*facultas*) is called by the jurists the right to one's own (*suum*); after this we shall call it a legal right properly or strictly so called.
>
> Under it are included power, now over oneself, which is called freedom, now over others, as that of the father (*patria potestas*) and that of the master over slaves; ownership, either absolute, or less than absolute, as usufruct and the right of pledge; and contractual rights, to which on the opposite side contractual obligations correspond.[5]

Rights of this kind—true natural rights—must be respected both within each nation and between nations.

In many instances, Grotius tells us, we ought not to insist on all that we may take as a matter of perfect right; rather, we ought to moderate our claims and exactions by reason of *humanity*. We must remember that "the rules of love are broader than the rules of law." A rich man who, intent on getting everything owed him, deprives a needy debtor of all his

---

[4] Ibid., p. 34.
[5] Ibid., pp. 35–36.

small possessions, "does nothing contrary to his right according to a strict interpretation"; yet he is guilty of heartlessness. It is honorable to practice humanity.[6] However, since Grotius finds that even the perfect rights are being wantonly violated by murderers, dishonest traders, and other criminals, while sovereigns are told by skeptics that might is right, what he emphasizes is perfect rights, rights relative to which acts can be denominated simply either right or wrong. So basic, indeed essential, to society is respect for these rights that Grotius feels obliged to show exhaustively that Christians have a duty to enforce them and to punish wrongdoers. Christ was not a pacifist. When he spoke of loving enemies, sheathing the sword, turning the other cheek, and the like, it was not his purpose to leave society—life, liberty, property—defenseless against murderers, robbers, and other wrongdoers; rather, he was instructing his followers not to exaggerate trifling offenses.[7]

Natural law, Grotius submits, contains all the rules required for the maintenance of society. Some of the rules are provided immediately: natural law confers certain well-defined rights—to life, liberty, chastity, and so on—and acts violating these rights are wrong. Some rights may be forfeited or restricted as a result of criminal misconduct, so that imprisonment, servitude, even death are just penalties. Moreover, where the defense of his natural rights has not been transferred to civil authorities, every person has the right to resist and punish those who invade his rights. Other rules are provided mediately: on certain matters, the law of nature is silent; relative to such matters, a society lawfully may erect civil institutions and make civil rules. If this has been done rationally, the principles of natural law will support the operation of those institutions and those subordinate rules; for example, to disobey a good civil law would be wrong under natural law.

The most notable example of an artificial institution of this kind is property. In early times, when life was simple, there was no such thing as property; rather, each person simply took whatever goods he needed, and without wrong, for God had conferred on humankind in general a right to use those goods. And it would have been possible to perpetuate that primitive state (of community of ownership) if people had been bound together by mutual affection, as were the early Christians, or had been satisfied with great simplicity, as were certain tribes in America; but this was not to be. Eventually, as a result of population pressure and an increase in productive skills, it became desirable to initiate a new kind of rights: those of property. Initially people "divided off countries, and possessed them separately." Later the flocks and herds, and still later the pas-

---

[6] Ibid., pp. 759–60.
[7] Ibid., pp. 20, 70–81.

tures and arable lands were divided among the families.[8] All this was accomplished by agreement. We can assume, Grotius tells us, that there must have been "a kind of agreement, either expressed, as by a division, or implied, as by occupation. In fact, as soon as community ownership was abandoned, and as yet no division had been made, it is to be supposed that all agreed, that whatever each one had taken possession of should be his property."[9] Subsequently, property rights are acquired by the rules of occupation, and so forth. Thus we see that although property is not an institution prescribed by natural law, it is a valid institution. It follows that theft is wrong; indeed, under the rules of simple expletive justice, we have a perfect right to kill robbers. Since natural law requires that parents support their children, once property has been introduced, the first right of succession is in the children.[10]

In a sense, property is simply an arrangement for the harmonious and efficient management of some of the goods given by God to all humankind collectively; it is neither all-inclusive nor ultimate. First, there are things—the open sea, for example—that cannot be appropriated; these things remain under the primitive common ownership. Second, in situations of extreme need, "the primitive right of user revives, as if community of ownership had remained, since in respect of all human laws—the law of ownership included—supreme necessity seems to have been excepted." Nor is this simply a matter of charity: "The reason which lies back of this principle is not, as some allege, that the owner of a thing is bound by the rule of love to give to him who lacks; it is, rather, that all things seem to have been distributed to individual owners with a benign reservation in favour of the primitive right."[11] Third, there is a natural right to innocent passage, for both persons and merchandise, by such land and water routes as are under the dominion of a city or nation; otherwise, one of the great ends of society, namely commerce, would be restricted. Here Grotius quotes Libanius: "God did not bestow all products upon all parts of the earth, but distributed His gifts over different regions, to the end that men might cultivate a social relationship because one would have need of the help of another. And so He called commerce into being, that all men might be able to have common enjoyment of the fruits of earth, no matter where produced."[12] Fourth, the primitive right to acquire goods applies even within a property system; this means that obstacles

[8] Ibid., pp. 186–89. Hume cites Grotius's explanation of the origin of private property, in *Enquiry* II, p. 307n.
[9] Ibid., pp. 189–90.
[10] Ibid., pp. 271–72.
[11] Ibid., p. 193.
[12] Ibid., pp. 199–200.

hindering the exchange of goods on mutually acceptable terms are not to be raised by either law or conspiracy.[13]

Natural law requires that perfect promises—those that conform to all the requirements of a genuine promise—be kept meticulously. Thus is provided the basis for the institution—based on agreed reciprocity— known as "contract." Contracts are inviolable. Natural law requires that they be fair, that is, that the goods or services exchanged be of equal value in the eyes of the contractors and have no hidden flaws or defects.[14]

Just as there can be society without property, society is possible without civic governance; however, since civic governance is not prohibited by natural law, it is permissible for a multitude to band together as a distinct society and then to establish a sovereign. The members of the society may lodge sovereignty in the whole society, or they may transfer it to some distinct person or body. "That power is called sovereign whose actions are not subject to the legal control of another, so that they cannot be rendered void by the operation of another human will."[15] Similarly, natural law does not pronounce on the legality of forms of government. This means that a people is free to establish whatever form it wishes; it may even establish an absolute monarchy.[16]

From time to time Grotius reminds us of the fact, noticed above, that there are natural-law obligations that lie outside the area of perfect rights; in addition, Christians are under the divine laws, by which the will of God was revealed to them in the form of explicit commands. We may decide, for example, that it would not be right (according to divine law) to exercise our natural-law right to kill a particular robber; however, if we kill him, his friends cannot expect to have us convicted in any human court. The members of society have rights as human beings, as owners, and as contractors. If they have set up a government, they will have the rights that go with their unequal places in the civil constitution. Quite apart from civil laws, all others are under the natural-law obligation to respect those rights. If a right is not respected, the injured party (in the absence of civil remedies and restrictions introduced by civil law) has a right to punish the wrongdoer.

The basic rule is this: preserve society. This end can be advanced in various ways, but above all by preventing and punishing offenses against perfect rights. Now, are we to act in conformity with the law of nature because conformity is commanded by God? This was a position Grotius wished to avoid, for the more dependent the law of nature was on Christian religion, the more its authority was put in question by contemporary

[13] Ibid., p. 203.
[14] Ibid., pp. 346–50.
[15] Ibid., p. 102.
[16] Ibid., pp. 103–4.

attacks on religion. He wished to show that the requirements of natural-law righteousness are binding in all times and places regardless of the prevailing strength of religious beliefs.[17] "The law of nature," says Grotius, "is a dictate of right reason, which points out that an act, according as it is or is not in conformity with rational nature, has in it a quality of moral baseness or moral necessity; and that, in consequence, such an act is either forbidden or enjoined by the author of nature, God."[18] God commands what natural law requires; He forbids what is wrong according to natural law. However, we must not conclude that the content of natural law results from God's will. To do so would be to confuse divine law and natural law: the former "does not enjoin or forbid those things which in themselves and by their own nature are obligatory or not permissible, but by forbidding things it makes them unlawful, and by commanding things it makes them obligatory."[19] In contrast, the law of nature is based, not on will, but on reason. Indeed, says Grotius, in his most famous sentence, "What we have been saying [about things 'by their own nature' either right or wrong] would have a degree of validity even if we should concede that which cannot be conceded without the utmost wickedness, that there is no God, or that the affairs of men are of no concern to Him."[20] Later he says,

> The law of nature, again, is unchangeable—even in the sense that it cannot be changed by God. Measureless as is the power of God, nevertheless it can be said that there are certain things over which that power does not extend; for things of which this is said are spoken only, having no sense corresponding with reality and being mutually contradictory. Just as even God, then, cannot cause that two times two should not make four, so He cannot cause that that which is intrinsically evil be not evil.[21]

Often it is said that Grotius launched modern natural jurisprudence by making it a science independent of God as supreme legislator. Strictly speaking, this is untrue: from the fourteenth century, the hypothesis of

[17] The view that Grotius broke sharply with a uniform scholastic theory of natural law and originated "modern natural law," a strictly rationalist theory, has been questioned by Charles Edwards, "The Law of Nature in the Thought of Hugo Grotius," *The Journal of Politics* 32 (1970): 784–807. In contrast, but not in contradiction, Richard Tuck emphasizes the determination of Grotius, Pufendorf, and the other modern natural lawyers to refute modern skepticism. See "Grotius, Carneades and Hobbes," *Grotiana* (n.s.) (1983): 43–62, especially pp. 56–58. Also Richard Tuck, "The 'Modern' Theory of Natural Law," in *The Languages of Political Theory in Early-Modern Europe*, ed. Anthony Pagden (Cambridge: Cambridge University Press, 1987), pp. 99–119.
[18] *On the Law of War and Peace*, pp. 38–39.
[19] Ibid., p. 39.
[20] Ibid., p. 13.
[21] Ibid., p. 40.

God's nonexistence or indifference had been used frequently in scholastic writings on morality. But Grotius was writing in the Calvinist part of Europe, where both the form and the content of all righteousness were traced to the will of God. This was a world in which nothing was seen as intrinsically reasonable or right. What was accounted reasonable and right was commanded by God, but not because it was reasonable and right; rather, first of all it was willed by God and thus it became reasonable and right.[22] By reverting to this old scholastic device, Grotius scandalized the faithful. In addition, he opened up questions about the nature of the obligation to observe natural law and to respect the rights conferred by natural law. If we say that natural law would be valid even if not backed by the will of God, how can we explain why these "laws" can be regarded as genuine laws, and how can we explain the obligation to obey them? Grotius himself does not have to answer these questions, for he believes both that these rules are intrinsically valid and that God, by giving His creation the nature it has, willed that they be obeyed. But would they be genuine laws for atheists, that is, for those who have no gods to give the rules the form of command, or for all those millions whose gods order or allow acts contrary to what Grotius and other Christians call "natural law"? How could Grotius or any other Christian convince those who do not presuppose the legislative authority of the Christian God that His commands are valid? After all, natural law applies to all humankind, to godless kings and pagan multitudes equally with Christian philosophers.

Thomas Hobbes

Hobbes, like Grotius, thinks of politics legalistically, in terms of authority, law, and rights. However, he focuses on society within one country, not all human society. While Grotius's great concern was to convince sovereigns, who have no superior on earth, that international peace is possible, Hobbes was out to show all the parties dividing England the way, the only way, to domestic peace. He had a remedy for their strife, that is, one absolute civil government.

For Hobbes the precivil condition is amoral. Nor are human beings drawn to work for great collective goals, for common goods. Before the

[22] The influential Puritan writer William Perkins, for example, asserted "that even the virtues of reasonableness or justice, as human beings conceive them, could not be predicated of God, for God's will, 'it selfe is an absolute rule both of justice and reason'; and that nothing could therefore be reasonable and just intrinsically, 'but it is first of all willed by God, and thereupon becomes reasonable and just.' " Perry Miller, *Errand into the Wilderness* (Cambridge: Harvard University Press, 1956), p. 52.

sovereign has made laws, every person is his own judge of good and evil: "[W]hatsoever is the object of any man's appetite or desire, that is it which he for his part calleth *good*: and the object of his hate and aversion, *evil*; and of his contempt, *vile* and *inconsiderable*. For these words of good, evil, and contemptible, are ever used with relation to the person that useth them: there being nothing simply and absolutely so; nor any common rule of good and evil, to be taken from the nature of the objects themselves."[23] What is natural is that each person should strive for his own good. Since the demand—avarice and ambition—for goods (riches, honor, and security) is insatiable, while the supply is limited, the result is, not a regime of peace and righteousness, but a condition of ruthless competition, in a word, war, in which conduct is neither just nor unjust.

It is true that human beings are rational: they are able to see that this state of affairs serves nobody well for long and that each individual would be far better off if all were to follow a common set of rules of conduct. They see these rules as good, desirable, not because the rules would benefit the public (society), but because they would benefit themselves. However, this selfish insight is not enough to make men and women behave lawfully; and even if a few did, they would be the victims of their own naiveté. These rules are mere precepts of reason; they may motivate some people sometimes, but since they depend for efficacy on individual insight, not on legislative authority, they cannot be expected to provide order to any significant degree. (This is not true, of course, in the case of those who believe that the rules are commands of God; for them, the rules are indeed true laws. How many such persons there are may be seen by surveying the sorry state of Christendom.) The rules of reason will not be realized in a state of nature; they will be realized and followed only when they have been embodied in the laws and institutions of a civil commonwealth and are enforced by prescribed punishments.

In the state of nature, every individual has the right to do whatever he thinks best for himself, for example, to defend himself as he sees necessary. The introduction of legitimate civil government and the beginning of society occur simultaneously; this happens when each person, suppressing his pride, contracts with every other person to create an absolute authority. Each contractor transfers to the person or body selected as sovereign his natural right to defend himself. (If the state of nature is utterly lawless, the terms "right" and "wrong" are unsuitable, and Hobbes ought not to write of a "right of nature." He does so because of the legalism of his thought: if the new civil government is to be an authorized agent, those who agree to create it must have rights to bestow upon it.)

[23] Thomas Hobbes, *Leviathan*, ed. Michael Oakeshott (Oxford: Basil Blackwell, 1955), p. 32.

For Hobbes, justice is the fair treatment of the several selfish competitors; it is not the principle of "the good society." Its basic rule is reciprocity of treatment: each person is to treat all others as he would wish to be treated by them. And, as we have seen, even this modest version of justice is realized, not in a precivil state of nature, but only in civil society. Hobbes moves away in both directions from the Grotian concept of *natural* society based on practical reason. For Hobbes, the precivil or natural situation is not society, but ruthless war waged by selfish competitors; the remedy is at the other extreme, the institution of civil society by the creation of a government to compel the restless warriors, not to love each other, but to conduct their competition fairly and peacefully.

For Hobbes, the civil government must be supreme within the society. Given the power of religion, if priests and prophets are permitted to set themselves up as promulgators of higher law, conflict between them and the government, even if there is only one church, and strife among them if there are many, are inevitable. Indeed, Hobbes believed that the English civil war had been caused chiefly by the rivalry among religious factions, each convinced that it alone possessed the true higher law.

Hobbes's theory was provocative. First, he had turned away from the traditional truth that by his nature man is a social animal. For Hobbes, each person is a selfish individual in competition with many other selfish individuals. Society is artificial; each society is established primarily as a local remedy. Second, his theory was atheistic in the sense that, except for His own people, direct intervention by God was not a factor at any stage after the Creation: the state of nature is naturalistic; the "laws of nature" are precepts of reason, not revealed commands; the civil government cannot claim to have been established by direct order of God. Clearly, since reason is a god-given faculty of human beings, it follows that civil authority is based ultimately on the will of God, but on the will of God as expressed by general, not particular, providence. Third, it was Erastian: none of those who claim to have been commissioned directly by God— bishops, prophets, and the like—has authority superior to that of the sovereign; indeed, given human religiosity, the government of a commonwealth ought to make suitable arrangements for the management of religion, assuring that worship is uniform, seemly, and peaceable, and that the clergy do not usurp the role of the government. Fourth, it was absolutist: given their inevitable selfishness, to allow any one of the avaricious, ambitious competitors access to the levers of power—placed by Hobbes in hands outside and above the struggle—would be to court injustice and disorder.

Hobbes was hard to refute. His picture of man as incorrigibly proud (that is, selfish in every way) followed the Calvinist view that fallen man, profoundly sinful, puts himself ahead of both his Creator and his fellow men, and cannot grow in virtue while living the life of "the world." Hobbes employs biblical language so powerfully that at times he seems a true believer in at least the sterner parts of the Old Testament. Again, his theory seemed scientific; it was consistent, at least superficially, with the recent advances in natural science. Both Aristotle and Hobbes regard man as a special province of nature. Aristotle sees man as moved to conform to nature's pattern—to grow to his end, his good, his idea, his perfection—and carries this way of thinking over from man into the other provinces of nature. Hobbes reverses the transfer. Galileo had revealed that nature was matter in motion, matter moving inertially endlessly. Hobbes applies this paradigm to man: while a person is alive, he is always moving, striving restlessly, never contented, always wanting to get ahead in the world, seeking no *summum bonum*, but victory after victory. Although the rhetoric was different, old theology and new science seemed to corroborate each other on one point: man is insatiable. Finally, Hobbes's prescription, however grim, was hard to dismiss in 1651. English society was disintegrating; if utter chaos was to be averted, if England was to escape the calamities that had befallen France during the previous century, the people of England would have to see the need to submit to an absolute government. To admit any right of resistance, other than that of the lonely individual to defend himself, would be to risk a return to the war of all against all.

Yet Hobbes was highly offensive. His description of the natural state as one of savage competition was basic to his argument for an absolute government; accordingly, it was rejected by all those who wanted either a full division of power or, more modestly, an element of genuine popular representation in the government. At the same time, his theory was offensive to those who believed in the divine right of kings, for he based the absolute power of the government, not on divine right, but on popular authorization, and because he did not endorse monarchy as the only genuine form of government. It was offensive to Christians of various denominations because it subordinated even the true church, their own, to the government in matters both spiritual and temporal. And his theory was offensive to all but the most rigorous Calvinists on the ground that his natural men lacked all the Christian virtues. Natural men were fallen men; indeed they had fallen so far that their only redeeming quality was the ability of each, when properly instructed in Hobbesian political science, to see somewhat dimly how things might be made better for himself, and even the motive for peaceful behavior thus provided was ineffective unless supplemented amply by sword and gallows. But even the rigorists, who could applaud Hobbes's somber picture of natural man, were appalled by the apparent atheism of his science.

By concentrating on the characteristics of the lonely, competitive man, always striving to get ahead, Hobbes had given his theory a sound, resilient core. Critics might denounce him for distortion, for equating selfish man with man; yet his theory had great strength. The core seemed sound; only the extreme contention that man—the saints apart—is *entirely* selfish in motivation was debatable. And no devout Christian could declare that Hobbes was utterly wrong without abandoning the doctrine of the Fall of Man. Hobbes's theory of human relationships stood strong in its hard-headed simplicity: it subordinated the warring religious factions; it seemed modern and scientific; it was enunciated with bold, blunt clarity.

Samuel Pufendorf

Natural law as an adequate basis for rights and duties had been badly mauled by Hobbes: for him, first, the "natural laws" do not have the force of law (except for those who find them confirmed in the Holy Scriptures), and, second, the will of the sovereign is the only source of genuine law. Although Samuel Pufendorf showed high respect for Hobbes's learning and acuity, as well as for his systematic method, he was out to restore and propagate the view that the basic rules of society are quite independent of and superior to the will of the rulers of particular countries. The result of his labors was a massive tome, *De Iure Naturae et Gentium*, published in 1672. In 1673 he brought out *De Officio Hominis et Civis*, a short restatement of his basic argument, unsupported and unadorned by the extensive quotations and examples that make the original work both long and engrossing. Both were to be highly influential during the next hundred years.[24]

If natural law is to be called "law" meaningfully, it must be effective; to an appreciable extent, it must oblige all human beings—they must feel

[24] Pufendorf published a revised and enlarged second edition of *De Iure Naturae et Gentium* in 1674. This work was edited and translated into French by Jean Barbeyrac. In a long prefatory discourse, Barbeyrac provided, "An Historical and Critical Account of the Science of Morality." I have used the fifth edition of Basil Kennet's translation of Pufendorf's work, to which is prefixed a translation of Barbeyrac's discourse. *The Law of Nature and Nations: or, A General System of the Most Important Principles of Morality, Jurisprudence, and Politics* (London: J. and J. Bonwicke and others, 1749). An edition of the compendium, *De Officio Hominis et Civis*, also edited and translated by Barbeyrac, was published in 1707. Another edition had been published at Cambridge in 1682. The latter edition, together with an English translation by Frank Gardner Moore was reprinted for the Carnegie Endowment for International Peace in 1927 by Oxford University Press, New York. I have used F. G. Moore's translation, entitled *On the Duty of Man and Citizen*. The influence of Barbeyrac as translator and commentator was very great; see James Moore, "Natural Law and the Pyrrhonian Controversy," in *Philosophy and Science in the Scottish Enlightenment*, ed. Peter Jones (Edinburgh: John Donald Publishers Ltd., 1988), pp. 20–38.

that they ought—to follow it without support from either divine law or civil law. Pufendorf undertakes to show that natural law is genuine law. He begins by accepting much of what Hobbes says about natural human motivation. Many good results can be achieved by cooperation, but given the pressure and diversity of human wants, fierce conflict is inevitable if not deliberately prevented: human beings need society, not only because society promotes the best kind of life, but because they need to be protected from each other by the rules of society. We find that

> man is indeed an animal most bent upon self-preservation, helpless in himself, unable to save himself without the aid of his fellows, highly adapted to promote mutual interests; but on the other hand no less malicious, insolent, and easily provoked, also as able as he is prone to inflict injury upon another. Whence it follows that, in order to be safe, he must be sociable, that is, must be united with men like himself, and so conduct himself toward them that they may have no good cause to injure him, but rather may be ready to maintain and promote his interests.
>
> The laws then of this sociability, or those which teach how a man should conduct himself, to become a good member of human society, are called natural laws.
>
> So much settled, it is clear that the fundamental natural law is this: that every man must cherish and maintain sociability, so far as in him lies. From this it follows that, as he who wishes an end, wishes also the means, without which the end cannot be obtained, all things which necessarily and universally make for that sociability are understood to be ordained by natural law, and all that confuse or destroy it forbidden.[25]

Nor are the laws of sociability mere precepts of reason, for (as Hobbes had said) reasonable counsel does not entail obligation; rather, they are commands of God and can be recognized as such without reliance on particular revelation. To anyone who will pay attention, reason discloses the reality of God as both the Creator and the Governor of nature. Reason also reveals that society is required by humankind. Reason then reveals the rules of sociability. Pufendorf rejects the essentialism of Grotius's famous doctrine:

> [T]o make the Knowledge of the *Law of Nature* . . . come up to the Measure and Perfection of *Science*, we do not think it necessary to assert, with some Writers, that there are several Things honest or dishonest of themselves, and antecedent to all Imposition. . . . And truly, as for those who would establish an eternal Rule for Morality of the Actions, without Respect to the Divine Injunction and Constitution, the Result of their Endeavours seems to us to

[25] *On the Duty of Man and Citizen*, p. 19. See also *The Law of Nature and Nations*, p. 134.

be the joining with GOD Almighty some coeval extrinsecal Principle, which He was oblig'd to follow, in assigning the *Forms* and *Essences* of Things. . . . From all that we have urg'd on this Head, it may appear, that the Sentence which is frequently in the Mouths of most Men, *That the Precepts of natural Law are of eternal Verity*, is so far to be restrain'd and limited, that this Eternity ought to reach no farther than the Imposition and Institution of GOD ALMIGHTY, and the Origin of human Kind.[26]

Both the form and content of the rules of sociability, that is, the natural law, have their origin in the will of God; these are no mere rules of prudence.

But to make these Dictates of Reason obtain the Power and the Dignity of Laws, it is necessary to call in a much higher Principle to our Assistance. For altho' the Usefulness and Expediency of them be clearly apparent, yet this bare Consideration could never bring so strong a Tie on Mens Minds, but that they would recede from these Rules, whenever a Man was pleas'd either to neglect his own Advantage, or to pursue it by some different Means, which he judg'd more proper, and more likely to succeed. . . . It is therefore, on all Accounts, to be concluded, and to be maintain'd, that the Obligation of *natural Law* proceeds from GOD himself, the great Creator and supreme Governor of Mankind; who, by Virtue of his Sovereignty, hath bound Men to the Observation of it. . . . Now this supreme Being having so form'd and dispos'd the Nature of Things, and of Mankind, as to make a sociable Life necessary to our Subsistence and Preservation; and having, on this Account, indued us with a Mind capable of entertaining such Notions as conduce to this End; and having insinuated these Notions into our Understandings, by the Movement of natural Things, deriv'd from him the first Mover; and, likewise, most clearly represented to us their necessary Connexion, and their Truth: Hence it follows, that it is the Will of GOD, Man should frame his Life according to that Disposition and Method, which he seems peculiarly to have assign'd him above the Life of Brutes. And since this cannot otherwise be atchiev'd and compass'd, than by the Observance of *natural Law*, it must be suppos'd that GOD hath laid an Obligation on Man to obey this *Law*, as a *Means* not arising from human Invention, or changeable at human Pleasure, but expressly ordain'd by GOD himself for the Accomplishment of this Design.[27]

Pufendorf explains the requirements of sociability (natural righteousness) by analyzing, not our rights, but our duties; first, our natural duties to God (that is, the requirements of natural religion); second, our duties

[26] *The Law of Nature and Nations*, pp. 16–19.
[27] Ibid., p. 141.

to ourselves; third, our duties to others. All three categories are related in whole or in part to sociability.

Our duties to others are of two kinds: some (those called "absolute") are duties to all other people; others (called "conditional") are duties integral to special relationships, such as husband and wife, master and servant. The cardinal absolute duty is to avoid injuring any other person. To be righteous, we must respect each other's natural rights.

> In the Series of *absolute* Duties, or such as oblige all Men antecedently to any human Institution, this seems, with Justice, to challenge the first and noblest Place, *that no Man hurt another; and that, in case of any Hurt or Damage done by him, he fail not to make Reparation.* For this Duty is not only the largest of all in its Extent, comprehending *all Men*, on the bare Account of their being *Men*; but it is, at the same time, the most easy of all to be perform'd, consisting, for the most part, purely in a negative Abstinence from acting; except that its Assistance is sometimes necessary in restraining the Lusts and Passions, when they fight and struggle against Reason; amongst which rebellious Desires, that boundless Regard which we sometimes shew to our own private Advantage, seems to be the Principal, and the Ringleader. Besides, it is the most necessary of human Duties, inasmuch as a Life of Society cannot possibly be maintain'd without it. For suppose a Man to do me no good, and not so much as to transact with me in the common Offices of Life; yet, provided he do me no harm, I can live with him under some tolerable Comfort and Quiet. And, indeed, this is all we desire from the greatest Part of Mankind; a mutual Intercourse of good Turns lying only between a few. But what Possibility is there of my living at Peace with him who hurts and injures me; since Nature has implanted in every Man's Breast so tender a Concern for himself, and for what he possesses, that he cannot but apply all Means to resist and repel him, who in either respect attempts to wrong him? Now, as the Strength of this Precept is a Guard and a Fence to those Things, which we receive from the immediate Hand of Nature, as our Life, our Bodies, our Members, our Chastity, our Reputation, and our Liberty; engaging Men to keep them sacred and inviolable: So must it be supposed to spread itself thro' all those Compacts or Institutions, by which the Propriety of any Thing is made over to us; since without it they could obtain no Force or Effect. Whatever, therefore, we can, on any good Title, call our own, Men are by this Precept forbidden to take away, to endamage, or to impair, or any way to withdraw it from our Use, in whole or in part.[28]

This duty is negative; it prohibits wrongs. Another absolute duty is positive: we are to practice *humanity*, that is, we are to do works beneficial to others. These may be done "indefinitely," that is, for no particular per-

[28] Ibid., pp. 211–12.

son or persons, as when we prepare our minds or bodies to be useful to the public; hence it appears "that those Persons are guilty of a Sin against Nature's Law, who neglect to exercise themselves in some honest Art or Employment, by living unprofitable to themselves, and troublesome to others, use their Soul only for Salt, to keep their Body from stinking."[29] Other good works are "definite"; that is, they are intended to be beneficial to particular persons. It is obvious that we are required to help others in ways that cost us nothing, as when we give directions to travelers. In this context, Pufendorf discusses with approval Grotius's prohibition against artificial restrictions on trade and commerce; such restrictions are contrary to the requirements of *humanity*. He summarizes Grotius's position as follows:

> [It is a duty of humanity] that we allow every Man the Privilege of procuring for himself, by Money, Work, Exchange of Goods, or any other lawful Contract, such Things as contribute to the Convenience of Life, and that we do not abridge him of this Liberty, either by any civil Ordinance, or by any unlawful Combination, or Monopoly. For that as Trade and Commerce highly promote the Interest of all Nations, by supplying the Unkindness of the Soil, which is not every where alike fertile, and by making those Fruits seem to be born in all Places of the World, which are to be found in any one: So it cannot be less than Inhumanity to deny any *Son of the Earth* the Use of those good Things, which our common Mother affords for our Support; provided our peculiar Right and Propriety be not injured by such a Favour.[30]

Pufendorf thought that Grotius had been too sweeping. The export of luxuries may be prohibited, and even necessities, but the latter only when there is a genuine domestic shortage.

A far more taxing duty of humanity requires that in certain circumstances we do good works that cost us money or painful effort. Such works "are called benefits *par excellence*, and they offer the best opportunity to gain praise, if only nobility of spirit and prudence duly control them."[31] Both what we can afford, taking our other commitments into account, and what really would be best for the potential beneficiary must be considered.

The virtue expressed by an appropriate response to beneficence is grat-

[29] Ibid., p. 241.

[30] Ibid., pp. 253–54. The way Pufendorf prepared the ground for the full recognition of commerce as a form of association has been examined by Istvan Hont, "The Language of Sociability and Commerce: Samuel Pufendorf and the Theoretical Foundations of the 'Four-Stages Theory'," in *Languages of Political Theory*, pp. 253–76.

[31] Pufendorf, *On the Duty of Man and Citizen*, p. 46. See also Pufendorf's discussion of the *higher* requirements of humanity—requirements of noble rank, stiled *benefits*—in *The Law of Nature and Nations*, p. 256.

itude. Strictly speaking, ingratitude does not injure, for, because no agreement or contract is involved, the right to gratitude is not a perfect right.

All Pufendorf's conditional duties originate in an express or tacit contract of some kind. The great examples relate to property. God did not confer on human beings, either severally or collectively, title to all the rest of creation; rather, he simply made all those things available to them. Without committing any wrong, each might help himself. There was "a negative Communion."[32] Here Pufendorf differs somewhat from Grotius, for whom all humankind collectively owned the sea, land, birds, and so on. It was not, says Pufendorf, until people had agreed to treat fields, flocks, and the like as proper to specific persons, which they did under the pressure of a growing population and to meet the requirements of new modes of production, that there were any property rights. The first appropriation took place by agreement: specified goods went to specified persons. Subsequently, all new original ownership comes about by occupation (first possession).

> We have sufficiently made it appear in our former Remarks, that after Men came to a Resolution of quitting the primitive Communion, upon the Strength of a previous Contract, they assigned to each Person his Share out of the general Stock, either by the Authority of Parents, or by universal Consent, or by Lot, or sometimes by the free Choice and Option of the Party receiving. Now it was at the same time agreed, that whatever did not come under this grand Division, should pass to the first Occupant; that is, to him who, before others, took bodily Possession of it, with Intention to keep it as his own.[33]

Once private property has been established, trade follows, with goods and services being exchanged at their natural (market) values. Eventually money is invented.

[32] *The Law of Nature and Nations*, p. 367. God, who had every kind of right to all creation, conferred on humankind a right to the fish, fowl, and so forth; thus from the beginning some kind of right was common to all human beings. What kind of right? By using the expression "negative Communion" to refer to the primordial order, Pufendorf means that nobody had an exclusive right to certain kinds of goods, such as land; each person might rightfully pick and gather from the common whatever he needed for his own immediate use. Property, the institution by which specific persons rightfully may use specific trees, fields, cattle, and their offspring and fruit, and alienate the same, was introduced later and by consent. In *Patriarcha*, republished in 1679, when the Whigs were seeking to have James, Duke of York, excluded from the succession to the throne by Act of Parliament, Sir Robert Filmer denounced both the notion of the primordial equality of humankind and the notion that property was instituted from below, by general consent. John Locke undertook to refute Filmer's patriarchalism. The political significance of the origin-of-property question has been made evident by James Tully, in *A Discourse on Property: John Locke and His Adversaries* (Cambridge: Cambridge University Press, 1980).
[33] Ibid., p. 386.

Here then we see human beings living in an advanced society without a civil government. It is a stage in which they have rights to life, liberty, reputation, and so on, and also, once property has been introduced, rights to their own external goods. They form families. They set up the master-servant relationship—at first by contract between "the wiser and richer Sort" and those of lesser parts and less wealth, and later by contracts between victors and vanquished in just wars—in which those in servitude have rights, as well as the masters.[34] It appears that the laws of sociability have been sufficient to bring about an idyllic situation, one far removed from Hobbes's war of all against all. However, the truth is that people neglect their obligations; corrupt, they fail to heed God's command-ments. Driven by avarice and ambition and, careless of the benefits they jeopardize by endangering society, as well as of the wrath of God, they show little concern for righteousness; instead, they neglect and violate each other's rights licentiously.

> [T]he Multitude act not by rational Motives, but by wild Impulse, mistaking Passion for Reason; chiefly through the Fault of Custom or Education, which stifle and suppress the Force of inward Reflection. As, also, because the great-est Part of Mankind are wholly intent upon the present, without any Care or Thought of the future; and are commonly moved by those Objects which thrust themselves upon their Senses, while those of a higher and nobler Na-ture are too refined for their Affections, and too remote for their Desires.[35]

Groups of people can deliver themselves from the sad results of human weakness by a covenant to unite as a distinct civil society, a city or com-monwealth with a government. Once that covenant has been made, the new city or commonwealth determines the form of its government by a decree. The third step is a second covenant: "After the Decree hath passed, to settle the particular Form of Government, there will again be Occasion for a new Covenant, when the Person or Persons, on whom the Sovereignty is conferred, shall be actually constituted; by which the Rul-ers, on the one hand, engage themselves to take care of the common Peace and Security, and the Subjects, on the other, to yield them faithful Obe-dience; in which, likewise, is included that Submission and Union of Wills, by which we conceive a State to be but *one Person*."[36] The supreme authority makes laws by focusing the principles of natural law on specific situations: it prescribes the punishments for wrongs; it decides controver-sies; it provides for the public worship of God and the education of the people; it organizes defence against foreign enemies.

[34] Ibid., pp. 611–13.
[35] Ibid., p. 630.
[36] Ibid., p. 636.

The contract with the rulers may be drawn so as to give them absolute power. If this has been done, the people have no right to try to change the constitution by revolution.[37] Nor is it true to say that the people have a right to apply force to their rulers to make them heed the popular will. However, to make these points is not to say that resistance is never right. For "there is in the People, or in particular Persons, a Right of defending their Life and Safety against their Prince, upon the Approach of extreme Danger, and when the Prince is manifestly turn'd an Enemy towards them."[38]

How successful was Pufendorf's attempt to restore natural jurisprudence? He had dealt with Hobbes's argument that precepts of reason are not laws by asserting that the natural laws are the commands of God, the supreme legislator. But does this assertion mean that superiority of authority is the criterion of righteousness, that, by definition, the commands of every superior are just? If not, if only the commands of God are always unquestionably just, what distinguishes His commands from those of Hobbes's "mortal Gods"? Is it, perhaps, His infinitely greater might? Or is it the fact that His will always conforms to eternal and immutable standards of righteousness? Pufendorf's account, according to Leibniz, was contradictory: in overcoming Hobbes, he had attributed the obligation to obey natural law to God's superior might; later he had said that to be obliging, the commands of the Almighty must be just; but he had failed to explain why righteousness binds the will of God. He made juridical obligations derive from the commands of a superior; yet he held also that the superior must have just cause. Commented Leibniz, "Consequently the justice of the cause is antecedent to this same superior, contrary to what had been asserted. Well, then, if the source of law is the will of a superior and, inversely, a justifying cause of law is necessary in order to have a superior, a circle is created, than which none was ever more manifest. From what will the justice of the cause derive, if there is not yet a superior, from whom, supposedly, the law may emanate?"[39]

[37] Ibid., p. 722.

[38] Ibid., p. 722.

[39] "Opinion on the Principles of Pufendorf," in *The Political Writings of Leibniz*, ed. Patrick Riley (Cambridge: Cambridge University Press, 1972), pp. 64–75, esp. 73–74. In another piece, "Meditation on the Common Concept of Justice," Leibniz states that the debate (in which Pufendorf had become entangled) was not new: "It is agreed that whatever God wills is good and just. But there remains the question whether it is good and just because God wills it or whether God wills it because it is good and just: in other words, whether justice and goodness are arbitrary or whether they belong to the necessary and eternal truths about the nature of things, as do numbers and proportions. The former opinion has been followed by some philosophers [including Pufendorf] and by some Roman [Catholic] and Reformed theologians: but present-day Reformed [theologians] usually reject this doctrine, as do all of our theologians and most of those of the Roman Church." He

Once a voluntarist concedes that to be binding the commands of his legislator must be just, he finds himself caught up in an infinite regression, commander above commander *ad infinitum*. Leibniz's own position is that justice is not a matter of will; rather, it belongs "to the necessary and eternal truths about the nature of things, as do numbers and proportions."

Pufendorf's works must be counted extremely influential, especially if the number of editions means much. Defective in principle they might be; but, as Leibniz himself admitted, they, especially *De Officio Hominis et Civis*, were readily available.[40] In Scotland during the 1690s, after the reform of the universities, natural jurisprudence gained an increasingly prominent place in that important part of the curriculum known as moral philosophy. In this development, the pioneer was Gerschom Carmichael (1672–1729), appointed a regent at Glasgow in 1694, and subsequently, in 1727, the first professor of moral philosophy. In 1718 Carmichael gave Pufendorf's *De Officio Hominis et Civis* new prominence and influence by publishing a carefully annotated edition of that work.[41] Therein he

---

goes on to comment that on the former view the will of the Devil would define justice if only he were the most powerful. *The Political Writings of Leibniz*, pp. 45–46.

[40] Leonard Krieger, *The Politics of Discretion: Pufendorf and the Acceptance of Natural Law* (Chicago: The University of Chicago Press, 1965), pp. 255–66. Krieger reports that in the case of *De Iure Naturae* and *De Officio Hominis et Civis*, listings can be found of thirty-five editions in Latin, thirty-nine in French, and fourteen in English. See also Knud Haakonssen, "Natural Law and the Scottish Enlightenment," in *Man and Nature*, in *Proceedings of the Canadian Society for Eighteenth-Century Studies* 4 (1985): 47–80.

[41] Although their views on political authority differed greatly, John Locke made extensive use of Pufendorf when writing *Two Treatises of Government*. "He took advantage of Pufendorf's arguments, he reproduced his positions, and he describes his major work 'as the best book of that kind', better than the great Grotius on *War and Peace*." Peter Laslett in his introduction to *John Locke: Two Treatises of Government* (Cambridge: Cambridge University Press, 1964), p. 74. The key role of Pufendorf, Carmichael, and the jurisprudential tradition in Scottish education in the early-eighteenth century has been shown by James Moore and Michael Silverthorne, "Gershom Carmichael and the Natural Jurisprudence Tradition in Eighteenth-Century Scotland," in *Wealth and Virtue: The Shaping of Political Economy in the Scottish Enlightenment*, eds. Istvan Hont and Michael Ignatieff (Cambridge: Cambridge University Press, 1983), pp. 73–87. For the content of Carmichael's teachings and his criticisms of Pufendorf, see the same authors' essay, "Natural Sociability and Natural Rights in the Moral Philosophy of Gerschom Carmichael," in *Philosophers of the Scottish Enlightenment*, ed. Vincent Hope (Edinburgh: Edinburgh University Press, 1984), pp. 1–12. Therein Carmichael's revision of Pufendorf's theory, to bring it into line with the best views of the new, post-1688, Scottish establishment, are examined. In sum, Carmichael's criticism of Pufendorf, although not expressed in this way, was that he had followed Hobbes too closely, accepting an absolute ruler as legitimate and tracing the obligation to follow natural law to God's omnipotence. The origins of intellectual liberalism in the Scottish universities, so that they ceased to be simply Calvinist seminaries, is examined by Peter Jones in "The Scottish Professoriate and the Polite Academy, 1720–46," in *Wealth and Virtue*, pp. 89–117.

undertook to correct certain defects in Pufendorf's theory: the latter (as Leibniz had said) had explained our obligation to obey natural law as a result of God's superior power and had neglected His justice and goodness; his account of the origin of private property had been superseded by Locke's; he had failed to denounce slavery. It appears that it was Carmichael who inaugurated in Scotland the practice of combining natural theology and natural jurisprudence: the former, of course, already had a well-established place in the university curriculum, but now, in addition, it came to be used as the basis for natural-law instruction on personal rights, the family, the economy, the role of governments, the right of resistance, and so forth.

Francis Hutcheson, who occupied the chair of moral philosophy at Glasgow from 1730 to 1746, writing in a preface to his *Introduction to Moral Philosophy*, explains to readers that the ancients divided moral philosophy into two parts. The first, ethics, taught the nature and regulation of the internal dispositions; the second, dealt with the law of nature. The latter "contained, 1. *the doctrine of* private rights, *or the laws obtaining in natural liberty.* 2. Oeconomicks, *or the laws and rights of the several members of a family; and* 3. Politicks, *shewing the various plans of civil government, and the rights of states with respect to each other.*" Hutcheson assures his readers that his own *Introduction* contains "*the elements of these several branches of moral philosophy,*" and will serve to give them access to the works of both the ancients, such as Plato and Cicero, and the moderns, "Grotius, Cumberland, Puffendorf, Harrington *and others.*"[42]

Scottish lawyers had become familiar with natural-law thought through the works of Grotius, Vinnius, Voet, and others in the continental universities, especially Leyden and Utrecht, whither they repaired to finish their training, and through Stair's influential *Institutions of the Law of Scotland.*[43] However, neither Grotius nor any other natural-law

[42] *A Short Introduction to Moral Philosophy, in three books; containing the Elements of Ethicks and the Law of Nature* (Glasgow: Robert Foulis, 1747), p. i.

[43] One scholar comments, "There was from 1681 (the publication year of the first edition of Stair's *Institutions*) a stretch of more than a hundred years in which the particular jurisprudence of Scotland flourished as never before or since, through the publication of a series of clear, comprehensive and principled scholarly elaborations of the private law and the criminal law of Scotland. There was also a flourishing in Scotland of jurisprudence in its more general sense, the philosophical study of the nature and fundamental principles of law and legality in themselves and in relation to morality, to social custom and to political economy." This contrasts sharply with the complacency of English lawyers of that period. Neil MacCormick, "Law and Enlightenment," in *The Origins and Nature of the Scottish Enlightenment*, eds. R. H. Campbell and A. S. Skinner (Edinburgh: John Donald Publishers Ltd., 1982), pp. 150–51. See R. G. Cant, "Origins of the Enlightenment in Scotland: the Universities" in the same volume of essays, pp. 42–64. Also, Alasdair MacIntyre, *Whose*

writer seems to have had any influence on instruction in moral philosophy in Scotland during the seventeenth century. It was Pufendorf's works, especially *De Officio Hominis et Civis*, that moved natural jurisprudence to the fore. Pufendorf was highly attractive: first, he based his theory on a foundation that, although flawed, did not repel orthodox Calvinists; second, his theory dealt directly with many questions of great interest in Scotland at a time when university education was being reformed to meet the requirements of a society that had thrown in its lot with England, then rapidly becoming the most commercialized and luxurious society in the world. Natural jurisprudence, with Grotius and Pufendorf as the authorities, was to provide the frame for discussion and instruction on most of the great topics of concern to Scots—most notably David Hume and Adam Smith—throughout the eighteenth century. The requirements of allegiance; the basis and rules of private property; the rights to buy and sell goods and services; the role of religion in society; the best form of society and government—all these were questions that Scots discussed keenly as their country was transformed.

Samuel Clarke and William Wollaston

Writing anonymously in his *Abstract*, Hume mentions that the author of the *Treatise* "talks with contempt of hypotheses; and insinuates, that such of our countrymen as have banished them from moral philosophy, have done a more signal service to the world, than *my Lord Bacon*, whom he considers as the father of experimental physicks. He mentions, on this occasion, *Mr. Locke, my Lord Shaftsbury, Dr. Mandeville, Mr. Hutchison, Dr. Butler*, who, tho' they differ in many points among themselves, seem all to agree in founding their accurate disquisitions of human nature intirely upon experience."[44] Two early-eighteenth century English writers who persisted in relying on reason alone were Samuel Clarke and William Wollaston. Although not named in the *Abstract* as relying on hypotheses, it was Hume's contention that they did not understand the method of true philosophy.[45]

Justice? Which Rationality? (Notre Dame: University of Notre Dame Press, 1988), pp. 209–59.

[44] Hume, *An Abstract of a Book lately Published, entituled, A Treatise of Human Nature, &c.*, reprinted with an introduction by J. M. Keynes and P. Straffa (Cambridge: Cambridge University Press, 1938). The *Abstract* has been reprinted with the second edition (the Selby-Bigge edition as revised by P. H. Nidditch) of *A Treatise of Human Nature*, pp. 641–62; my quotation is from p. 646.

[45] The theories of Clarke and Wollaston are analyzed succinctly in J. L. Mackie, *Hume's Moral Theory* (London: Routledge & Kegan Paul, 1980), pp. 15–23. See also Stanley Twey-

Clarke, perhaps the most eminent English philosophical theologian of the early-eighteenth century, argues, in *A Discourse of Natural Religion*, the Boyle Lectures (1705), that to make obedience to a superior the basis of righteousness is to deprive righteousness of its essential quality and to make power the ultimate principle. Let us think of human life as a great play. According to Clarke, each role in the play has its rights and duties; those rights and duties constitute the role. Even if the play had never been put into production by the act of creation, the rights and duties would have remained exactly the same. They are the fundamentals of justice, the principles of righteousness. Even God himself, who willed the production, could not have altered the rights and duties—not because He is under a superior authority, but because He himself is just or righteous; the eternal reason (the eternal law or *logos*) is an essential element of His character. Clarke finds the original of righteousness, not in the will of God, but in the eternal law, the eternal reason; as a result, for Clarke the requirements of righteousness are to be known by reasoning, not simply by obeying commands, as with orthodox Calvinists. The requirements of moral duty can be known directly from the definitions of the roles: king, husband, friend. Moreover, the roles are their own justification; while it is true that the players find their fulfillment (happiness) in their roles, all consequences for the players, whether natural, such as good health, or extrinsic, such as crowns in Heaven, are secondary to the great play.

Clarke constantly uses the analogy of mathematics. Each person is to be treated justly. To treat equal persons unequally would be as inconsistent or absurd as to treat the sum of three and four as other than seven; similarly, to treat unequals equally would be absurd. To treat persons without appropriate attention to their different roles, places, or stations in life would be an absurdity or inconsistency comparable to treating acute angles as if they were obtuse, circles as squares, or triangles as hexagonals. Justice requires that we give each person his due, and each person's due is a function of his role. Consistency obliges us to be just. We ought not to permit subjectivism, in the form of particular loves and hatreds, to distort our conduct.

The several players are in different relationships with each other; what is fit and unfit, right and wrong, follows from those relationships. God himself necessarily is just; men likewise ought

> to govern all their actions by the same rules, for the good of the public, in their respective stations. That is; these eternal and necessary differences of things make it *fit and reasonable* for creatures so to act; they cause it to be their *duty*, or lay an *obligation* upon them, so to do; even separate from the

man, *Reason and Conduct in Hume and His Predecessors* (The Hague: Martinus Nijhoff, 1974), pp. 73–99.

consideration of these rules being the *positive will* or *command of God*; and also antecedent to any respect or regard, expectation or apprehension, of any *particular private and personal advantage or disadvantage, reward or punishment*, either present or future; annexed either by natural consequence, or by positive appointment, to the practising or neglecting of those rules.[46]

In short, what is most important is the play itself; the players are under obligation to perform it faithfully regardless of the fact that they thereby enjoy happiness or win applause and laurels.

Clarke complains that Hobbes and all those who begin with positive law, either divine or human, as the original of justice make right merely the product of might. The truth is that the difference between right and wrong is independent of power; it is based on necessary and eternal relationships. It is as clear as a mathematical proposition that there is "a fitness or suitableness of certain circumstances to certain persons, and an unsuitableness of others; founded in the nature of things and the qualifications of persons, antecedent to all positive appointment whatsoever; also that from the different relations of different persons one to another, there necessarily arises a fitness or unfitness of certain manners of behaviour of some persons towards others."[47]

If there were no difference between good and bad before positive laws are made, Clarke argues, there would be no valid reason for making positive laws, and there would be no difference between good and bad positive laws. It may be asserted by some, he says, that while all is indifferent in terms of justice, governors decide to make some conduct obligatory for "the public benefit of the community." But, says Clarke, this is a contradictory assertion. If a certain kind of conduct is beneficial to the community, all was not indifferent: "For if the practice of certain things tends to the public benefit of the world, and the contrary would tend to the public disadvantage; then those things are not in their own nature indifferent, but were good and reasonable to be practised before any law was made,

---

[46] Samuel Clarke, *A Discourse of Natural Religion*, in *British Moralists: 1650–1800*, ed. D. D. Raphael, 2 vols. (Oxford: Clarendon Press, 1969) 1:192. We should remember that rationalist moral theory went hand in hand with rationalist (or natural) religion, as the book titles often proclaim. Hume could trace rationalist moral theory back no farther than Father Nicholas Malebranche, whose three-volume work came out in the 1670s. *Enquiry* II, p. 197n. On Hume's early interest in Malebranche, see Charles J. McCracken, *Malebranche and British Philosophy* (Oxford: Clarendon Press, 1983). Henning Graf Reventlow provides a valuable history of rationalist religion in England shortly before and after 1700; his notes contain comprehensive bibliographical information on Shaftesbury, Toland, Clarke, Butler, and others. *The Authority of the Bible and the Rise of the Modern World*, translated from the German by John Bowden (London: SCM Press Ltd., 1984).

[47] *A Discourse of Natural Religion*, p. 192.

and can only for that very reason be wisely enforced by the authority of laws."[48]

The understanding is convinced absolutely by a demonstration in arithmetic or geometry; likewise, the understanding is convinced absolutely by a demonstration of the requirements of justice. True, human beings sometimes do not see clearly what is morally right, but it is true also that often they do not understand Euclid's theorems until they have been adequately instructed. Also, people may be blind to what is just when their own interest is involved, but when they are impartial spectators, they see clearly far more readily. The truth is "that the mind of man naturally and necessarily assents to the eternal law of righteousness."[49] This is shown better

> from the judgement that men pass upon each *other's* actions, than from what we can discern concerning their consciousness of their *own*. For men may dissemble and conceal from the world, the judgement of their own conscience; nay, by a strange partiality, they may even impose upon and deceive *themselves*; (for who is there, that does not sometimes allow himself, nay, and even justify himself in that, wherein he condemns another?) But men's judgements concerning the actions of *others*, especially where they have no relation to themselves, or repugnance to their interest, are commonly impartial; and from this we may judge, what sense men naturally have of the unalterable difference of right and wrong.[50]

Once we know what is right, we ought to act conformably. We are here to perform the play and ought not to allow ourselves to be distracted by personal whims or off-stage commotions; unfortunately, however, often we are swayed, contrary to our consciences, by "unaccountable arbitrary humours, and rash passions, by lusts, vanity and pride; by private interest, or present sensual pleasures."[51] Those who allow themselves to be distracted, so that their performance is defective, stand convicted in the court of their own conscience. It is a person's own conscience that puts him under obligation to act his part properly; other motives are secondary.

> The original *obligation* of all, (the ambiguous use of which word as a term of art, has caused some perplexity and confusion in this matter,) is the eternal reason of things; that reason, which God himself, who has no superior to direct him, and to whose happiness nothing can be added nor any thing diminished from it, yet constantly obliges himself to govern the world by: and

[48] Ibid., p. 196.
[49] Ibid., p. 204.
[50] Ibid., pp. 204–5.
[51] Ibid., p. 201.

the more excellent and perfect any creatures are, the more cheerfully and steadily are their wills always determined by this supreme obligation, in conformity to the nature, and in imitation of the most perfect will of God.[52]

When he analyzes the eternal law of righteousness, the law of right reason, Clarke finds that it has three great branches. One of these relates to one's own life: a person is to strive to make and preserve himself healthy in mind and body so as to be able to perform his role. He is to restrain his appetites and govern his passions. Moreover, just as he may not depart "wilfully out of this life, which is the *general station* that God has appointed him; he is obliged likewise to attend the duties of that *particular station* or condition of life, whatsoever it be, wherein Providence has at present placed him; with diligence, and contentment: without being either uneasy and discontented, that others are placed by Providence in different and superior stations in the world; or so extremely and unreasonably solicitous to change his state for the future, as thereby to neglect his present duty."[53]

A second branch of righteousness relates to our dealings with other human beings. This branch is subdivided: the first part requires equity; the second, benevolence. First, we are to treat each person equitably; we are to deal with him no different than "as in like circumstances we could reasonably expect he should deal with us." Equity requires, not that everybody be treated alike, but that every person in a particular role be treated the same as every other person in that role. Reason requires that we take all the elements of the situation, including the public good, into account. For example, the magistrate should not think how he would wish to be dealt with if he were the criminal, but "what *reason* and the *public good* would oblige him to *acknowledge* was fit and just for him to *expect*."

> And the same proportion is to be observed, in deducing the duties of parents and children, of masters and servants, of governors and subjects, of citizens and foreigners; in what manner every person is obliged by the rule of equity, to behave himself in each of these and all other relations. In the regular and uniform practice of all which duties among all mankind, in their several and respective relations, through the whole earth; consists that *universal justice*, which is the top and perfection of all virtues.[54]

The other part of the second branch requires that we go beyond justice and act generally with "*mutual love and benevolence*." Once we have seen that whatever is good ought to be sought, we are committed to seek

[52] Ibid., p. 202.
[53] Ibid., p. 212.
[54] Ibid., pp. 207–9.

the greatest good of mankind. For the confirmation of this principle, Clarke turns from reason to experience. Human beings need society for many reasons; as a result, they form many groups "till by degrees the affection of single persons, becomes a friendship of families; and this enlarges itself to society of towns and cities and nations; and terminates in the agreeing community of all mankind. The foundation, preservation, and perfection of which universal friendship or society, is *mutual love and benevolence*." Men need society, and "mutual love and benevolence is the only possible means to establish this society in any tolerable and durable manner."[55] Hobbes notwithstanding, each person ought, as Cicero asserted, "to *love all others as himself*."[56] The last branch of righteousness, which Clarke (like Pufendorf) puts first, is that we are to love, honor, and worship God.

As mentioned, Clarke dismisses all the benefits the players may gain by stellar performances, also all punishments, as only consequential, secondary, and auxiliary. It is true that good conduct often has good results: one who avoids gluttony and drunkenness will be healthier. It is true also that good conduct is beneficial for the whole of humankind, but there are serious practical difficulties in using public utility as the measure of goodness.

> And true indeed it is, in the whole; that the good of the universal creation, does always *coincide* with the necessary truth and reason of things. But otherwise, (and separate from *this* consideration, that God will certainly cause truth and right to terminate in happiness;) *what* is for the good of the whole creation, in very many cases, none but an infinite understanding can possibly judge. Public utility, is one thing to one nation, and the contrary to another: and the governors of every nation, will and must be judges of the public good: and by public good, they will generally mean the private good of that particular nation. But truth and right (whether public or private) founded in the eternal and necessary reason of things, is what every man can judge of, when laid before him. It is necessarily one and the same, to every man's understanding; just as light is the same, to every man's eyes.[57]

What is right inevitably rules the moral judgment: no one "willingly and deliberately transgresses this rule, in any great and considerable instance; but he acts contrary to the judgement and reason of his own mind, and secretly reproaches himself for so doing." But if he does what is right, his own mind congratulates him for executing "what his conscience could not forbear giving its assent to, as just and right." It is to this that St. Paul

[55] Ibid., p. 210.
[56] Ibid., p. 211.
[57] Ibid., pp. 216–17.

refers when he says that when the Gentiles, who have not the law, do what the law requires, they are the law unto themselves, which shows "the work of the law written in their hearts, their conscience also bearing witness, and their thoughts the mean while *accusing*, or else *excusing* one another."[58]

Clarke finds that Hobbes cannot avoid admitting the relevance of the difference between right and wrong to his amoral state of nature; in explaining why human beings seek peace, Hobbes has to admit that the lawlessness of that state leads to disastrous results. When all behave utterly selfishly, everybody suffers—this fact shows that Hobbes's state of nature is contrary to the nature of things; it is both bad and wrong. But, we may ask, is Clarke's own theory totally different? Hobbes's argument is that human beings will not follow the precepts of reason in the state of nature, not because the precepts would not make for an improvement, but because each person cannot be sure his fellows also will heed them. The main effect of the establishment of a government is that one can feel reasonably sure the precepts will be followed by one's fellow subjects. If Clarke were quite different from Hobbes, he would have to adopt the Stoic position that righteous conduct, regardless of all consequences, in fact is its own sufficient obligation; yet he explicitly rejects that position as unrealistic. He finds that, unfortunately, man and the world being as they now are, righteousness although obligatory, is rarely found compelling. For this reason, rewards and punishments, both temporal and eternal, are required to convince people to make an effort to practice righteousness. In short, the fact of the Fall cannot be ignored. This means that insofar as practical results are concerned, Hobbes and Clarke are not all that far apart. They differ radically, however, on the nature of the basic obligation to follow what Hobbes calls the precepts of reason. For Hobbes, those precepts are recommended by their usefulness; the observance of them by the individuals who constitute a society makes for peace and commodious living. For Clarke, a sufficiently rational person would observe the precepts regardless of all consequences.

Clarke does not distinguish between the good, the right, and the true. A good person is one who is perfectly genuine; he is true to his part, role, or idea. Shaftesbury, as we shall see, regards the play (society) as the result of the players' healthy passions; once the play has been thoroughly rehearsed, so that all the roles have been conclusively determined, any deviations or wrongs are attributable to aberrant passions. Clarke, in contrast, takes the play as the primordial datum. He asserts that human beings, called to be players, ought to play their parts regardless of their passions. There is nothing contingent about the play, nothing arbitrary in

[58] Ibid., p. 203.

the distinction between right and wrong conduct. Obviously, God is omnipotent, and we may be tempted to think of the rules of the play as commands of God; however, we should obey the rules, not because God orders us to do so, but because the rules are rational (or good).

Clarke relies on the idea of roles: every character in the play (whether the play is produced or not) is essential; accordingly, each participant is to be respected by both himself and others. This means that suicide, murder, injury, and the like necessarily are wrong; sound laws, divine and human, simply specify and confirm primordial right. He relies also on the idea of human beings as equal individuals; this is the basis of equity. What one person claims as a human being, either as a member of the cast or as proper to his particular role, he cannot deny to any other without being irrational. Hume, as we will see, does not dispute Clarke's conclusions, but he denies that we come to them by reason alone.

William Wollaston is the other rationalist moralist Hume dealt with directly. Wollaston's aim is to provide the correct definition of moral good and evil. Some say, follow "common sense"—but the opinions of humanity are neither uniform nor consistent. Some say, follow "nature"—but this is an unsatisfactory maxim, because it is too naturalistic (pagan) and may be interpreted as meaning that the irrational appetites and passions are to be given free rein. Some say, follow "right reason"—but whose reason is right? All these definitions are subjective; what is required is one that emphasizes the fact that the standard is not in the knower, but in the known. Wollaston's own definition is this: *"No act (whether word or deed) of any being, to whom moral good and evil are imputable, that interferes with any true proposition, or denies any thing to be as it is, can be right."*[59] To act contrary to one's promise is to deny the fact that one made a promise, which is untrue. To take another's horse without permission is to deny the fact that the owner has title to the horse, which is untrue. To commit murder is to pretend to have a right to do so, which is untrue. To act righteously is to act truthfully, that is, in conformity with things as they are, and to act wrongfully is to act falsely, in conflict with things as they are.

What Wollaston says has the merit of rejecting certain popular maxims as defective. Righteousness does entail conformity; otherwise, right as a standard is indefinite, which is a contradiction. But, we must ask, what are the credentials of "things as they are"? Why is it good always to act in conformity with one's promises? Why are old titles always to be respected? Even if his theory did not have this difficulty, the basic difficulty of all positivistic theories of right, his definition does not explain either

[59] *The Religion of Nature Delineated*, in *British Moralists*, 1:243.

moral obligation or moral motivation. Why ought we always to act truthfully? What moves us to act as we do, either rightfully or wrongfully?

The Dilemma

The dilemma of the modern natural-law theorists now was obvious. For Hobbes, a society is an arrangement established to protect selfish individuals from each other; this is achieved within each society by laws made by the person appointed the sovereign of that society. In contrast, the natural-law theorists insist on a basic sociability; however, since most societies do not operate automatically, these writers, like Hobbes, need sovereigns. Then, in making their case for natural law—a body of law binding on all sovereigns, Christian, infidel, and godless alike—they enter hazardous theological waters. Grotius uses both the available tacks, but neither is successful. If, as Clarke argues, natural law is a set of eternal precepts of reason, why, apart from God's will, is anybody obliged to heed those precepts? To say that they ought to be followed because they are right simply begs us to ask, first, why we should do what is right, and second, how we can know that they are right. Moreover, we seem to be placing God under an even higher authority. The alternative, the other tack, is to adopt a position of divine positivism, a position which has no difficulty in explaining the obligation to obey, but which deprives righteousness of moral virtue. We are obliged to obey because of God's power to reward the obedient and punish the disobedient. But this is to say that righteousness is the best policy: it is prudent to obey natural law, not because it is intrinsically good, but because of attendant sanctions. The dilemma arose from the fact that these theorists approached morals legalistically. They started with law, with right.

Pufendorf tried to wriggle off the horn he had chosen by adducing gratitude as an additional reason for obeying God. He wrote,

> It must be acknowledg'd . . . as a certain Truth, That neither Strength, nor any other natural Pre-eminence, is alone sufficient to derive an Obligation on me from another's Will; but that it is farther requisite, I should either have receiv'd some extraordinary Good from him, or should voluntarily have agreed to submit my self to his Direction. . . . For, as we naturally yield and give up ourselves to some singular Benefactor, so if it appears that this Benefactor both intends my Good, and can consult it better than I myself am able, and, farther, doth actually claim the Guidance of me, I have no Reason in the World to decline his Government and Sway. Especially if it so happen, that I am beholden to him for my own very Being.[60]

[60] *The Law of Nature and Nations*, p. 64.

Since covenants with God are instruments, not of natural law, but of divine law, we must conclude that Pufendorf means that we are obliged to obey natural law, not because natural law is right, but because we owe a debt of gratitude to the legislator. However, while our gratitude to the legislator may help explain our sense of obligation, this, as Hutcheson was to argue, gives us no basis for stating that his laws are good.[61]

[61] Hutcheson, *An Essay on the Nature and Conduct of the Passions and Affections*, a facsimile edition of the 1728 (first) edition, in *Collected Works of Francis Hutcheson* (Hildesheim: Georg Olms Verlagsbuchhandlung, 1971), pp. 221–22.

2

THE ARGUMENT BEFORE HUME:

BEGINNING A NEW SCIENCE

IN HIS POLITICAL TRACT, *The Second Treatise of Government*, John Locke rejects Hobbes's view of man's condition without government as strife-riven and amoral. In the state of nature, human beings already had rules; they lived, not as isolated individuals, but in society with established moral rights and duties. Thus Locke provided a stable base for both a house of representatives elected by "the people" and for a right to dismiss bad governors. But in another work, *An Essay concerning Human Understanding*, a work in which he carried no partisan brief, Locke dismisses the notion of innate ideas. Does this dismissal mean that natural man, unless guided by revealed commandments, can have no knowledge of the distinction between virtue and vice? Are all moral rules, apart from revelation, merely the result of government legislation, persuasive education, and custom? Or are laws, customs, and maxims valid only when and to the extent that they conform to and embody a certain (valid) content?

Shaftesbury

Anthony Ashley Cooper, the third Earl of Shaftesbury, concluded from Locke's denial of innate ideas that the former was his old teacher's view. As a result, he regarded Locke as a moral skeptic. Both Locke and Hobbes, each in his own way, Shaftesbury complained, had denied that there is any fundamental (or natural) difference between virtue and vice.[1]

[1] According to Shaftesbury, "It was Mr. Locke that struck the home blow [against objective natural morality]: for Mr. Hobbes's character and base slavish principles in government took off the poison of his philosophy. 'Twas Mr. Locke that struck at all fundamentals, threw all order and virtue out of the world, and made the very ideas of these (which are the same as those of God) *unnatural*, and without foundation in our minds." Locke, says Shaftesbury, made virtue either (a) the result of will and law, or (b) simply a matter of fashion and custom. *The Life, Unpublished Letters, and Philosophical Regimen of Anthony, Earl of Shaftesbury*, ed. Benjamin Rand (London: Swan Sonnenschein & Co., Lim., 1900), pp. 403–4. According to John Dunn, Locke sought, from the epistemology of the *Essay concerning Human Understanding*, to produce a rational moral theory compatible with his *Two Treatises of Government*; however, says Dunn, "[T]he final position developed

Both had been led into error by the desire, all too common among philosophers, to erect a system. They should have observed and described accurately the complexity of human motivation, even if they were unable to fit everything into one neat structure. Shaftesbury, like Hobbes, resorted to introspection; but the human nature he discovered and described was very different from Hobbes's amoral, selfish man. Man, he found, has natural moral characteristics. Locke, too, had erred: he had made too much of his rejection of innate ideas. Whether or not human beings are born with innate ideas is irrelevant: the truth is that humans are gregarious and that as they grow up in society they acquire valid moral ideas.

Unlike Grotius and Pufendorf, Shaftesbury did not think in terms of laws, rights, duties, contracts, property, sovereignty, and the like; rather, he wrote *An Inquiry concerning Virtue or Merit*, first published in 1699, chiefly to examine in an unprejudiced way the relationship between religion ("piety") and sound morality ("virtue"). Is religion the true foundation of virtue, or, alternatively, are religions to be evaluated by the standards of sound morality? For our purposes, two points are important: first, his insistence that nature is the only true basis of moral rules, and, second, his rejection of the calculating selfishness central to Hobbism. Both these points follow from his rejection of the doctrine of the Fall.

Popular theology in England, Shaftesbury found, depicted nature as the fallen creature of a remote God; consequently, it concentrated on the supernatural commands of God—"the divine law"—and paid little attention to the moral laws implicit in nature, that is, natural law properly understood. Man was regarded as sinful and depraved, hopelessly selfish, beyond salvation except by supernatural Grace. In contrast, for Shaftesbury sound morality is based on nature. It can be advanced and supported powerfully by religion, but only if the concept of the deity propagated by religion is one of a perfectly good and benevolent god, that is, a god who conforms to nature. Unfortunately, he finds, religion often has fostered immorality. It has depicted God as demonic—arbitrary, petulant, partial to a chosen few, open to flattery, susceptible to being bribed or placated by gifts and sacrifices—with the result that His representatives, who alone know His will, have been advanced in place, power, and riches, while sound morality has been blighted. Shaftesbury's virtuous man lives in conformity with nature. Piety is a powerful force, but it is secondary. It ought to support virtue; unfortunately, history shows that piety often has been virtue's chief enemy.

Shaftesbury regarded much popular religion as fictitious, as a kind of fanciful mythology, a mythology elevating the unknown at the expense

in the *Reasonableness of Christianity* reverts to a sort of fideist voluntarism." *The Political Thought of John Locke* (Cambridge: Cambridge University Press, 1969), pp. 187–88.

of nature, the known. Divinity is presented as a perfect, but remote, Creator, while nature is treated at best as dull and commonplace, at worst as fallen or corrupted; thus wonder at the divinity present in nature is stifled. According to Shaftesbury, once a person sees nature as the One, the Absolute, he comes to regard it with profound awe and reverence—unless he falls into the ridiculous atheistic error of thinking of nature as a mindless mass of atoms. The wise man sees the whole as a great, orderly, integrated rational system. In that system, every "wise and virtuous man" takes his place joyfully, enthusiastically, unperturbed by whatever short-term troubles and pains occur. Such troubles and pains distress the unphilosophic, those who fail to comprehend the harmony of the universe.

Human conduct is primarily the expression of "the affections" (or motivating feelings). It is a person's temper or character—the constellation of his affections—that we rate as morally good or bad. Good affections are those that cause people to act in ways appropriate to human beings, that is, in ways beneficial to those of the human race. Such affections are "natural" or "kindly"; they are appropriate to humankind. Accordingly, Shaftesbury calls them "the natural affections" or "the kindly affections" (and also "the public affections"). Only acts good for human beings are morally good. This does not mean that Shaftesbury is concerned with only the good of others; the actor's feelings for himself, those feelings that move him to act for his own good, are important. The "private affections" (or "self affections") are not to be quashed, for private affections strong in the appropriate degrees—"moderate" is the word Shaftesbury generally uses—are necessary if the general good is to be promoted. For example, someone who ruins his health by working excessively long hours in public office, or a mother who kills herself tending her child, cannot be said to have acted correctly; in the long run those served will suffer. A good person must have private affections strong in the appropriate degree. Nobody can serve others effectively for long unless he takes care of himself. But if a person's private affections are unrestrained, he is selfish, and consequently seeks to serve himself rather than his kind.

What distinguishes the good person is not the results of his conduct, but his generous affections for others. Neither unintended good results nor good works done for ulterior reasons—to gain rewards or to avoid punishments in this life or the next—qualify a person as good.[2]

In addition to the public affections, which are good, and the private affections, which are good when consistent with public good, there are certain "unnatural affections"—inhumanity, destructiveness, disinter-

[2] Anthony Ashley Cooper, Earl of Shaftesbury, *Characteristics of Men, Manners, Opinions, Times*, ed. John M. Robertson, 2 vols. (New York: The Bobbs-Merrill Company, Inc., 1964) 1:249.

ested malice, envy, and the like—which in any degree are always vicious. These cause acts against the well-being of human beings.

The standards of human goodness are inherent in human nature. They are objective, not in the sense that they have been made known through either reason or supernatural revelation, but in the sense that they pertain to the species and remain as constant as human nature. What is good is not a matter of opinion; rather, "it is really something in itself, and in the nature of things; not arbitrary or factitious (if I may so speak); not constituted from without, or dependent on custom, fancy, or will; not even on the supreme will itself, which can no way govern it; but being necessarily good, is governed by it and ever uniform with it."[3] Every living being strives to achieve its potentiality, that is, to be a perfect unit, instance, or example of its kind. A good (or true) horse is one that conforms to the idea of a horse; a good (or true) person is one who conforms to the idea of a person. Any living thing—a tree, a horse, a person—that as it grows conforms to its idea is found beautiful by observers and is admired by them. The true (genuine), the good, and the beautiful are the same.

The goodness of a person is apprehended just as readily as the beauty of a tree or a horse. The *observer* senses his quality. "No sooner are actions viewed, no sooner the human affections and passions discerned (and they are most of them as soon discerned as felt) than straight an inward eye distinguishes, and sees the fair and shapely, the amiable and admirable, apart from the deformed, the foul, the odious, or the despicable."[4]

Human beings differ from other animals in that they can be virtuous, as well as good. They are rational. This means, first, that self-consciously they can reflectively survey both their own actions (and the affections that cause those actions) and those of others. It means, second, that they can know what affections (and actions) are appropriate (or most beneficial) in the diverse relationships of life. As a result, they can state explicitly the previously implicit standards of righteousness; they can state the ideal. To do this they need not be learned philosophers; in the school of nature, even the untaught quickly acquire the basic notion of what is morally good; instinctively human beings give their approval to conduct good for beings of their kind, humankind. The basic notions are innate—in the sense that they have their inevitable origin in life, and are neither revealed by prophets nor contrived by politicians.[5] Human rationality means, third, that human beings can evaluate their own affections (and actions) by those standards, and, fourth, that they can try to repress their bad affections and try to express their good affections. Shaftesbury's *virtuous*

[3] Ibid., 2:53.
[4] Ibid., 2:137.
[5] Ibid., 2:134–39.

man, as distinguished from a merely *good* man, whose conduct is good because of his unmanaged natural temperament, knows consciously what is right; and, because he knows the right (the orderly or beautiful), he loves it.[6] He loves conduct that is "equitable" (i.e., just, in the sense of right or appropriate) and beneficial. In other words, he loves "virtue, which is itself no other than the love of order and beauty in society."[7] He is moved by his love of righteousness, by what Shaftesbury in one place calls his "rational affections," both to rein in any misleading "sensible affections," that is, any disposition to selfishness, and to quash any unnatural affection. The virtuous person acts conscientiously. The person who commits wrongs is indicted by his own conscience; he is not at peace with himself unless his conscience has been perverted by "custom and education in opposition to Nature."[8] The descriptive standards of what is good conduct for human beings have become prescriptive rules for him. The indicative mood has been replaced by the imperative.

For Shaftesbury the sense (knowledge) of right and wrong is as natural and basic to human beings as is the general sense of beauty. Experience reveals to people the difference between moral good and evil; as a result, they can learn the rules of morality. This will happen naturally in the case of every child reared in natural circumstances. However, the development of the mind can be warped and distorted by unhealthy influences. Just as the body can be developed to the ideal by proper exercise, or deformed by restraints and poisons, the mind can be made rational by a healthy, natural life, or twisted by false beliefs, unrealistic speculation, and bad practices.

What effect has religion had on morality? Has religion been the mother of morality? What history shows, Shaftesbury contends, is that far from being the sure source of sound morality, religion often has been morally corruptive. Consequently, religious teachings ought to be tested rigorously against the eternal standards of right and wrong in the courts of natural morality. Natural morality, learned through undistorted experience, is far more reliable than "divine laws," which depend for their validity on the beliefs and values of the priests and prophets. What they teach may be demonic. The fact that the devotee believes that flagellation, human sacrifice, treachery against infidel rulers, and the persecution of unbelievers is pleasing in the sight of his god or gods does not make those practices virtuous.

According to Shaftesbury, two historical facts explain the distortion of moral education in Christendom. First, the Romans expanded their em-

[6] Ibid., 1:252–53.
[7] Ibid., 1:279.
[8] Ibid., 1:261, 304–5.

pire and stifled diversity: they "spread an universal tyranny and oppression over mankind." Second, philosophy and religion were confounded, producing theology. "[T]he schools of the ancient philosophers, which had been long in their decline, came now to be dissolved, and their sophistic teachers became ecclesiastical instructors, the unnatural union of religion and philosophy was completed, and the monstrous product of this match appeared soon in the world." The mysterious was reduced to a set of dogmas. This new science, theology, gave rise to controversy and strife, to dogmatism and heresy, to bigotry and intolerance.[9] The time now has come, Shaftesbury argues, when moral philosophy and instruction ought to be set free from the unreliable guidance of religion.

In popular religion, nature is treated as the creature of a deity. In turn that deity is thought of as having two elements: first, the eternal law, and, second, the creative will. If it is believed that the eternal law is consistent with natural law, and that the will of God is controlled completely by eternal law, popular religion will serve to strengthen natural morality. However, if the will of God is regarded as uncontrolled, the commands of God, the divine laws, are necessarily arbitrary; that is, whatever God's spokesmen, often self-appointed, wish to command is promulgated as a command of God. In that case popular religion is potentially a powerful enemy of natural morality. Moreover, the view that God's laws are to be obeyed chiefly because of particular divine rewards and punishments in this world or the next is scandalous: first, it is strongly tainted with demonism in that it emphasizes "the mere will or fancy" of the deity; second, it makes virtue mercenary, to be practiced for a price; third, by emphasizing gains and losses, it appeals to and fosters selfishness, a principle directly hostile to sound morality; and, fourth, by representing God as less than perfectly good, it makes even the alternative, a grim, blind atheism—the idea of "forlorn Nature and a fatherless world"—seem attractive.[10] Shaftesbury has rejected both forms of traditional natural law: the rationalists cannot explain either the content or the obligation of moral rules; the voluntarists are positively dangerous.

His conclusion is that true religion—that is, religion made to conform with his own type of natural law—is a valuable ally of morality. Atheism, being inert, has no power to pervert morality, but it deprives moral standards of the religious support they need with the multitude. Shaftesbury, like many other Whigs, favored religious toleration; yet he followed James Harrington in thinking that England should have an official national church. As the institution by which the people of England worship God publicly, the church should not be independent of the government.

[9] Ibid., 2:204–8.
[10] Ibid., 1:29.

An established church with a sound theology—a latitudinarian theology—would promote sound morality. Moreover, it would be the best defense against political and moral disorder caused by religious panics: "One may with good reason call every passion panic which is raised in a multitude and conveyed by aspect or, as it were, by contact or sympathy." Although he himself worshipped chiefly by private contemplation, Shaftesbury regarded provision for the performance of decent, seemly religious rites as necessary to prevent outbursts of wild enthusiasm, spread sympathetically among the vulgar. This had been "ancient policy."[11]

Another of Shaftesbury's concerns was to refute the notion, which he attributed to Hobbes among others, that "the common interest or public good" is different from the interest of the individual, and is to be upheld only because of a contract into which selfish individuals were forced, not to achieve positive benefits, but to avoid conflict. The idea of a presocial "state of nature" inhabited by strictly selfish individuals is ridiculous.[12] His own position is that man is naturally a political animal; that "to be well affected towards the public interest and one's own is not only consistent but inseparable; and that moral rectitude or virtue must accordingly be the advantage, and vice the injury and disadvantage of every creature."[13] Society is not a mere remedy; it is not the result of a contract to refrain from hostilities so as to avoid death and destruction; rather, society is necessary for the individual's happiness, and this for two distinct reasons. First, much of our pleasure comes about, not privately, but by sympathetic communication. Human beings in company participate in shared feelings; they echo and re-echo the joy of their comrades. They need society because, isolated from each other, they become empty, lonely, and depressed. We must recognize "how many the pleasures are of sharing contentment and delight with others; of receiving it in fellowship and company; and gathering it, in a manner, from the pleased and happy states of those around us, from accounts and relations of such happinesses, from the very countenances, gestures, voices and sounds, even of creatures foreign to our kind, whose signs of joy and contentment we can anyway discern. So insinuating are these pleasures of sympathy, and so widely diffused through our whole lives, that there is hardly such a

[11] Ibid., 1:13–14. See also Stanley Green, *Shaftesbury's Philosophy of Religion and Ethics* (Athens: Ohio University Press, 1967), pp. 110–19.

[12] *Characteristics*, 1:281–82. Shaftesbury anticipates Hume's criticism of the contract theory of government. That theory rests on the availability of the promise as the instrument by which human beings can remove themselves from an asocial state of nature. Says Shaftesbury, "Now the promise itself was made in the state of nature; and that which could make a promise obligatory in the state of nature, must make all other acts of humanity as much our real duty and natural part. Thus faith, justice, honesty, and virtue, must have been as early as the state of nature, or they could never have been at all." Ibid., 1:73.

[13] Ibid., 1:282

thing as satisfaction or contentment of which they make not an essential part."[14]

Second, much of the pleasure we gain from our own goodness, whether expressed in notable achievements or everyday behavior, is the result of the approval and esteem, not of ourselves, but of those around us. In summary, Shaftesbury contends that by far the greatest part of human pleasure comes from society: "[W]ere pleasure to be computed in the same way as other things commonly are, it might properly be said, that out of these two branches (viz. community or participation in the pleasures of others, and belief of meriting well from others) would arise more than nine-tenths of whatever is enjoyed in life."[15] Even the pleasures of the body, for example, eating and drinking, are enjoyed most when experienced in company. Human beings are social animals, not by treaty, but by their nature. It is only when they are playing a valued role in society that their lives are orderly and healthy, as is shown by the fact that a lazy opulence and wanton plenty—that is, idle luxury—leads to dissolute irregularities.[16]

Shaftesbury is out to refute Hobbes's famous view—that the basic human passions are selfish and that civil society is only an artificial arrangement to suppress conflict—not simply in order to put the theory right, but because he holds that false beliefs about human nature and about how happiness is to be achieved have bad practical effects. They lead to immoral conduct. Such beliefs may cause people to act selfishly; they are almost as dangerous as perverse religion.

In *An Inquiry Concerning Virtue or Merit*, we are told that the human commitment is to the entire species, not to any sect or party; if one's basic affections for others are partial, if they are limited to "some one part of society, or of a species," both the happiness produced by participation, through sympathy, in the feelings of others and the happiness caused by a sense of merit are diminished. But in a later work, *An Essay on the Freedom of Wit and Humour* (1709), Shaftesbury recognizes that partial groups are common; indeed, he adduces the rise and vitality of such groups—sects, factions, parties—and the discord and violence they often cause, as convincing evidence of man's social nature. Far from wishing to remain isolated, people tend to herd into groups, to which they often are fiercely loyal. Why do they not think and act as citizens of the world, as

[14] Ibid., 1:298. It is not only pleasant feelings that are communicated by sympathy. See Shaftesbury's description of panics. Ibid., 1:13.

[15] Ibid., 1:299.

[16] Although he disagreed radically with Hobbes's contention that human beings naturally are strictly selfish, Shaftesbury thought there was something to be said for the practical results of Hobbes's approach. Hobbes puts us on our guard against those who pose as our friends and benefactors so as to be able to fleece us. Ibid., 1:64.

members of one great society, humankind? The answer is that there are few occasions when the interest of all mankind can be taken as a goal in action and when specific ways to achieve such a goal are readily available. In contrast, both what is good for partial groups and the means of attaining that good often are known. Accordingly, a sense of partnership in a company, sect, or faction arises readily, but a sense of partnership with all humankind only rarely.

> Universal good, or the interest of the world in general, is a kind of remote philosophical object. That greater community falls not easily under the eye. Nor is a national interest, or that of a whole people, or body politic, so readily apprehended. In less parties, men may be intimately conversant and acquainted with one another. They can there better taste society, and enjoy the common good and interest of a more contracted public. They view the whole compass and extent of their community, and see and know particularly whom they serve, and to what end they associate and conspire.[17]

Thus, paradoxically, the devastation of war is due in large part to man's sociability, that is, to public affections unduly confined. Similarly, civil war is a threat in every large state, because people tend to turn to partial groups to gain that sense of involvement of which they are deprived in such states.

> Vast empires are in many respects unnatural; but particularly in this, that be they ever so well constituted, the affairs of many must, in such governments, turn upon a very few, and the relation be less sensible, and in a manner lost, between the magistrate and people, in a body so unwieldy in its limbs, and whose members lie so remote from one another and distant from the head.
>
> 'Tis in such bodies as these that strong factions are aptest to engender. The associating spirits, for want of exercise, form new movements, and seek a narrower sphere of activity, when they want action in a greater. Thus we have wheels within wheels.[18]

His conclusion is that "the very spirit of faction, for the greatest part, seems to be no other than the abuse or irregularity of that social love and common affection which is natural to mankind."[19]

We might expect from this that Shaftesbury would deplore all division or faction within mankind, indeed, that he would advocate a world state. But he does not. For him, as for Aristotle, a polity is the correct "whole," and the correct size of a polity is fixed by practical considerations. The members must be able to comprehend both the common interest and the

[17] Ibid., 1:75.
[18] Ibid., 1:76.
[19] Ibid., 1:77.

means for its achievement, and they must have a sense of company or fellowship; otherwise, an effective notion of a *public* is impossible. Accordingly, the factions he deplores are those that frustrate the achievement of the public interest within particular states. States or countries of a proper size are legitimate expressions of the public affections. For example, he dismisses absolute governments as perversions, because they lack a true sense of community; indeed, in them there is little or no sense of a public. At the same time, he rejoices, with almost republican fervor, that in England there exists, first, a notion of a public; second, a conception of a proper constitution; and, third, a high degree of public spirit.[20]

Shaftesbury's main contention against Hobbists is that human beings have strong public affections, that they feel frustrated when they cannot express those affections adequately, and that if constitutional ways to do so do not exist, they will find other ways. They are political or social animals. The other side of the coin, he asserts, is that humans are miserable when the private affections are too strong. Selfishness makes a person unhappy. The private affections are necessary; they are good when moderate. But when they grow too strong, they become harmful to the individual: the love of life becomes cowardice; the resentment of injury becomes vengefulness; the love of pleasure becomes luxury; the love of economic gain becomes avarice; the love of honor and praise becomes obsessive ambition and vanity; the love of ease becomes sloth. Bad for others, these passions are bad for the individual also. The wise and virtuous person sees the importance of an equitable and generous attitude toward his fellows and of temperance in his own appetites. He knows that this is the way to achieve his greatest happiness. He knows that since he is a political animal, there is no basis for conflict between his private good and the good of his society.

Where worldly goods are concerned, a person can strive moderately to gain wealth without damaging either himself or society. Such conduct is compatible with virtue; indeed, it is beneficial to society. "The public as well as private system is advanced by the industry which this affection excites." But if someone's drive for "a settlement or fortune in the world" becomes too strong, if he becomes avaricious, not only does the public suffer, but the person himself is doomed to perpetual discontent.[21] Similarly, someone who seeks social approval promotes his own happiness as well as the good of society, but if his need for praise swells to "an enormous pride and ambition," he damages himself as well as others. Shaftesbury sums this up: "Thus have we considered the self-passions, and what the consequence is of their rising beyond a moderate degree. These affec-

[20] Ibid., 1:72–73.
[21] Ibid., 1:326.

tions, as self-interesting as they are, can often, we see, become contrary to our real interest. They betray us into most misfortunes and into the greatest of unhappinesses, that of a profligate and abject character."[22]

The virtuous man—the man who combines strong public affection and moderate private affection and is free from any unnatural affection—is the happy man. Virtue brings its own reward, as vice entails its own punishment. As well as being vicious, selfishness is highly unprofitable. Human nature being as it is, we would be most unhappy in a Hobbesian state of nature, not only because we would lack protection from invasion by others, but because we would lack company, collaboration, and sympathy—in short, because we would lack society.[23]

It is important to notice that Shaftesbury does not speak of a struggle between evil passions and virtuous reason. The passions or affections, both public and private, are benign; what is required is the appropriate balance. Reason, as the conscious observer and monitor, operates to maintain that balance for the virtuous person. Hobbes oversimplifies; he begins with one part of a person's passions, the self-affections, making for a "cool and deliberate selfishness," and consequently depicts all the passions as divisive, with the result that society can be achieved only by following reason's counsel that the passions be restrained by means of the awesome power of a politically irresponsible sovereign.[24] For Shaftesbury, rationality enables human beings to do deliberately, consciously, what is for the good of their species or public, a cause to which their natural passions inevitably would commit them if they were not misled by false religion, bad customs, deforming education, and inaccurate beliefs. Shaftesbury's ideal is "the wise and virtuous man," not the simple good man, but the man who reflects on his own conduct, rejects perverse customs and teachings, and lives so that his conscience is easy.

It is important to notice also exactly how Hobbes and Shaftesbury disagree. Shaftesbury does not assert that most people do not behave selfishly; what he says is that the selfishness prevalent in contemporary society springs from the erroneous belief that selfishness is the way to happiness. Hobbes helped propagate that belief. Shaftesbury agrees that there is a great deal of selfish striving among people but insists that this arises from an egregious error, from a mistake he undertakes to correct. Misled, humans do not see that the greatest happiness comes from serving, not themselves, but their kind. Hobbes accepted people as they are, in their fallen state. Shaftesbury admits that there is an element of truth

[22] Ibid., 1:329.

[23] Grean argues that Shaftesbury was no mere modern Stoic, that he was influenced strongly by the Cambridge Platonists and the latitudinarians. Grean, *Shaftesbury's Philosophy*, pp. 161–63.

[24] Shaftesbury, *Characteristics*, 1:78.

in Hobbes's account, but, denying that this is their natural state, contends that they can be restored to their genuine character by a reformation of moral and religious thought.

To advance the argument, let us agree with Shaftesbury that Hobbes's picture of the strictly selfish individual is an exaggeration, a caricature. But then, anticipating Hume, we must ask if Hobbes's view is not the more useful. Let us concede to Shaftesbury that human beings are not strictly selfish, that they do have strong social affections, and that as a result they strive for the good of others. From this, as Shaftesbury himself says, it does not follow that they are moved to serve the general public, that is, all humankind, or even their own commonwealth; rather, it is likely to mean that they will compete with others on behalf of their own families, their own trade unions, their own sects, their own parties, their own regions, their own nations. The boundary between private good and public good has been moved. It has been relocated far from Hobbes's lonely individual; yet it has been retained. And, again anticipating Hume, is Shaftesbury's explanation of moral obligation adequate? Do not our moral obligations extend to many for whom we feel little or no effective affection? Indeed, is it not precisely in such cases—those that make up the sphere of what Hume, in the *Treatise*, calls the artificial virtues—that moral duty, restraining our natural motivation to strive for the well-being and happiness of those near and dear to us at the expense of those to whom we are indifferent, is most important in a large society? Moral motivation has to be set apart more distinctly; it cannot be mere "natural affection."

In summation we can make three comments. First, Shaftesbury overturned the traditional Judaeo-Christian relationship—accepted by Grotius, Pufendorf, and other natural-law writers—between religion and morality; he assigned priority to the latter. Given the danger that religion, always a powerful force, will be arbitrary, expressing the fancies of enthusiasts, or ideological, serving the worldly interests of factions, provision ought to be made to assure that public religion conforms to sound morality. Second, he accepted the old doctrine that man is a social animal; but he did so, not by stressing the need for peace and prosperity, benefits to be gained by observing the rights of others, but by insisting that society is necessary for human happiness. His concern is psychological, not legal and economic; given the strength of the public affections, life without society would be morally, intellectually, and spiritually impoverished. Human beings cannot fulfill themselves without genuine society. Third, because he was not expounding morality as law (command), he had no need for a source or principle external to nature, either eternal reason or divine will, to make his moral rules legitimate; this meant that he did not have to cope with the dilemma that tormented the modern natural-jurisprudence theorists. However, it did not mean that he did not require an explanation of moral obligation; in respect of this requirement, his theory was found defective by Butler.

Bernard Mandeville

A second wave of high controversy in British moral philosophy was brought on by the brisk realism of Bernard Mandeville, a Dutch physician who had settled in London in the 1690s. Mandeville took as his lifelong avocation the exposure of delusion and hypocrisy in contemporary English moral teaching, preaching, writing. An enemy of cant, his strategy was to emphasize the conflict between genuine Christian morality and the values prevalent in English society. Drawing upon the Augustinian tradition, familiar to him from his Calvinist upbringing and education, he posed as accepting fully the view that man is thoroughly depraved, far fallen from his primordial perfection. From this he drew the conclusion, not that the world must be saved, but that genuine Christians must reject the world and the flesh, electing to live obscure lives of ascetic sanctity. Alas, most Englishmen, he found, wished to enjoy the world and the flesh abundantly, all the while insisting that England was, or rather ought to be, a Christian society. They loved the robust wines of Babylon, but smuggled them home in Jerusalem water jugs. Mandeville found this both amusing and dangerous; they were not being honest, even with themselves. He was ready to accept both the candidly Babylonian and the truly regenerate; what he deplored was that the people of England should pretend to take or, worse, actually take Jerusalem as the model for a better Babylon. Mere pretenders were hypocrites; genuine reformers were subversive. For some thirty years, he remonstrated against the advocates of a virtuous England, many of whom were low churchmen or Protestant dissenters, who, like himself, inclined to the Whig side in politics; against their preachy moralism he defended the ethics, the values, the institutions, and the practitioners of the new commercial socioeconomic order.

Fallen man, he asserted, is selfish, proud. Avaricious for worldly goods, addicted to luxury, ambitious for power, ravenous for praise and honor, he seeks chiefly his own gratification and delectation. Envy and falsehood and pride are basic to society. Contrary to Shaftesbury's flattering view, man has no public affections, no natural motivation that makes him want to serve his fellows gratuitously. It is true that people live in society; but society is a utility, an artificial arrangement produced by reason of necessity, not by either natural gregariousness or Christian love. It is true that people generally behave justly and peaceably, as civilized men; in large part this is so because, driven to live and work together by necessity, they have gradually learned ways of behavior—manners or morals—that made cooperation and association possible and tolerable. Like their language, their civility is acquired and conventional. Slowly, over many generations, baited and driven by their needs, they became tame, civilized, polished. Conformity to the rules of civility is promoted by moralists, who lavish praise upon orderly, just, and obedient conduct, and denounce nonconformists, thus exploiting human vanity to a good end. People also behave in civilized ways because of fear; those in power know, as did Hobbes, how salutary it is to keep the sword and the gallows in plain sight. What makes for order, prosperity, and national strength in Babylon is a clutch of notorious self-serving vices: pride, envy, avarice, ambition, the love of luxury. In contrast, the citizens of Jerusalem, who live in humility studying to mortify the flesh, in fact promote unemployment, depression, and national poverty. The two cities are worlds apart. The moral reformers should choose; if they really want Jerusalem, they should retire from the world, leaving the people of England to live happy, natural, worldly lives, free from the torments of a guilty conscience. Alternatively, if they want a better England, as they insist they do—that is, a stronger, wealthier England—they should appraise candidly the passions that drive postlapsarian society and learn how to manage them. They should free themselves from deception and from cant; otherwise, they will adopt misconceived institutions, bad laws, vain policies. Although Mandeville was more than ready to poke fun at those who preached, "Be good that ye may grow rich," he was deadly serious in his efforts to reform English morality by making it realistic.[25]

The society examined by Mandeville was undergoing rapid change. In 1688–1689, the leaders of the nation had concluded that James II, who took seriously the duties of a Roman Catholic monarch, was unacceptable as head of the English church and state; they replaced him (and his son) with Mary, his daughter, and her husband, William of Orange, both Protestants. William did not let English isolationism deter him from involving his adopted country in his diplomatic and military campaigns to frustrate Louis XIV's efforts to create a vast Bourbon empire; from 1688 to 1697, under William, and then from 1702 to 1713, under Mary's sister, Anne, England was at war on the continent. In 1701 Parliament determined that Anne's successor would be, not James II's heir, but another

[25] The recent books on Mandeville are especially helpful. I have used Hector Monro, *The Ambivalence of Bernard Mandeville* (Oxford: Clarendon Press, 1975); Thomas A. Horne, *The Social Thought of Bernard Mandeville* (New York: Columbia University Press, 1978); and M. M. Goldsmith, *Private Vices, Public Benefits: Bernard Mandeville's Social and Political Thought* (Cambridge: Cambridge University Press, 1985). See also *Mandeville Studies: New Explorations in the Art and Thought of Dr. Bernard Mandeville*, ed. Irwin Primer (The Hague: Martinus Nijhoff, 1975).

foreign Protestant; consequently, in 1714 the Elector of Hanover came to the throne as George I. Throughout this entire period, beginning in 1688 and continuing for years, perhaps until 1745, the Tories were uncertain and divided: they favored the Stuart family; they professed to believe that kings inherit their thrones by divine ordinance; they disliked and distrusted foreign Protestants as heads of the Church of England; yet thrice God had failed—in 1685, 1689, and 1714—to provide an Anglican Stuart. The Whigs, in contrast, were prepared to rely on human agency, on Parliament, to give England a Protestant king. The Tory attitude toward kings made for royal favor, but only when the king believed that the Tories accepted him as the rightful king: under William, the Whigs at times were ascendant; even under Anne, an Anglican Stuart, they managed to gain royal favor for a time. The first two Hanoverians, kings by act of Parliament, were loyal to the Whigs, and this, together with able ministers, the unreformed representation of the people, the threat of Jacobitism, and inept Tory leadership, enabled the Whigs to establish themselves as the government party, despite the strength of the Tories in the country.

With the passing years, differences of other kinds had arisen. The Whigs favored religious toleration, at first for Protestant dissenters, later for others; the Tories were stubborn defenders of Anglican monopoly, at least as far as public office was concerned. The Whigs, full of admiration for the prosperity of the Dutch, were ready to wage war against their enemy Louis XIV, who, as part of his imperial design, hoped to bring about a Stuart restoration. The Tories, although not prepared to have a Roman Catholic king, had no great zeal for interminable wars with France, especially wars brought on and perpetuated largely by the interests of their foreign kings and continental allies, interests far beyond the ken of English squires.

In addition, England was agitated by great economic and social, that is, moral, issues. Throughout the seventeenth century, but especially after 1660, the English economy had been changing rapidly as overseas and colonial trade increased. Now the decision to become directly involved in continental politics by armies and subsidies accelerated the tempo of change and brought in new arrangements and institutions: the Bank of England was established; the debt contracted to pay the costs of war was made an obligation, not of the king, but of the nation; taxation techniques were improved; parliamentary control of revenue was reformed; the machinery of government was modernized; a stock exchange was opened. London, the seat of government, flourished and expanded.[26]

[26] A detailed description of the rapid transformation of the financial infrastructure of the English economy after 1689, with emphasis on the national debt, is to be found in P.G.M. Dickson, *The Financial Revolution in England: A Study of the Development of Public Credit, 1688–1756* (London: Macmillan and Company Limited, 1967). For the impact of

Great fortunes were gained through commerce and manufacturing and by speculation in stocks and bonds. The pace of business quickened, opulence increased, the ports swarmed with shipping. All this meant that the English way of life was being transformed. The good, old days, when land was the main form of wealth and the basis of power, were slipping away as commerce, war industries, and the money and credit businesses presented opportunities for "new men," as well as industrious "men of rank," to enrich themselves quickly and greatly, thus gaining the wherewithall to acquire estates, build fine houses, and enjoy new luxuries. At the same time, far less attention was being given, especially in London and the seaports, to keeping the Sabbath holy and to all the other essentials of godly living. More and more, it was said, the English were living for themselves, putting their own worldly good, their pleasure, foremost. One way to attack this individualistic materialism (or luxury) was to demand a return, possibly voluntary but probably compulsory, to Christian values. Another was to warn the people of England that by pursuit of luxury at the expense of the general good, they, but especially their government, had set the country, like the ancient Roman republic, on the road to gross moral depravity, social disintegration, tyranny in government, and disastrous defeats abroad. Both attacks, Christian and civic alike, emphasized to the public the dire consequences of private vice; the wages of private sin, whether meted out by God or by fate, would be paid by the people of England collectively.

Even during the early years, 1689 to 1714, although Tory politicians often were in office and had close relations with the City, the Whigs, with considerable justification, were regarded as the real friends of business and commerce. After 1714 the Whigs, then the government party, became the target of almost all discontents. Malcontented landowners, together with high-flying clergy, found their parliamentary spokesmen—condemning the promotion of commerce and luxury, condemning the continental wars and the land tax, condemning toleration, indeed everything that was deplorable—on the opposition benches. The roles had been reversed: the Whigs, originally a country party, had become the court party, while the Tories, originally the party of strong executive government, had donned the guise of a country party.

The Whig ministers were depicted as traitors to Christian England: true successors to those who had murdered Charles I, they had no commitment to old England, to its divine-right principles and its apostolic church. However, a richer, fresher, more sophisticated rhetoric of denun-

expanding commerce and the new institutions for managing money on the politics of London, see Gary Stuart De Krey, *A Fractured Society: The Politics of London in the First Age of Party, 1688–1715* (Oxford: Clarendon Press, 1985).

ciation was supplied by a third party, the exponents of classical republicanism, the True or Real Whigs. This was a party—or rather a movement—that had had its beginnings at the middle of the previous century, when the troubles of the 1640s and 1650s raised the possibility that England would adopt an entirely new social and political constitution. Its English fountainhead was James Harrington; behind Harrington stood Machiavelli, not Machiavelli of *The Prince*, but Machiavelli of *The Discourses*. Disgusted by the sordid pettiness of Italian politics, which he attributed in large part to the otherworldly focus of Christianity, Machiavelli had looked back beyond the Christian era to far better times. There he beheld the glorious Roman Republic, a republic with a constitution firmly based on a healthy social structure and sustained by the patriotic devotion, the civic virtue or public spirit of its citizens. Harrington carried the Machiavellian vision of the virtuous republic into England in his project for the reform of Oceana. Even after the Restoration, the republican tradition remained alive, setting up the ideal of a republic in which authority ascends from a virtuous people, a republic with a social structure made stable by an agrarian law, as a rebuke to the decadent politics of the times.[27] Republicans participated in the vain attempts to fend off the threat posed by James, Duke of York—Algernon Sidney died for their cause. At the Glorious Revolution, the republicans asserted that with the departure of James II political power had reverted to "the people," who could and should establish a new constitution; however, the Whig and Tory magnates moved rapidly to a compromise settlement with William, thus quickly closing the awkward hiatus in legality, an opportunity for radicals, occasioned by James's flight.[28] In the decades after 1689, as com-

[27] In 1959 Caroline Robbins demonstrated how radical reform ideas current in England during the civil war persisted for generations and remained influential until the American and French Revolutions. Among those included by Robbins in "the Whig canon" are the third Earl of Shaftesbury; Francis Hutcheson's friend, Robert, Viscount Molesworth; and Hutcheson himself. For a succinct statement of Country grievances, see Isaac Kramnick, *Bolingbroke and His Circle: The Politics of Nostalgia in the Age of Walpole* (Cambridge: Harvard University Press, 1968), pp. 39–83. Kramnick interprets Bolingbroke's politics as a civic-tradition protest against commercialization.

[28] The revival of genuine Whiggism, a cause reaching back to the 1640s and also forward into the next century, occasioned by the Revolution of 1688–1689 has been examined by Mark Goldie, in "The Roots of True Whiggism 1688–94," *History of Political Thought* 1 (1980): 195–236. The old view that Locke's *Two Treatises of Government* state accurately the views of those who led the Whigs in 1688–1689 has been successfully challenged by recent scholarship. This does not mean that Locke was a republican; it does mean, however, that he saw the Revolution as an opportunity for a reconstruction of the civil and ecclesiastical order far more radical than that sought by the Whig Parliamentary leaders. James Tully, for example, shows that, far from being the happy apologist of the post-1688 settlement, Locke revived an older, more egalitarian view of society. *A Discourse on Property: John Locke and His Adversaries* (Cambridge: Cambridge University Press, 1980). See also

mercial capitalism spread in England, the ideal of a noble republic was employed, not as a serious alternative to the existing constitution, but as a convenient rhetorical weapon, useful for denouncing all that seemed wrong: the rising power of commercial interests; the spread of luxurious living; the prosperity of parasitic speculators, stockbrokers, and monied men; the influence of the ministers over the House of Commons, the body that ought to have made effective the people's will that England remain virtuous. The Real Whigs saw the Whig ministers—the Junto and afterwards Walpole—as renegades who had abandoned true revolution principles.

In Real Whig ideology, the Tories found a well-stocked magazine from which to borrow both arguments and rhetoric. The result was that the Whig ministers were denounced by their critics, Real Whigs and Tories alike, for corrupting England. That was the omnibus charge: by omission and commission, the ministers were hastening the corruption of virtuous old England. The drama of the last years of the Roman Republic was being repeated, for Caesar, Catiline, and Sejanus were alive and dominant in the Privy Council. The charge of corruption included many particulars: the English people were being seduced from their ancient civic virtue, the companion of plain living, by the selfish pleasures of luxurious indulgence; the importation of luxuries was reducing the money England earned by foreign trade; soft living was enervating the race; the balance of society was being upset by the new wealth and power of the commercial interests; the values of gentlemen were being jostled aside by those of traders and stockbrokers; greedy foreigners were far too influential at Court; the country was being despoiled by wars and alliances brought on by foreign causes; the balance of the constitution was being upset by ministerial bribery; immorality was rife; the liberty of Englishmen was threatened by the standing army; the polite arts and the sciences were decaying. Only the fall of the Roman Republic was sufficiently cataclysmic to serve as an instructive parallel.

Mandeville was an advocate of the new order in politics and economics, which, growing rapidly after 1660, came of age at the Glorious Revolution. In spirit and connections, he was a Whig. At the same time, although he scorned the concept of English society fostered by high-church Anglicanism, he deplored the moralism of the Protestant dissenters and their low-church cousins, who tended to be Whigs. As he saw the situation, the people of England placed a high value on worldly goods; they wanted full employment, economic plenty, and national power. That being so, consistency required that they should give hearty welcome to the

Richard Ashcraft, *Revolutionary Politics and Locke's Two Treatises of Government* (Princeton: Princeton University Press, 1986).

new economic order. Trade, by reason of the division of labor it promotes, increases the supply of goods; it makes goods both better and
cheaper. The proponents of virtue denounce luxurious living. But what is
luxury? Are we to return to dank caves and huts, to raw meat, to smelly
skins; these were the necessities with which our first ancestors made do.
Even the most ordinary shirt is the product of many arts and skills and so
must be regarded as a luxury, not a necessity. The patriotic argument that
England would earn more money in foreign trade if the importation of
luxuries was stopped is false: England's exports would fall if England's
imports were reduced. The private citizen need not be a civic-minded patriot: let him apply himself diligently to his own business, and, provided
the government too does its job, the whole will benefit. The wealthy are
not the keepers of the nation's treasure; if they spend their money on
goods and services for themselves, the economy will grow. The state is
not the individual writ large; frugality may enable a family to amass
wealth, but it is not to be thought that frugality by all will bring about
national wealth. Old Babylon is being replaced by a new, bigger, more
efficient Babylon. Englishmen, or rather, Britons—to use the Whig term—
should rejoice greatly.

According to Mandeville, a truly Christian society cannot be either
prosperous or strong. If all the citizens make do with the bare necessities,
if they eschew all conveniences and refinements, the economy will be
primitive, unemployment high, poverty endemic, trade minimal, and
hardly any money will circulate. In condemning luxury, the moralists
overlook the effect of each person's conduct on others. The virtuous person who turns away from the goods of the world and saves his money
deprives many others of work and income, while even the profligate who
wastes his inheritance feeds them, albeit unintentionally. Society is a great
web of interdependence. The grandee who erects a huge mansion, keeps
a coach and six, collects statuary and paintings, and searches the world
for rare delicacies to astonish his guests gives employment to many.
Health is a plague to physicians and undertakers, as is peace to shipwrights and gunsmiths, honesty to lawyers and locksmiths, and sobriety
to brewers. With no buyers, there can be no sellers in either domestic or
international trade. Those who think to make England great by plain living should anticipate the effects of their prescription. Mandeville is not
recommending drunkenness, murder, theft, or profligacy, although without them the plight of brewers, hangmen, and pawnbrokers would be
sorry; rather, he is insisting on the complex interconnection of a division-
of-labor society.

Similarly, those who assert that the national good is the proper concern
of the virtuous should appraise the claims and motives of such public-
spirited patriots, and also the likely upshot of their good works. Who is

to say what is best in the public interest, beyond certain obvious fundamentals such as order and peace? As for private good, while intelligent,
experienced persons—taught by practice, rather than by "authorities"—
will be able to give sound advice to those who turn to them, no private
person has any right to tell others how to live their lives; by nature each
person is his own keeper. Even the government should intervene as little
as possible. Moreover, those who would rush in, proclaiming hot zeal for
the public good, are really knaves. They are moved by selfishness; they
have no superior motivation, for there are no public affections.

All human beings are moved by "self-love," by good will to themselves.
They are moved also by a more basic affection, by "self-liking." Each
person instinctively holds himself in high esteem, setting himself above all
else in the world. Accordingly, his goals and purposes are important, his
opinions valuable. The loss of self-liking entails the loss of self-love;
someone who loses his sense of his own worth will do nothing for himself; he may even commit suicide. In one dialogue, Mandeville has Cleomenes tell Horatio,

> That Self-love was given to all Animals, at least, the most perfect, for Self-
> Preservation, is not disputed; but as no Creature can love what it dislikes, it
> is necessary, moreover, that every one should have a real liking to its own
> Being, superior to what they have to any other. . . .
>   . . . I fancy, that, to encrease the Care in Creatures to preserve themselves,
> Nature has given them an Instinct, by which every Individual values itself
> above its real Worth; this in us, I mean, in Man, seems to be accompany'd
> with a Diffidence, arising from a Consciousness, or at least an Apprehension,
> that we do over-value ourselves: It is this that makes us so fond of the Ap-
> probation, Liking and Assent of others; because they strengthen and confirm
> us in the good Opinion we have of ourselves.[29]

In another dialogue, Horatio complains that since by "self-liking" Cleomenes really means pride, he should have used that familiar word. Cleomenes replies that he means something more than pride. Having heard
the explanation, Horatio states Cleomenes's reason for coining the word
"self-liking" as follows:

> You are of Opinion, that we are all born with a Passion manifestly distinct
> from Self-love; that, when it is moderate and well regulated, excites in us the
> Love of Praise, and a Desire to be applauded and thought well of by others,
> and stirs us up to good Actions: but that the same Passion, when it is exces-
> sive, or ill turn'd, whatever it excites in our Selves, gives Offence to others,
> renders us odious, and is call'd Pride. As there is no Word or Expression that

[29] *The Fable of the Bees or Private Vices, Publick Benefits*, ed. F. B. Kaye, 2 vols. (London:
Oxford University Press, 1924), 2:129–30.

comprehends all the different Effects of this same Cause, this Passion, you have made one, *viz.* Self-liking, by which you mean the Passion in general, the whole Extent of it, whether it produces laudable Actions, and gains us Applause, or such as we are blamed for and draw upon us the ill Will of others.[30]

Self-liking, then, is essential to life; what is bad is pride, self-liking run wild. What distinguishes civilized people is that they check their self-liking; thus active pride is reduced.

Mandeville has no time for those who define virtuous conduct as rational conduct and vicious conduct as passionate conduct. All conduct, virtuous and vicious alike, is caused by the passions: "Man never exerts himself but when he is rous'd by his Desires: While they lie dormant, and there is nothing to raise them, his Excellence and Abilities will be for ever undiscover'd, and the lumpish Machine, without the Influence of his Passions, may be justly compar'd to a huge Wind-mill without a breath of Air."[31] Reason, of course, has a role to play in society, helping to show the ways and means to achieve the goals selected by the passions.

It is wise to remember that men tend to be knaves. The word "knave," he tells us, comprehends "every Body that is not sincerely honest, and does to others what he would dislike to have done to himself."[32] Self-nominated patriots are no better than their fellows; indeed, the form in which their pride expresses itself, a presumptuous eagerness to run other people's lives, makes their knavery especially odious.

What England needed was a larger, cheaper, more diligent, more docile labor force. With such a labor force, she would win the war of international trade.[33] What she did not need was the perpetuation of religious strife by means of schools for the poor set up in rivalry by the Church of England and the dissenting sects. Mandeville's *Essay on Charity and Charity-Schools* is an earnest discussion of education and the social order. The main conclusion is that all education—perhaps not in Russia, where Peter the Great has to deal with a population "next to Brute Beasts," but certainly in England—should be left to depend on market forces. The market should be allowed to recruit the young into the various trades and callings; they should not be schooled, and for ulterior reasons at that, in subjects for which there is no demand. The bulk of the population, since they must be poor, should also be ignorant.[34]

[30] *An Enquiry into the Origin of Honour and The Usefulness of Christianity in War*; 2d ed. (reprinted London: Frank Cass & Co. Ltd., 1971), pp. 6–7.
[31] *The Fable of the Bees*, 1:184.
[32] Ibid., 1:61.
[33] Ibid., 1:316–17.
[34] Ibid., 1:288.

The free spending that Mandeville applauded was spending by the rich and the great. The vast bulk of the population, those "that bear the Brunt of every Thing, the meanest Indigent Part of the Nation, the working slaving People," must be kept in straightened circumstances; otherwise there will be nobody to do the heavy, dirty work.[35] He summarizes,

> I have laid down as Maxims never to be departed from, that the Poor should be kept strictly to Work, and that it was Prudence to relieve their Wants, but Folly to cure them; that Agriculture and Fishery should be promoted in all their Branches in order to render Provisions, and consequently Labour cheap. I have named Ignorance as a necessary Ingredient in the Mixture of Society: From all which it is manifest that I could never have imagined, that Luxury was to be made general through every part of a Kingdom.[36]

His main criticism of charity schools was not that the children of the poor should never move up in society, but that education imposed on them by do-gooders interferes with the natural percolation of society: "[T]here is a prodigious Difference between debarring the Children of the Poor from ever rising higher in the World, and refusing to force Education upon Thousands of them promiscuously, when they should be more usefully employ'd. As some of the Rich must come to be Poor, so some of the Poor will come to be Rich in the common Course of Things. But that universal Benevolence, that should every where industriously lift up the indigent Labourer from his Meanness, would not be less injurious to the whole Kingdom than a tyrannical Power, that should, without a Cause, cast down the Wealthy from their Ease and Affluence."[37] The few who are very rich are those who, according to Mandeville, by choosing between virtuous temperance and vicious luxury, control the health of the economy. The many who are poor have no choice; they spend all they earn. But the few who are rich may live plainly, thus causing economic depression; alternatively, they may live luxuriously, thus causing prosperity. What the poor need from the rich is profuse spending, not charity.

And if there is to be economic growth, entrepreneurs must be industrious. Contentment with one's fortune, not laziness, is the great enemy of progress. Mandeville distinguishes between diligence and industry: "A poor Wretch may want neither Diligence nor Ingenuity, be a saving Painstaking Man, and yet without striving to mend his Circumstances remain contented with the Station he lives in; but Industry implies, besides the

---

[35] Ibid., 1:119.

[36] Ibid., 1:248–49.

[37] Ibid., 2:352–53. Mandeville published his *Essay on Charity, and Charity-Schools* late in 1723. He elaborated his views in *The Fable of the Bees; Part II*, published in 1729.

other Qualities, a Thirst after Gain, and an Indefatigable Desire of meliorating our Condition."[38]

Shaftesbury's picture of the wise and virtuous man, a man serene and lofty, far above the spurs of avarice and ambition, a patriot intent upon serving the people, was an irresistable target for Mandeville. So complacent, so Olympian a figure stood in sharp contrast to Mandeville's industrious man striving restlessly to get ahead in the world. In his later writings, beginning in 1723, Mandeville turned upon His Lordship's works. The stoic aristocrat understood the world for which he prescribed no better than the Christian reformers. Men are led to behave morally, not by some natural moral sense, but by necessity aided by vanity, custom, and coercion. Nor are they naturally concerned to advance the good of the public; if England's government were to decide to rely on public spirit, on civic virtue, the nation soon would perish. Contrary to Shaftesbury's vision of public-spirited citizens freely dedicating their lives to the common interest, it is chiefly the passions, the "vices" of the high and the low alike, which make for peace, prosperity, and good government. It is avarice and pride—a passion for riches coupled with a passion for public approval—that make people ingenious and industrious. It is ambition—the love of dominion and applause—together with the tangible fruits of office, that makes the politician do his job. The public interest is not served intentionally, but as the by-product of self-love. What Mandeville emphasizes in his criticism of Shaftesbury is the artificiality of civil society. Society is historical; its rules and institutions were worked out over time. He denies that there are "standards of moral truth firmly established in nature herself," standards to be perceived by a natural moral sense. Outside society, every person perceives and evaluates actions from his own particular standpoint; within society, he limits his selfishness by rules of conduct learned from experience or through education.

As Maurice Goldsmith has shown, Mandeville gives two quite different accounts of the origin of morality.[39] The first is an ironic version of the founder or legislator theory. In 1709 the splendid contribution to the public of truly great men, those who "ever invented anything for the Publick Good," was extolled by The Tatler in a manner reminiscent of Pufendorf's praise for those who conform to the highest requirements of humanity. Such men are really human; unlike the walking dead who encumber the streets around us, they are genuine, living men. Now, the classic case of the great-man theory of history is that made famous by Machiavelli: men such as Moses, Romulus, Lycurgus, Theseus, and Solon, by providing laws to their followers, gave them their distinctive char-

[38] The Fable of the Bees, 1:244.
[39] Goldsmith, Private Vices, Public Benefits, pp. 47–77.

acter as a nation or city; speaking for the gods, they bestowed moral systems upon their people. First, in 1709, in *The Female Tatler*, and subsequently, in 1714, in "An Enquiry Into the Origin of Moral Virtue," Mandeville casts doubt on the whole idea of great public benefactors, by giving a perverted account of the work of "legislators." In the state of nature, human beings had needs that could best be met by cooperation and had latent social potentialities; however, they lacked both any interest in the welfare of others and any social affection. They were initiated into society, made moral beings, by great legislators, whose good works are continued even to this day by moralists and philosophers. The legislators contrived laws or rules and then lavished praise on all who obeyed them and contempt on those who broke them. Thus, by exploiting the pride of man, they tamed him. And why? This was no work of benevolence; rather, it was done out of avarice and ambition. "This was (or at least might have been) the manner after which Savage Man was broke; from whence it is evident, that the first Rudiments of Morality, broach'd by skilful Politicians, to render Men useful to each other as well as tractable, were chiefly contrived that the Ambitious might reap the more Benefit from, and govern vast Numbers of them with the greater Ease and Security."[40] It was, then, crafty politicians who first tamed mankind. The truth is that "the Moral Virtues are the Political Offspring which Flattery begot upon Pride."[41] Mandeville's works contain many references to skilfull politicians and to philosophers and moralists, who, by playing on love of praise and fear of contempt, have carried on the manipulative task of civilizing men. No doubt Mandeville believed that moralists, teachers, and the like love dominion; however, as Goldsmith proposes, Mandeville's chief purpose here is not to give a serious account of the origins of morality, but to blacken the reputations of the "legislators" by revealing that they were knaves.

The second account of the origin of morals appears in the dialogues published in 1729 as part 2 of *The Fable of the Bees*, and in *An Enquiry into the Origin of Honour, and the Usefulness of Christianity in War*, published in 1732. Both the substance and the manner of its presentation indicate that here Mandeville is being serious, taking us behind the scenes to explain what irony and satire had obscured in his earlier account. He rejects the idea that the rules of morality were introduced by legislators and also the idea that the rules were deliberate prescriptions. The civilization of man, where it has occurred, was an evolutionary process: it was neither planned nor intended by any politician, moralist, or philosopher, although men such as Solon and Lycurgus, having studied extensively the

[40] *The Fable of the Bees*, 1:46–47.
[41] Ibid., 1:51.

lessons of the past, were able to compile good codes. Man was endowed by Nature, or rather the Creator, with great potentialities; the challenge of the human situation brought forth his talents. Before the evolutionary process began, human beings were like scattered grapes; potentially they were wine, but a "critical mass," interaction, and a process (change or time) were required to bring them to the higher state. Speaking, thinking, and reasoning are prime examples of *results* of the development of man caused by interaction over time.[42]

Primitive humans needed to cooperate to fend off beasts of prey, also to improve their productive skills through the specialization made possible by a division of labor. At the same time, each was endowed with a strong sense of his own worth; he liked himself supremely; this was, and is, essential for self-preservation, but unrestrained it made association and thus cooperation impossible. What happened was that over many generations human beings gradually learned to control and conceal their self-liking, not consciously or reflectively, but as a way adopted instinctively to achieve their ends, just as children, without thought, learn by experience to walk and jump. Gradually, incrementally, wonderfully complex, subtle rules of conduct accumulated. A moral system, a civilization, is the result of the experience of many people, most of them quite unreflective. It is a common error to praise human lucubration for what is the work of nature over time. We tend to ascribe "to the Excellency of Man's Genius, and the Depth of his Penetration, what is in Reality owing to length of Time, and the Experience of many Generations, all of them very little differing from one another in natural Parts and Sagacity." This is true in the practical arts and trades, such as ship building, soap boiling, and cloathing, which "from mean Beginnings [are] brought to great Perfection; but the many Improvements, that can be remembered to have been made in them, have for the Generality been owing to Persons, who either were brought up to, or had long practis'd and been conversant in those Trades, and not to great Proficients in Chymistry or other Parts of Philosophy, whom one would naturally expect those Things from." The philosopher comes on the scene only after the fact. He describes and tries to

[42] Ibid., 2:319. Again and again Mandeville insists on the wonderful complexity of both natural and historical causation and on the good results achieved without human planning, indeed because of the absence of human planning. He was intrigued and delighted by the perversity of Providence as revealed by the confounding rebukes delivered to those who rely on human reason: they pronounce something evil, but its consequences are beneficial; they rush to intervene in people's lives, and disaster results; just down from Oxford, they elbow aside the old practitioner, and the patient dies. Learned authorities pretend to know *why* things happen; the modest empiric knows only *that* they happen. One important aspect of Mandeville's thought, "his sensitivity to the complex processes that produce and sustain society," is examined by J.A.W. Gunn in "Mandeville and Wither: Individualism and the Workings of Providence," in *Mandeville Studies*, pp. 98–118.

understand civilization; he does not prescribe it. For example, says Mandeville, the science of navigation recently has been set forth by Chevalier Reneau; yet shipwrights and sailors have been building and sailing ships for centuries without knowing Reneau's principles. It is clear that since "the People, who first invented, and afterwards improved upon Ships and Sailing, never dream'd of those Reasons of Monsieur *Reneau*, it is impossible, that they should have acted from them, as Motives that induced them *a priori*, to put their Inventions and Improvements in practice, with Knowledge and Design." The same can be said of good conduct. The truth is that

> the raw Beginners, who made the first Essays in either Art, good Manners as well as Sailing, were ignorant of the true Cause, the real Foundation those Arts are built upon in Nature; but likewise that, even now both Arts are brought to great Perfection, the greatest Part of those that are most expert, and daily making Improvements in them, know as little of the *Rationale* of them, as their Predecessors did at first: tho' I believe at the same time Monsieur *Reneau*'s Reasons to be very just, and yours as good as his; that is, I believe, that there is as much Truth and Solidity in your accounting for the Origin of good Manners, as there is in his for the Management of Ships. They are very seldom the same Sort of People, those that invent Arts, and Improvements in them, and those that enquire into the Reason of Things: this latter is most commonly practis'd by such, as are idle and indolent, that are fond of Retirement, hate Business, and take delight in Speculation: whereas none succeed oftener in the first, than active, stirring, and laborious Men, such as will put their Hand to the Plough, try Experiments, and give all their Attention to what they are about.[43]

Driven by the imbalance between the demand for goods and the available supply, people became industrious and law-abiding, and as they prospered, yesterday's luxuries became today's necessities. The ultimate basis of modern civil society is not a public affection peculiar to human beings, not sociability, but economic requirements: "There are great Blessings that arise from Necessity; and that every Body is obliged to eat and drink, is the Cement of civil Society."[44]

Societies operate and civilizations are shaped because of the drives implanted in human beings by divine wisdom, not by human stratagems. By nature man is equipped with passions suitable to move him to play his part, not by his foresight, but instinctively. He feels hunger, thirst, and lust; by these nature spurs him to do what is necessary to maintain himself and his race. He is endowed with self-liking: this makes him strive

[43] *The Fable of the Bees*, 2:139–45.
[44] Ibid., 2:350.

"to ameliorate his condition," with good results for all. He desires dominion; without this "vice," who would spend himself in politics, where calumny, ingratitude, and constant crisis are the only certainties? According to Mandeville, it is to the unsung practitioners that we are indebted for advances in medicine, the arts, law, politics, and the like. Such persons do not pretend to know the ultimate principles behind their inventions and discoveries; indeed, they are content to know *how* to achieve results and seldom think to ask *why* the remedies and devices work. To go behind the observed causal relationships is the vocation of speculators, theorists. Let them speculate all they like, but keep them well away from the real world.

Mandeville, the London doctor trained abroad, had a special contempt for the "metaphysicians" he found practicing medicine in England. He specialized in nervous disorders, ostensibly the subject of his *Treatise of the Hypochondriack and Hysterick Diseases* (1711); however, this work is essentially a polemic against bad teaching and practice in medicine. The Oxford professors theorize grandly about the ultimate causes of diseases. Their students read Galen and learn latin (to maintain the mystery) and mathematics (the latest scientific fad), but never approach a sickbed; then, at twenty-five or so, equipped with degrees and hypotheses, they come down to London to enrich themselves. Contemptuously shouldering aside the experienced practitioners, they are a menace to health and purse. Mandeville's attack on "metaphysicians," who, proud of their theories and refusing to observe, obstruct "the Progress of the glorious Art, that should teach the Recovery as well as Preservation of Health," seems to anticipate Hume's introduction to *A Treatise of Human Nature*.

But Mandeville sees that by presenting extremes—speculative theorists versus drudging empirics—he may mislead: the truth is that the ideal physician does not scorn reason; rather, he combines observation and reflection. What, exclaims Misomedon to Philopirio (Mandeville), are you then an empiric? Philopirio replies,

That is an odious Name, especially in *England*; but then you know that the Word is much abus'd, and that the *Empyricks* among the Physicians of all Ages have been as famous a Sect as any, that ever were distinguish'd by a Name: That the first Author of it, *Heraclion*, was a Physician of Renown, and abundance of his Followers Men of great Parts and Learning. They were of Opinion, that the Art of Physick consisted in downright Observation, and a world of Experience; and that all manner of reasoning about the Causes of Distempers, and being Witty in deducing the Symptoms from 'em, were very insignificant toward curing People that were sick: So far I am an *Empyrick:* But then there are several things said of 'em, that are worse; as their denying, that the Knowledge of natural things, and the Body itself, were any ways material to the Profession, and that their Experience, (as an Author that preaches very much for Moderation among Physicians calls it,) was *mere Stupida, non repetita, casu non ductu inventa, & prorsus Circumsoranea* [Altogether stupid, not repeated, acquired by chance not with design, and entirely such as that of our Mountebanks.] Here I should differ from them.[45]

Later, when charged by Misomedon with having banished reason from the medical art, Philopirio replies,

When you ask'd me, how I could without the Help of some *Hypothesis* or other reason about the Symptoms, Causes, &c. of Distempers; because I would by no means have you expect from me those nice Explications of unsearchable Nature, which your witty *Theorists* rack their Brains for from a bare Supposition, I answer'd you at once, that I did not reason about them at all; but now I have shew'd you the demonstrable Error of the Ingenious People of our Age, who are so fond of their Parts, as to think, that besides Anatomy and Philosophy, a Man of Sense wants no other Helps to penetrate into the Causes of the most intricate Distempers, if he is but once acquainted with the Symptoms: Now I have shew'd you this, I say, I shall not scruple to tell you that I would not make a Step without Reason, more than those Philosophers, to which Title I don't pretend, whatever I may to the Reality of its meaning: I would not have you think, that I speak of that lofty self-sufficient Reason that boldly trusts to its own Wings, and leaving Experience far behind mounts upon Air, and makes Conclusions in the Skies; what I make use of is plain and humble, not only built upon, but likewise surrounded with, and every way limited by Observation, from view of which it never cares to stir.

Misomedon now understands: "I am satisfy'd, and thought my self answer'd as soon as you condescended to join Reason to Observation. For as to the other reasoning, that both begins and ends in Speculation, I told you Yesterday, that I had done with it my self."[46]

Shaftesbury made the mistake of studying books, not people: "[I]t cannot be denied, that the Ideas he had form'd of the Goodness and Excellency of our nature, were as romantick and chimerical as they are beautiful and amiable; that he labour'd hard to unite two Contraries that can never be reconcil'd together, Innocence of Manners and worldly Greatness; that to compass this End he favour'd Deism."[47] Mandeville's own purpose was to show how remote the received moral theories were from

[45] *A Treatise of the Hypochondriack and Hysterick Diseases*; 2d ed., corrected and enlarged by the author (London: J. Tonson, 1730 [Reproduced by Scholars' Facsimiles & Reprints, Delmar, New York, 1976]), pp. 56–57. (The first edition, 1711, has been reproduced, by Arno Press, New York, 1976.)

[46] Ibid., pp. 129–30.

[47] *The Fable of the Bees*, 2:357.

reality: "[T]he National Happiness which the Generality wish and pray for, is Wealth and Power, Glory and Worldly Greatness; to live in Ease, in Affluence and Splendour at Home, and to be fear'd, courted and esteem'd Abroad . . . [yet] such a Felicity is not to be attain'd to without Avarice, Profuseness, Pride, Envy, Ambition and other Vices."[48]

Mandeville is not an advocate of laissez faire. His contention that nature has put each person under his own care, that society should be permitted to percolate naturally, that luxurious living is turned to public benefit by the market—all these point that way. But Mandeville is not out to write economic theory; rather, his purpose is to show that certain old moral values are impeding clear thought and candid speech. He does not contend that a society will run itself without government. Laws are needed; therefore the origin of a constitution and a system of law is part of the process of civilization. There is work to be done by those ambitious individuals who turn to politics. Driven by their own motives, they can serve the public well if they understand people and society accurately. Mandeville wants a strong, active government, a government that will make laws, regulate trade for the national good, encourage agriculture and the fisheries, undertake vast works (dredging rivers, cutting canals, draining fens), protect the people from overweening priests, keep the laboring poor quiet and diligent, and hang delinquents with dispatch. Bad policies, neglect, and mismanagement, not the "vices" of the people, are what need correction. For example, it was because of good governance, not virtue, that the Low Countries prospered. "The *Dutch* may ascribe their present Grandeur to the Virtue and Frugality of their Ancestors as they please; but what made that contemptible Spot of Ground so considerable among the principal Powers of *Europe*, has been their Political Wisdom in postponing every thing to Merchandize and Navigation, the unlimited Liberty of Conscience that is enjoy'd among them, and the unwearied Application with which they have always made use of the most effectual means to encourage and increase Trade in general."[49]

What is called "vice" cannot be extirpated, but it can be managed and made productive. In "A Vindication of the Book," he makes this point explicit: "*[P]rivate Vices by the dextrous Management of a skilful Politician, may be turn'd into publick Benefits.*"[50] Earlier, in "The Grumbling Hive," he had made the same point in a way that anticipates Hume's discussion of the function of justice: "So Vice is beneficial found, / When it's by Justice lopt and bound."[51] Selfishness is natural; justice is the result of civilization. The rules of justice restrain and harness the power of self-

[48] Ibid., 2:106.
[49] Ibid., 1:185.
[50] Ibid., 1:411–12.
[51] Ibid., 1:37.

ishness. And good governance entails more than the maintenance of justice; it requires intervention in the economy.

> The great Art then to make a Nation happy and what we call flourishing, consists in giving every Body an Opportunity of being employ'd; which to compass, let a Government's first care be to promote as great a variety of Manufactures, Arts, and Handicrafts, as Human Wit can invent; and the second to encourage Agriculture and Fishery in all their Branches, that the whole Earth may be forc'd to exert it self as well as Man; for as the one is an infallible Maxim to draw vast Multitudes of People into a Nation, so the other is the only Method to maintain them.[52]

According to Mandeville, human beings are moved by "self-liking"; however, the goods and security they want for themselves can be attained only in civil society, which cannot exist unless their "self-liking" is restrained and channeled. One of Mandeville's explanations of the origin of good social conduct relies on contrivance by knavish legislators. The other, the one to be taken as his own, describes such conduct as learned behavior, as an unscientific adjustment promoted by necessity, built up incrementally, chiefly by obscure practitioners.

Francis Hutcheson

In his first major work, *An Inquiry into the Original of our Ideas of Beauty and Virtue*, published in 1725, Francis Hutcheson, who was to be Carmichael's successor as professor of moral philosophy at Glasgow, undertook to explain "the Principles of the late Earl of Shaftesbury" and thereby to show the errors of "the Author of the *Fable of the Bees*." Hutcheson, like Shaftesbury, found the self-love explanation of morality theoretically wrong and also practically dangerous. It raises doubts about the goodness of God and of our fellow men "by instilling into us some ill-natur'd, cunning, shrewd Insinuations, 'That our most generous Actions proceed wholly from *selfish Views*.' This wise *Philosophy* of some Moderns, after EPICURUS, must be fruitful of nothing but *Discontent, Suspicion*, and *Jealousy*; a State infinitely worse than any little transitory *Injurys*, to which we might be expos'd by a good-natur'd *Credulity*."[53]

[52] Ibid., 1:197.

[53] *An Inquiry into the Original of our Ideas of Beauty and Virtue*; 4th ed. (London, 1738), pp. 211–12 (republished by Gregg International Publishers Limited, Westmead, Farnborough, England, 1969). See also Francis Hutcheson, *An Essay on the Nature and Conduct of the Passions and Affections. With Illustrations on the Moral Sense* (London, 1728), pp. 207–208 (republished as vol. 2 in *The Collected Works of Francis Hutcheson* [Hildesheim: Georg Olms Verlagsbuchhandlung, 1971]. The first edition of Hutcheson's

Hutcheson's immediate goal was to vanquish the self-love theory of morality, explicit in Mandeville's writings and implicit in the sermons of those Christian clerics who, urging virtue, dwelt long upon divine rewards and punishments; however, beyond this his great purpose, following Shaftesbury's lead, but as a sincere Christian, was to reverse the generally accepted relationship—the relationship presupposed by Pufendorf, for example—between natural morality and religion. Contemporary moral thought was vitiated by a fundamental error, namely, the presupposition that man is a fallen creature, that is, that he is thoroughly selfish. With the sinful nature of man presupposed, many Christian philosophers saw the rules of morality as laws imposed by God; thus they confronted themselves with the famous dilemma. Other philosophers—Hobbes and Mandeville—treated morality simply as rules contrived to make possible the coexistence of selfish human beings. As for himself, Hutcheson found the presupposition shared by all three schools—the self-love theorists and both the natural-law positions (the voluntarist and the rationalist)—contrary to the facts of ordinary life. He dismisses the self-love theorists as dangerously wrong. As for the two other schools—especially the voluntarists, who were prone to denounce all who strayed from voluntarism as horrid heretics—they are to correct their ways; instead of scandalizing the faithful by noisy disputes about the Creator, they are to apply themselves diligently to studying the Creation. When they have achieved an adequate understanding of natural morality, they may be ready to say something about the Creator. As a practical concern, Hutcheson was more interested in the voluntarists: Hobbists in vestments, they spread their pernicious, divisive doctrines—the seeds of suspicions, persecutions, wars, and other barbarities—from far too many pulpits.

In *An Inquiry into the Original of Our Ideas of Beauty and Virtue*, Hutcheson makes a stand against the rationalists, but his main purpose there is to refute, first, those who (with Epicurus) trace morality to self-love, and, second, their religious fellow travelers, who (with Pufendorf) teach that moral virtue is simply obedience to God. Later, in 1728, in *An Essay on the Nature and Conduct of the Passions and Affections. With Illustrations on the Moral Sense*, he deals extensively, but respectfully, with the rationalists, especially Clarke and Wollaston. The great concern of Clarke and Wollaston, as we have seen, was to show that morality is not simply custom, or alternatively whatever the ruler commands, even when the ruler is God. Hutcheson agrees but holds that the rationalists are wrong in their reliance on reason. They have accepted the simplistic view that man is the locus of a struggle between two opposite forces,

---

Inquiry, published in 1725, appears as vol. 1 in the *Collected Works of Francis Hutcheson*). All my quotations from the *Inquiry* are from the fourth edition.

passion and reason, and think that the more that passionate motivation is supplanted by rational motivation the better. Presupposing that the passions are bad, they fall into two other errors: first, they abandon love of others as a basis of morality, thus leaving love (in the form of self-love) to the self-love theorists; second, they themselves then rely on reason alone for both the content of morality and all genuine moral motivation. They tell us, says Hutcheson, that human beings have "two Principles of Action, *Reason*, and *Affection*, or *Passion* (i.e. strong Affection): the *former* in common with Angels, the *latter* with Brutes: No Action is wise, or good, or reasonable, to which we are not excited by *Reason*, as distinct from all *Affections*; or, if any such Actions as flow from *Affections* be good, 'tis only by *chance*, or *materially* and not *formally*."[54] Hutcheson disagrees. Reason is the faculty by which we seek truth, that is, true propositions about reality; when we act, reason guides us in the choice of means but does not instruct us in the choice of ends, goals, or purposes. These are defined by the affections (or passions) and by morality.

By "true" Hutcheson means "accurate," as in "true propositions" about what was, is, or will be, and about causation. He has no use for "the true" in the sense of "the genuine" or "the good," because this meaning begs the question how the good (the genuine or the ideal) acquired its high status in the first place. His main argument is that truth alone, true propositions alone, can never move us either to act to acquire a "natural good" (e.g., an apple) or to do "moral good" (e.g., good works).

Although Hutcheson was a Presbyterian minister, he rejected the somber picture of fallen man presented by writers in the Augustinian tradition, writers such as Hobbes, La Rochefoucauld, and Bayle. These tell us only half the truth, perhaps not even that. Man is influenced by self-love; yet he has also a good measure of active love (benevolence) for others. Following Shaftesbury, Hutcheson holds that love for others, passion for "public good," is the basis of virtue. Prior to any sense of moral obligation—prior to any knowledge of rules—we are moved to try to promote the happiness of others. Acts caused by this passion, *benevolence*, win our approval. The result is a whole complex of moral obligations, obligations to do good works appropriate to the various relationships in which we find ourselves.

Hutcheson undertakes to develop a theory of natural morality, a theory based on a moral sense natural to man. He begins the *Inquiry* with an explanation of beauty. This tactic alerts us to the fact that for Hutcheson the common distinction between "the subjective" and "the objective," between the knower and the known, is misleading. We know an external

---

[54] *Illustrations*, pp. 216–17.

world, but we know it as human beings. Through the five senses called "external," we know the world around us as formed and extended, but also as full of things that look colorful, make sounds, taste sweet or bitter, and feel hot, sharp, or soft—all more or less pleasant or painful. How we know the world is a function of our nature as human beings; other beings with these senses tuned differently may hear different sounds, taste different tastes. What is cold for us may be hot for them; sounds pleasant for us may be painfully high-pitched for them; they may starve although surrounded by what we find delicious. The external senses do not simply bring before us the world as it exists out there; rather, they contribute to our perception of the world.

But, says Hutcheson, we use yet another sense in perceiving the world. We evaluate in terms of beauty the things presented by the five senses. We perceive some things as shaped and colored; then we pronounce them beautiful or ugly. We perceive certain vibrations as sounds; then we pronounce those sounds musical (beautiful) or not. All human beings have a sense of beauty, more or less well developed. In addition, just as what we perceive by the five external senses is not "subjective," what we perceive as beautiful or ugly by the inner sense of beauty is not "subjective." The things that all human beings find beautiful have the same specific characteristics: whether we are perceiving a cathedral, a painting, a quartet, or a human form, we find "uniformity amidst variety" beautiful. Custom, education, and example cause differences in taste, but the basic criterion, uniformity amidst variety, remains the same the world over. Some prefer the Gothic to the classical in architecture, but both styles conform to the criterion. We are not to think, following Locke, of the mind as a *tabula rasa*: there are natural *internal* senses.

Nothing is more ordinary among those, who after Mr. LOCKE have rejected *innate Ideas*, than to alledge, 'That all our Relish for *Beauty* and *Order*, is either from Prospect of *Advantage, Custom*, or *Education*,' for no other Reason but the *Variety* of *Fancys* in the World: and from this they conclude, 'That our *Fancys* do not arise from any *natural Power of Perception*, or *Sense*.' And yet all allow our *external Senses* to be *Natural*, and that the Pleasures or Pains of their Sensations, however they may be increas'd or diminish'd by *Custom* or *Education*, and counterbalanc'd by *Interest*, yet are really antecedent to *Custom, Habit, Education*, or Prospect of *Interest*. Now it is certain, 'That there is at least as great a Variety of Fancys about their Objects, as the Objects of *Beauty*:' Nay, it is much more difficult, and perhaps impossible, to bring the Fancys or Relishes of the *external Senses* to any general Foundation at all, or to find any Rule for the *Agreeable* or *Disagreeable:* and yet we all allow, 'that these are *natural* Powers of *Perception*.'

Both the external and the internal senses are *"natural* Powers of *Perception,* or *Determinations* of *the Mind* to receive necessarily certain Ideas from the Presence of Objects. The *Internal Sense* is, a *passive Power of receiving Ideas of Beauty from all Objects in which there is Uniformity amidst Variety."*[55] In other words, the inner senses approve or disapprove the quality of their objects.

The sense of beauty is both evaluating and demanding. We want, not mere sounds, but beautiful sounds; not just clothes and buildings, but beautiful clothes and buildings. Very little wealth or power suffices to provide the crude essentials of life required by hunger, thirst, and so forth; the only use of a great competence (apart from doing good works for others) is to buy "the Pleasures of *Beauty, Order,* and *Harmony."*[56] We admire beautiful theorems in geometry, beautiful histories, and beautiful government constitutions, as well as beautiful buildings; they too are orderly and harmonious, accommodating all the complexity of particularity within one integrated plan.

Hutcheson argues that the order of the universe—the presence of causes, both natural and moral, sufficient to produce good results— shows, proves, not only that the theists are correct, but that God is benevolent. At the end of the first part of the *Inquiry,* he asks why God chose to create an ordered universe, one based on uniformity or general laws. After setting forth various other valid answers, he comes to the main one, namely, that uniformity or predictability in the world around us is a prerequisite of virtue. To act virtuously people must be able to understand the physical and moral worlds in which they live. "As to the Operations of the DEITY by *general Laws,* there is still a farther Reason from a *Sense* superior to these already consider'd, even that of VIRTUE, or the *Beauty* of *Action,* which is the Foundation of our greatest Happiness. For were there no *general Laws* fix'd in the Course of *Nature,* there could be no *Prudence* or *Design* in Men, no *rational Expectation* of Effects from Causes, no *Schemes* of Action projected, or any *regular Execution."*[57]

Having introduced us to one inner or evaluative sense, the sense of beauty, Hutcheson advances, in the second part of the *Inquiry,* to a second internal sense, a sense that causes us to give approval to acts of moral value. Here he begins by taking cognizance of the basic difference between that which is naturally good and that which is morally good.

---

[55] *Inquiry*, pp. 78–79, 80, 129. For a defense of the view that morality, according to Hutcheson, is not the result of custom, self-interest, or commandment, see David Fate Norton, "Hutcheson's Moral Realism," *Journal of the History of Philosophy*, 23 (1985): 397–418.

[56] *Inquiry*, p. 94.

[57] Ibid., pp. 102–3.

Things or acts that give us pleasure either immediately (themselves) or mediately (as means) fall in the first category: they are sought "from a View of *Interest*, or from *Self-Love*."[58] This does not mean that they are morally bad. Second, acts that when we observe them give us pleasure because they express love for others—for humankind—fall in the second category; we find them morally good. Acts motivated by love for others command the approval of an inner, evaluative sense, just as a fine ship commands the approval of our sense of beauty. Inevitably, we give approval to acts of moral beauty. The term "moral goodness" denotes "our Idea of *some Quality apprehended in Actions, which procures Approbation*." The apprehended quality is benevolent motivation; the apprehending faculty is the moral sense.[59]

A person in society is moved by four affections (or passions): by self-love and self-hatred; by love and hatred for others. Contrary to Mandeville, there is a natural moral passion, specifically, love for others; society is not simply a useful arrangement achieved by restraining "self-liking" by legislation or convention. The other positive affection, self-love, is bad only when it overwhelms our love for others; the self-love of a person alone on an island would be amoral, rather than immoral. Self-hatred, the desire of private misery, Hutcheson almost dismisses as impossible. Hatred for others, as we shall see, is only ancillary; it can exist only as a flaw or deficiency in our love for others.[60]

Love for others is of two kinds: esteem (or complaisance), caused by approbation of a person by the moral sense, and benevolence, which moves us to work for the happiness of others. Esteem itself is not a passion; however, esteem ordinarily entails benevolence, which does move us. Love is both original and reactive. We love a virtuous person. We hold him in high esteem; accordingly, if possible, we act benevolently toward him. But why do we perceive him as virtuous and hold him in esteem? Because of his original love, that is, his original benevolence, for others. Thus we see that the moral sense operates so as to enhance natural benevolence: acts of natural benevolence win the spectator's esteem; the result is that the spectator acts benevolently toward the benevolent person, thus causing gratitude (and more benevolence). Once we have moved beyond the initial act of natural benevolence, the relationship has become moral.

Hatred of others, too, may be either dislike, a mere perception, or malice, a passion that causes action. Logically, hatred, like love, is both original and reactive, but in reality, the Devil excepted, hatred is never substantive. Since all beings are the creatures of God, no creature is

[58] Ibid., p. 107.
[59] Ibid., p. 105.
[60] Ibid., p. 152.

motivated by original or disinterested hatred, and thus is utterly vicious. The hatred we see around us is reactive; it is occasional, not "sedate" or calm: when people are hated and treated malevolently, it is because of some flaw (selfishness) in the hater or in themselves; either he who hates or he who is hated is deficient in love.[61] Consequently, although active hatred—malice—is all too common, our analysis focuses on love (or rather on active love, benevolence). The virtuous person loves others greatly; the vicious person is somewhat deficient in his love for others, either because his self-love is too strong—he is "selfish"—or because he has been led, misled, to believe, perhaps by his religious or political masters, that their rivals are utterly vicious.

The struggle between vice and virtue is the result of two desires to do good: first, a desire to achieve good on behalf of others; second, a desire to do the same for ourselves. The struggle is between public and private good; it is a struggle between benevolence and excessive self-love; it is not attributable to malice, which is only the reverse side of selfishness, either ours or theirs. Says Hutcheson, "The ordinary Spring of *Vice* then among Men, must be a *mistaken Self-Love*, made so violent, as to overcome *Benevolence*; or *Affections* arising from *false*, and *rashly form'd Opinions of Mankind*, which we run into thro' the Weakness of our *Benevolence*."[62] In another passage, he states that the springs of vicious acts are never ultimate deliberate malice, but "only sudden Anger, Self-Love, some selfish Passion or Appetite, some kind Attachments to Parties, or particular kind Passions."[63] The main cause of man's inhumanity to man is not sedate malice, but generally "an *injudicious, unreasonable Enthusiasm* for some kind of *limited Virtue*."[64] As with Shaftesbury, the competition is between the good of a part—ourselves alone or those dear to us—and the good of the whole. Hutcheson's favorite example of hatred induced by partiality is the hatred for heretics caused by sectarian religion, a sentiment he found widespread in Ireland and Scotland. Although he deplores Shaftesbury's deism, again and again Hutcheson, like Shaftesbury, denounces the immoral consequences of false religion.

We may work for public good because we see that this redounds to our own happiness, and we may work for public good because a benevolent ruler has commanded us to do so, with prescribed rewards and punishments. But quite aside from all such considerations, which appeal to our interest, we have an affection, indeed a strong affection, a passion, for the happiness of other human beings. The only acts that win the approval of the moral sense are acts caused by this passion, benevolence. This is the

[61] Ibid., pp. 152, 172–73.
[62] Ibid., p. 175.
[63] Ibid., p. 191.
[64] Ibid., p. 213.

object, the "quality apprehended in actions," that, whether we wish it or not, procures our moral approbation. Moreover, we find benevolent acts morally good immediately, and not because we see them as useful in promoting the happiness of some great public.

Our moral sense may be blurred by interest, for when we are directly involved, our self-love distorts our perception. We see moral beauty far more accurately when, as observers or spectators, we consider actions involving others. A spectator is pleased by benevolent conduct, just as he is pleased by a beautiful sight. He approves, not because the act gives him pleasure, although it does, but because the actor conforms to the criterion. The spectator recognized the person's moral beauty. Although Hutcheson does not make much of the spectator, he assumes throughout that the interest (self-love) of a participant in an act will tend to distort his evaluation. The moral sense works best either when we are spectators of the conduct of others or when we are reflecting on our own conduct. To the rationalists' contention that a moral sense is too particularistic to provide a standard of moral value, Hutcheson's reply is that the moral sense of every man is the same (in approving benevolence), and that the moral sense operates, not from the viewpoint of a participant, but from that of an observer or spectator.[65]

Like the sense of beauty, the moral sense is antecedent to all local legislation, convention (custom), and education. The moral sense, like the sense of beauty (and the five external senses), is basically the same for all human beings. This does not mean, however, that morality is always the same. Opinions differ from time to time and from place to place as to what kinds of conduct are truly benevolent; but if a particular disagreement is not due to differences in the prevailing circumstances, what the disagreement shows is, not the absence of a common moral sense, but the weakness of reason. Human knowledge about *how* to be most benevolent in any given circumstance is subject to error; as a result, instead of relying on old opinions, we ought to study how best to promote public good. Travelers' tales about the strange ways of faraway peoples are evidence, not that the moral sense is not a universal human faculty, but that human reason is fallible. False and foolish opinions abound; these give rise to weird and perverse customs.

> Men have *Reason* given them, to judge of the Tendencys of their Actions, that they may not stupidly follow the first Appearance of *publick Good*; but it is still some Appearance of *Good* which they pursue. And it is strange, that *Reason* is universally allow'd to Men, notwithstanding all the stupid ridiculous Opinions receiv'd in many Places; and yet absurd Practices, founded upon those very *Opinions*, shall seem an Argument against any *moral Sense*,

[65] *Illustrations*, pp. 235–36; also *Inquiry*, pp. 244–45.

altho' the bad Conduct is not owing to any Irregularity in the *moral Sense*, but to a wrong *Judgment* or *Opinion*. . . . Our *Sense* of *Virtue* generally leads us exactly enough according to our Opinions; and therefore the absurd Practices which prevail in the World, are much better Arguments that Men have no *Reason*, than that they have no *moral Sense* of *Beauty* in Actions.[66]

The basis of all moral goodness, as we saw, is original love for others: each of the cardinal virtues—temperance, courage, prudence, and justice—is approved, not because it is beneficial for the virtuous person, but because it is beneficial for others. Self-love that harms no other person is morally neutral; indeed, a proper degree of self-love is morally good, for unless people take reasonable care to preserve themselves, the good of the whole, the body, the system of which they are parts, may be damaged, even ruined; also, they have a moral obligation to make themselves as able as possible to serve others. But it is their importance to the whole, to the body, not their importance to themselves, that makes their preservation morally good. What is required is a proper balance between concern for one's own good and concern for the good of others. When we denounce "self-love," we are denouncing, not mere self-love, but selfishness.[67]

Hutcheson, like Shaftesbury, thinks of the whole as "a rational system" in which each person has his place. Often he refers to "public good," but he is not referring to the good of a particular body, a body comparable to "the nation" or "the people." We ought to be concerned for the public good of our club, public good of our neighborhood, the public good of our country, the public good of all humankind. Public good is the alternative to private good. The two are not incompatible, but selfishness draws too strongly toward the latter. Members of lesser bodies are susceptible of partiality (or selfishness) simply because those bodies are only parts.

Hutcheson undertakes to prove that all self-love theories are wrong; this he does by showing that the difference and conflict between what is naturally good for one's self or one's faction and what is accounted morally good are far too great for both to be expressions of the same affection, self-love. What is good from the selfish viewpoint of one person, one party, a sect, a country, often in fact is condemned by that same person, party, sect, or country. We do distinguish, at least when we are spectators, between what is selfishly good and what is morally good. Everybody knows from his own experience that the standard of virtue is quite independent of interest. We form an idea of the virtuous person; we hold in esteem anyone who conforms to the idea, even if he has been dead for

---

[66] *Inquiry*, pp. 207–9.
[67] Ibid., pp. 175–76.

centuries, lives in a distant country, or happens to be our opponent. If morality simply followed interest, no explanation of morality would be necessary. But once we admit that people sometimes follow rules of morality in preference to their interest, we have to explain both the origin of those rules and why the rules often overpower interest. Consider, says Hutcheson, the English reaction to the conduct of France and Holland. The government of France persecuted the Huguenots, many of whom fled to England, bringing with them their manufacturing skills; England benefited greatly as a result. The Dutch showed great resolve in throwing off the Spanish tyranny and then in setting up an industrious republic, which competes keenly with England. Yet the English scorn the French and admire the Dutch.

Moreover, the self-love theorists make a mistake characteristic of philosophers in that they depict human beings as much more far-sighted and contriving than they are. To trace all acts of charity, generosity, gratitude, and the like back to a remote motive of self-love requires much subtle, ingenious ratiocination. Philosophers may have the time and skill to construct such chains or schemes, but most people act impulsively, without much careful thought. Similarly, they form moral judgments spontaneously, by "immediate perception," without arduous calculation.[68] Providentially, we do not have to rely on slow, feeble human reason; rather, we are led to judge and act without a clear perception of ultimate consequences.

> It is perhaps true, that *Reflection*, and *Reason* might lead us to approve the same Actions as *advantageous* [as are found good by the moral sense]. But would not the *same* Reflection and Reason likewise generally recommend the same *Meats* to us, which our *Taste* represents as pleasant? And shall we thence conclude, that we have no *Sense* of *Tasting*, or that such a *Sense* is *useless*? No: The Use is plain in both Cases. Notwithstanding the mighty *Reason* we boast of above other Animals, its Processes are too slow, too full of Doubt and Hesitation, to serve us in every Exigency, either for our own Preservation, without the *external Senses*, or to influence our Actions for the *Good* of the *Whole*, without this *moral Sense*.[69]

Although a disinterested desire for the happiness of others is the basis of morality, other factors, of course, often reinforce original benevolence. First, the benevolent person is made happy reflectively by his own virtue. Second, we feel pleasure when we observe his moral beauty. Third, virtuous conduct makes for private happiness in this life—an important

[68] *Illustrations*, pp. 209, 247.
[69] *Inquiry*, pp. 271–72.

truth overlooked by the self-love theorists.[70] Fourth, it has been revealed that eternal rewards have been appointed. However, all these factors only concur; much of the error of modern moral teaching arises from treating one or more of them as fundamental, when in truth they are only secondary. The primary basis is "*some Determination of our Nature to study the Good of others*; or *some Instinct, antecedent to all Reason from Interest, which influences us to the Love of others*; even as the *moral Sense*, above explain'd, determines us to *approve* the Actions which flow from *this Love* in ourselves or others."[71]

Hutcheson scoffs at the notion that the rules of morality were originated by "legislators," who by exploiting human pride and shame tricked the multitude into accepting the rules. If self-love is man's basic drive, it is far too powerful to be tamed by mere opinion. Having summarized the view set forth by Mandeville in "An Enquiry into the Origin of Moral Virtue," he proceeds to comment:

> 'These wondrous cunning Governors made Men believe, by their *Statues* and *Panegyricks*, that there was *publick Spirit*, and that this was in itself *excellent*; and hence Men are led to admire it in others, and to imitate it in themselves, forgetting the Pursuit of their own *Advantage*.' So easy a matter it seems to him, to quit judging of others by what we feel in ourselves!—for a Person who is wholly *selfish*, to imagine others to be *publick-spirited!*—for one who has no Ideas of *Good* but in his own *Advantage*, to be led by the Persuasions of others, into a Conception of *Goodness* in what is avowedly detrimental to himself, and profitable to others; nay, so intirely, as not to approve the Action thorowly, but so far as he was conscious that it proceeded from a *disinterested Study* of the *Good* of others!—Yet this it seems *Statues* and *Penegyricks* can accomplish![72]

It is important to notice that Hutcheson distinguishes in his own way between, first, our benevolence for our children, our friends, our party, our country, and, second, our benevolence for humankind. He distinguishes between both calm self-love and calm benevolence, on the one hand, and particular passions. Calm self-love is different from hunger, ambition, or lust; similarly, calm benevolence is different from parental affection, friendly affection, and party affection. Calm benevolence is wide in scope, particular benevolence is narrow; accordingly, calm benevolence is more virtuous than particular benevolence. Our love for humankind at large is more virtuous than our love for our families, friends, party, or country.[73]

[70] Ibid., pp. 195–96.
[71] Ibid., pp. 159–60.
[72] Ibid., pp. 125–26.
[73] Hutcheson regarded some "parties" as desirable. He states, "Associations for innocent

BEGINNING A NEW SCIENCE 87

From these Observations, we may see what Actions our *moral Sense* would most recommend to our Election, as the most *perfectly virtuous: viz.* such as appear to have the most universal unlimited Tendency to the *greatest* and *most extensive Happiness* of all the *rational Agents*, to whom our Influence can reach. All *Beneficence*, even toward a *Part*, is amiable, when not inconsistent with the *Good* of the *Whole:* But this is a smaller Degree of *Virtue*, unless our Beneficence be restrain'd by want of Power, and not want of Love to the *Whole*. All strict Attachments to Partys, Sects, Factions, have but an imperfect Species of *Beauty*, even when the *Good* of the *Whole* requires a stricter Attachment to a *Part*, as in *natural Affection*, or *virtuous Friendships*; except when *some Parts* are so eminently useful to the *Whole*, that even *universal Benevolence* does determine us with special Care and Affection to study their Interests. Thus *universal Benevolence* would incline us to a more strong Concern for the Interests of *great* and *generous Characters* in a high Station, or make us more earnestly study the Interests of any *generous Society*, whose whole Constitution was contriv'd to promote *universal Good*.[74]

The reason why limited affection is inferior to wider affection, far inferior to the love of all humankind at the extreme, is that the smaller groups involve fewer numbers. It is that "the more limited *Instincts* tend to produce a smaller Moment of Good, because confined to small Numbers. Whereas the more *extensive calm Instinct* of Goodwill, attended with Power, would have no Bounds in its good Effects, and would never lead into any Evil, as the particular Passions may."[75] This does not mean that we are obliged to strive directly for the happiness of everyone everywhere. Hutcheson, like Shaftesbury, recognizes that there are reasons why our benevolence can be directly beneficial for only relatively small groups: our families, our neighborhoods, our own society.

Now because of the great Numbers of Mankind, their distant Habitations, and the Incapacity of any one to be remarkably useful to great Multitudes; that our *Benevolence* might not be quite distracted with a Multiplicity of Objects, whose equal Virtues would equally recommend them to our Regard; or become useless, by being equally extended to Multitudes, whose Interests we could not understand, nor be capable of promoting, having no Intercourse of Offices with them; NATURE has so well ordered it, that as our Attention is more raised by those good Offices which are done to ourselves or our

---

Commerce, or *Manufactures*; Cabals for Defence of *Liberty*, against a *Tyrant*; or even lower Clubs for *Pleasantry*, or *Improvement* by Conversation, are very amiable and good." However, selfish parties, which aim to aggrandize themselves at the expense of others, are bad. He singles out religious sects for special denunciation. *Inquiry*, pp. 210–11.

[74] Ibid., pp. 184–85.
[75] Ibid., pp. 185–86.

Friends, so they cause a stronger Sense of Approbation in us, and produce a stronger Benevolence toward the Authors of them. This we call *Gratitude*. And thus a Foundation is laid for *joyful Associations* in all kinds of *Business*, and *virtuous Friendships*.[76]

While we have goodwill for all humankind, we benefit from the benevolence of only a few; to them we respond with gratitude. Universal benevolence, Hutcheson says, is like gravity "which perhaps extends to all Bodys in the *Universe*; but *increases* as the Distance is diminish'd, and is *strongest* when Bodys come to touch each other."[77] Given that the whole world is one system, there should be no conflict between what is good for benign small associations and what is good for larger ones; however, in principle what produces the greatest happiness for the greatest number is what is morally preferable.

The fact that Hutcheson thinks of benevolence as analogous to gravity is revealing. As the numbers and distances increase, the effective power of benevolence decreases, but at no point—at the nation's boundary, for example—is there a clear break. This continuity provides Hutcheson with the basis for a kind of felicific calculus based on the greatest happiness of the greatest number. Hume, as we shall see, distinguishes sharply in the *Treatise* between two quite different kinds of relationships: first, natural relationships, such as the family; and, second, artificial relationships, such as civil society. Only the former have their beginning (or original) in love. This difference gives rise to his distinction between the natural and the artificial virtues. For Hutcheson, instinctive love for *all* others is the basic virtue. In contrast, Hume has to focus on the evaluative process, which has to explain the moral duties of the artificial relationships as well as those of the natural relationships. This is why Hume differentiates clearly between particular benevolence (toward family, friends, etc.) and general benevolence (toward all our kind). Hutcheson comes very close to this distinction with his comments on particular benevolence and calm benevolence, but since he does not have artificial relationships to explain, he does not make much of the distinction. In contrast, for Hume it is fundamental.

We saw that because of their sense of beauty, people are not content with mere food, drink, and shelter; they want handsome houses, fine clothes, graceful ships, glorious music, delicious food served on splendid dishes. The sense of beauty is practical; it causes people to make and seek things of beauty. Much the same happens in society and would happen even more if people were not misled by bad preachers and mistaken philosophers. The various human relationships are held together by basic

[76] Ibid., pp. 220–21.
[77] Ibid., pp. 221–22.

benevolence. These relationships may have the provision of natural goods as their crude and obvious ends, but it is the fact that the relationships— families, and so on—give their members the joys of mutual esteem and benevolence, not the fact that they provide them with natural goods, that is the source of their greatest value. The moral sense is practical; it gives people a desire for the good life. Living and working with others ought to be a great moral adventure. Excessive self-love, selfishness, is a corruptive force, which impoverishes human relationships. Accordingly, Hutcheson, like Shaftesbury, denounces as pernicious all philosophers who spread the theory—such theories tend to be self-fulfilling—that society is an association of people who live and work together only because this is the way they get more and more natural goods for themselves. Human beings share, *sympathetically*, each other's joys and sorrows. This sharing, even when the emotion shared is painful, is of great value.[78] The relationships in which they are involved, give people a chance to develop toward their perfection and to enjoy the moral beauty of both themselves and their associates. They can be partners not only in life, but in the good life.

Hutcheson's rejection of the theory, set forth ironically by Mandeville—that politicians, by a stratagem, led the multitude to believe that whatever advances public good is virtuous—does not mean that Hutcheson thinks that public opinion is of little or no consequence in determining conduct. Man is a political animal, a creature who needs society; accordingly, the appraisal of others is important to him. Human beings crave honor, especially merited honor; they fear shame, especially merited shame. Unfortunately, the multitude's opinions about the kinds of conduct that are virtuous often are incorrect; this is the result, not of a failure of the moral sense, but of misinformation as to how to do good, misinformation resulting either from the inadequacies of reason or from false views propagated by sects, parties, and other "interests."

The respectful obedience of the multitude to their rulers, Hutcheson speculates, is a result of the honor always paid to benevolent people. Those who have great wealth and power can do much good for others; they possess "the great *Engines* of *Virtue*." As long as it is expected that they will use them for the benefit of others, they attract honor. There is a standing "general Presumption of a good Application"; accordingly, when we see their pomp and glory, we revere the rich and great. Mandeville contends that princes and statesmen insist on magnificence chiefly because they enjoy it. Hutcheson, in contrast, suspects that the apparatus of power has a useful function.

This ordinary Connexion in our Imagination, between *external Grandeur, Regularity* in *Dress, Equipage, Retinue, Badges* of *Honour*, and some *moral*

[78] Ibid., p. 252.

Abilitys greater than ordinary, is perhaps of more Consequence in the World than some *recluse Philosophers* apprehend, who pique themselves upon despising these external Shews. This may possibly be a great, if not the only Cause of what some count *miraculous, viz.* That *civil Governors* of no greater Capacity than their Neighbours, by some inexpressible *Awe* and *Authority*, quell the Spirits of the *Vulgar*, and keep them in Subjection by such small Guards, as might easily be conquer'd by those Associations which might be rais'd among the *Disaffected*, or *Factious* of any *State*; who are daring enough among their *Equals*, and shew a sufficient Contempt of Death for undertaking such an Enterprize.[79]

We can say, in summary, that Hutcheson sees human beings as moved by two basic instinctive affections: self-love and benevolence. Moral approval is given to benevolent acts, acts for public good, but since the public good of a body requires the health and prosperity of its members, not all self-love is morally bad. Those who slight their own interest skew the balance; however, there is far less danger of this happening than that selfishness on behalf of oneself, one's friends, one's sect, or one's party will obscure the public good of the greater whole.

Hutcheson has answered two questions. First, what is the essential quality of virtuous conduct? Benevolence. Second, why do we approve of benevolence? Because naturally, or rather providentially, we find it immediately admirable. For Hutcheson, virtuous conduct expresses love for others. The virtuous person expresses his love for others by good acts suitable to (a) the relationships in which he stands to particular persons, and (b) the prevailing circumstances. The natural pleasure caused by two acts, one done for pay and the other done from benevolence, may be exactly the same; however, the latter gives moral pleasure also. The spectator senses that it is morally good. There is nothing "subjective" about Hutcheson's theory: the moral sense of all healthy human beings, like their other senses, is much the same, and the essential quality of virtuous conduct is the same everywhere.[80]

[79] Ibid., pp. 236–37.

[80] J. L. Mackie draws attention to two possible interpretations of Hutcheson's definition of moral goodness. The first is that the quality of moral goodness is objective, that is, it is in the observed action. The other is that human nature is such that we react with approval to benevolence. Since we would react differently if our nature were different, Mackie says that on this, the second interpretation, the moral quality of goodness is "subjective." He says that Hutcheson "opted firmly for the subjective interpretation, and so, as we shall see, did Hume." See J. L. Mackie, *Hume's Moral Theory* (London: Routledge & Kegan Paul, 1980), p. 33. Mackie's use of the term "subjective" may be misleading; it implies that moral goodness is strictly particular, varying from place to place, from time to time, and even from person to person. Hutcheson, as Norton shows, was writing with a keen awareness of the Cartesian divide between the mind and external objects. For Hutcheson, all perception involves both a subject and an object, and the subject contributes to all perceptions of quality,

Hutcheson was a deeply religious man, but, as we have seen, he turned to human nature to find, first, the content of morality, and, second, the explanation of moral obligation. He did so, not because he thought that morality and religion are distinct and separate matters, but because he believed that those who sought to derive morality from religion were harming morality, while doing little or nothing to advance religion. Clearly, the candid self-interest theorists, such as Hobbes and Mandeville, were wrong and pernicious. The same was true, but far less obviously and therefore more dangerously, of those moralists, such as Pufendorf and Barbeyrac, who defined righteousness as obedience to the great legislator, God. First, by making all natural morality dependent on the dubious assumption that all moral agents, even pagans, have an adequate idea of a good law-making deity, they put the status of moral standards in question.[81] Second, such moralists advance neither sound morality nor true religion: for "to call the *Laws* of the *supreme* DEITY *good*, or *holy*, or *just*, if all *Goodness, Holiness*, and *Justice* be constituted by *Laws*, or the *Will* of a *Superior* any way reveal'd, must be an insignificant Tautology, amounting to no more than this, 'That GOD *wills* what he *wills*.' "[82] Third, by defining righteousness as habitual obedience to an all-powerful legislator, virtue is reduced to mere prudent self-interest. The voluntarist horn of the dilemma, grasped resolutely by Hutcheson's conservative opponents in Glasgow, subverts both religion and morality.[83]

While Hutcheson regarded the rationalists as allies against the followers of "the old Epicureans," he found that they, too, had been misled by the paradigm that represents virtue as conformity to the laws of an au-

---

that is, to perceptions of color, heat, and beauty, as distinct from perceptions of number and duration. See David Fate Norton, *David Hume: Common-Sense Moralist, Sceptical Metaphysician* (Princeton: Princeton University Press, 1982), pp. 83–87. For Hutcheson moral goodness is entirely a matter of mind: a perception of moral good invariably involves (a) a benevolent intention, and (b) reactive approbation. Neither of these is variable: the basic quality of all virtue is benevolence; and benevolence always is approved by everyman's moral sense.

[81] *Illustrations*, pp. 317–18.

[82] *Inquiry*, p. 275.

[83] Ibid., pp. 142–45, 277. Hutcheson was charged with heresy by the presbytery of Glasgow on the ground that he taught, "first that the standard of moral goodness was the promotion of the happiness of others; and second that we could have a knowledge of good and evil, without, and prior to a knowledge of God." See W. R. Scott, *Francis Hutcheson: His Life, Teaching and Position in the History of Philosophy* (Cambridge: Cambridge University Press, 1900), pp. 15, 20–21, 83–84. See also J. K. Cameron, "Theological Controversy: A Factor in the Origins of the Scottish Enlightenment," in *The Origins and Nature of the Scottish Enlightenment*, eds. R. H. Campbell and A. S. Skinner (Edinburgh: John Donald Publishers Ltd., 1982), pp. 116–30. For an account of fundamentalist Calvinism in Scotland, see H. G. Graham, *The Social Life of Scotland in the Eighteenth Century*, 2 vols. (London: Adam and Charles Black, 1899), 2:1–150.

thority beyond nature. To ascertain the content of genuine morality, we do not have to undertake an *a priori* analysis of the eternal law; rather, we need only observe what is approved by the natural moral sense, the moral sense provided by the Creator. We can rely, *in fact* we always do rely, on the moral sense for the content of valid morality. The rationalists, Hutcheson asserts, constantly make use of the moral sense without acknowledgment, proudly praising their own reason for the morality discovered by the moral sense. For example, some of them assert, " *'Tis our Duty to study publick Good.*" But why is this our duty? What is presupposed is either self-love or the moral sense; they are saying either that to study public good is necessary for the good of the agent, or that "*every Spectator, or he himself* [the agent] *upon Reflection, must approve his Action* [in studying public good], *and disapprove his omitting it, if he considers fully all its Circumstances.*"[84] Since the first alternative is unacceptable to the rationalists, they must take the second. Rationalists use the words "rational" and "reasonable" as synonomous with "virtuous"; there are, Hutcheson finds, several explanations why this misleading usage is common. For example, when we act without reasoning (as to whether our ends can be achieved, and by what means) we often are unsuccessful; this leads us to say that we acted unreasonably. Again, the truth that publicly useful acts are found good by both every spectator and by the agent is so generally and so strongly believed that anybody who acts otherwise is immediately pronounced wrong-headed, unreasonable, or irrational. The truth that there is a moral sense and that it reacts with approval to benevolence is so fundamental that we take its judgments for granted and then proceed to pronounce "irrational" all those who act selfishly.

Indeed, all the fashionable moral theories are parasitic. Their teachings, insofar as valid, were learned through the moral sense. Lacking anything solid of their own, the rival theories expropriate from the true theory with neither notice nor thanks.

> The Writers upon opposite Schemes, who deduce all Ideas of *Good* and *Evil* from the *private Advantage* of the *Actor*, or from Relation to a *Law*, and its *Sanctions*, either known from *Reason* or *Revelation*, are perpetually recurring to this *moral Sense* which they deny; not only in calling the *Laws* of the DEITY *just* and *good*, and alledging *Justice* and *Right* in the DEITY to govern us; but by using a Set of Words which import something different from what they will allow to be their only Meaning. *Obligation*, with them, is only such a *Constitution, either of Nature, or some governing Power, as makes it advantageous for the Agent to act in a certain manner.*[85]

[84] *Illustrations*, p. 229.
[85] *Inquiry*, p. 274.

Why they fail to see man's basic benevolence and the power of the moral sense is evident. All share the false presupposition that man's basic motivation is selfish, that to oblige him to be good he must be convinced that thereby he will make a selfish gain in this world or the next. From this premise, it follows that the only acceptable definition of moral obligation is one based on imposition, constraint, and coercion, a definition that implies that if human beings are to act virtuously, their natural motivation must be overcome. Given this presupposition, their definition of moral obligation follows:

> [I]f our *moral Sense* be suppos'd exceedingly weakened, and the *selfish Passions* grown strong, either thro' some general Corruption of Nature, or inveterate Habits; if our *Understanding* be weak, and we be often in danger of being hurry'd by our *Passions* into precipitate and rash Judgments, that *malicious Actions* shall promote our Advantage more than Beneficence; in such a Case, if it be inquir'd what is necessary to engage Men to *beneficent Actions*, or induce a steady Sense of an *Obligation* to act for the *public Good*; then, no doubt, 'A *Law* with Sanctions, given by a *superior Being*, of sufficient Power to make us happy or miserable, must be necessary to counterbalance those apparent Motives of *Interest*, to calm our *Passions*, and give room for the Recovery of our *moral Sense*, or at least for a just View of our *Interest*.'[86]

However, contends Hutcheson, ordinary-life facts show that man is basically benevolent. True, we see much wickedness around us; that, however, is largely the result of the self-fulfilling presupposition that man is selfish, or the result of perverse religion. Those moralists and preachers who harp on man's sinfulness make him worse, not better. The primary requirement is liberation from the pervasive false teaching that people find the fruits of self-love sweet; this belief implies that self-love is to be practiced up to, but not beyond, the point where the costs in this world and the next outweigh what is gained. The proper task of the moral philosopher is to put moral philosophy on a sound footing.

In addition to its disastrous effects on morality, the traditional view that religion is the mother of morality is bad in that it fosters religious skepticism. When it is taught that religion is the basis of morality, many are led to ask that the validity of religion be shown. They demand a strict demonstration, settling for nothing less than would satisfy them in geometry. And when they see that demonstrative proof cannot be given, they turn away from religion. It was Hutcheson's considered opinion that the philosopher should eschew both (a) the voluntarism of Hobbes, Pufendorf, and the conservative Calvinists and (b) the rationalism of Gro-

[86] Ibid., p. 269–70.

tius, Clarke, and the like. Rather, beginning with the facts of morality, he should advance thence to religion, drawing on the former, where conclusive evidence is available, to strengthen and deepen the latter.[87]

Hutcheson's insistence that the moral philosopher must begin with human nature rather than with imposed laws does not imply that Hutcheson rejected the idea of God-given natural laws.[88] If we believe that God created human nature, it is understandable, he allowed, that we should see the rules of morality as laws of God. However, we should be on guard to keep the idea of *laws* from reimposing the deceptive old paradigm in which God imposes His will on fallen men. The word "laws" tends to give the wrong idea of moral obligation.

> This word [obligation] has two senses, 1. We are said to be *obliged* to act, or perform to others, 'when the inward sense and conscience of each one must approve such action or performance, and must condemn the contrary as vitious and base:' in like manner we conceive an obligation to omit or abstain. This sort of obligation is conceived previous to any thought of the injunction of a law. 2. Obligation is sometimes taken for 'a motive of interest superiour to all motives on the other side, proposed to induce us to certain actions or performances, or omissions of action.' Such motives indeed must arise from the laws of an omnipotent Being. This latter meaning seems chiefly intended in these metaphorical definitions of great authors [Pufendorf, Barbeyrac], who would have all obligation to arise from the law of a superior, '*a bond of right binding us by a necessity of acting or abstaining*' or an '*absolute necessity imposed upon a man, to act in certain manner.*'[89]

The first usage refers to obligation correctly understood; the second refers to constraint or compulsion. To say that God's laws oblige us to do what the moral sense approves is entirely suitable; but to say that His laws constrain us to act contrary to the moral sense is to assert that God is evil. "The Difference is plainly this: When any Sanctions co-operate with our *moral Sense*, in exciting us to Actions which we count *morally*

---

[87] Ibid., pp. 303–4. See the account of Hutcheson's life, character, and writings by William Leechman, the professor of divinity at Glasgow University and sometime tutor to Hume's friend William Mure of Caldwell. *Collected Works of Francis Hutcheson*, 5:iv–vi; also xiii–xvi.

[88] On the coherence of Hutcheson's thought, especially on the relation between (a) his theory of morality as set forth in his first two major works and (b) the content of *A System of Moral Philosophy* (1755) and the other later works, see James Moore, "The Two Systems of Francis Hutcheson: On the Origins of the Scottish Enlightenment," and Knud Haakonssen, "Natural Law and Moral Realism: The Scottish Synthesis," both in *Studies in the Philosophy of the Scottish Enlightenment*, ed. M. A. Stewart (Oxford: Clarendon Press, 1990).

[89] *A Short Introduction to Moral Philosophy* (translated from the Latin) (Glasgow: Robert Foulis, 1747), pp. 121–22. Both Pufendorf and Barbeyrac are mentioned in a footnote. For a longer discussion of the two meanings of obligation see the *Inquiry*, pp. 267–69.

good, we say we are *oblig'd*; but when Sanctions of Rewards or Punishments oppose our *moral Sense*, then we say we are *brib'd* or *constrain'd*. In the former Case we call the *Lawgiver good*, as designing the *publick Happiness*; in the latter we call him *evil*, or *unjust*, for the suppos'd *contrary* Intention."[90] It is easy to see why the principles of morality came to be called laws of God. Benevolence is a natural human motivation; the moral sense is an attribute of human nature. Since God created human nature, it follows that He stands behind, endorses, supports, the findings of the moral sense.[91]

When Hutcheson sets down the basic moral rules, he does so in terms of rights and duties in the natural-law way; however, he gives explicit notice that we are to regard the content of natural law as immediately the result of moral sense, and only mediately as required by God. With this understood, he proceeds to conduct us along highways made thoroughly familiar by Grotius and Pufendorf. He describes "the several duties of life" by explaining "the several *rights* belonging to men, and the corresponding obligations, in all the several states and relations they stand in to each other."[92] Here, of course, Hutcheson continues to reject legalistic morality. Our first ideas of morality do not depend on law. Good and evil, not right and wrong, are the basic moral categories. The good is the only valid end of law in any form. The right, established by law, is subordinate; the purpose of rights is to promote and maintain the good. Our ideas of rights, says Hutcheson, derive from the moral sense: "Whenever it appears to us, that *a Faculty of doing, demanding, or possessing any thing, universally allow'd in certain Circumstances, would in the Whole tend to the general Good*, we say, that one in such Circumstances has *a Right to do, possess*, or *demand that Thing*. And according as this Tendency to the *publick Good* is *greater* or *less*, the *Right* is *greater* or *less*."[93]

---

[90] *Inquiry*, p. 277.

[91] *A Short Introduction*, pp. 110–12. Hutcheson gives a clear account of why, and how, it is correct to speak of *laws* of nature (and laws of God)—that is, imperative laws, not descriptive laws—in *A System of Moral Philosophy*. There he begins with the distinction between right and wrong. This fundamental distinction is made by the moral sense. In his words, "From the constitution of our *moral faculty* above-explained, we have our notions of *right*, and *wrong*, as characters of affections and actions." This distinction is the foundation of the notion of rights and wrongs, that is, what is right (or wrong) in specific relationships and situations. Only thereafter does Hutcheson advance—with a reference to "Leibnitz's censure on Puffendorf and Barbeyraque's defence of him"—to the argument that rights are to be observed, and wrongs rejected, because what is right and what God wills are the same. "When we have arrived at this persuasion [that God stands behind our moral faculty], these practical conclusions receive new enforcements upon our hearts, both from our *moral faculty*, and from our interest." *A System of Moral Philosophy* 1:252–65. (*Collected Works of Francis Hutcheson*, vol. 5.)

[92] *A Short Introduction*, p. 139.

[93] *Inquiry*, pp. 277–78.

Using this criterion, the relative strength of their tendency to the public good, rights can be divided into three kinds. First, *perfect rights* are "of *such Necessity to the publick Good, that the universal Violation of them would make human Life intolerable.*"[94] These are defensive rights; in a state of nature a person has a right to his life and limbs, to the fruits of his innocent labor, to the performance of contracts, and so forth. Second, *imperfect rights* are claim rights; a person has a right to certain good works—prompted chiefly by gratitude to benefactors and humanity to all mankind—but may not force others to perform them. Perfect rights, we may say, relate to life, while imperfect rights relate to the good life. Respect for another person's perfect rights is so essential that it wins no praise, but disrespect for them brings on resistance and punishment. In contrast, disrespect for imperfect rights entails no punishment, but respect for them is positively virtuous and praiseworthy. Third, some rights are *external*. Where there is a conflict between what is good as a general rule and an imperfect right, there is an external right. Hutcheson uses an unfair contract as an example: one party has a perfect right to insist on performance, while the other party has an imperfect right to be relieved of his obligation. The right of the former prevails, but only as an external right. Contract is too important an institution for us to let it be eroded by permitting people who believe, perhaps correctly, that particular contracts are unfair to renounce their obligations; however, a good person would forgive the obligations of the disadvantaged.

Hutcheson divides rights in another way: the inalienable and the alienable. We cannot surrender either our private judgment or our internal affections; they are not within our control. We may not alienate our rights to our lives and limbs. Nor may we alienate our right to serve God as we think best, because "it can never serve any valuable Purpose, to make Men worship him in a way which seems to them displeasing to him."[95] Our public institutions and laws ought to be based on a recognition of these truths. On the other hand, we may put ourselves, and our possessions, presumably, under the direction of governors, if thereby some good purpose, such as the enforcement of perfect rights, can be achieved.

Hutcheson bases the right of property on utility. Once the population had grown to a size so great that the needs of all were no longer met by nature's bounty, labor became necessary. But calm benevolence is not a sufficiently strong motive to induce humans to work for the benefit of all; they need to be spurred on by the knowledge that they themselves, their families, and their friends will benefit from their efforts, and that they will be honored because of their riches. Self-love without a property system

[94] Ibid., p. 278.
[95] Ibid., p. 283.

would discourage industry; a person, because of his self-love, would not work if others, because of their self-love, were simply waiting to consume the fruits of his labor. But within a property system, self-love spurs the people to work. Not only does a person have a right to the fruits of his own innocent labor, but he has the right to trade those goods, to give them away, and to bestow them in his last will and testament.

Like Shaftesbury, Hutcheson rejects the view that morality is merely factitious, made arbitrarily by a legislator, either divine or human; on this both agree with the rationalists. As Shaftesbury stated in 1699, "If the mere will, decree, or law of God be said absolutely to constitute right and wrong, then are these latter words of no significancy at all."[96] However, in contrast to the rationalists, both Shaftesbury and Hutcheson contend that the rules of morality are to be discovered, not by logical demonstration, but by observing natural moral motivation, that is, human nature free from distortion by false education, bad customs, or wrong theories. A good person is one whose motivation conforms to genuine human nature. In explaining Shaftesbury's principles, Hutcheson employs considerable technical sophistication and presents human nature as the creation of the God of the Judaeo-Christian tradition. Where the former writes of "kindly affections," the latter includes all these under the umbrella of Christian goodwill: "Thou shalt love thy neighbor as thyself." However, there is a difference—not to be overstated—between them on the importance of rationality. Shaftesbury says that man can be virtuous because he is rational; because he is rational (self-conscious or reflective), he can control himself in accordance with the rules of morality. In contrast, Hutcheson, who felt obliged to show the basic error of rationalist moral epistemology, is careful to treat reason, not as reflective capacity, but as a faculty to be used to gain information.

Joseph Butler

The analysis of morality given by Joseph Butler—chiefly in *Fifteen Sermons Preached at the Rolls Chapel*, published in 1726—although terse, is especially subtle and perceptive. The intention of this learned Anglican divine is practical: to convince his audience to go beyond a superficial, conventional commitment to virtue and Christianity. Although he is a true believer in both the eternal and the divine law and does not criticize Clarke's approach, his preferred strategy, as he states in his preface, is to begin with facts of human nature he thinks a candid intelligent audience simply cannot deny, and then to show the perfect consistency between

[96] *Characteristics*, 1:264.

natural truth and Christian theology. By studying the attributes and constitution of human nature, he argues, we can discover the kind of life God intends for humankind. Although the young Hume was predisposed against theologians, he respected Butler highly; Butler was one of those who had begun "to put the science of man on a new footing."[97]

Butler's style seems excessively succinct and often convoluted; he himself, in the preface to the second edition of the *Fifteen Sermons*, describes it as abstruse and difficult, although suitable to the subject. Moreover, each sermon has the relatively limited purpose of adducing natural truth in support of a biblical text. Neither the sermons alone nor the sermons taken together with his other writings constitute an integrated, systematic statement of his moral theory; as a result, the reader has to draw the argument together and order it for himself. Our purposes may best be served by setting forth the relevant parts of his theory in a series of points.[98] Because these points are interrelated, some repetition cannot be avoided.

First, as mentioned, Butler focuses mainly, not on the play, as does Clarke, but on the players, not on eternal fitnesses and unfitnesses, not on roles in a great drama knowable quite apart from the participants, but on the attributes of the players, the attributes of human nature. Man, he contends, was constituted and equipped by the Creator so as to be able to live a good life on earth. Butler's aim is to base his sermons, which show the eminent desirability of that good life, on an accurate analysis of human nature.

Second, he holds that the popular dichotomy of (evil) passions versus (good) reason is wrong and dangerously misleading. God gave human beings the passions for a good purpose: they provide the goals of action; they motivate people to seek those goals. They are basically good, although often they need to be guided by reason and conscience, also provided, in selecting efficient ways and means for attaining human ends or purposes.

Third, Butler contends that it is a fundamental mistake to think that the individual ought not to be concerned about his own happiness. Inevitably, when he thinks about his life, his happiness is his great concern; if to be interested in one's own happiness is to be under the rule of self-love, then self-love is indeed the dominant principle in human life. To accept the idea that there is a basic conflict between virtue and the individual's desire for happiness, his self-love, is to concede victory to vice even before

---

[97] *Letters*, 1:25, 27, 43.

[98] I used two excellent commentaries. The older of these, the more expository, is Austin Duncan-Jones, *Butler's Moral Philosophy* (Harmondsworth: Penguin Books, 1952). The other, a more evaluative study, is Terence Penelhum, *Butler* (London: Routledge & Kegan Paul, 1985). See also Scott, *Francis Hutcheson*.

the battle starts.[99] Butler, of course, does not dismiss benevolence; he makes it an important source of happiness.

Fourth, man is a social being by his nature. The distinction between private good (private happiness) and public good (the happiness of others) is analytically useful; in practice, however, private good cannot be achieved to a high degree unless one promotes the good of others, and one will be unable to promote the good of others unless one gives some attention to one's own good. Both self-love and benevolence are basic in human nature, with benevolence essential to efficacious self-love. This raises an important question. Is benevolence simply an inclusive category comprising those various affections—family love, friendship—that cause us to do good works for some others? If so, it would stand to those public-good "under affections" as self-love stands to the various private-good "under affections." Or does benevolence include something more, something properly called benevolence, without any confusion of family love, and the like? Butler gives the latter reply. Benevolence is the virtue to which we are enjoined by the commandment, "Thou shalt love thy neighbor as thyself." Benevolence is expressed in works intended for the good of one's neighbor, with "neighbor" meaning *anybody* within reasonable reach. While Butler does not exclude works prompted by special ties such as family love, benevolent works proper are works for the happiness of *neighbors*.

Individuals, then, are moved, or rather, ought to be moved, by cool self-love. Also, they are moved naturally by a basic benevolence; the commandment simply recalls them to their genuine nature. Conversely, as there is no basic self-hatred, there is no basic malevolence.[100] Fundamentally, the whole creation is good. While we may be offended by defects in ourselves and in others and may act in ways harmful to ourselves and to others, these facts, while serious, are not to be taken as evidence that mankind's post-fall condition is hopeless. These defects and errors are only disorders.

Fifth, although Butler recognizes our desire for happiness, for both ourselves and others, he contends that the desire for happiness does not prescribe what we should do. Happiness is a condition, not a specific end or goal. Just as the captain of a ship at sea in a storm has a keen interest in safety, the idea of safety does not tell him how safety is to be achieved. But, as we have seen, wise Providence has furnished us with various passions; these define for us our goals and purposes. We seek to satisfy these passions. When they are gratified, we are happy. Just as safety is not a

---

[99] Joseph Butler, *The Works of the Right Reverend Father in God Joseph Butler*, ed. Samuel Halifax, 2 vols. (Oxford: The University Press, 1844) 2:146–47.

[100] Ibid., 2:12–13.

safe haven, but the result of entering a safe haven, happiness is not sufficiently specific to be a goal or purpose; rather, it is a result. Providence
did not launch us with the vague injunction, "Be happy"; rather, we were
furnished with very powerful drives to show us what we should do (with
the guidance of reason and conscience) if we are to be happy.[101] Some of
those drives are private passions and affections, for example, hunger.
Others are public, for example, friendship, compassion, gratitude. It is by
the gratification of his passions and affections, both private and public,
that a person achieves his own happiness. This means that a person has
to be benevolent—to love his neighbor—if he is to be happy to any considerable degree. One who is a good member of society is *virtuous*. In
other words, virtue is essential to the individual's own happiness. In the
sermon, "Upon Compassion," Butler emphasizes the providential nature
of the passions.

> It is manifest our life would be neglected, were it not for the calls of hunger,
> and thirst, and weariness; notwithstanding that without them reason would
> assure us, that the recruits of food and sleep are the necessary means of our
> preservation. It is therefore absurd to imagine, that, without affection, the
> same reason alone would be more effectual to engage us to perform the duties
> we owe to our fellow-creatures. One of this make would be as defective, as
> much wanting, considered with respect to society, as one of the former make
> would be defective, or wanting, considered as an individual, or in his private
> capacity.[102]

In other words, man was equipped by his Creator with particular social
passions, assistants to benevolence, so as to be an integral member of
society; he is a sociable creature. Society is not, as Hobbes thought, an
arrangement devised and introduced by humans for the advancement of
their private good.

Butler's dismissal of happiness (or the general enjoyment of good) as a
specific goal opens the way for him to emphasize the several affections
and passions, those he calls "the under affections." It enables him to point
out that some of an individual's affections and passions lead him to act
in ways that result in his private good, while others lead him to act in
ways that result in public good. Butler can then argue that since all these
passions are the passions of one individual, that individual can be happy
in a high degree only when all his "under affections," the public as well
as the private, are given satisfactory expression.

Butler's insistence that happiness is not a specific goal means that for
him neither self-love (the individual's desire for his own happiness) nor

101 Ibid., 2:134–35.
102 Ibid., 2:60.

benevolence (the individual's desire that neighbors be happy) is of much direct practical importance for unreflective people. What is important to them as driving forces are the particular passions, both private and public. However, the reflective person ought to evaluate and compare the various passions in terms of their contribution to happiness. Some havens are safer than others, and not all, especially not those highly touted by men of the world, offer much protection. One of Butler's main points in his rebuttal of the theory that narrow self-love is the main principle of human conduct is that it is a fact, denied by no candid observer, that most people act with little or no attention to their own happiness; rather, they tend to act rashly, thoughtlessly, impulsively; indeed, often their conduct would be morally far better if they gave more thought to their own happiness.

Sixth, the individual's conduct ought to be guided by his conscience. The old adage, "Do whatever is natural, for what is natural is right," is sound, but it is not an open licence to a careless life of pleasure; the whole, the system or constitution of human nature is assumed. In that constitution, the reflective capacity, conscience, ought to preside as the highest authority. Conscience informs people when their thoughts and acts are right or wrong. That the conscience is a part of the human constitution, Butler submits, nobody is likely to deny; it is also generally agreed that the conscience does pass judgments. From this we can conclude, he argues, that to judge and superintend is its constitutional role; the conscience is supposed to function as the governor. By nature it has *de jure* power, authority, although often it lacks sufficient *de facto* power in flawed human beings. The passions are good, but frequently, even when guided by reason, they need to be restrained, balanced, and guided by the conscience. Man is, he was created as, a conscientious being, a moral being; he feels obliged to follow the directions of his conscience. Nor are the judgments of conscience to be confused with other value judgments: the latter distinguish between good and bad, between beauty and ugliness, but the judgments of conscience distinguish legalistically, between right and wrong, between what conforms to and what violates a role; thus the basic notion of an entire drama emerges as the result of particular roles. Conscience is basic to human nature; it is not simply an attribute of those in the Judaeo-Christian tradition. When St. Paul wrote, "For when the Gentiles, which have not the law, do by nature the things contained in the law, these, having not the law, are a law until themselves," he was referring to the conscience; although they lack the divine law, at times the Gentiles, guided by conscience, meet the requirements of that law.

Seventh, what conscience requires is not contrary to true happiness. The real cause of vice is not cold, calculating self-love, far from it, but ungoverned passions and ignorance of the fact that virtue is essential to happiness. People often act contrary to their own happiness by reason of indifference or thoughtlessness; turning a blind eye to their happiness, they indulge in gluttony and drunkenness, for example. And they act contrary to their own interest as a result of failing to see, perhaps because of false theories, that the satisfaction of their public affections is necessary to any high degree of happiness. To blame either the passions or self-love, as many philosophers do, is to conceal the real cause and thus prevent correction. The individual's desire for his own happiness is not to be blamed, for the number of people who seriously put their minds to the attainment of their own good is just as small as is the number of those who make a conscious effort to do good works for others.[103]

Eighth, Butler acknowledges that to be good members of society we must accept restrictions on our conduct; however, what we forego is of little long-term worth. Our real interest and our duty prescribe the same lines of conduct. "Reasonable self-love and conscience are the chief or superior principles in the nature of man: because an action may be suitable to this nature, though all other principles be violated; but becomes unsuitable, if either of those are. Conscience and self-love, if we understand our true happiness, always lead us the same way. Duty and interest are perfectly coincident; for the most part in this world, but entirely and in every instance if we take in the future, and the whole; this being implied in the notion of a good and perfect administration of things."[104] It is important to notice that Butler is not prepared to assert that interest and morality are perfectly harmonious in this world: the virtuous person may have to wait for full redress in the next world.

Ninth, in modern times, says Butler, there is "open scorn of all talk of public spirit, and real good-will to our fellow-creatures."[105] It is thought that if someone is acting for the good of the public, he must be giving up his own private good to a reciprocal degree. If one pan of the scales goes down, the other, it is said, must go up. This is a twisted, misleading notion. Any expedition to find and capture private happiness is certain to fail, because it is based on a false conception of the nature of happiness. Happiness, as we have seen, is not a specific goal, but a condition. An individual who sails hither and yon searching for happiness will never find it; meanwhile, blinded by his obsession, he will be oblivious to many sources of pleasure, which would make him happy. Moreover, this kind of thinking is based on the mistake of thinking that self-love excludes the gratification of the public passions and affections. Life is not a zero-sum

103 Ibid., 2:13–14.
104 Ibid., 2:36.
105 Ibid., 2:131.

game, a game involving only a limited quantum of happiness: by making others happy, we contribute also to our own happiness.

Tenth, Butler undertakes to show why we often think that private good and public good are in conflict. The explanation is that happiness is regarded as analogous to property. This is misleading, because property is an exclusive concept: if one person has an unqualified title to a field, nobody else has any right whatsoever in relation to that field. As one person's dominion increases, the dominion of all others must decrease. Applied to the relationship between private and public good, the analogy of property is horrendously false.[106]

Eleventh, modern men, at least men of the world, have come to think that the increase of their own riches and power, together with pleasure (mere sensual gratification) will make for their greatest happiness. It is this particular interpretation of how an individual may attain happiness that masquerades as "self-love," and by imposture gains compelling strength. These men are sadly mistaken: experience has shown conclusively that the rich, the powerful, and the men of pleasure often are anxious and miserable, while those who work for the good of others generally are happy.

Twelfth, the commandment that we are to love our neighbor as ourselves is to be obeyed, Butler submits, not blindly, but under the guidance of reason.

> Thus, when benevolence is said to be the sum of virtue, it is not spoken of as a blind propension, but as a principle in reasonable creatures, as so to be directed by their reason: for reason and reflection comes into our notion of a moral agent. And that will lead us to consider distant consequences, as well as the immediate tendency of an action: it will teach us, that the care of some persons, suppose children and families, is particularly committed to our charge by Nature and Providence; as also that there are other circumstances, suppose friendship or former obligations, which require that we do good to some, preferably to others.[107]

Moreover, we ought to remember that the commandment does not require us to strive officiously to do good for everybody in the world. It applies to us in our place and situation, whatever these be. To assume responsibility for the well-being of all humankind, or even of our own country, is beyond our competence. God is omniscient; therefore perfect benevolence is a virtue suitable to Him. The love of God can embrace the whole universe without endangering it; ours cannot, for when we act beyond our ken, we know not what we do.

[106] Ibid., 2:137.
[107] Ibid., 2:162.

The object is too vast. For this reason moral writers also have substituted a less general object for our benevolence, mankind. But this likewise is an object too general, and very much out of our view. Therefore persons more practical have, instead of mankind, put our country; and made the principle of virtue, of human virtue, to consist in the entire uniform love of our country: and this is what we call a public spirit; which in men of public stations is the character of a patriot. But this is speaking of the upper part of the world. Kingdoms and governments are large; and the sphere of action of far the greatest part of mankind is much narrower than the government they live under: or however, common men do not consider their actions as affecting the whole community of which they are members. There plainly is wanting a less general and nearer object of benevolence for the bulk of men, than that of their country. Therefore the scripture, not being a book of theory and speculation, but a plain rule of life for mankind, has with the utmost possible propriety put the principle of virtue upon the love of our neighbour; which is that part of the universe, that part of mankind, that part of our country, which comes under our immediate notice, acquaintance, and influence, and with which we have to do.[108]

Butler was concerned that the traditional virtues not be pushed into oblivion by the exaltation of benevolence. It is not enough, he said, to reduce all virtue to benevolence, as some seem to; probably it was chiefly Hutcheson whom he had in mind. We need other, more specific virtues: we need to be just, to be truthful, to observe our unequal obligations to the members of our families, to help our friends, to love our neighbors, and others.

I am not sensible that I have, in this . . . observation, contradicted what any author designed to assert. But some of great and distinguished merit have, I think, expressed themselves in a manner, which may occasion some danger, to careless readers, of imagining the whole of virtue to consist in singly aiming, according to the best of their judgment, at promoting the happiness of mankind in the present state; and the whole of vice, in doing what they foresee, or might foresee, is likely to produce an overbalance of unhappiness in it: than which mistakes, none can be conceived more terrible. For it is certain, that some of the most shocking instances of injustice, adultery, murder, perjury, and even of persecution, may, in many supposable cases, not have the appearance of being likely to produce an overbalance of misery in the present state; perhaps sometimes may have the contrary appearance. . . . The happiness of the world is the concern of him, who is the lord and the proprietor of it: nor do we know what we are about, when we endeavour to promote

[108] Ibid., 2:150–51.

the good of mankind in any ways, but those which he has directed; that is indeed in all ways not contrary to veracity and justice.[109]

Butler's moral theory amounts to a denial of the Augustinian-Calvinist view that the Fall devastated human nature. For him, as for St. Thomas Aquinas, post-Fall nature does not need to be supplanted by Grace; rather, the function of Grace is to supplement (to perfect) nature. Butler, like Shaftesbury and Hutcheson, looks back to the ancients; indeed, his analysis is somewhat reminiscent of Plato's: there are both private-good and public-good drives, and both kinds, although good, need to be governed. When each of the elements of the constitution plays its proper part, a person (or a state) is sound, just, and happy. But where Plato would have reason rule, Butler enthrones conscience (with its known prohibitions and requirements).

Points of Departure

Hume recognized writers such as Locke, Shaftesbury, Mandeville, Hutcheson, and Butler as his modern precursors: they had seen that all scientific endeavors not based on fact must be vain, and that incessant, inconclusive squabbling among eminent philosophers had instilled in the multitude an aversion to abstruse thought on moral subjects. Consequently, they had "begun to put the science of man on a new footing."[110] The result, Hume hoped, would be that those who advanced this science would not be dismissed as "metaphysicians," but would be seen as useful, contributing to the improvement of society. From studying their works, Hume seems to have come to the following conclusions about the moral sciences.

The moral philosopher must focus on human nature, for morality, politics, criticism, and natural religion are phenomena of mind. In morality, for example, there are rules, as the great natural law writers said—and

[109] Dissertation 2: "Of the Nature of Virtue," in *The Works*, 1:325–26. This dissertation and another, "Of Personal Identity," initially were incorporated in *The Analogy of Religion*. Later Butler placed them after the conclusion of the *Analogy*. Hutcheson, in the preface to his *Essay on the Nature and Conduct of the Passions* (1728), had mentioned Butler's Sermons as having done "much Justice to the wise and good Order of our Nature"; probably it was to quash any notion that he subscribed to Hutcheson's theory, of which benevolence is the foundation, that Butler, in the preface to the second edition of *Fifteen Sermons* (1729), insisted on the primary importance of conscience. See Scott, *Francis Hutcheson*, pp. 96–97.

[110] Hume was influenced by writers other than those mentioned in his famous footnote. His debt to Cicero, Bayle, Malebranche, and others is examined by Peter Jones in *Hume's Sentiments: Their Ciceronian and French Context* (Edinburgh: Edinburgh University Press, 1982). See also R. H. Popkin, *The High Road to Pyrrhonism* (San Diego: Austin Hill Press, Inc., 1980), pp. 103–80.

for the most part they stated those rules accurately—but those rules arise from human experience. Begin with ascertainable fact; the standards and rules of morality cannot be discovered by any other method. Religion is not the mother of morality.[111] Whether, once discovered and enunciated, the standards and rules learned from nature are to be attributed to a Creator depends on one's religious beliefs.

In *A Letter from a Gentleman to his friend in Edinburgh*, written to refute the charges made against him by those opposing his candidacy for the chair of ethics and pneumatical philosophy at the University of Edinburgh, Hume deals with the accusation that in the *Treatise* he had sapped the foundations of morality "by denying the natural and essential Difference betwixt Right and Wrong." He denies the charge, contending that he had allied himself with Hutcheson and others in trying to put the moral sciences back on a factual basis. "He hath indeed denied the eternal Difference of Right and Wrong in the Sense in which *Clark* and *Woolaston* maintained them, viz. That the Propositions of Morality were of the same Nature with the Truths of Mathematicks and the abstract Sciences, the Objects *merely* of Reason, not the *Feelings* of our internal *Tastes* and *Sentiments*. In this Opinion he concurs with all the antient Moralists, as well as with Mr. *Hutchison* Professor of Moral Philosophy in the University of Glasgow, who, with others, has revived the antient Philosophy in this Particular."[112] The factual approach requires that morality be dis-

---

[111] In the *Treatise* Hume strove to refute chiefly the excessive claims of moral rationalism; yet he, like Hutcheson, was completely opposed to the voluntarists. See David Fate Norton, "Hume, Atheism, and the Autonomy of Morals," in *Hume's Philosophy of Religion*, the sixth (1985) James Montgomery Hester Seminar lectures (Winston-Salem: Wake Forest University Press, 1985), pp. 97–144.

[112] *A Letter From a Gentleman to his friend in Edinburgh*, eds. E. C. Mossner and J. V. Price (Edinburgh: The University Press, 1967), pp. 18, 30. Clearly, Hume's case was being put in the best light. He had heard that Hutcheson thought him unfit for the post. At the same time, Hutcheson, Leechman, and the like were being denounced as heretics on the ground that instead of being preachers of the Word of God, they were mere "moralists," even worse, moralists who followed the teachings of heathen writers. The first choice of the town council for their vacant chair was Hutcheson himself. When he declined, the council turned to the ministers of Edinburgh for guidance; twelve of the fifteen ministers advised against Hume. At this point Hume, hoping to sway the council, wrote his *Letter from a Gentleman*; but to no avail. Evidently Hume did not intend that *A Letter from a Gentleman* should be published, at least not in the form in which it was published. See *New Hume Letters*, p. 15. Moreover, it is possible that Henry Home (Lord Kames) or some other of Hume's friends may have revised the *Letter from a Gentleman* to make it more effective. See Norton, *David Hume*, p. 44n. Hume attributed his defeat to misunderstanding and misrepresentation of his writings. To an acquaintance he wrote, "the matter was brought to an issue, and by the cabals of the Principal, the bigotry of the clergy, and the credulity of the mob, we lost it." *Letters*, 1:62. The opening at Edinburgh had been brought about by the resignation of John Pringle. The fact that Pringle's courses "dealt mainly with the moral theory of Cicero, Marcus Aurelius, Pufendorf, and Bacon," but with some attention to nat-

cussed initially in terms of virtues and vices, not rights and wrongs. While it is true that virtuous conduct comes to be recommended, even required, by maxims, rules, and laws, to begin with these, especially with laws, and thus rights and wrongs, would be to revert to the old theological dilemma. The good, not the right, is the fundamental concept. Rights are established, by convention and legislation, as means to the good.

A philosopher must center his attention on the passions (the "under affections"), rather than on the desire for happiness; people are moved largely by particular feelings, not by elaborate calculations about how happiness is to be achieved.

Undoubtedly the affection commonly called benevolence is an important moral virtue, but, as Butler showed, it cannot be the guiding principle of human life: (a) its range is short; (b) our capacity to plan or achieve happiness for others is limited; and (c) while we have a right and duty to care for our children, we have no title to set ourselves up as paternalistic masters over even our closest friends and neighbors. Besides, we deal with many toward whom we feel neither benevolence nor malevolence; an explanation of the rules of conduct we feel obliged to follow in those dealings is required. Here Carmichael and Hutcheson, and, behind them, Grotius and Pufendorf, have paved the way by explaining justice, the negative virtue, which requires, not that we do good works, but that we refrain from wronging others by injuring them in life, liberty, reputation, property, and the like. What has not been given is an explanation of why we feel morally obliged to follow the rules of a form of association that, unlike even the neighborhood, is not based on affection. When we understand why the moral sense reacts with approbation to just conduct, we may have a deeper understanding of why one who is benevolent to his neighbors is regarded as virtuous.

Reason plays an important role in conduct, but it is not conscience; to equate reason and conscience is to beg the question, what is right reason, and why do we feel obliged to heed it? On the other hand, while the moral-sense theory gives an explanation of why we distinguish between good and evil acts, it only hints at why we feel obliged to do what is right. What is the origin of the feeling of moral obligation, of the sense of ought? The key role of conscience is recognized by Butler, but he relies on religion to explain both the authority of conscience and its requirements.

---

ural theology and politics, suggests that Hume would have been on familiar ground. See R. B. Sher, *Church and University in the Scottish Enlightenment* (Edinburgh: Edinburgh University Press, 1985), p. 29. Carlyle of Inveresk, who studied under Pringle, comments, "His lectures were chiefly a compilation from Lord Bacon's works; and had it not been for Puffendorf's small book, which he made his text, we should not have been instructed in the rudiments of the science." *The Autobiography of Dr. Alexander Carlyle of Inveresk, 1722–1805* (Edinburgh: T. N. Foulis, 1910), p. 55.

Unless we accept Butler's religious presuppositions, another explanation of our knowledge of right and wrong, and of our sense of obligation, is required.

Given the fact that we are moved by our affections and values, with reason only helping by showing the best ways and means, when we undertake to explain someone's acts, we should try to discover the causes, not the reasons, behind his behavior; often he has no reasons. The same is true, but far more so, in the case of economic, social, and political changes. Perhaps Fortune, Fate, or Providence has comprehensive purposes, plans, and reasons; however, the historian—of the advent of civil liberty in England and Scotland, for example—is able to analyze only effective causes.

While the natural-law writers make the mistake of explaining the obligation to observe certain rights and duties by asserting that we must act in conformity with either the will of God (Pufendorf) or the eternal reason (Grotius), the content of natural law teaching on private property, allegiance, and the like, with its emphasis on individual rights, seems to be generally correct. This is readily understood: far from letting their fancies fly wild, to a great extent these writers relied on the factual world for the content of their jurisprudence.

Now that the notion that the standards and rules of morality can be discovered by speculation on the eternal reason or on the will of God has been dismissed, we must recognize that human beings formulate those standards and rules as the result of experience. In some areas of moral conduct, few new discoveries are likely; in others—politics and political economy, and the latter far more than the former—many false beliefs still prevail, so that what would be best is not done. Bad laws, false maxims, and erroneous policies are common. The task of the moral philosopher is to advance morality. This he can do by the experimental method of reasoning, which combines experience and reflection.

3

MORALITY EXPLAINED

The Origin of Moral Sentiments

The Passions

PEOPLE GENERALLY conduct themselves, both privately and publicly, according to rules and standards of morality. Ordinarily they do what is regarded as right; misconduct, although not infrequent, is not usual. What, Hume asks, is the origin of these rules and standards, and why are they observed? He is not prepared to treat them as laws of Allah or any other god, or as the commands of lieutenants to whom a deity has delegated legislative authority; as St. Paul saw, even Gentiles often practice sound morality. Are they then, perhaps, laws of reason, as Grotius and Clarke said? To lay the foundation for an answer to this question, Hume, in the first book of the *Treatise*, examines the nature of the understanding. His conclusion is that we know the moral and physical worlds beyond the present by believing, a form of knowing not to be confused with the way we know demonstrable systems, and that we remain dependent on belief even when we consciously conduct and control our thinking by adhering to the rules of authentic understanding. Animals, too, engage in a kind of thinking; in performance they are not all that far below the vulgar, and, being afflicted with neither vanity nor false religion, they suffer from far fewer harmful beliefs. Reasoning about the real world, in contrast to analysis of complex ideas such as geometric models, aims only at understanding; it aims only at achieving beliefs about existences: what did exist, what exists, what will exist. What causes produce particular effects? How can certain effects be achieved and others prevented? Whether particular existences and effects are good or bad is quite another matter. Yet we constantly make all kinds of value judgments—about policies, constitutions, human behavior, houses, apples, and so on—pronouncing them good or bad. If reason is concerned with existences and with causes and effects, not with discovering the basic difference between the good and the bad, we have no alternative but to turn to the other great aspect of human nature, the passions. The truth is, not that the passions ought to be ruled by reason, but that ultimately reason ought to serve the passions. The old paradigm of divine reason ruling the base passions is misleading.

It is perhaps not surprising that *A Treatise of Human Nature* was not a great success during Hume's lifetime. The content of the work is both novel and difficult; the arguments are complex and cumulative, liable to overwhelm the reader. Much of the subtlety of the second and third books, "Of the Passions" and "Of Morals," is missed unless one already has mastered "Of the Understanding"; that in itself is a major achievement. What is not obvious is that "Of Morals" is founded directly on "Of the Passions." Indeed, the *Treatise* might have fared better if Hume had published "Of the Understanding" alone and brought out "Of the Passions" and "Of Morals" together later, instead of bringing out "Of the Understanding" and "Of the Passions" together in 1739, and then "Of Morals" separately in 1740. By proceeding in that way, the close relationship between the two books would have been made evident, at least to those who had read Hutcheson and Butler.[1] Hume wished to show the errors of the rationalist approach: there are moral "fitnesses and unfitnesses," but what they are is learned, not by reason alone, but by experience and reflection, after which it is possible to formulate "laws of nature"; moreover, even if we could see a priori the fitness or unfitness of certain kinds of conduct, we would not feel morally obliged to respect the related rights and duties. For Hume the requirements of morality are an emanation of human nature, one of the phenomena of mind; the rules and standards guide us in achieving those ends that we, being human, find good. This is why we must analyze the passions.

Hume begins "Of the Passions" by distinguishing between original and reflective feelings: the former are "all the impressions of the senses, and all bodily pains and pleasures"; the latter are "the passions, and all other emotions resembling them." He then focuses on the reflective impressions; these, unlike sensations, are brought on in part by thought or per-

[1] See J. A. Passmore, *Hume's Intentions* (Cambridge: Cambridge University Press, 1952), pp. 1–17. Eugene Rotwein has given what I think is the chief reason why Hume thought of Book I and Book II as one unit and Book III as a second unit. The first two books are analytic; they give Hume's account of (a) the cognitive and (b) the psychological elements of human nature. In the third book, "Of Morals," Hume moves on to the second or synthetic stage of his work, where he seeks, in Rotwein's words, "by considering the impact of specific stimuli on 'human nature,' to establish laws of human behavior which would explain how, in various realms of experience, man responded to different sets of conditions." See his "David Hume, Philosopher-Economist," in *David Hume: Many-Sided Genius*, eds. K. R. Merrill and R. W. Shahan (Norman: University of Oklahoma Press, 1976), p. 119. See also James Noxon, *Hume's Philosophical Development* (Oxford: Clarendon Press, 1973), pp. 4–8.

I traverse "Of the Passions" and "Of Morals" in a way somewhat different from that followed by Páll S. Árdal; my purposes are different. His account remains the best demonstration of the relationship of those two books; it is especially valuable because it points out errors that cause major distortions in the interpretation of Hume's moral theory. Páll S. Árdal, *Passion and Value in Hume's Treatise* (Edinburgh: Edinburgh University Press, 1966).

ception. Next, he distinguishes between calm and violent reflective impressions. His only example of the calm reflective impressions is approbative, and points forward to his theory of morals; of this kind, he says, is "the sense of beauty and deformity in action, composition, and external objects" (T., 276). The violent reflective impressions are quite different: joy and grief, love and hatred, pride and humility, and the like. The latter, commonly called "passions," are either *direct* or *indirect*; they are the subject of the second book of the *Treatise*.

The first two thirds of the book are given over to an exposition of the indirect passions. These are the main *social* feelings: love and hatred (together with pity, generosity, envy, and malice) directed toward others, and pride and humility (together with ambition and vanity) for ourselves. These passions, the indirect passions, immediately influence our "personal" relations with others, and mediately influence our economic and political relations.

Since Hume's main concern is not with individual psychology, but with conduct in society, he examines the direct passions only briefly, in "Of the Passions," part 3, section 9. They provide our primary motivation. They are either active or reactive. The active direct passions—original (unaccountable) impulses or instincts—comprise the bodily appetites and the desire to make our friends happy and to punish our enemies. These are "drives" or "needs"; they are not brought on by the attractiveness or repulsiveness of things or situations. "These passions, properly speaking, produce good and evil, and proceed not from them, like the other affections."[2] Consistent with contemporary usage, by "good and evil" Hume means pleasure and pain, not specifically moral good and moral evil. The other direct passions—which I have called reactive—are variants of the general desire for whatever has been found to be "good"—either as agreeable (immediately pleasant) or as useful—or of the general aversion to whatever has been found to be "evil," that is, whatever causes pain of any kind, either immediately or mediately. The passion of joy is brought on by present good, grief by present evil. Hope and fear are caused by anticipated good and evil respectively. Since we desire to achieve whatever is good (pleasant) and to avoid whatever is bad (painful), we will be moved to act if we believe that thereby we can achieve the good or avoid the bad in ways not excessively taxing or costly. Here Hume, perhaps following Butler, is rejecting the notion that human beings regularly act with happiness as their goal; rather, they are moved by certain instincts or by desire for specific goods. We mislead ourselves if we say that they act with

---

[2] *Treatise*, p. 439. In a passage in *Enquiry* II, perhaps based on Butler, Hume mentions, in addition to bodily appetites, certain primary mental passions "by which we are impelled immediately to seek particular objects, such as fame or power, or vengeance without any regard to interest" (*Enquiry* II, p. 301).

happiness as their end; besides, different people—soldiers and scholars, for example—are made happy by very different goods.

Some of the factors that influence the strength of desire and aversion, and thus influence the will are custom and repetition, the specificity (or, alternatively, the indefiniteness) of the prospective good or bad, and the proximity in time and place of the particular good or bad in question.

As mentioned, Hume distinguishes between calm and violent passions. It really is to the violent passions that rationalist moralists refer when they assert that "the passions" should be controlled by "reason." The calm passions, says Hume, are of two kinds: first, "the general appetite to good, and aversion to evil, consider'd merely as such"; second, "certain instincts originally implanted in our natures, such as benevolence and resentment, the love of life, and kindness to children" (T., 417). The moral sentiments are included among the calm passions: they express, in relation to conduct, the general approval of what is morally good and aversion to what is morally bad (T., 276).

It is not to be thought that the calm passions are always weak and the violent always strong (T., 419). Whether a calm passion, often mistakenly called "reason," will prevail over a violent passion depends on the general character of the person and his present disposition. What is called "strength of mind" implies "the prevalence of the calm passions above the violent" (T., 418). The strong-minded man, mistakenly called "the rational man," resists the allure of goods that tempt him to deviate from the rules of beauty in action.

We turn now to the indirect passions. As we have seen, according to Hutcheson's schema the social passions are love and hatred for others, and self-love and self-hatred. Hume, most significantly, replaced these with love and hatred, pride and humility; these are the elementary social passions or affections. By abandoning the familiar self-love versus love-of-others schema, Hume reveals that for him virtue is not simply a matter of intention (good or bad will), with love of others (or benevolence) as the preeminent virtue. As we shall see, according to Hume, there are virtues that are not moral, and not even all the moral virtues can be explained in terms of love for others.

Hume's four principal indirect passions are based on comparison. Why are we proud or humble? We are proud or humble for the simple reason that when we compare not "selves" but "goods," we find that we have more goods or fewer than others, that is, more or less in the way of natural talents, beauty, moral virtues, external goods, reputation. We have more or less cause to be happy than they have, according to our values. Similarly, we love (in some degree) those of our acquaintance who give us pleasure either immediately or mediately because of their goods. We tend to have hatred for, to hold in disesteem, all those who cause us pain because they fall short in goods: the dull, the morally defective, the poor, the ugly. Often our hatred is only dislike, as when we flee those who bore us; our hatred is most intense when our pain results from injuries inflicted on us viciously.

Three points should be noticed about Hume's schema. First, all his indirect passions are human feelings about people in society; they are the feelings of humans about themselves or others in a social setting. A man living alone on a remote island would have none of these feelings. This is true of Hutcheson's schema also. Second, all these passions, unlike Hutcheson's, result from evaluation. For example, love for others, apart from our families, is not an instinct; rather, it is evoked by the pleasure caused by their "goods." Hatred results from the pain we feel because of the vices and other defects of others. In both loving and hating others, we are reacting to their worth or value. In the case of pride or humility, how we feel results from our evaluation of our own worth or value. Hutcheson begins with primary love and hatred for self and for others. Hume, in contrast, regards all these passions as reactive to what is found good and bad. Pride and humility are the *basic* feelings of a person about himself in comparison with others; love and hatred are the *basic* feelings of a person for others. Pride and love follow approval; humility and hatred follow disapproval. Since moral virtue stands high among the causes of pleasure—that is, high among the "goods"—Hume's analysis of these four passions in "Of the Passions" is fundamental to the argument of the next book, "Of Morals." Third, for Hume each of us is at the center of his own system of relationships. For example, if we come to know someone who has many "goods"—moral virtues, external goods, and the like—we have pleasant feelings because of his goods; consequently, we come to love him in some degree. This means that while anybody with goods is eligible for our love, in fact the number we love is relatively small, for we know only a few. Similarly, we hate very few. Contrary to what Hutcheson says, we have no love for all mankind—no love for all beings of the human kind—simply as such. We can love or hate only those whose qualities we know or know about.

Love brings on another passion, benevolence, the desire to promote the happiness of the beloved, if we see that this can be done by our efforts. Similarly, hatred brings on anger (or resentment), an aversion to the happiness of those we hate because of their viciousness. Benevolence and anger are distinct passions, not to be confused with love and hatred; indeed, as we noticed above, they are direct passions and are conjoined with the indirect passions of love and hatred only "by the original constitution of the mind" (*T.*, 368). Given the limited number whom we love, the benevolence that follows love extends to only a few; the same is true of anger.

Most people live well beyond the range of both our love (and consequent benevolence) and our hatred (and consequent anger).

Hume deals separately with four special cases of love. First, we love (probably beyond what their worth merits) those connected with ourselves in any way. We love those of our family and also "our countrymen, our neighbours, those of the same trade, profession, and even name with ourselves" (*T.*, 352). Second, we love old acquaintances. Both these phenomena Hume attributes to familiarity, which makes *sympathy* strong. Third, we love the rich and the powerful, to the degree called "esteem," even though we expect no benefit for ourselves, no immediate pleasure, from their riches and power. This, too, is due to *sympathy*. Fourth, the strong bond between lovers is a compound of three factors: sexual appetite, the pleasure given by beauty, and generous benevolence, each fostering the others.

As we have seen, our basic indirect passions for others are caused by (a) their good qualities and possessions, and (b) their bad qualities and deficiencies. We love those whose goods cause us pleasure in some way; we hate (or hold in disesteem) those who cause us pain because they are lacking in goods. But what about the important passions of pity (compassion) and malice? These passions seem to refute Hume's analysis. Pity brings on benevolence, while malice brings on anger; however, we have seen that benevolence moves us to work on behalf of those who have goods, and our anger moves us against those whose evils cause us pain. Moreover, those for whom we feel pity or malice may be almost unknown to us. Here, says Hume, we must not make the misleading mistake, a mistake made by Hutcheson, of regarding pity as an expression of love, and malice of hatred. "*Pity* is a concern for, and *malice* a joy in the misery of others, without any friendship or enmity to occasion this concern or joy. We pity even strangers, and such as are perfectly indifferent to us: And if our ill-will to another proceed from any harm or injury, it is not, properly speaking, malice, but revenge"(*T.*, 369). Pity arises from a kind of reversal in the causal relation among the passions; it is brought on, not by love (the result of the beloved's virtues and other goods), but through *sympathy* with great misfortune. Similarly, malice must not be confused with basic hatred. Like pity, it involves a reversal. Genuine hatred is caused by the defects of the hated person, especially as revealed by wrongs done to ourselves. In contrast, malice is caused by the envy aroused by the putative good fortune of some other person. If we feel malice towards somebody, it is as a result of envy brought on by comparing our own worth and circumstances with those of a person whom we regard as far better off. It is true that pity brings on benevolence, and malice anger; this is why pity and malice are of practical importance. But both are only sporadic and occasional. To regard pity as a variety of love and malice as a kind of hatred is misleading; thereby we obscure the real cause of our loving or hating persons not close in some way to us, that is, their known good or bad attributes.

Hume found that personal relations can be analyzed in terms of pride (in self) and love (for others). In contrast, "self-love" is misleading (T., 329). The term is prejudiced; moreover, its meaning is uncertain. Hume uses it occasionally in the *Treatise*, but "self-love" there almost always has an obvious economic meaning: the self-loving person is an interested person; he wants to acquire economic goods for himself and those dear to him (T., 480). This does not mean that Hume thinks that "self-love," in the sense of Mandeville's "self-liking," does not exist. It is what Hume calls "pride."

We must not be mislead by this rejection of the term "self-love." Hume was determined to treat moral subjects, not by declamation or exhortation, but by analysis, firmly grounding his arguments and conclusions on observed facts. His philosophy, in true post-Lockian manner, is based on an analytic description of perception. What we know are our own perceptions, and, he contends, we have two kinds of perceptions: ideas (or thoughts without power to make us take them seriously) and impressions of either sensation or reflection. The rationalist moralists focused on ideas; in contrast, Hume, following Hutcheson, puts his emphasis on impressions. They are fundamental to both knowledge and evaluation: our *beliefs* are impressive ideas, and our distinction between the good and the bad is the result of our feelings in reaction to features of the objective world. Since it is the self that perceives, the self is central to Hume's whole philosophical system. One's perception is basically self-centered; each has his own "peculiar position." Both our physical and our social world center upon ourselves; each sees the world from his own station or viewpoint in time and place. What is close to him looms large. What affects a person, or comes near, is more important to him than what happens far away. For him, his present is the present, his good the good. "Contiguous objects," says Hume, "must have an influence much superior to the distant and remote. Accordingly we find in common life, that men are principally concern'd about those objects, which are not much remov'd either in space or time, enjoying the present, and leaving what is afar off to the care of chance and fortune"(T., 428). Moreover, when a person compares himself with others, as he does constantly in society, he has a natural bias, a partiality, in his own favor. His love is limited in scope, seldom reaching with strength beyond those in some way near himself, as blood relatives, friends, partners. This natural egocentrism, this "self-ishness" or *particularity* of natural perception, is a fact, not a sin or a wrong; but it has to be restrained, by rules and standards of conduct, if people are to live together in society. What is needed is an accommodation between desire for the particular (private) good, which desire is necessary if human beings are to be moved to accomplish anything, and respect for the general (public) good, which is necessary if they are not to destroy each other, let alone be helpful to each other. The person who does not restrain his natural "self-ishness" is guilty of the moral offense called selfishness.[3]

How are rules and standards of what is good from a general or public standpoint possible? So far we have taken into account only primary perception. To stop here would be a mistake; it would be to ignore what we may call sympathetic perception. Primary perception involves only our own sensations, passions, and ideas. By sympathetic perception, however, we are able to know what or how others are feeling. We are far from being isolated from, and indifferent to, their feelings. As a result of seeing the outward and visible signs of their impressions—grief, joy, love, anger, and so on—we perceive the appropriate ideas; consequently, each of those ideas brings on for us the impression related to that idea. Thus we acquire a second set of feelings. Sympathy, as described in the *Treatise*, is part of a process of perception, a process by which feelings are shared; it is not a particular feeling, and, of course, it is not to be confused with either compassion (pity) or benevolence. Sympathy relieves us from perceptual isolation. Here Hume follows Shaftesbury, Butler, and others. We are joyful as a result of our companions' joy; their sadness makes us sad. In the course of his explanation of the indirect passions, Hume gives us long, almost lyrical descriptions of sympathetic perception, using it to explain various phenomena—the hunger for company, the love of fame, our partiality to our relatives and friends, our esteem for the rich; thus he drives home the great importance of sympathy. Without sympathetic perception, we would be isolated, lonely, distraught. It is by sympathetic perception that we are liberated from the prison of our own particularity; it makes objective evaluation possible. As we shall see, according to Hume, sympathy provides the perceptual basis for moral evaluation. However, it is important to notice that although we can sympathize to some extent with any other human being, and even with animals, sympathetic perception, too, is self-centered. We sympathize more readily and more fully with those with whom we share character traits, manners, country, or language, and with those we know well, than with those whom we find different and strange (*T.*, 318). Moreover, sympathetic perception works best when the other person is in our presence.

---

[3] *Treatise*, p. 486. Because the word "selfish" generally has a moral connotation, I have hyphenated the word when I have wanted to make it clear that I am using the word without that connotation. Those who exhibit *excessive* self-ishness, extreme egocentricity, are judged morally bad by judicious spectators; they are found to be selfish.

Hume's Strategy in "Of Morals"

Hume begins "Of Morals" with a recapitulation of his famous discussion of the relative importance of reason and passion as determinants of moral distinctions, and consequently of conduct. By "reason" Hume means here not "the calm passions," but the faculty by which we acquire knowledge about the real world and about systems of ideas; his conclusion is that ultimately moral sense, not reason, makes the distinction between moral good and evil. In the course of this discussion, he mentions casually a distinction between *natural* and *artificial* virtues. Then, in "Of Morals," part 2, he turns abruptly to the artificial virtues and gives us a long, important analysis of those virtues. What is Hume's strategy? He seems simply to be jumping from one controversial topic to another. What is his basic concern? Toward the end of *Enquiry* II, in an appendix on some verbal disputes over free will, he says, "Every one may employ *terms* in what sense he pleases: but this, in the mean time, must be allowed, that *sentiments* are every day experienced of blame and praise, which have objects beyond the dominion of the will or choice, and of which it behoves us, if not as moralists, as speculative philosophers at least, to give some satisfactory theory and explication" (*E.*, 322). In other words, it is the task of moral philosophers, or at least of speculative philosophers, not simply to praise and recommend virtue while denouncing vice, but to explain the difference, recognized every day, between virtue and vice. It is a fact that human beings have moral sentiments; they have beliefs about morals; they make moral judgments. Here, then, is the basic question dealt with in "Of Morals": what mental qualities are virtues; why and how are those characteristics approved and called virtues? In discussing the indirect passions, we saw that many different kinds of goods and bads influence our relations with others. Some of these goods are personal characteristics called "virtues"; some of the bads are personal characteristics called "vices." But why do we regard some qualities of character as morally good (virtuous) and others as morally bad (vicious)? The relationship of "Of Morals" to "Of the Passions," we now see, is relatively simple: our joy or grief, our love or hatred of others, and our pride or humility all involve goods and bads. Virtues and vices—qualities of human character—are one kind, a most important kind, of goods and bads. We need an explanation of why some characteristics are regarded as good and others as bad. The purpose of much of "Of Morals" is to provide that explanation.

To answer these questions—what are the virtues; what is virtue; what kinds of conduct are virtuous—Hume turns to moral conduct, an area in which there are moral obligations, that is, duties. Some ways of behaving are judged good in a special way, so that consequently we are expected to act in those ways from a sense of moral duty, if we do not do so from other motives. What distinguishes such ways of behaving? In answering this question, we must focus our attention on our relations with others, for we have no duties to ourselves. What is virtuous conduct in such relations? As we ponder the question, we see—this, of course, is not Hume's final answer—that in "personal" relations, what we expect to be done as the result of natural motivation is what is pronounced morally good. Someone who does not have love at the expected level for his son, his nephew, or his partner will feel a sense of duty to act as if he had such a motive; yet someone whose motives are normal will be good, but will feel no distinct sense of duty. In other words, because duty and normal natural affection may lead to exactly the same behavior, an analysis of the "personal" relationships would not be especially helpful to our philosophical endeavor. To facilitate our investigation, we need a situation in which the sense of duty can be clear and distinct, a situation where the effects of natural motivation cannot be mistaken for the effects of moral obligation at least some of the time.

There is just such a situation; moreover, it is precisely the situation treated most inadequately by those, such as Hutcheson, who hold up benevolence as the great social virtue. A person's love for others and the benevolence that follows love can extend only to those whom he knows: his family, his friends, his partners, perhaps those from his own country, and those whom he holds in high esteem. But we participate in a vast impersonal relationship, namely, the economic system, in which feelings—love and hatred—for the other participants are irrelevant. Moreover, in modern times, economic society is supported by a second impersonal system, the political order. In both the economic and the political orders, we have moral obligations to many for whom we have no personal feelings. What is there about certain kinds of conduct in these relationships that is good in such a way that such conduct is regarded as morally obligatory? Our natural inclination is to seize the land, food, jewels, and other goods we want for our beloved families and friends; yet we resist this natural inclination because we feel that it is our moral duty to act justly. We restrain our benevolence from a sense of justice. What, then, is justice, and how does it influence us?[4]

[4] If we think of Hume as having adopted Hutcheson's moral realism and as then proceeding to improve Hutcheson's theory, we see that Hume would have found Hutcheson far less satisfactory on the artificial virtues than on the natural virtues. Justice cannot be an expression of benevolence unless one distinguishes clearly between particular benevolence and general benevolence; this Hume, unlike Hutcheson, does. D. D. Raphael suggests that Hume began with the artificial virtue, justice, because this was where the ethical rationalists, against whom he was arguing, were at their strongest in criticizing Hutcheson. See "Hume's

As we have seen, in "Of the Passions" Hume introduces us to conduct based on the four basic social feelings: love and hatred, pride and humility. Then he turns away from these to discuss the direct passions. "Of Morals," part 1, is given over to the reason-versus-moral-sentiment debate. When he resumes his discussion of social relationships, in "Of Morals," part 2, he directs our attention to those social relationships that are based on the artificial virtues of justice and allegiance. Why he proceeds in this way, and why he calls justice "artificial," now is clear: he wishes to begin his examination of morals with relationships in which moral obligation and natural affection are not likely to be confused, where indeed they are often opposed. Later, in the third and final part of "Of Morals," after the answers to his questions about moral obligation and the nature of virtue have been found, as a result of examining the artificial relationships, he brings those answers to bear on the natural virtues. There he explains, for example, why a father has a moral duty to treat his children as if he loves them in the degree proper to a father.

We now can see the portal by which Hume entered the complex maze of moral philosophy. He, like Butler, saw clearly that, despite its high reputation with moralists, love of others (and benevolence based on love) is not the foundation of morality. First, even where benevolence operates, it is not a totally reliable guide; for example, usually parents feel benevolent toward their children, but they also feel morally obliged to observe standards, and thus they give to their children perhaps less, perhaps more, than their benevolence prompts. There are standards of duty to which even benevolence ought to conform. Second, we love (and so feel benevolent toward) only a few; yet we are morally obliged to be just in all our dealings. One reason Mandeville scandalized those moralists who thought that benevolence is fundamental to all society was that he showed beyond refutation that vast tracts of modern society cannot be comprehended by a moral theory that insists that love and goodwill are enough. Hume saw that the facts of economic and political society—civil society—cannot be ignored by any moral theory that aspires to credibility. The cardinal question in morals, he saw, relates to duty or obligation. Why do we feel that it is fitting, indeed imperative, to act with appropriate benevolence toward those we are assumed to love (our children, friends, etc.) or pity (the poor and afflicted at our gates), but justly toward all others? In Butler's language, first, why does conscience speak authoritatively; second, what does conscience command for relationships—the family and the market, for example—that are radically different?

Critique of Ethical Rationalism," in *Hume and the Enlightenment*, ed. W. B. Todd (Edinburgh: Edinburgh University Press, 1974), pp. 14–29.

Moral Sentiments, Natural and Artificial

For Hume the term "society" often, perhaps generally, has an inclusive meaning. When human beings live peaceably together, collaborating to achieve various goals, they are living socially, they are living in society. It is by society—we might say, by associating or by association—that they attain goods of many kinds unavailable to solitary persons: companionship, education, security, economic goods, and so forth. At other times, "society" refers to specific kinds of associations. "Without justice," we are told, "society must immediately dissolve." Again, justice is the principle of "the laws of society." Here "society" refers primarily to what we might call "the economic system" or "the economic order." When the economy is supported by a government, the economic order and the governmental (the state) taken together constitute "civil society," or "political society." Hume also applies the term to small associations. For example, he writes of "the society of marriage" and says that the birth of additional children produces "a more numerous society."[5] Society involves many kinds of relationships; however, for present purposes we can distinguish between, first, relationships structured by particular affections and circumstances, and, second, relationships structured by the rules of justice and allegiance. In order to explain the artificial virtues, Hume frequently contrasts civil society, which is artificial, with the family and other natural relationships.

The natural relationships involve those persons whom we love. Some we love because they are immediately useful or agreeable to us. Others, as we have seen, we love because of ties of family, profession, and so on. All these relationships involve variants of love; moreover, as we already know, love brings on benevolence, that is, a will to promote the well-being or happiness of the beloved when a higher level of well-being or happiness is thought possible. "Love is always follow'd by a desire of the happiness of the person belov'd, and an aversion to his misery" (T., 367). The virtue proper to the natural relationships is "private benevolence"; certain persons are loved for special reasons, and benevolence, "a regard to the interests of the party concern'd," follows (T., 482). Because benevolence is a motive, a passion that finds expression in action, in the Treatise Hume normally refers to benevolence, not to love, as the basic virtue of the natural relationships.

All the natural relationships are person-to-person relationships: the actor loves his benefactor, his wife, his child, his friend. These relationships do not have to be justified to the actor as the best means to a self-interested end; for him they are good per se. Each member is related by love

[5] Treatise, pp. 308, 486.

to a circle of others, and also by benevolence if it is believed that the others' happiness can be increased. Most people are not narrowly selfish; they strive more for the happiness of those dear to them than for their own happiness. Because these are standardized kinds of natural conduct, and not restraining or costly means employed to attain pleasant ends outside the relationship, they can be described as *natural*.

In contrast, economic society is an *artificial* relationship. At bottom it is either a person-service-person relationship, or a person-external-goods-person relationship. Acts in these relationships are done, not because the other person is loved, but to gain services or external goods. They are done for the good of one's self or those whom one loves. They are acquisitive or "interested." Participants in economic society are related primarily as owners, producers, and consumers of economic goods and services; they meet as traders. The sustaining virtue of economic society is *justice*; economic society becomes civil society when justice is supplemented by *allegiance* (or obedience to a particular government). Benevolence is not essential here. True, over time one may become friendly with one's butcher or come to adore the prime minister, but such emotional ties are not essential to either the economic or the political relationship. Neither just nor obedient conduct is based on love for the other participants; rather, such conduct is good as a means.

Although the natural relationships provide opportunities for us to love certain other people and to enjoy the benefits of their help and company, those relationships do not always provide an ample supply, let alone a bountiful supply of economic goods. What is needed is a relationship designed specifically to produce and distribute economic goods. What is needed is a system of cooperative economic production far more extensive and efficient than the family, the friendship, and the like. When people work alone or in small groups, says Hume, their strength is small, they forego the advantages of an extensive division of labor, and they are entirely dependent on themselves and fortune for their economic security. The remedy is a special kind of society, economic society.

However, economic society is impossible unless we respect private property and keep our contracts. In a sense such conduct, just conduct, is unnatural. Our natural motivation is always partial and uneven; it favors not the whole, the public, but ourselves and those dear to us; it prompts us to seize goods for our families, friends, cities. But we learn by experience that the goods we need can be acquired only through economic society, that such society requires stable possession and internal peace, and that these are impossible without an established order of ownership and exchange, a system that permits no exceptions and in which rules of ownership and exchange are followed equally, impartially, even blindly, in every transaction. An economic society is a kind of game or play into which we enter, not because the parts, roles, or positions are intrinsically good for us, but because by participating we can get what we want, namely a more copious supply of economic goods and services. The *primary* motive to behave justly, the motive behind the *moral* motive or obligation, is our interest in the economic goods to be gained by means of such society. The primary motive is self-love. (As mentioned, Hume uses the term "self-love" instead of "self-interest" a few times in the *Treatise*, perhaps because it seems stronger, but that he means "self-interest" is evident.[6] For Hume "interest" is almost always an economic term: someone who acts because he is "interested" is not acting benevolently, but neither is he acting in anger or malevolently.)

How does the moral evaluation of conduct take place? Acts in conformity with the rules are right; acts that break the rules are wrong. Why is right conduct morally good and wrong conduct morally evil? When a member of society, misled by a violent passion, breaks the rule that property is to be respected—by stealing, for example—he causes pain to the aggrieved person; this pain is perceived sympathetically, without "selfish" (or "subjective") distortion, by any spectator. Moreover, since the wrongdoer has made an attack on the principles of society, the spectator perceives—sees and feels—the threat to the well-being of all who benefit from the social order. The pain thus produced causes the spectator to censure the theft and to regard with disesteem the one who did the unjust deed; that person has acted against the good of humankind. The spectator's moral sense reacts with disapprobation. Thus the offender becomes the target of remonstrance, denunciation, and punishment. In this way, by experience, the offender learns that certain kinds of conduct, unjust acts, are found bad when viewed from the general or objective viewpoint. Over and above their motive from interest in following the rules, human beings come to feel morally obliged to do what is right and to avoid what is wrong. The rules, now moral rules, specify what we ought not to do. When people follow the rules, they are praised; when they break them, they are blamed. Moreover, our concern for our reputation strengthens the moral sentiments "after the opinion, *that a merit or demerit attends justice or injustice*, is once firmly establish'd among mankind" (*T.*, 501). Each person now has a new kind of motive, a moral motive, a motive brought on by third-party evaluation, to refrain from unjust acts. The primary motive for just conduct, long-term individual interest, has been confirmed and shrouded by morality. Unjust conduct has been evaluated objectively; it has been pronounced morally evil.

When the content of morality has been learned within a family, a tribe, or a community and has been stated in the form of general rules, these

---

[6] Ibid., pp. 480, 529.

rules become part of that people's culture; by discipline and education the young are civilized; the rules are drilled into them by parents, moralists, and politicians (*T.*, 479). This means that the young acquire their moral sentiments in large part, not from direct experience, but vicariously, from others through education. Because of their teachers' authority, they accept the rules the teachers recommend to them. Hume, in a manner reminiscent of the argument for obedience given by Socrates in the *Crito*, emphasizes the formative power of education—education by teachers, laws, customs, and language. Since there is no immediate natural motive to act justly, "we must allow, that the sense of justice and injustice is not deriv'd from nature, but arises artifically, tho' necessarily from education, and human conventions" (*T.*, 483). However, contrary to the great-legislator hypothesis, the content of *genuine* morality is not contrived by "skilful politicians"; for Hume there is nothing arbitrary about what is morally right and wrong in either civil society or the natural relationships.

Hume believes, unlike Hobbes, that a relatively small society can operate without a government, just as a simple game can be played without an umpire. The participants are motivated to follow the rules of justice by moral obligation, and perhaps also by insight into the primary motive, self-interest, now overlaid by morality. But in a large, rich society, a government is necessary: the players' interest in maintaining the whole system will have been obscured by the society's size and complexity; in addition, the moral obligation is not as strong as when the group was smaller and more closely integrated. As a result, it is in the interest of all that there be a government to enforce justice. The basic political rule is that those to whom we bear allegiance are to be obeyed. As in the case of justice, there is a primary motive for obedience, namely, the long-term self-interest of each individual. And, again, as in the case of justice, this primary motive, through the reaction of spectators to acts of disobedience, gives rise to another motive, a moral motive, to obey the government. The spectator, always sensitive to what is good for humankind (the public), feels pain when he sees disobedience; he feels pleasure when he sees obedience. Thus the basic political rule, requiring allegiance (obedience) to a good government, becomes a moral rule. Thereafter obedience is morally right, disobedience morally wrong. In the case of justice, "man in his civiliz'd state, and when train'd up according to a certain discipline and education" ordinarily acts justly; likewise, he obeys the laws (*T.*, 479).

What have we learned from this investigation of civil society that will advance Hume's general moral theory? First, we have seen that sympathy enables us to perceive a good other than our own private good. This is the good "consider'd merely as such," the good seen from the viewpoint of the spectator. Second, we have learned that in explaining morality we must distinguish between primary motives and moral motives; the latter seek the good as seen from the impartial viewpoint. And, third, while politicians, as well as parents and moralists, perform a necessary role in civilizing the young, the rules of sound morality are not contrived by them; the rules are not factitious.

Hume flatly rejects the proposition that the obligation to act justly results from love for an anonymous group, the public, either severally or collectively. Justice does advance the good of humankind, the good of the public, the whole; however, the range of our love is limited. One can be perfectly just without ever willing or even conceiving the public good. Says Hume, "there is no such passion in human minds, as the love of mankind, merely as such, independent of personal qualities, of services, or of relation to ourself. 'Tis true, there is no human, and indeed no sensible, creature, whose happiness or misery does not, in some measure, affect us, when brought near to us, and represented in lively colours: But this proceeds merely from sympathy, and is no proof of such an universal affection to mankind, since this concern extends itself beyond our own species" (T., 481).

Indeed, we can have no idea of a public, a whole—in the sense of an economic society—until after we have learned the principles of justice. The nature and benefit of just conduct are learned originally step by step in particular instances by participants. This gives rise to the moral rules. Over time we come to follow the rules of justice in our dealings with all those with whom we do business. The only whole or public known to us, the only public or whole for whose good we might be concerned, is the totality of those individuals. In short, any concern we have for public good is a result, and not the cause, of the obligation to act justly. The interest of the several players precedes the establishment of the league; however, once the league has been established, the league does have a general interest, an interest of importance to each and all players. But even then, few of the players are concerned to keep that general interest clearly in mind. The truth of the matter, says Hume, is that even in a well-established economic society, where the idea of the good of that society is quite conceivable, most people act justly for other reasons, generally from a sense of moral obligation seconded by the civil laws, and sometimes from a sense of private interest. The public good by itself is far too remote an end to motivate them.

In the case of the natural virtues, what we pronounce virtuous are certain natural motives at normal levels, motives that at those levels make people behave in ways that, viewed from a general (or impartial) standpoint, have been found good for humankind. Here we are pronouncing on people's natural motivation as modified by their learned sense of obligation to conform to relevant *standards*.[7] In contrast, in the case of the artificial virtues—justice, allegiance, chastity, and the like—what we pronounce virtuous is an effective sense of obligation to behave contrary to natural motivation. That is, it is being virtuous that is virtuous; however, as Hume says, this is circular. What is really meant is that the good of humankind, not as a whole, but as individuals, which always concerns spectators, but rarely ourselves when we are party to an act, has given rise to a set of *rules*, and we feel obliged to heed those rules, that is, to be virtuous, despite the fact that they require conduct contrary to our thoughtless natural motivation.

Benevolence and justice are the cardinal virtues of all stable human relationships. Benevolent conduct and just conduct are approved by spectators because these kinds of conduct sustain society, and society is necessary if we are to live good lives. Love, or rather the benevolence that attends love, is the virtue fundamental to the family, the friendship, and the like, while justice is the virtue fundamental to civil society. Hume sometimes refers to these two virtues as "the social virtues." Certain other characteristics are approved by spectators as useful to others. These characteristics also foster society and consequently are ranked as virtues, for example, meekness, clemency, moderation; however, while these are valued highly, they do not rank with justice and benevolence.

Although Book III is entitled "Of Morals," Hume therein undertakes to show why *all* those characteristics of mind called virtues are approved from the general viewpoint; he does not limit himself to the moral virtues. We now have established that justice, benevolence, meekness, clemency, and the like are virtues because they are *useful to others*. Are there other kinds of virtues, some moral, others nonmoral? First, are there mental qualities that are *useful* not primarily to others, but *to the possessor him-*

---

[7] Mackie comments that the fact that good conduct in the natural relationships is conduct approved from an impartial standpoint because it is good for "society" is "rather devastating for Hume's theory," since it means "that his natural virtues are, after all, a further set of artificial virtues." J. L. Mackie, *Hume's Moral Theory* (London: Routledge & Kegan Paul, 1980), p. 123. This comment is misleading. Hume recognized the role of what Butler called "conscience"; consequently, he wanted to explain why we feel that we ought to behave morally, something he contended had not been explained by those writers who simply jumped from "is" to "ought." In other words, Hume, whether discussing the natural or the artificial virtues, always distinguishes between primary motivation and moral motivation. That he makes the distinction is not devastating for his theory; indeed, his main undertaking was to explain how moral motivation, which is something quite different from primary motivation, comes about. Second, Hume uses the term "artificial" to make the point that while in the case of the natural virtues, moral obligation merely fine-tunes our natural motivation, in the case of the artificial virtues, it prohibits flatly what we might do naturally. The requirements of the standards of natural virtue are more conveniently expressed positively: "Thou shall love thy neighbor as thyself." Those of the rules of artificial virtue take the form of prohibitions: "Thou shall not steal."

self, and that, since usefulness approved from the general viewpoint is a relevant test, qualify as virtues? Indeed there are: prudence, temperance, frugality, industry, assiduity, enterprise, dexterity (*T.*, 587). We have no reason to expect any direct gain when strangers have these characteristics, but by sympathy a spectator will enter into the pleasure they produce for the possessor and consequently will approve them. Again, are only those qualities that *tend* to the happiness of the possessor or those affected by his conduct—that is, qualities that are *useful*—properly called virtues? Or are there qualities that *on their mere appearance* are found good and that spectators approve as virtues? Again, Hume's reply is affirmative: there are *agreeable* virtues, characteristics that are agreeable to the possessor and characteristics agreeable to others (*T.*, 590). However, his contention is that insofar as moral virtue is concerned, usefulness is far more important than agreeableness, determining "all the great lines of our duty."

Hutcheson's moral theory focuses on intention; the moral sense appraises acts as evidence of good or bad will. In contrast, Hume goes behind the will to natural or acquired attributes of character. He focuses on the characteristics subsequently revealed by word or deed. Of course he asks whether or not a man acts benevolently when his situation calls for "good will." Does that person, from either love or a sense of duty, behave properly? But he asks also whether a person is just, wise, courageous, temperate, moderate, loyal, and industrious. The virtues are those qualities of character—some called "abilities"; others, like justness and moderation, moral traits—that enable us to lead good lives both as individuals and as participants in society. Hume sums up his analysis of virtue as follows: "Every quality of the mind is denominated virtuous, which gives pleasure by the mere survey; as every quality, which produces pain, is call'd vicious. This pleasure and this pain may arise from four different sources. For we reap a pleasure from the view of a character, which is naturally fitted to be useful to others, or to the person himself, or which is agreeable to others, or to the person himself" (*T.*, 591). Thus we see that the virtues, defined broadly to include both moral virtues and natural abilities, are those human characteristics that produce pleasure (and the avoidance of pain) sympathetically for spectators because they (the virtues) cause pleasure either indirectly (as useful goods) or directly (as agreeable goods) to beings of the human kind.

Misleading Teachings

Are humility and benevolence the great, inclusive virtues, as many moralists teach? We have seen that Hume has replaced self-love by pride (self-esteem), as the chief self-regarding passion. Likewise, we have seen that one who has many moral virtues, natural abilities, and external goods has ample cause for pride. Is it vicious to be proud and virtuous to have great humility? Or was Mandeville correct when he said that "self-liking" is of cardinal importance? Again, is it always virtuous to be benevolent, or are there occasions for anger? Hume has told us that the spectator's moral sense pronounces good those qualities of mind that satisfy a fourfold test: usefulness to others or self, agreeableness to others or self. When this test is applied, do we find that pride in one's self and anger toward others are always disapproved?

When, through sympathy, we are exposed to the lofty opinion a very proud person has of himself, we feel reduced or diminished. This is painful for us. In contrast, someone who speaks and acts with modesty causes us to feel good; certainly, he ingratiates himself with us. The result is that overweening pride is found vicious, and modesty virtuous; the former being immediately *disagreeable* to others, and the latter immediately *agreeable* to them. Thus we see that the moralists have an important point. But life is not so simple; we have overlooked utility. Confidence, a good opinion of himself, is a prerequisite if one is to accomplish anything of importance; success requires assurance. "Whatever capacity any one may be endow'd with, 'tis entirely useless to him, if he be not acquainted with it, and form not designs suitable to it" (*T.*, 597). Pride provides the vigor and spirit, the drive, without which great goals are not attained. On the other side, genuine deep humility makes a person useless, impotent; in addition, it is painful. Obviously, an accommodation is required; both excessive pride and extreme diffidence are vicious, as disutilities for the person himself and as disagreeable to him. As Mandeville said, it is by rules of good manners—to be dealt with in chapter 4—that we overcome the clash between the *usefulness* and *agreeableness* of pride to the person himself and the *agreeableness* of modesty to others.

Some moralists, says Hume, try to quash all pride as "purely pagan and natural" (*T.*, 600). If this monkish view were to prevail, it would render us incapable of achieving much in this world. However, by long experience, practical people have learned the value of well-regulated pride; indeed, magnanimity, or greatness of mind, that inclusive quality attributed to all the greatest heroes, is "either nothing but a steady and well-establish'd pride and self-esteem, or partakes largely of that passion." Besides, "a genuine and hearty pride" is essential to society: there are various ranks or stations, fixed by "our birth, fortune, employments, talents or reputation," that must be maintained if a society is to function. A feeling of pride in his role and work is necessary if a person is to take his rank or station seriously and to perform well. Too much humility weakens the very structure of society and makes life chaotic and unproductive.

Having shown the error of those moralists who exalt humility as a great virtue, Hume turns, in "Of Morals," part 3, section 3, to love and hatred, our basic feelings for others. What is required to make someone eligible for the accolade, "a good person"? First, we are realistic; as Hutcheson said, we do not disqualify someone on the ground that his benevolence is limited in scope.

> When experience has once given us a competent knowledge of human affairs, and has taught us the proportion they bear to human passion, we perceive, that the generosity of men is very limited, and that it seldom extends beyond their friends and family, or, at most, beyond their native country. Being thus acquainted with the nature of man, we expect not any impossibilities from him; but confine our view to that narrow circle, in which any person moves, in order to form a judgment of his moral character. (T., 602)

Second, we bring the spectator's moral sense to bear on him: "When the natural tendency of his passions leads him to be serviceable and useful within his sphere, we approve of his character, and love his person, by a sympathy with the sentiments of those, who have a more particular connexion with him" (T., 602). A person's benevolence directs all his other qualities, both his natural abilities and his moral virtues, to the good of those dear to him. In addition, love itself—quite aside from the benevolence that always accompanies love if an improvement in well-being is seen as possible—is immediately agreeable to the beloved; therefore, it too is approved as a virtue.

Benevolence, like justice, fosters society. Does this mean, as those moralists who exalt benevolence above all else imply, that its opposite, anger (resentment), the motivating passion brought on by hatred, is always vicious? Hume's answer is that anger is vicious as an active passion; it impairs society. Yet, anger is not to be extirpated; on appropriate occasions it may be virtuous as a reactive passion, as a passion resisting or negating evil. A virtuous person will feel anger when vicious men steal or disobey the laws of the land; otherwise, he would be thought to show "weakness and imbecillity" (T., 605). However, there is no need, Hume finds, to spend time and effort instilling hatred and anger; people feel these passions readily enough and are quick to spring to the defence of those they love and their own interests. Accordingly, we find that people are usually praised, not for their hatred of evil, expressed through anger, but for moderation in those passions.

A Grammatical Question

Sections 4 and 5 of "Of Morals," part 3, deal directly with the question whether natural mental abilities such as wit should be included in the list of virtues, along with the moral qualities. Hume's concern here is to defend his analysis of the virtues as good qualities of character against those who define virtue as obedience to laws. Natural abilities are qualities that are useful to the possessor or his associates; they, too, like the moral qualities, cause love and hatred, pride and humility. Nor can we say that natural abilities are under necessity, while moral qualities are in the realm of free will.[8] The difference between these two sets of mental characteristics, says Hume, is that natural abilities are not the subject of moral obligation. A person's natural abilities can only be developed, but his character, while not perfectly malleable, can be formed, especially in youth, by parents, teachers, and associates. However, ordinary people regard both natural abilities and moral virtues as important determinants of one's worth. This fact, Hume submits, shows that his fourfold analysis of virtue is accurate.

The Objectivity of Beauty

Hume makes much of the similarity between the comeliness of virtuous conduct and the beauty of things. The approval given to both is a reactive judgment, a calm reflective impression. In chapter 4 we will examine why the beauty of things—horses, castles, coaches, ships, vestments, and so on—has important social consequences. As an introduction, let us now notice what "beauty" means for Hume. His definition is a variant of his definition of goodness. A judgment that something is beautiful, like any other value judgment, is a human commentary. Just as there can be no moral judgment without a spectator, there can be no judgment of beauty without a judging observer. The quality or characteristic evaluated, and on the merit of which the object is pronounced beautiful, is found valuable by the beholder. Both the quality and the beholder are necessary. So far Hume follows Hutcheson.

However, Hume undertakes to go behind our approval of certain qualities as beautiful; he undertakes to explain why the form of certain objects evokes applause. It is not enough to say that some characteristic gives us pleasure—for example, uniformity amidst variety—but we must say why it does so. Hume gives the beautiful a human reference. Whatever brings pleasure when used by people is called "good" by them. Any object that when only observed promises to be highly *useful* by reason of the order

---

[8] In the appendix, "Of some Verbal Disputes," Hume explains why he does not attempt to distinguish precisely between moral virtues and talents (*Enquiry* II, pp. 312–23). What Hume denies is not the liberty of spontaneity, which for him is of great psychological and political value—violence is its enemy—but the liberty of indifference, the notion of uncaused acts. Regardless of all the harangues on free will, we all believe, he submits, that all human acts result from causes. See the succinct discussion of this point in D.G.C. MacNabb, *David Hume: His Theory of Knowledge and Morality* (London: Hutchinson's University Library, 1951), pp. 199–203.

and constitution of its parts is also found good, but in a different way; such an object is "beautiful." It appears apt, well contrived, well suited to serve the purpose to which it may be put by human beings. It is to the potential usefulness, to the potential advantageousness of the praised object, that Hume attributes most of its beauty. The goodness of beauty is largely the goodness of promised utility, the goodness of aptness as a means. Nor does the object have to be put to use to be valued: things are valued, found beautiful, even when only admired from a distance. Moreover, beauty, like virtue, is judged from an impartial standpoint: the test is whether or not the object judged is suitable to be good for potential human users. And the evaluation is impartial: the potential users may even be our enemies, whose formidable fortresses and men-of-war we admire and covet.

The form of things—the shape of ships, race horses, shade trees, and so forth—is not appraised anew every time such things are seen. As a result of experience, certain standards of beauty prevail within a society; they have become the received, conventional standards. Good design is governed by general principles. Because of the similarity found by Hume between the general rules of morality and the general rules of beauty, it is worth noticing that the latter may become obsolete. An eleventh-century knight, constantly concerned for security, suddenly placed in the eighteenth century would probably find ugly the wide windows of a Palladian mansion. Similarly, the standards may be out of place. A lady of fashion, the toast of Mayfair, would probably cause boistrous hilarity on the American frontier by reason of her flimsy apparel and haughty airs.

Aspects of Hume's Moral Theory

Hume presents polished, finished analyses of free will, reason and the passions, justice, allegiance; there are, however, important aspects of his theory of morals that for one reason or another, do not stand out in sufficient prominence, at least not for a twentieth-century reader unfamiliar with the writings of Shaftesbury, Mandeville, Hutcheson, and Butler. Some of these aspects are implied in long trains of argument, but are not proclaimed in summaries; some are touched upon repeatedly, but always only incidentally; some are treated as simply obvious. Now that we have traced the broken course of the argument in "Of the Passions" and "Of Morals," we can go back to explore some of these important points.

First, neither the fact that sympathetic perception provides an escape from the egocentricity (or particularity) of primary perception nor the full implication of this fact is stated explicitly. Particularity was not a problem for those writers for whom moral laws were either divine commands or logical axioms, but it was a problem for theorists who undertook to derive morality from the basic distinction between pain and pleasure. Since primary perception is private or self-centered, one approach was to begin with what was found good by the perceiver and then attempt to show that the rules of society are the result of longheaded selfishness. Alternatively, they could find humans to be endowed with love (and thus benevolence) for all human beings; that approach, however, could not be used to explain how society is possible among those who love only a few others and who want their own lives to be free from meddling, self-appointed benefactors intent on doing good works. Hume has his own solution: while our primary perception is self-centered, we also receive, indeed are greatly dependent on, the perceptions of others. The human mind simply cannot survive prolonged isolation without deteriorating. Man is not a hermit crab; he lives and works with others, and not only for reasons of convenience. Remove him from his family, from company, from society, and you have destroyed him. Hume provides fairly long accounts of sympathetic perception, but always only incidentally, in the course of explaining phenomena important in their own right. The first of these accounts is given when he explains the love of fame in "Of the Passions." There we are told, "When any affection is infus'd by sympathy, it is at first known only by its effects, and by those external signs in the countenance and conversation, which convey an idea of it. This idea is presently converted into an impression, and acquires such a degree of force and vivacity, as to become the very passion itself, and produce an equal emotion, as any original affection" (*T.*, 317). Four paragraphs later, he shows how sympathetic perception of the feelings of others parallels the operation of the imagination in originating beliefs about reality.

It has been remark'd in the beginning of this treatise, that all ideas are borrow'd from impressions, and that these two kinds of perceptions differ only in the degrees of force and vivacity, with which they strike upon the soul. The component parts of ideas and impressions are precisely alike. The manner and order of their appearance may be the same. The different degrees of their force and vivacity are, therefore, the only particulars, that distinguish them: And as this difference may be remov'd, in some measure, by a relation betwixt the impressions and ideas, 'tis no wonder an idea of a sentiment or passion, may by this means be so inliven'd as to become the very sentiment or passion. The lively idea of any object always approaches its impression; and 'tis certain we may feel sickness and pain from the mere force of imagination, and make a malady real by often thinking of it. But this is most remarkable in the opinions and affections; and 'tis there principally that a lively idea is converted into an impression. Our affections depend more upon ourselves, and the internal operations of the mind, than any other impressions;

for which reason they arise more naturally from the imagination, and from every lively idea we form of them. This is the nature and cause of sympathy; and 'tis after this manner we enter so deep into the opinions and affections of others, whenever we discover them. (*T.*, 318–19)

In yet another passage, he describes the process of sympathy as almost mechanical: "The minds of all men are similar in their feelings and operations, nor can any one be actuated by any affection, of which all others are not, in some degree, susceptible. As in strings equally wound up, the motion of one communicates itself to the rest; so all the affections readily pass from one person to another, and beget correspondent movements in every human creature" (*T.*, 575–76).

It is sympathetic perception, not love or the benevolence that follows love, that ties all humankind together. In order for sympathy to operate most effectively, there must be a well-established acquaintance. This is why sympathy between blood relatives who live together, old neighbors, close friends, those with similar interests, and so on is easy and strong. Our sympathetic perception with strangers is strong enough to produce moral evaluation—to produce esteem or disesteem—but not strong enough to make us love the virtuous (so as to be moved by benevolence) or to hate the vicious (so as to be moved by anger). The critical case is the Samaritan relationship: the good Samaritan, out of pity, not love, acts benevolently toward a stranger, but that is because the stranger is in his presence. One starving child at our door moves us more than reports of ten million starving children far away in another continent.

Nor is sympathetic perception a faculty to be turned on and off at will. It makes man by his nature a social animal: he needs the economic cooperation of others; he needs their good offices; but most of all he needs their company. In the course of explaining why we love our relatives, Hume tells us that the mind is insufficient to entertain itself:

[I]t naturally seeks after foreign objects, which may produce a lively sensation, and agitate the spirits. On the appearance of such an object it awakes, as it were, from a dream: The blood flows with a new tide: The heart is elevated: And the whole man acquires a vigour, which he cannot command in his solitary and calm moments. Hence company is naturally so rejoicing, as presenting the liveliest of all objects, *viz.* a rational and thinking being like ourselves, who communicates to us all the actions of his mind; makes us privy to his inmost sentiments and affections; and lets us see, in the very instant of their production, all the emotions, which are caus'd by any object. (*T.*, 353)

A person needs others for biological and economic reasons, but most remarkably because he needs to be part of a great network of perceptions, a world of mind, rich in beliefs, values, and affections. Apart from such a world, a person is poor and lonely; he suffers from mental and spiritual anemia. Hume traces the fact that there are distinct nations, each with its own values, customs, manners, and styles—its own character—mainly to the influence of sympathetic perception among the people (T., 316–17).

Hume regarded his use of the transfer or communication of impressiveness as a notable philosophical advance. In epistemology it explains much of our knowledge of reality. And here, as we have seen, it goes a long way toward explaining morality. Hidden away in a discussion of why the rich and powerful are held in high esteem, we find the following passage:

> In all creatures, that prey not upon others, and are not agitated with violent passions, there appears a remarkable desire of company, which associates them together, without any advantages they can ever propose to reap from their union. This is still more conspicuous in man, as being the creature of the universe, who has the most ardent desire of society, and is fitted for it by the most advantages. We can form no wish, which has not a reference to society. A perfect solitude is, perhaps, the greatest punishment we can suffer. Every pleasure languishes when enjoy'd a-part from company, and every pain becomes more cruel and intolerable. Whatever other passions we may be actuated by; pride, ambition, avarice, curiosity, revenge or lust; the soul or animating principle of them all is sympathy; nor wou'd they have any force, were we to abstract entirely from the thoughts and sentiments of others. (T., 363)

Sympathetic perception explains how objective judgments of conduct are possible. Since everyone sees and evaluates from his own viewpoint, particular evaluations will differ widely and never can be the basis of standards of goodness. Sympathy enables us to evaluate acts, and the characteristics behind acts, from a general or objective viewpoint. To the moral philosopher's first question—how are moral judgments made?—Hume's answer is this: not by reasoning, but by feelings; and not by the "self-ish" feelings of each participant, but by the feelings of spectators. There can be no moral evaluation without impartiality, and no spectator without sympathetic perception. Hume does not pretend to have discovered sympathy; Shaftesbury and Butler were only two of his predecessors. But he makes extensive use of the concept, finding it important in many contexts.

The second general point, one we have anticipated somewhat, travels close with the first: the moral judgment is the judgment of the spectator. Hume takes this as obvious; probably it was obvious to his contemporaries; for Clarke had made the point that the reason of impartial observers is best, and Hutcheson had relied on the moral sense of the "spectator." Hume assumes also that, by definition, a spectator is disinterested; indeed, only once does he use an adjective, namely, "judicious" (*T.*, 581). What is important is Hume's explanation of the achievement of objectivity. To qualify as a spectator, one must have been dislodged from one's own natural self-centered view, from one's particularity. What has to be overcome is the partiality of primary perception, the natural magnification of what is present or close to ourselves. In "Of the Passions," Hume providently puts down a foundation for his discussion of this problem (*T.*, 427–38). Later, in "Of Morals," he tells us that a feeling must be of "a peculiar kind" to serve as the basis of a moral judgment.

> The good qualities of an enemy are hurtful to us; but may still command our esteem and respect. 'Tis only when a character is considered in general, without reference to our particular interest, that it causes such a feeling or sentiment, as denominates it morally good or evil. 'Tis true, those sentiments, from interest and morals, are apt to be confounded, and naturally run into one another. It seldom happens, that we do not think an enemy vicious, and can distinguish betwixt his opposition to our interest and real villainy or baseness. But this hinders not, but that the sentiments are, in themselves, distinct; and a man of temper and judgment may preserve himself from these illusions. (*T.*, 472)

Again, we are told that "virtue is distinguished by the pleasure, and vice by the pain, that any action, sentiment or character gives us by the mere view and contemplation" (*T.*, 475). Not until we come to the last part of the *Treatise*—III.3.1—do we find passages in which Hume explains why and how we achieve an evaluative viewpoint different from our own natural viewpoint. There he compares this change of viewpoint with the correction we make in our perception of the physical world. Nobody, he says, fails to alter his natural view of the physical world by an act of mind; perhaps small children think that windows are bigger than the moon, but they soon correct their view. Exactly the same happens in value judgment. Necessity in various forms—irate parents, outraged brothers and sisters, and so on—teaches us that the egocentric values of early childhood are quite impractical. A society of "self-ish" idiots simply cannot work. Society requires order and coordination; this means that there must be at least an elementary agreement on rules and standards of conduct; and the only good on which there is any possibility of agreement is the good as perceived from the judicious or impartial viewpoint. Experience forms our minds; the result is that no longer are we simply particular beings who can see only our own good; we become able to make relatively objective judgments of both our own behavior and that of others. Our moral formation, however, is not radical: we remain particular human beings, but we learn how to speak the lines prescribed by morality, and to some extent to play the roles.

In general, all sentiments of blame or praise are variable, according to our situation of nearness or remoteness, with regard to the person blam'd or prais'd, and according to the present disposition of our mind. But these variations we regard not in our general decisions, but still apply the terms expressive of our liking or dislike, in the same manner, as if we remain'd in one point of view. Experience soon teaches us this method of correcting our sentiments, or at least, of correcting our language, where the sentiments are more stubborn and inalterable (*T.*, 582)

Then, after reminding us that our admiration for Brutus is high although he lived long ago, Hume continues: "Such corrections are common with regard to all the senses; and indeed 'twere impossible we cou'd ever make use of language, or communicate our sentiments to one another, did we not correct the momentary appearances of things, and overlook our present situation" (*T.*, 582). He resorts to the same explanation in "Of Morals," part 3, section 3, where he applies to the good man his conclusion that virtues are qualities useful or agreeable to the possessor or to others. We seem, he says, to have forgotten ourselves, what is useful or agreeable to ourselves. Do we not count? His answer is that we do not. What is useful or agreeable to ourselves especially is irrelevant in moral evaluation because inevitably it is partial. We all know that we cannot take our self-centered view of external bodies as reliable; the same is true here.

In like manner, tho' sympathy be much fainter than our concern for ourselves, and a sympathy with persons remote from us much fainter than that with persons near and contiguous; yet we neglect all these differences in our calm judgments concerning the characters of men. Besides, that we ourselves often change our situation in this particular, we every day meet with persons, who are in a different situation from ourselves, and who cou'd never converse with us on any reasonable terms, were we to remain constantly in that situation and point of view, which is peculiar to us. The intercourse of sentiments, therefore, in society and conversation, makes us form some general inalterable standard, by which we may approve or disapprove of characters and manners. And tho' the *heart* does not always take part with those general notions, or regulate its love and hatred by them, yet are they sufficient for discourse, and serve all our purposes in company, in the pulpit, on the theatre, and in the schools. (*T.*, 603)

The natural evaluation is a self-centered evalution; in contrast, the moral evaluation ignores particular interests. By taking an impartial standpoint, the spectator sets free his public (general) benevolence, his basic preference for what is good "consider'd merely as such," that is, good for beings of the human kind; he frees it from the distorting influ-

ence of both self-interest and private benevolence. That we make evaluations from the two viewpoints is shown by the fact that we have two
distinct vocabularies, one the vocabulary of partiality, the other the vocabulary of morality (E., 272).

Third, the virtues are all those qualities that cause (or would cause if
not prevented) effects good for humankind—not humankind as a collec-
tivity, a public or a whole, but humans as individuals. We do not love all
humankind as we love our families, partners, and so on; yet sympathetically we can perceive the feelings of any other person. Because we too are
human, we find good what other humans find good, and bad what they
find bad. "Sympathy interests us in the good of mankind" (T., 584).
Therefore, we find good whatever is useful or agreeable to human beings.
For example, we may approve someone's sobriety—as good for him,
given his nature as a human being—although we foresee no benefit whatsoever for ourselves, perhaps harm if he is a rival. Nobody whose values
have not been distorted by bad formation would suggest seriously that
what is ultimately disadvantageous or disagreeable to our species, what
causes beings of the human kind, not pleasure, but pain, is good (E., 280–
81). Benevolence and justice are "the social virtues"; they are necessary
for "the good of mankind." Even the nonsocial virtues, those approved
as useful or agreeable to the possessor, are good for humankind, not because they advance the well-being of all people throughout the world, but
in the sense that anyone who has those qualities will benefit from them.

How does a spectator's perception differ from that of a person affected
by an action so that we can say that the judgment made from the spectator's viewpoint, and not the latter's, is a moral judgment? (It is possible
for someone to make a moral evaluation of his own character and conduct, but only if he imaginatively takes up a spectator's viewpoint, seeing
himself as others see him.) One difference is that the spectator is judicious, that is, impartial. But is impartiality enough? Or, to put the question another way, what difference does the spectator's impartiality make
if it only lets the spectator have a perception that is the same as an interested participant's, only weaker? The spectator must distinguish between
what is good and what is bad on the basis of some principle. The answer
is that as a *person*, as one who shares the human nature, he finds that
those human qualities that are seen as good for beings of the human kind
are virtues. Human nature is the ultimate test. Qualities found good for
human beings are virtues.

We must recall that we love those who have goods, specifically in this
case, virtues. Here is a virtuous person; because he is a complete stranger,
I have no private interest in his happiness; his happiness affects me only
by sympathy. "From that principle, whenever I discover his happiness
and good, whether in its causes or effects, I enter so deeply into it, that it

gives me a sensible emotion. The appearance of qualities, that have a *tendency* to promote it [his happiness and good], have an agreeable effect upon my imagination, and command my love and esteem" (*T.*, 588–89). This means that we will have some degree of benevolence even toward particular strangers, provided that they are virtuous. However, Hume does not want us to take this love and the consequent benevolence for virtuous strangers too seriously. We have "extensive sympathy" but only "limited generosity." We must not confuse the love (esteem) produced by a high moral evaluation and the love we have for those related to us in some special way. "My sympathy with another may give me the sentiment of pain and disapprobation, when any object is presented, that has a tendency to give him uneasiness; tho' I may not be willing to sacrifice any thing of my own interest, or cross any of my passions, for his satisfaction" (*T.*, 586).

The importance of our "humanity," our desire for "the good of mankind"—that is, our desire for what is good for beings of the human kind—to Hume's moral theory as set forth in the *Treatise* is easily overlooked because of his insistence that we have no "love of mankind merely as such, independent of personal qualities, of services, or of relation to ourself." But it comes to the fore clearly in "Of Morals," part 3, section 1, in the section entitled "Of the origin of the natural virtues and vices." Given its title, this section might be regarded as only the short consort of the twelve previous sections on the artificial virtues, rather than as crucial in the exposition of Hume's moral theory. Moreover, the section is both extremely complex and succinct. What was emphasized in the discussion of justice was our lack of love for people in general; now, however, we are told that when we make a truly disinterested judgment of good and evil, we always approve that which is "good for mankind." This seems contradictory until we remember that in the first case Hume is writing about our love of those related to us in some special way, and in the second case about the fact that when spectators make moral evaluations they do so free from partiality. Justice, we are told here, "is a moral virtue, merely because it has that tendency to the good of mankind." Sympathy causes us to approve all the artificial virtues: "From thence we may presume, that it also gives rise to many of the other virtues; and that qualities acquire our approbation, because of their tendency to the good of mankind" (*T.*, 578). There is, then, what may be called a public or *general* benevolence, but unlike private or *particular* benevolence, it accompanies, not love, but sympathetic perception. Hume dismisses the system that teaches that moral rules are mere arcana contrived by politicians and preachers; then he says, "But tho' this system be erroneous, it may teach us, that moral distinctions arise, in a great measure, from the tendency of qualities and characters to the interest of society, and that 'tis our concern for that interest, which makes us approve or disapprove of them. Now we have no such extensive concern for society but from sympathy; and consequently 'tis that principle, which takes us so far out of ourselves, as to give us the same pleasure or uneasiness in the characters of others [that are useful or pernicious to Society]" (*T.*, 579, 672).

Here Hume is following Shaftesbury. The basic test of what is morally good or bad is what is good or bad for beings of the human kind, and the danger is that we may do what presently seems good for ourselves at the expense of what is good for individuals of the human kind, that is, both ourselves and others. Hume differs from Shaftesbury in that he distinguishes clearly between primary motivation and moral motivation. As noticed above, this distinction is easy to discern in the case of the artificial virtues. But Hume agrees with Hobbes and Mandeville in thinking that economic man is self-interested; as a result, economic society is different from those relationships in which private benevolence is appropriate. Yet the dome of morality covers both spheres: both justice and private benevolence are virtues. Both are beneficial to beings of the human kind.

Although our basic concern for what is good for our kind is essential to Hume's moral theory in the *Treatise*, in that work he does not call that concern benevolence; obviously he wished to keep clear his distinction between private benevolence and justice, a distinction necessary if he was to show the difference between primary and moral motivation. In contrast, in *Enquiry* II, he announces that there are two kinds of benevolence.

> Benevolence naturally divides into two kinds, the *general* and the *particular*. The first is, where we have no friendship or connexion or esteem for the person, but feel only a general sympathy with him or a compassion for his pains, and a congratulation with his pleasures. The other species of benevolence is founded on an opinion of virtue, on services done us, or on some particular connexions. Both these sentiments must be allowed real in human nature: but whether they will resolve into some nice considerations of self-love, is a question more curious than important. The former sentiment, to wit, that of general benevolence, or humanity, or sympathy, we shall have occasion frequently to treat of in the course of this enquiry; and I assume it as real, from general experience, without any other proof. (*E.*, 298n)

Elsewhere in the *Enquiry*, he again excuses himself from providing an explanation of why "we have humanity or a fellow-feeling with others." The presence of humanity can be taken as a basic principle of moral science (*E.*, 219–20n). On one occasion, he refers to general benevolence as our "natural philanthrophy" (*E.*, 227). His preferred term, however, the one he came to use again and again, especially in the *History of England*, is "humanity." It is our humanity that leads us to distinguish between virtue and vice.

Although Hume begins *Enquiry* II by stating that little is to be gained by arguing with those who explain morals as simply the effect of long-headed self-love, the work turns out to be a running battle, in which Hume defends his system of morals, based on humanity, against moral skeptics. After three or four engagements, in which the self-love theorists are raked and battered, in the "Conclusion," he closes on them, delivering two lethal salvos; thus he wins the victory for humanity. First, assuming that by self-love we mean selfishness, it is ridiculous to propose that a sound moral order, a genuine society, could ever be based on avarice, ambition, or any other strictly self-serving passion. Moral obligation always modifies or restricts natural motivation to some extent, and it is precisely the difference between natural motivation and moral obligation that must be explained. The very concept of morality requires, first, a sentiment that causes all to approve the same conduct, and, second, a sentiment so universal as to interest us in the well-being of every person, no matter how far removed he is from ourselves (*E.*, 272). Avarice, ambition, and the like are strong passions, but they are particularistic: these passions lead people to compete and conflict; the victory of one is not the victory of all. These passions are divisive, not cohesive. The players in a game may be driven by such self-serving passions, but there will be no game for them to play unless the rules are supported by a basic, general agreement or presupposition that the game is good for all. Here, again, as in the *Treatise*, Hume has resorted to the universalism of individualism; true moral sentiment interests each in the well-being of all, and must find good for each what it finds good for all.

It is, says Hume, as if there were two parties of passions. Arrayed on one side are avarice, ambition, vanity, and so forth, all divisive passions: some people, but not all, have cause to rejoice when somebody has achieved the gratification of any one of these passions. On the other side is concern for the well-being of humanity, humankind, not just as embodied in ourselves, but as such. Here we think of ourselves, at least when we can manage to achieve an impartial viewpoint, as individual human beings. This concern for, this sympathy with, this benevolence for, humankind musters "the *party* of human kind." It may be thought that avarice, and the like will always win the day; that, however, would be a serious error. A passion such as avarice, being selfish, can never be the principle of general cooperation; it has no common end, no common goal. Humanity, in contrast, has support everywhere, even in the camp of avarice and ambition, with the result that rules and standards of morality, based on what is seen as good for humankind—the good on which everybody as an individual can agree—come to be established. Additional strength is given to the rules and standards by the fact that people love fame, and human beings delight to sing the praises of those whom they see as their true friends and champions. The principles that give rise to moral sentiment are not to be underestimated.

> [T]hey form, in a manner, the *party* of human-kind against vice or disorder, its common enemy. And as the benevolent concern for others is diffused, in a greater or less degree, over all men, and is the same in all, it occurs more frequently in discourse, is cherished by society and conversation, and the blame and approbation, consequent on it, are thereby roused from that lethargy into which they are probably lulled, in solitary and uncultivated nature. Other passions, though perhaps originally stronger, yet being selfish and private, are often overpowered by its force, and yield the dominion of our breast to those social and public principles. (*E.*, 275–76)

Humanity or general benevolence, not self-love, is the feeling by which we are led to approve some characteristics, motives, and actions as morally good, and to denounce others as evil.

The fourth point relates to how the spectators' judgments, distinguishing between what is good and what is bad from a general viewpoint, influence subsequent conduct. Here we move from a finding as to what is good, and what is bad, to a statement of how we ought to act; we move from the language of *good* (and bad) to the language of *right* (and wrong). This transition Hume attributes to the rise of rules and standards. These rules and standards translate good into right and bad into wrong. They speak imperatively, instructing us to do what is declared right and to avoid what is declared wrong. Let us take an example. When one of Hume's primitive human beings learns by experience that theft is contrary to his own interest, he forms a rule that he will refrain from theft. To conform to that rule is to do right, to break it is to do wrong. At this point, this rule is only a rule of expediency: the person has concluded that theft is contrary to his interest and should be avoided. But when spectators find that acts that break such a rule are bad, being contrary to the good of human beings, while acts in accord with the rule are good for them, the rule takes on a new and different status. It becomes a moral rule. Conformity becomes morally right; disregard for the rule, morally wrong.

Here we must notice an important implication of Hume's distinction between the natural and the artificial virtues. Someone strong in the artificial virtues does not break the rules prohibiting injustice, disobedience, and so on; rather, he respects the moral *rules*. In a sense his virtue is negative: it keeps him from doing the wrongs proposed by his natural motivation; it does not move him to do good works. In contrast, the natural motivation of someone strong in the natural social virtue, that is, particular benevolence, is only modified by moral obligation; his motivation to do good works for his children, friends, neighbors, and the like is adjusted so that his performance conforms to the moral *norms* or *standards*. We must recognize that "we always consider the *natural* and *usual* force of the passions, when we determine concerning vice and virtue; and if the passions depart very much from the common measures on either side, they are always disapprov'd as vicious. A man naturally loves his children better than his nephews, his nephews better than his cousins, his cousins better than strangers, where every thing else is equal. Hence arise our common measures of duty, in preferring the one to the other" (*T.*, 483–84). As a result of this difference, the basic requirements of morality are far easier to state in the case of the artificial virtues. These requirements are stated as absolute prohibitions.

Fifth, reason is indispensible in establishing and improving morality. In those passages in the *Treatise* where Hume is out to refute the extreme rationalist view—that virtuous conduct is conduct that conforms to an eternally valid pattern knowable by reasoning, conduct in which men perform their assigned parts or roles with total indifference to, even contempt for, their passions—the contribution of reason is played down, even derided. There he contends that moral evaluation, like all other evaluation, is concerned with distinguishing between good and bad, not with distinguishing between the truth and falsity of propositions about what was, is, or will be real. At bottom it is a matter of the impartial approval (or disapproval) of those human characteristics that cause pleasure (or pain) to the players severally and collectively. However, Hume's famous assertion on the instrumentality of reason ought not to be read out of context. "Reason is," he says, "and ought only to be the slave of the passions, and can never pretend to any other office than to serve and obey them" (*T.*, 415). Here Hume is giving an extreme response to the extreme view that the passions, being brutish, ought to be ruled, perhaps even extirpated, by angelic reason. He is denying that reason (or science) has a title to sovereign power, that "reason alone" can either discover "eternal fitnesses and unfitnesses" or provide the motivation, moral or otherwise, to act righteously. He never says that reason is unnecessary.

The basic cause of the distinction between good (the reactive judgment to pleasure) and bad (the reactive judgment to pain) remains the same over time and from place to place; it is as constant as human nature. Accordingly, the qualities found good because they are *agreeable* will change little. However, if the subject's knowledge of the consequences of an act changes, his evaluative reaction also will change. As reason provides us with new or better information, as we understand better, we perceive new goods, and also new ways to achieve good. Moreover, any change in the values of a society will be expressed in the conduct of the members of that society. It is the superiority of their reason, says Hume, that makes human beings superior to beasts.

One way reason helps is by activating the calm passions, those passions that move us to seek what is found good from an impartial, objective, or general viewpoint. The violent passions, too, seek good in various forms, but these goods are momentary goods, goods of the present, the here and now. If to gain a momentary good we risk or forego a greater long-term good, as does someone who risks his life in an impetuous attempt to avenge some slight injury, we have acted foolishly. Momentary goods are easy to perceive; we are deluged constantly by their entreaties and demands. They will move us to act unless they are countered by calm passions. Now, although it is the prospect of pleasure or of avoiding pain that makes the long-term good attractive, it is reason that opens our eyes to the distant prospect. Reason gives us our perception of what probably lies in the future, out beyond the present. It shows us the greater goods; without reason, the violent passions generally would prevail.

In the *Treatise*, the great example of a major change in morals caused by changes in knowledge is the rise of the artificial virtues. People need economic cooperation but cannot cooperate because of the looseness of external goods. The understanding shows the way out: "The remedy, then, is not deriv'd from nature, but from *artifice*; or more properly speaking, nature provides a remedy in the judgment and understanding, for what is irregular and incommodious in the affections" (*T.*, 489). That remedy is property. Similarly, people learn in war how useful political authority can be; later they apply political authority to the task of maintaining justice. Hume leave no doubt about the importance of reason: "Human nature being compos'd of two principal parts, which are requisite in all its actions, the affections and understanding; 'tis certain, that the blind motions of the former, without the direction of the latter, incapacitate men for society" (*T.*, 493).

In *Enquiry* II, Hume makes a determined effort to ensure that the power of reason to change morality is not overlooked. We are not to focus narrowly on the moral sense. Reason can change our moral judgment of an act, a policy, a law; it can change the *content* of morality. Hume uses beauty judgments to make his point. We call houses, horses, and ships beautiful because we see the suitability of their forms to their uses. From this it follows that we may make a mistake in evaluating something if we do not understand fully how it works. Our medieval man would find eighteenth-century buildings ugly because of their broad windows, but after he had learned that domestic warfare had ceased, his judgment would change. The form of beautiful steel structures is different from the form of beautiful stone structures. Since most acts, policies, laws, and rules are morally good because of their utility, new insight into their effects may lead us to change our judgments, approving what we formerly deplored, and deploring what we formerly approved.

> In all determinations of morality, this circumstance of public utility is ever principally in view; and wherever disputes arise, either in philosophy or common life, concerning the bounds of duty, the question cannot, by any means, be decided with greater certainty, than by ascertaining, on any side, the true interests of mankind. If any false opinion, embraced from appearances, has been found to prevail; as soon as farther experience and sounder reasoning have given us juster notions of human affairs, we retract our first sentiment, and adjust anew the boundaries of moral good and evil. (E., 180)

Hume's examples are almost as interesting as the argument they support. At first glance, he says, it may seem virtuous to give alms freely to beggars, but once we see that in modern circumstances begging ordinarily is unnecessary, and that indiscriminate alms giving only encourages idleness and debauchery, we decide that casual alms giving is not authentic charity. Second, at one time tyrannicide was accounted praiseworthy, but as people began to discern its bad effects, they came to denounce it.[9] Again, liberality in princes may be accounted virtuous until it is seen that thereby the bread of "the honest and industrious" often becomes cake for greedy, indolent courtiers. Finally, those who do not understand political economy may persist in regarding luxury as vicious; yet the truth is otherwise.

> Luxury, or a refinement on the pleasures and conveniences of life, had long been supposed the source of every corruption in government, and the immediate cause of faction, sedition, civil wars, and the total loss of liberty. It was, therefore, universally regarded as a vice, and was an object of declamation to all satirists, and severe moralists. Those, who prove, or attempt to prove, that such refinements rather tend to the increase of industry, civility, and arts regulate anew our *moral* as well as *political* sentiments, and represent, as laudable or innocent, what had formerly been regarded as pernicious and blameable. (E., 181)

The essay "Of Refinement in the Arts"—originally "Of Luxury"— draws together neatly Hume's stand on the role of reason, his rejection of

---

[9] Hume's interest in the theory of tyrannicide may have been caused by the trial and death of Charles I. *History of England,* 5:544–46. The question of the right of tyrannicide, a question with a long history, had been given new prominence by the advent of heretical rulers; see Roland Mousnier, *The Assassination of Henry IV: The Tyrannicide Problem and the Consolidation of the French Absolute Monarchy in the Early Seventeenth Century* (London: Faber and Faber, 1973). For a summary account of Roman Catholic views on tyrannicide, see Guenter Lewy, "A Secret Papal Brief on Tyrannicide during the Counterreformation," *Church History* 26 (1957): 2–8.

monkish morality, and his contention that "humanity" is the basis of moral distinctions. By exercise and application in the arts of commerce and manufacturing, human reason is aroused and refined. Thus mobilized, reason sets to work to promote the liberal arts and to reform government. The general result is a vast increase in humanity; consequently, people advance from barbarity to civility. In other words, if we are to regard reason as the slave of the passions, it must be as an enlightening guide, not a menial servant. Although reason does not speak imperatively, it does speak indicatively.[10] More experience and sounder reflection, by showing the true effects of constitutions, practices, policies, and laws, may turn vices into virtues, and virtues into vices. This is why reason is central to the improvement of public morality. It is quite understandable that the unphilosophic make much of "reason" in morality, for disputes and debates commonly are not over ends, but means, not over what is good and what evil, but over the tendencies and results of particular constitutions, laws, practices, and policies.

We must not misunderstand the way reason advances the process of civilization in Hume's theory. We are not to think that in the beginning reason held up the prospect of the good of a society, a public—the good of the British, the French, or any other public—and then prescribed justice and allegiance as means for the achievement of that good. Rather, prolonged experience, enlightened by "thought and reflexion," drove home to many the truth that in economic and political dealings their self-interest could best be served by resisting thoughtless impulse. Hence the rules of justice and allegiance. These rules, when applied within a particular kingdom or nation, provide the constitution for a genuine civil society. In other words, initially the scientific analysis of the principles of civil society was descriptive, not prescriptive; the philosophers who made the analysis arrived on the scene, not before the rise of civil society, but relatively late. This is not to say, however, that economic and political science cannot subsequently be used to reform the beliefs, customs, and laws of backward kingdoms and nations.

Sixth, Hume's refusal to explain moral sentiments as a refined variety of love (or particular benevolence) enables him to be realistic about the requirements of morality. Moral sentiments, he tells us, arise from the feelings of spectators; both their humanity and impartiality are presupposed. Now, the spectator recognizes the fact that the scope of our particular benevolence is limited; consequently morality does not require that

---

[10] For a convincing statement of a similar interpretation, see David Fate Norton, *David Hume: Common-Sense Moralist, Sceptical Metaphysician* (Princeton: Princeton University Press, 1982), pp. 126–33. On the role of reason in the origin of civil society, see Knud Haakonssen, *The Science of a Legislator: The Natural Jurisprudence of David Hume and Adam Smith* (Cambridge: Cambridge University Press, 1981), pp. 18–21.

we undertake to do good words for all humankind. The ordinary person is regarded as virtuous if he acts appropriately, that is, with suitable benevolence toward those within his narrow circle, and treats others justly. He is a safe companion, an easy friend, a gentle master, an agreeable husband, a good neighbor. Beyond those relationships, he governs himself by "the cautious, jealous virtue of justice" (*E.*, 184). What is more, this is for the best, because (as Shaftesbury, Hutcheson, and Butler had said) if we loved everybody equally, we would accomplish little for anybody. "It is wisely ordained by nature," says Hume, "that private connexions should commonly prevail over universal views and considerations; otherwise our affections and actions would be dissipated and lost, for want of a proper limited object."[11] Ordinary people work to achieve the good they comprehend. What about those with public roles, the politicians? We do not expect even them to assume responsibility for human beings everywhere.

> When the interests of one country interfere with those of another, we estimate the merits of a statesman by the good or ill, which results to his own country from his measures and councils, without regard to the prejudice which he brings on its enemies and rivals. His fellow-citizens are the objects, which lie nearest the eye, while we determine his character. And as nature has implanted in every one a superior affection to his own country, we never expect any regard to distant nations, where a competition arises. Not to mention, that, while every man consults the good of his own community, we are sensible, that the general interest of mankind is better promoted, than by any loose indeterminate views to the good of a species, whence no beneficial action could ever result, for want of a duly limited object, on which they could exert themselves. (*E.*, 225n)

Seventh, although the rules and standards are given their moral status by society, they can be internalized; they can become the requirements of conscience. One result of sympathetic perception is that the approval, esteem, respect, and admiration of others—all variants of love—are of the highest importance to people. They want goods—external goods, beauty, talents, virtues—because these things are valuable per se, but often they want them even more for their social results; that is, for the approval, reputation, and deference these things bring with them. While some goods are only intrinsically good, others are valuable both intrinsically and socially. For example, good health ordinarily is not a cause of pride and mutual congratulation among the young; with them it is too common

---

[11] *Enquiry* II, p. 229. Adam Smith, too, applauds nature's wise arrangement, which makes the politician's responsibility commensurate with his ability. *The Theory of Moral Sentiments* (Oxford: Clarendon Press, 1976), pp. 227–34.

a good even to be noticed. But other goods—provided that they are closely related to the person; provided that they are his constantly, not accidentally; provided that they are conspicuous; and provided that they are recognized as good by the standards or conventions of the society— may be sought more for their social than their intrinsic value. The same is true, but in reverse, of deprivations and vices. In short, people's lives are shaped greatly by the conventional values of their peers; the more closely knit the society, the stronger the influence of those values (T., 323).

What is true of goods in general is true of moral virtues. These virtues are good in both ways: they are intrinsically good, but they are good also because someone thought to be morally virtuous does not suffer disapproval, and may even be rewarded with esteem and admiration. The feeling of moral obligation originates with others, who exert themselves through example and language, through education, and through pressure to conform. A reputation of viciousness causes pain: the pain of being hated and the pain of humiliation. Conversely, a good reputation, a reputation of virtue, "a character," brings both the love of others and the rapture of pride. In addition, Hume tells us tersely in the *Treatise*, the morally virtuous person is at peace with himself (T., 620). Hume amplifies this point in *Enquiry* II. There he tells us, in a passage reminiscent of Butler's explanation of the ancient precept "Reverence thyself," that there are those, just how many he does not say, for whom conduct based on humanity becomes a matter of "reflection."[12] Anxiety to do only what the

[12] In explaining the constitution of human nature, Butler emphasizes the role of reflection or conscience. "The practical reason of insisting so much upon this natural authority of the principle of reflection or conscience is, that it seems in great measure overlooked by many [including Shaftesbury], who are by no means the worse sort of men. It is thought sufficient to abstain from gross wickedness, and to be humane and kind to such as happen to come in their way. Whereas in reality the very constitution of our nature requires, that we bring our whole conduct before this superior faculty; wait its determination; enforce upon ourselves its authority, and make it the business of our lives, as it is absolutely the whole business of a moral agent, to conform ourselves to it. This is the true meaning of that ancient precept "Reverence thyself." Butler, *The Works of the Right Reverend Father in God Joseph Butler*, ed. Samuel Halifax, 2 vols. (Oxford: The University Press, 1844), 2:xvi. Commenting on the character of Sir Thomas Fairfax, Hume stressed the distinction between conformity to public standards and true virtue. "Fairfax," he wrote, "was a person equally eminent for courage and for humanity, and not more guided by that *honor*, which regards the opinions of the public, than by that nobler principle of *virtue*, which seeks the inward satisfaction of self-approbation and applause." *The History of Great Britain*, ed. Duncan Forbes (Harmondsworth: Penguin Books Ltd., 1970), p. 579. (This is a reprint of the first edition of vol. 1 of the *History*, which volume was published in 1754. The same passage appeared in the second edition, 1759, but was modified in the 1763 edition.)

The principal reason given in the *Treatise* for hoping that rulers will perform well is that, given their neutrality, to do so is in their own interest. However, in *Enquiry*, the possibility of benevolent rulers is raised. There we are told that when truly generous people, people of

public approves leads to self-examination; thus the achievement of what the standards and rules prescribe becomes a matter of conscious striving.

> By our continual and earnest pursuit of a character, a name, a reputation in the world, we bring our own deportment and conduct frequently in review, and consider how they appear in the eyes of those who approach and regard us. This constant habit of surveying ourselves, as it were, in reflection, keeps alive all the sentiments of right and wrong, and begets, in noble natures, a certain reverence for themselves as well as others, which is the surest guardian of every virtue. The animal conveniences and pleasures sink gradually in their value; while every inward beauty and moral grace is studiously acquired, and the mind is accomplished in every perfection, which can adorn or embellish a rational creature.
>
> Here is the most perfect morality with which we are acquainted: here is displayed the force of many sympathies. Our moral sentiment is itself a feeling chiefly of that nature, and our regard to a character with others seems to arise only from a care of preserving a character with ourselves; and in order to attain this end, we find it necessary to prop our tottering judgement on the correspondent approbation of mankind. (*E.*, 276)

In noble natures, then, the pressure of public opinion as a cause of moral conformity is supplanted by a desire for the self-respect, the self-approbation, without which such people cannot be happy. Most people act morally because of custom and education, but some, those of great nobility of character, those of generous minds, become morally autonomous in some degree. Theirs is a happiness far beyond the dreams of avarice and ambition. They are "wise and virtuous men." For them, general benevolence (humanity) serves not only as the basis of moral judgment, but as the motive for good works. It is true that general benevolence is inseparable from human nature, but "they are only the more generous minds, that are thence prompted to seek zealously the good of others, and to have a real passion for their welfare. With men of narrow and ungenerous spirits, this sympathy goes not beyond a slight feeling of the imagination, which serves only to excite sentiments of complacency or censure, and makes them apply to the object either honourable and dishonourable appellations" (*E.*, 234n).

Eighth, the marriage of religion and morality may impede the moral sciences. Theological moralists, "treating all morals as on a like footing with civil laws, guarded by the sanctions of reward and punishment, were necessarily led to render this circumstance, of *voluntary* or *involuntary*, the foundation of their whole theory" (*E.*, 322). Thus they propagated a

---

very great humanity, find themselves in high places, their benevolence displays itself in "the good government or useful instruction of mankind." *Enquiry* II, p. 176.

dangerous doctrine, the doctrine of free will. By obscuring the importance of factors that shape the characters of individuals and peoples, factors which should be the chief concern of moral philosophers, the doctrine of free will tends to obscure the task of moral philosophy.

Moral obligation is prodigiously powerful. Children undergo moral formation in the family. In civil society, people are just and obedient, even though such conduct crosses their natural motivation. Indeed, says Hume, so powerful is morality that if someone realizes that he lacks some normal motive, he may, from guilt, undertake to reform himself: "When any virtuous motive or principle is common in human nature, a person, who feels his heart devoid of that principle, may hate himself upon that account, and may perform the action without the motive, from a certain sense of duty, in order to acquire by practice, that virtuous principle, or at least, to disguise to himself, as much as possible, his want of it" (T., 479). When a person does an act, not accidentally, but intentionally, we regard that act as evidence of his character; and it is sound evidence "unless repentance and a change of life have produc'd an alteration in that respect" (T., 349). Always we must remember that a person can turn his back on his past, for "repentance wipes off every crime, especially if attended with an evident reformation of life and manners" (T., 412).

Given the power of moral causes to shape people's characters, the moral philosopher should fix his attention on those causes. "Are the manners of men different in different ages and countries? We learn thence the great force of custom and education, which mould the human mind from its infancy and form it into a fixed and established character."[13] The moral philosopher should focus on the need for good laws and institutions, a healthy socioeconomic structure, salutary customs, sound education, and a religious regime that discourages superstition and enthusiasm. He should never forget that the most powerful influence on people's characters is not precepts or sermons, but good laws and well-contrived institutions (Essays, 55). The voluntarist system of morals, taught by those who see virtue as obedience, is misleading.[14] What has to be shaped, as every wise parent, educator, and reformer knows, is not the will, but the character, for the will may be bribed by rewards and punishments.

Hume ends "Of Morals" with a disclaimer aimed at any notion that he aspires to inculcate morality. He has tried, he says, to be no more than an exact anatomist, a careful analyst, not a painter out to recommend by the artful use of line and color. Yet perhaps, he reflects, the moral anatomist can play a part in improving morality, by informing those who teach and preach. There is something more than contemplative acquiescence or conservative complacency in the sentences with which Hume concludes the

[13] An Enquiry concerning Human Understanding, pp. 85–86.
[14] Treatise, pp. 312, 404; An Enquiry concerning Human Understanding, pp. 90–99.

Treatise: "We must have an exact knowledge of the parts, their situation and connexion, before we can design with any elegance or correctness. And thus the most abstract speculations concerning human nature, however cold and unentertaining, become subservient to *practical morality*; and may render this latter science more correct in its precepts, and more persuasive in its exhortations."[15]

Hume's Achievements

If just after he had finished the *Treatise*, the young author had been asked what he regarded as his main achievements in moral philosophy, what would he have listed? Obviously, he would not have claimed to have made the distinction between the good and the right, but probably he would have said that he had shown the importance of keeping that distinction clearly in mind (*T.*, 469). To speak of good and bad is to make a value judgment—of an apple, of a deed. To speak of right and wrong is to speak a different language, a language that presupposes rules and standards of conduct—perhaps of a game, perhaps of economic transactions, perhaps of political conduct—to which all participants ought to conform.

It is evident that the young Hume thought that many writers on moral subjects had taken mere ideas as their proper subject matter, while neglecting impressions; consequently, the systems of morality contrived by them tended to be divorced from the real world. Indeed, the purpose of the entire *Treatise* is to focus attention back on reality and away from the realm of mere ideas. What counts most is the impressiveness of a perception. Beginning with the sense of beauty, about which he had learned much from Shaftesbury and Hutcheson, he had gone on to explore and analyze the entire spectrum of the impressions: the feeling of necessity in causation; conviction in belief; pain and pleasure in sensation; the passions of joy, hope, pride, love, anger, and the like; the sense of moral obligation. This, the shift of focus from idea to impression so as to make philosophy realistic, he might have put first on the list of his achieve-

---

[15] *Treatise*, p. 621. In response to a request from Hume for comments on the manuscript of "Of Morals," Hutcheson had complained that the book wanted "a certain Warmth in the Cause of Virtue." In his reply, Hume stated that he had sought deliberately to avoid "Warmth" so as to preserve the scientific quality of the work. "Any warm Sentiment of Morals, I am afraid, wou'd have the Air of Declamation amidst abstract Reasonings, & wou'd be esteem'd contrary to good Taste. And tho' I am much more ambitious of being esteem'd a Friend to Virtue, than a Writer of Taste; yet I must always carry the latter in my Eye, otherwise I must despair of ever being servicable to Virtue." He expressed a hope that Hutcheson would take his point, but then went on to say that he intended "to make a new Tryal, if it be possible to make the Moralist & Metaphysician agree a little better." *Letters*, 1:32–33. Hume, as we have noted, begins *An Enquiry concerning Human Understanding* with a defence of his abstruse approach.

ments. We use ideas properly when we employ them to help us know and deal with the real world; we misuse them if we try to make the real world conform to our fanciful utopias.

The implications of this shift are important. The paradigm of society basic to a system of morality may be incompatible with human nature and man's circumstances. Just as Galileo had recourse to experience to test the accuracy of the Ptolemaic paradigm, Hume had recourse to experience to test the content of contemporary teachings about morals. He found that much of the morality taught from pulpits was false: founded on corrupt religion, that teaching recommended the "monkish virtues" of humility, mortification, and so forth. The truth is that these "virtues" are vices: suitable for only "gloomy, hair-brained enthusiasts," they "neither advance a man's fortune in the world, nor render him a more valuable member of society; neither qualify him for the entertainment of company, nor increase his power of self-enjoyment"(E., 270). The anatomist proposes to put morality on a sound basis; thereby he will open up the possibility of reform.

Hume would have included on his list of accomplishments the refutation of the doctrine of free will. Understandably, the voluntarist theory of morality, which defined virtue as obedience to commands, made much of "free will": the virtuous man was the obedient man, and each man was free to obey. That doctrine, Hume contended, implies that moral virtue is mere obedience. For example, by rewards and punishments, a king might cause a cowardly person to act as if he were courageous, but nobody would think that thereby the person showed courage. We must not look upon the will as the site of minor miracles; rather, we must look behind it to the various causes that taken together shape the will, and those causes include the qualities of a person's character, as well as any announced rewards and punishments. By dismissing "the free will" as the original cause of acts, Hume sought to direct the attention of moralists back to the virtues and vices as understood by the ancients. The practical moralist's question once more would be this: to what extent can virtuous character be formed, and how?

The young Hume also would have listed his distinction between primary and moral motivation. Hutcheson had confused these somewhat; for him the primary virtuous motive in all areas of human activity is love (or benevolence). Hume contends that benevolence based on love extends to only those within a person's own sphere, and that in our dealings with most others we are motivated basically by self-interest, which ought to be governed by justice. Although justice is a result of reason, it, like benevolence, is a great moral virtue. Therefore, we must conclude that moral motivation cannot be a primitive natural instinct. We have become moral beings, adhering to rules and standards, as a result of the experience of living with others.

He would have included his discovery that it is sympathetic perception that enables us to make the impartial evaluation of conduct that is basic to morality. The insistence on impartiality, implying the judicious (or impartial) spectator, was a stock feature of moral theories. But how is impartiality possible? The fact of sympathy, too, had been recognized by earlier writers. Hume saw that sympathetic perception could be used to explain how impartial or objective value judgments are possible.

Next, he would have stated, perhaps boastfully, that he had explained the authority of conscience. Butler had shown that reliance on the simple maxim "Be benevolent" is far from adequate, that benevolence must be controlled by both reason and conscience. Hume set out, not to dismiss conscience, but to explain its authority, and to do so without resort to religion. He believed that he had been successful. He had explained the transition from *is* to *ought*, how judgments recognizing what is good give rise to rules and standards of morality. Conscience enforces those rules and standards. Who, he asks at the end of the *Treatise*, revealing for a moment some warmth in the cause of virtue, can regard "any advantages of fortune a sufficient compensation for the least breach of the *social* virtues, when he considers, that not only his character with regard to others, but also his peace and inward satisfaction entirely depend upon his strict observance of them; and that a mind will never be able to bear its own survey, that has been wanting in its part to mankind and society?" (*T.*, 620). The reflective (conscientious) person strives for "inward beauty and moral grace."

He would have emphasized his refutation of moral subjectivism. He had shown that good and evil when defined, with Hobbes, in terms of self-love are divisive, promoting, not society, but unrestrained competition and hostility. Nor is group moral subjectivism much better than individual moral subjectivism. The morals of a group—a tribe, city, or nation—perhaps lauded as immemorial and sacred by the members, may lead to primitive and barbarous conduct, both domestically and externally. When judged by the spectator, they may be found, not good, but bad for humankind.

Finally, he would have noted that as a result of exploring the distinction made by natural-law writers between perfect and imperfect rights, he had been able to show the difference between the sphere of justice, in which we may strive for our own good freely as long as we respect the rights of others, and the sphere of particular benevolence, in which we ought to do good works for certain others, and thus he had cleared the ground for both a science of economics and a science of government.[16]

[16] It has been argued that in his theory of rationality and justice Hume turned away from the Scottish tradition in moral philosophy, still retained, although presented in a novel way, in Hutcheson's theory. Alasdair MacIntyre, *Whose Justice? Which Rationality?* (Notre Dame: University of Notre Dame Press, 1988), pp. 207–325.

4

CIVIL SOCIETY

The Principles of Justice

MAN BY HIS nature and circumstances is a social animal. From this it follows, Hume submits, that rules of conduct are required; without such rules, society would be impossible by reason of conflict and strife. Lacking divine omniscience and benevolence, people need the guidance of generally accepted rules, whether they are rowing boats, playing games, passing on the road, walking in procession, selecting kings, appropriating land and houses, or engaging in conversation. Even when killing each other, they resort to rules: those who break the rules of war or dueling are held in contempt (*E.*, 210–11). These rules are the constitution of society. It is not enough to distinguish impartially between good and bad conduct; a set of moral rules, directives establishing right and thus prohibiting wrong, is required.

Hume was keenly interested in the prerequisites and characteristics of "the progress of society." But what is "society"? When we read Hume carefully, we find that the love, companionship, and cooperation we need are provided in several kinds of relationships, all different kinds of "society." Can we sort out these relationships? Let us think of society as a body of stratified water. At the very bottom, we see small natural structures—families, friendships, and so on. For most of us, these compose the circle, the narrow circle, to which our particular benevolence is confined. This is one kind of society. In the stratum immediately above, we see that people are also related as owners, producers, traders, and consumers of economic goods. At this level, "society" takes the form of what we would call an economy. Here the rules of justice are fundamental. In any large, rich society, a government is needed to enforce justice; thus, the next stratum is governmental. Taken together, these two strata, the economy and the government, constitute "civil society." Then, fourth, superimposed on civil society, is the structure of social ranks, headed by the social and political elite, "the great." Fifth, a society is a community with common rules of conduct regulating the casual relations between and among the members, the rules of civilized behavior, that is, rules of good manners, courtesy, and decorum. In many passages, Hume couples benevolence and justice together as "the social virtues"; indeed, what he generally has in mind as functioning groups are, first, people combined in families, friendships, and so on; and, second, people combined in particular civil societies, for example, France, Britain. The rules of good manners apply within natural groups and civil societies alike. Rank is important in civil societies.

Although only the duties of the natural relationships and of civil society entail full moral obligation, social rank is sustained by something like natural moral obligation, while good manners involve something like artificial moral obligation. Yet Hume would not expect us to call a someone virtuous merely because he is polite in conversation and meetly deferential to noble lords. My chief concern in this chapter is with the second and third strata, the economic and political strata. When it seems advisable for the sake of clarity, I shall refer to society at the second-stratum level as "economic society" or as "the economy." I shall follow Hume's practice in using "civil society"—sometimes he writes "political society"—to refer to the economic stratum supplemented by the government stratum. At the end of the chapter, we will come to social rank and good manners. We should bear in mind that although Hume refers to these five varieties of society, he does so in some cases only incidentally while discussing other matters: in the *Treatise*, for example, he deals with the natural relationships, with civil society, and with polite society to show that the rules and standards of approved conduct are based on what from an impartial standpoint is found to be good for human beings. Besides, we must remember that one person may have several hats: he may love his brother, yet treat him equally with others in the market, and although he may shudder at the thought of buying dear and selling cheap, away from the market he may give his hard-won money liberally to those in need.

What Hume tells us about civil society in the *Treatise* is to be found in his discussion of two virtues, justice and allegiance. Since justice is a negative virtue, requiring only that we refrain from wrongs, and not that we do good works for others, he does not give us a direct description of economic society; instead, what we find in the *Treatise* is chiefly a statement of what men must not do if there is to be an economy. However, by analyzing what the rules of justice prohibit, we can put together a fairly complete idea of economic society. Then we can consider why Hume thinks that an economic society requires the support of a government.

When he looks beyond those for whom we do good deeds because we love them, Hume finds that relations among people are primarily economic. Human beings have great economic requirements, and each alone is incapable of satisfying his own needs. Moreover, although the natural relationships, especially the family, entail some economic support and assistance for their members, especially the young and the old, the prime purpose of those relationships is not the efficient production and distribution of economic goods. What is needed is a strictly economic relationship: a production system based on a division of labor, with an extensive market on the distribution side. By participating in such a system, people can combine their strength; they can gain the advantages of a division of labor; and they can escape from the insecurity of economic independence. This new relationship, a cooperative production system coupled with a market, is economic society. As producers and traders of goods and services, people are completely indifferent to each other; they neither love nor hate one another. They participate in the economy as interested people, not because they are gregarious, and not as people of good will, but because the economy is the most efficient means by which to achieve a secure, copious supply of goods and services.

The rules of economic society are moral rules; they have moral status because of the very great importance of economic society.

> 'Tis by society alone he [man] is able to supply his defects, and raise himself up to an equality with his fellow-creatures, and even acquire a superiority above them. By society all his infirmities are compensated; and tho' in that situation his wants multiply every moment upon him, yet his abilities are still more augmented, and leave him in every respect more satisfied and happy, than 'tis possible for him, in his savage and solitary condition, ever to become. When every individual person labours a-part, and only for himself, his force is too small to execute any considerable work; his labour being employ'd in supplying all his different necessities, he never attains a perfection in any particular art; and as his force and success are not at all times equal, the least failure in either of these particulars must be attended with inevitable ruin and misery. Society provides a remedy for these *three* inconveniences. By the conjunction of forces, our power is augmented: By the partition of employments, our ability encreases: And by mutual succour we are less expos'd to fortune and accidents. 'Tis by this additional *force, ability*, and *security*, that society becomes advantageous. (*T.*, 485)

There is one great obstacle to the establishment of economic society, namely, the strife that inevitably results when there is a strong demand for goods, but only a limited supply. The game cannot be played unless there is peace among the players. The goods in question are not the goods of the mind or the goods of the body, but external goods, that is, "such possessions as we have acquir'd by our industry and good fortune" (*T.*, 487). The goods of the mind cannot be carried away, and the goods of the body cannot be transferred from one person to another; these goods, therefore, are not disruptive in an economy. "The last only [external goods] are both expos'd to the violence of others, and may be transferr'd without suffering any loss or alteration; while at the same time, there is not a sufficient quantity of them to supply every one's desires and necessities. As the improvement, therefore, of these goods is the chief advantage of society, so the *instability* of their possession, along with their *scarcity*, is the chief impediment" (T., 487–88).

There must be a *primary* motive behind acts before, as a result of evaluation "on the general survey," there can be a moral motive. Is benevolence the primary motive that overcomes the problem of instability of possessions? No. Clearly, public (general) benevolence is not available as the primary motive, for, as we already have seen, "there is no such passion in human minds, as the love of mankind, merely as such." Nor is private (particular) benevolence the answer: it extends only to those we love or pity. It is true that as a result of sympathetic perception, not love, we are not indifferent to the happiness or misery of strangers, but this will move us to do good works for them only when their plight has been brought home to us, chiefly by proximity (T., 481). Indeed, far from being a motive that might sustain an economic society, private benevolence is somewhat antisocial. Hume has no patience with the notion that human beings are moved only by narrow selfishness; in fact, says he, most men tend to spend themselves and their goods readily for those dear to them, especially their wives and children. But this partiality to a few would destroy society, not sustain it: "Benevolence to strangers is too weak for this purpose [of sustaining society]; and as to the other passions, they rather inflame this avidity [for economic goods], when we observe, that the larger our possessions are, the more ability we have of gratifying all our appetites" (T., 492). In another place, he makes the same point in the following way: "But tho' this generosity [to wives, children, friends, and the like] must be acknowledg'd to the honour of human nature, we may at the same time remark, that so noble an affection, instead of fitting men for large societies, is almost as contrary to them, as the most narrow selfishness. For while each person loves himself better than any other single person, and in his love to others bears the greatest affection to his relations and acquaintance, this must necessarily produce an opposition of passions, and a consequent opposition of actions" (T., 487). How, then, can people acquire the benefits of economic society? Hume's answer is, by bringing in, by instituting, rules of private property. They must stop behaving naturally with regard to external goods. They need not, cannot, extirpate their avidity for such goods, but by setting limits on their conduct, they can lay the foundation of an economic system. They can check avidity for short-term gain by a system designed to produce far greater long-term gain. Avidity, "the interested affection," must be channeled, harnessed, made more productive by appropriate rules.

To make all external goods abundantly plentiful would be one way to prevent conflict; if that could be done, justice would be unnecessary; that, however, is only a poetic fancy. Therefore, the only solution, human nature remaining unchanged, is to stabilize possession. This is done by establishing rights, that is, by demarcating ways of possessing and using goods, ways upon which others may not trespass. Hume defines property, not as items of external goods, but as the rights to goods a person has vis-à-vis other persons. Property is a specific kind of relation of intelligent and rational beings to external goods (*T.*, 527). It may be defined as "*such a relation betwixt a person and an object as permits him, but forbids any other, the free use and possession of it, without violating the laws of justice and moral equity*" (*T.*, 310). Because it is difficult to think of property as rights to goods rather than as the goods themselves, when we transfer the rights to buildings or fields, which, unlike apples or clocks, cannot simply be handed over, we often perform a symbolic deliverance, transferring a key or a handful of earth, to help our imaginations follow the transaction. The key, the earth, stands for the transferred right or title.

If there is to be a stable society, there must never be loose or unappropriated economic goods; such goods would precipitate conflict. There must be a set of rules applicable to all, "universal and perfectly inflexible" rules, by which to identify the rightful owner of every economically valuable thing. Inevitably, there will be disputes over the application of these rules, but there must never be occasion for a substantive debate, a debate about whether it would be good to transfer ownership because of need, suitability, or virtue; every claim of need, suitability, or virtue would look different from each player's own viewpoint.

> 'Twere better, no doubt, that every one were possess'd of what is most suitable to him, and proper for his use: But besides, that this relation of fitness may be common to several at once, 'tis liable to so many controversies, and men are so partial and passionate in judging of these controversies, that such a loose and uncertain rule wou'd be absolutely incompatible with the peace of human society. The convention concerning the stability of possession is enter'd into, in order to cut off all occasions of discord and contention; and this end wou'd never be attain'd, were we allow'd to apply this rule differently in every particular case, according to every particular utility, which might be discover'd in such an application. Justice, in her decisions, never regards the fitness or unfitness of objects to particular persons. (*T.*, 502)

In short, there must be a rule of laws (defining what is right), not of men (debating the good). These laws must direct the original allotment of goods, and thereafter appoint the rightful possessor of every economic good within the bounds of the society.

The basic reason for the acceptance of a set of property rules is that property is useful, indeed indispensible, if the members of a society are to be prosperous. Once a property system has been introduced, industrious people can bring about distribution and redistribution by industry and trade. To attempt an administered distribution of goods and services—

based on particular utility, need, or merit, or on equality—would be to revert to a rule of men, with all the dangers of conflict and violence such a regime would entail.

How then are particular fields, orchards, cows, scritoires, and so on, to be allotted among potential owners? In the *Treatise*, Hume sets forth five general rules. These were the standard rules accepted by traditional jurisprudence. Here Hume is not trying to be inventive; rather, he is trying to explain the ordinary, to reveal the causes behind what usually happens. These rules, he contends, seem "natural," thus they make for the unchallenged acceptance of the allotment. They arise from human nature; they conform to the way the human imagination associates ideas. Moreover, at least some of them have the added advantage of being immediately useful—for example, parents will work harder if their estates are to pass to their children—but this subordinate utility must not be confused with the primary utility of the stable possession of all economic goods. Three of the rules relate to an original person and *an old good*, for example, a cow, an apple tree, a field by a river. The first of these three rules is present possession. This operates only when the very first appropriation of goods is made. Thereafter the other principles always override present possession; otherwise, mere *de facto* possession would confer title, and successful thieves would be respectable property owners. The other rules are as follows: first possession (discovery) when relevant; otherwise, long possession. When *a new good* appears by reproduction, growth, or alluviation, it goes by accession to the owner of the parent, the owner of the field or tree, or the owner of the adjacent land. The fourth principle, then, is accession. Fifth, when goods are to be assigned after the death of a former owner, the rule is that they go to his children. This last principle, succession—inheritance by law, not by testament—carries ownership within a family from one generation to another. One result of this, we may note, is that if the rank structure is based on wealth—as Hume says it often is—it will be perpetuated from one generation to another unless the family's wealth is lost or superior new wealth arises. Private property and inheritance, Hume finds, go a very long way to shape the social order. He explains the right of inheritance as follows:

> The right of *succession* is a very natural one, from the presum'd consent of the parent or near relation, and from the general interest of mankind, which requires, that men's possessions shou'd pass to those, who are dearest to them, in order to render them more industrious and frugal. Perhaps these causes are seconded by the influence of *relation*, or the association of ideas, by which we are naturally directed to consider the son after the parent's decease, and ascribe to him a title to his father's possessions. Those goods must become the property of some body: But *of whom* is the question. Here 'tis

evident the persons children naturally present themselves to the mind; and being already connected to those possessions by means of their deceas'd parent, we are apt to connect them still farther by the relation of property. (*T.*, 510–13)

As mentioned, in the *Treatise* the five rules result primarily from the normal operation of the human imagination. At least one of them, succession, is highly useful immediately, but that is a retrospective judgment: primitive human beings did not deliberately select and adopt these particular rules because they are the most useful; they did not select these because they saw them as more efficient than other rules as means by which to bring about prosperity. Rather, they followed them because they seemed "natural." In the *Treatise*, Hume is exploring and expounding his novel theory of how we think, his theory of how ideas run together in the imagination. Here is a person and his tree; the tree is laden with apples; we think of the tree as the main cause of the apples; consequently, we think of the person (who has the right to the tree) as having the right to the apples. Later, when expounding the five rules in *Enquiry* II, Hume plays down the association-of-ideas explanation and shifts his emphasis to utility: each of the rules is good and is adopted because it is useful.

These are only the basic rules: if they are to be effective in any complex society, they must be made far more specific by statutes and precedents. So necessary is a rule of law, to prevent disputes, that if in particular cases no applicable law or precedent can be found, we are quite ready to let judges pretend that they are revealing relevant law when in fact they are simply making it up.[1]

Private property in goods is the first, the basic, and the greatest requirement if we are to live in economic society; however, it alone is not sufficient. Justice encompasses two other principles, both permitting transfers of goods *inter vivos* consistent with private property. The second requirement is that economic goods are to be transferred only after the former owner has conveyed his rights to the person who is to receive the goods. This may take place by gift, but in economic society it takes the form of an exchange in which one good (perhaps money) is traded for another. This is the basic principle of a market: one good is exchanged for another because of economic reasons, and not because of any form of social or political pressure. Since different people and different parts of the earth produce different goods, it can be said that the trading of goods is based on "a law of nature" (*T.*, 514). The third principle is that contracts, by which transfers of goods and services outside barter are made possible, are to be kept meticulously.

The basic characteristics of a member of economic society are that he

---

[1] *Treatise*, p. 531; *Enquiry* II, p. 308.

is not a thief, that he trades when it is advantageous to do so, and that he does not break his promises. He is just and honest. When Hume is discussing noneconomic relationships, he is prepared to use the word "justice" with the common, wider definition, but that is of little importance to us now. What is relevant is that here he is describing a far-flung relationship, a relationship extending far beyond the reach of private benevolence, in which all scarce goods—crown lands and the like aside—are held as private property. On the production side, there is an intensive division of labor; on the distribution side, owners exchange goods at market value either by swapping them or by contract. Hume is fully aware that other virtues—industriousness, perseverance, frugality, and various abilities of mind and body—are highly desirable if a society is to prosper; these relate, however, only to how well the players will play; they are not prescribed by the rules of the game.

A society served by a government is a civil society. The domestic *raison d'être* of government, its function within its borders, is to make laws based on the principles of justice, laws carrying the principles down to particular situations; to establish law courts to apply these civil laws in cases where litigants are uncertain about either the law or the facts; and to maintain private property and contracts by penalties. Initially the three principles are rules of reason, not of demonstrative reasoning, but of that process, reasoning, by which we form beliefs about the real world. They are not categorical rules comparable to the commands of a king. Initially they are hypothetical imperatives: they inform us how we can live in society, thus gaining the economic benefits of an extensive system of production. However, because they are highly beneficial to humankind they are approved by spectators, who always approve what is seen as beneficial for human beings. Consequently, they become moral rules; we feel a moral obligation to act in conformity with them.

Justice is not the motive that moves us to work industriously and to bargain keenly. The dynamic of this kind of society, the force that drives it, is the desire for economic goods and the esteem attracted by conspicuous wealth. However, justice is required if that dynamic is to be productive, not destructive.

Hume's second principle of justice—that we are to take goods from others only when we acquire also the title to those goods—is more important than one might think at first glance. What the principle presupposes is that we ought to engage in trade when to do so is mutually advantageous. As we have noticed, Hume states this emphatically: the trading of goods is based on "a law of nature." The clear implication, as we shall see in chapter 6, is that laws and policies preventing or restricting mutually advantageous trade between nations are "unjust," or "vicious," or "violent."

The Progress of Civil Society

Economic society is an ongoing game. How and why do we come, both when the game first started and nowadays, to respect private property and contracts? Hume, unlike John Locke, does not begin with preestablished rights of any kind. For him rights exist only in society, and the origin of rights has to be explained as a function of human nature and natural circumstances; they cannot be taken as ordained by supernatural authority. Moreover, again unlike Locke, he does not begin with the sanctity of promises already established; this means that he cannot say that we ought to respect private property, or to obey our government, because we have promised to do so. Where Locke began with the fundamentals of morality already in place, Hume's primary undertaking is to explain the origin of morality; accordingly, he must show us a primary motive for respecting private property and contracts, a primary motive that gives rise to the moral obligation to be just. We know already that the primary motive has to do, not with human nature alone, but with human beings in the economic circumstances of their times. Hume's basic argument is that we can produce the goods we need or want only in an economy, and that the institutions of private property, the market, and contract are prerequisites of an economy; thus we see that, quite distinct from moral obligation, there is a primary motive, an interested motive, for respecting these institutions.

One very important implication of the fact that justice is a negative virtue—restricting natural avidity—is that civil society has a history. The three principles of justice are not arbitrary; when Hume refers to justice as an artificial virtue, he does not mean that the content of the rules of justice is indefinite; rather, he means that, like Aristotle's polis, which although "natural" has to be established, the rules have to be realized, brought into operation, by human beings. It is only as humans collectively, as groups, come to behave justly and obediently that civil society comes into existence. There are five distinct steps beyond the family, the basic natural group, to civil society: preconvention; convention; society based on the primary motive alone; society with justice established as a moral duty; finally, civil society. Hume thought of civil society as having developed historically, but he did not believe that the logical sequence was followed exactly, that is, that the progress of civilization followed exactly the logical order in each distinct society. First, for him the family is a natural or nonhistorical relationship; it is a constant; it always underlies the development, the progress, of society. Generation after generation, every child, to become civilized, must undergo the process of moral formation up to the level of his times. Second, there is no reason why one stage must be completed before the next can be started; for example, although the maintenance of justice is the primary task of governments, this does not mean that people must have achieved the full realization of justice before the first rudiments of government appeared. However, Hume uses the logical stages in analyzing and explaining history, that is, what actually happened. Many kinds of causes had their influence, but the main plot is the development called "civilization." What he gives us in the *Treatise* is a brief natural history of civil society, a kind of conjectural account of civilization.

This genre, conjectural history, was used extensively in the eighteenth century to provide natural explanations—replacing theological explanations—of specific institutions, practices, and cultural phenomena, for example, language, literary forms, the state, society, natural religion, morals. The writer of conjectural history writing about, for example, "the modern state" deals with the archetypical or authentic modern state as he conceives it, and not with one or more actual states. Instead of describing a fully-developed state, he explains it by tracing its most probable progress from its simplest stage to its fullest development. He is not interested in the details of what happened in this country or that, but in basic causes, why the modern state came to be as it is. This method, the genetic method, makes demands, not on the writer's skill as a researcher, but on his analytic powers. He has to start with sufficient resources in his envelope—in Hume's case, for example, sympathetic perception is an essential resource—to carry him through to the final stage of the development; he has to be able to advance from stage to stage in a creditable way, that is, by adducing creditable causes. A conjectural history may explain a "rise," an advance; it may go on to tell of a decline and fall, as in the case of excessively great empires; it may tell of ebbs and flows—the term "progress" being used to describe declines as well as advances.[2] A conjectural history is likely to reveal what the author thinks is most important; for example, when Hume says that the first task of government is to maintain justice, he means that this is the most important task, not that it must have come first chronologically. Let us now review his conjectural account of the rise of civil society.

The family prepares the young for society. In the family, which originates in and is sustained by natural affection, they are taught by their

[2] R. L. Emerson, "Conjectural History and Scottish Philosophers," in *Historical Papers/ Communications historiques, 1984* (Ottawa: The Canadian Historical Association), pp. 63–90. Emerson contends that it is a mistake to see the Scottish conjectural historians, including Hume, as expressing "a nascent economic determinism." Moreover, he cautions (p. 65n) against equating "progress" with improvement: "Development and progress were used synonymously by eighteenth century Scots for whom progress did not usually imply a necessarily better state but only a change."

parents, and learn from experience, that they cannot live entirely "self-ishly," that they cannot say and do exactly as they please. From their parents, who have both strength and parental authority on their side, and from experience, which shows them repeatedly that narrow egocentricity entails painful results, they learn that if they are to get along with their fellows, they must adopt another approach, that is, learn their places and perform the duties of their places with some objectivity. Their parents allot beds, garments, and toys to each of them as his own, and subsequently enforce the rights of private property within the family. To a great extent, the children cease to behave as (unequal) particular children and begin to act as (equal) individuals, that is, as members of an artificial relationship, a society of persons. They learn the basic idea of society, namely, that as members of society, as individuals, they can claim no more for themselves than their places entail, and this regardless of how precious and wonderful they find themselves. As the children multiply in number and develop in personality, the family undergoes a partial metamorphosis; to some extent it becomes a small society, a hybrid form, what Hume at one point calls a "family-society" (E., 190). In the *Treatise*, he describes what happens as follows:

> Now as 'tis by establishing the rule for the stability of possession, that this passion [of self-interest] restrains itself; if that rule be very abstruse, and of difficult invention; society must be esteem'd, in a manner, accidental, and the effect of many ages. But if it be found, that nothing can be more simple and obvious than that rule; that every parent, in order to preserve peace among his children, must establish it; and that these first rudiments of justice must every day be improv'd, as the society enlarges: If all this appears evident, as it certainly must, we may conclude, that 'tis utterly impossible for men to remain any considerable time in that savage condition, which precedes society; but that his very first state and situation may justly be esteem'd social. (T., 492–93)

Hume then remarks that he has no objection to writers using the device of a presocial state of nature, provided they announce that it is an abstraction, a fiction, employed to show the results of allowing one aspect of human nature, the violent passions, to run free, unrestrained by reason. Since for Hume growing up in a family is a process of socialization, the only stage to which the label "state of nature" could be applied is that of the very young child, the child in the utterly particularistic stage. Early in life, children come, in the family, to value company and cooperation; they are introduced to private property; they begin to think and act as individuals; and they experience the beneficial influence of authority. They are formed as *persons* by instruction, experience, and habit.

We come next to Hume's explanation of how people came to participate in economic society. In his philosophical history, there is a precon-vention stage. At that stage, humans confront others who have desirable external goods, but who are not moved by benevolence to turn them over, and who are ready to seize the goods they themselves want. Natural af-fection no longer provides the basis of their relations with the others around them. In the family, as we have seen, each has learned the value of peace and cooperation. In addition, each has learned that private prop-erty is a basic prerequisite for peace and cooperation. They now wish to have private property respected generally, but initially they do not be-lieve, at least not strongly, that all the others, the strangers, are of the same mind. Hume speaks of a long period during which the need for jus-tice was driven home to all by experience, a period during which mutual confidence gradually grew and spread (T., 490). Increasingly, those who acted justly in the hope that others would do the same were not disap-pointed.

At some moment, whenever the belief that the others—either singly or as tribes or clans—are not going to seize one's possessions has set in suf-ficiently, we may say that a new relationship, society, has started. This shared belief or convention is not the result of a promise or anything like a promise, for at this period there is no preestablished basis for feeling confident that a promise will be kept; rather it is the result of prolonged experience. No longer is *de facto* possession what counts; people are now prepared to heed certain prior claims to external goods; in short, private property has been instituted, and increasingly the five rules for allotting particular goods to particular persons become effective. Afterwards, as each generation emerges from the family, it passes directly into a society based on justice. Hume gives two accounts of the origin of the social con-vention.

> I observe, that it will be for my interest to leave another in the possession of his goods, *provided* he will act in the same manner with regard to me. He is sensible of a like interest in the regulation of his conduct. When this common sense of interest is mutually express'd, and is known to both, it produces a suitable resolution and behaviour. And this may properly enough be call'd a convention or agreement betwixt us, tho' without the interposition of a promise; since the actions of each of us have a reference to those of the other, and are perform'd upon the supposition, that something is to be perform'd on the other part. Two men, who pull the oars of a boat, do it by an agree-ment or convention, tho' they have never given promises to each other. Nor is the rule concerning the stability of possession the less deriv'd from human conventions, that it arises gradually, and acquires force by a slow progres-sion, and by our repeated experience of the inconveniences of trangressing it. (T., 490)

The second account follows his assertion that, although single acts of justice may have bad effects, the private property system as a whole is beneficial.

> When therefore men have had experience enough to observe, that whatever may be the consequence of any single act of justice, perform'd by a single person, yet the whole system of actions, concurr'd in by the whole society, is infinitely advantageous to the whole, and to every part; it is not long before justice and property take place. Every member of society is sensible of this interest: Every one expresses this sense to his fellows, along with the resolution he has taken of squaring his actions by it, on condition that others will do the same. No more is requisite to induce any one of them to perform an act of justice, who has the first opportunity. This becomes an example to others. And thus justice establishes itself by a kind of convention or agreement; that is, by a sense of interest, suppos'd to be common to all, and where every single act is perform'd in expectation that others are to perform the like. (*T.*, 497–98)

What brings the property rules into operation is neither a promise nor any other kind of formal commitment; rather, it is each person's belief that the others, or at least almost all of them, see how useful it is to respect private property.[3] Private property is an institution; it becomes operative because of belief—each person's belief that the others also believe that private property is useful. Private property rests on shared belief, on public opinion.

Since rights to economic goods result from a belief common within a society, it follows that such rights are possible only in a social situation; this is one reason why Hume rejects Locke's theory. For Locke someone living alone on an island has a right to his labor, and so to such goods as he has acquired by his labor. For Hume, since rights influence how people behave in relation to others, rights arise only through and from interaction.

Closely tied to the convention that makes possessions stable is a second convention, that is, that contracts (promises) are inviolable. The members of economic society are not moved by benevolence to help each other; this means that goods can be acquired from others only for "reciprocal

---

[3] Jonathan Harrison argues that a commitment can be given by a course of action even though no promise is spoken, and therefore that Hume's argument that the origin of property is not based on a promise but is analogous to the cooperation of two persons rowing a boat is defective. We must remember, however, that Hume was seeking to convince his readers of two points—that there is a primary motive behind the moral motive, and that the idea that only a government based on a contract has moral authority is misleading—neither of which is damaged by Harrison's argument. See Jonathan Harrison, *Hume's Theory of Justice* (Oxford: Clarendon Press, 1981), pp. 57–59.

advantage." This gives us trade, but only in the form of barter; therefore, just as they were led to institute private property, people are led by experience to discover the contract. They put the idea of contract into practice, not because some philosopher demonstrated to them the theory and merit of contract, but because in specific instances the advantages of contracts were obvious. Practice preceded theoretical understanding. The contract is an institution of the market, a forum where self-interested people meet to buy and sell goods and services; it is not an institution of the family, the friendship, and the like. Hume makes this point as follows:

> But tho' this self-interested commerce of men begins to take place, and to predominate in society, it does not entirely abolish the more generous and noble intercourse of friendship and good offices. I may still do services to such persons as I love, and am more particularly acquainted with, without any prospect of advantage; and they may make me a return in the same manner, without any view but that of recompensing my past services. In order, therefore, to distinguish those two different sorts of commerce, the interested and the disinterested, there is a *certain form of words* invented for the former, by which we bind ourselves to the performance of any action. This form of words constitutes what we call a *promise*, which is the sanction of the interested commerce of mankind. When a man says *he promises any thing*, he in effect expresses a *resolution* of performing it; and along with that, by making use of this *form of words*, subjects himself to the penalty of never being trusted again in case of failure. (*T.*, 521–52)

In short, the promise, like property, is a social institution. A person alone on an island cannot make a contract, a promise. Promising is not an act of a mind in isolation; there has to be another person who by the words, "I promise," is led to expect performance. That the promise is social is shown by the fact that if someone utters the words, "I promise," intending to be taken seriously by another person, but with no intention to keep his promise, he is as fully committed as if he had intended to keep it. By using words with a certain public meaning, he has put himself under obligation to the other person. Both an intentional act by the promiser and legitimate expectation by the other person are required. In this case, the deceitful person intended to cause the other person's legitimate expectation.

Whether or not the promise as an institution is in effect depends on the state of public opinion: if people have come to believe that the usefulness of promises is known adequately by the others, they will rely on promises. The growth of this shared belief, this convention, is the result of (a) insight into the usefulness of promises, and (b) adequate experience with those with whom one is dealing. Hume comments that "the shortest experience of society," or "but a very little practice of the world," suffices to show people the value, the usefulness, of the general rule that a promise is to be kept regardless of the consequences in particular instances.

Now, with private property, trade, and contract introduced, the game can be played at an advanced level. The motive that led people to begin respecting private property and contract is enlightened self-interest. In the logical sequence, this is the only motive supporting those institutions immediately after the conventions have set in. The next step in the development is that private property and contracts come to be reinforced by moral obligation. (Historically, the advance undoubtedly was far more ragged; for example, theft probably became morally wrong within a tribe before much was known about contracts, and within a tribe contracts probably became morally binding while those successful in robbing strangers were still regarded as heroes.) The moral judgment that theft and breach of contract are evil is made as a result of unjust acts; if everyone always acted justly, there never would have been an occasion for disapprobation by spectators. Here we come to the question raised earlier. Does Hume think that there was a historical period, after the justice conventions and before their first violation, when justice prevailed perfectly, or does he think that there never was such a historical period? My submission that he is writing conjectural history implies that for him there never was such a historical period. It is because he is arguing that there must be a primary motive before there can be a moral motive that such a stage is needed in his logical account. The passage in which he describes how moral obligation arises is worth careful examination.

After men have found by experience, that their selfishness and confin'd generosity, acting at their liberty, totally incapacitate them for society; and at the same time have observ'd, that society is necessary to the satisfaction of those very passions, they are naturally induc'd to lay themselves under the restraint of such rules, as may render their commerce more safe and commodious. To the imposition then, and observance of these rules, both in general, and in every particular instance, they are at first mov'd only by a regard to interest; and this motive, on the first formation of society, is sufficiently strong and forcible. But when society has become numerous, and has encreas'd to a tribe or nation, this interest is more remote; nor do men so readily perceive, that disorder and confusion follow upon every breach of these rules, as in a more narrow and contracted society. But tho' in our own actions we may frequently lose sight of that interest, which we have in maintaining order, and may follow a lesser and more present interest, we never fail to observe the prejudice we receive, either mediately or immediately, from the injustice of others; as not being in that case either blinded by passion, or byass'd by any contrary temptation. Nay when the injustice is so distant from us, as no way to affect our interest, it still displeases us; because we consider it as prejudicial to human society, and pernicious to every one that approaches the person guilty of it. We partake of their uneasiness by *sympathy*; and as every thing, which gives uneasiness in human actions, upon the general survey, is call'd Vice, and whatever produces satisfaction, in the same manner, is denominated Virtue; this is the reason why the sense of moral good and evil follows upon justice and injustice. . . . *Thus self-interest is the original motive to the* establishment *of justice: but a* sympathy *with public interest is the source of the* moral approbation, *which attends that virtue.* (T., 498–500)

Here we have the idea of a stage, before "society had become numerous," when everybody was just because of self-interest alone. Then, after a time, when the society has grown large, people are no longer confident that a perfect respect for justice on their part serves their own ends. At that point, something like the Fall occurs; thereafter unjust acts, wrongs, are sometimes committed; this leads to the moral disapprobation of theft and breach of contract. Such acts are found morally bad, evil, because they are contrary to the welfare of humankind. Thereafter wrongs are censured as morally wrong.

Once it has been learned that unjust conduct is found evil when viewed impartially, the family takes up the task of teaching the young, generation after generation, the *moral* duty to respect private property and to keep promises.[4] So influential is this education, supplemented by the exhortations of moralists and politicians, that in a civilized state the primary motive for just conduct is entirely submerged and hidden by morality, with the result that philosophers who ask why justice is a virtue are likely to be regarded as idle, perhaps subversive. Clearly, once justice has become a moral virtue, few young men and women, if any, will have to be shown that justice is good (useful); rather, they will grow up in a community with common moral values, in "a society," and be equipped for participation in that society by their belief that just conduct is morally right.

The principles of justice are not the results of either the artifice of skillful politicians or accidental accretion. Hume refers to the principles of justice as artificial, because there is no natural instinct that causes short-sighted people to respect private property, and so forth, and because the principles are *discovered* by the understanding and put into effect by convention, habituation, education, and the like. But that does not mean that the content of artificial virtue is arbitrary. The content of justice is not merely a matter of custom or fiat like the rules concerning hats in church and driving on the left or right side of the road. The principles of justice are "obvious and necessary." To dispel any notion that his term "artificial virtues" implies arbitrariness, Hume in the *Treatise* adopts the expres-

[4] *Treatise*, pp. 500, 523.

sion, "laws of nature." He states emphatically, "Tho' the rules of justice be *artificial*, they are not *arbitrary*. Nor is the expression improper to call them *Laws of Nature*; if by natural we understand what is common to any species, or even if we confine it to mean what is inseparable from the species" (*T.*, 484). In another place he says, "The interest, on which justice is founded, is the greatest imaginable, and extends to all times and places. It cannot possibly be serv'd by any other invention. It is obvious, and discovers itself on the very first formation of society. All these causes render the rules of justice stedfast and immutable; at least, as immutable as human nature" (*T.*, 620). Again, when we descend to the next level, to the basic rules for the assignment of titles to economic goods, we find that these rules, too, are not arbitrary; rather, they are the rules because they conform to the operation of the human imagination, and, what is highly reassuring, of all possible rules they are the ones most useful to humankind. There is nothing arbitrary, merely customary, about the sanctity of private property, the trading of goods, and the obligation of contracts. These institutions are essential to genuine society.

A civil society is much the same as an economic society except that there is a government to make more certain the observance of justice. Hume, unlike Hobbes, thought that in fact there can be societies without governments. Where goods are few and simple, as in primitive America, self-interest and moral obligation are sufficient to maintain justice. Indeed, Hume traces the first rudiments of government, not to eruptions of injustice, but to war. While self-interest and morality suffice to maintain justice in simple societies, there is nothing except the fear of violent death to prevent strife between different societies. Government was first introduced to organize and conduct resistance to invaders. It was in coping with this kind of desperate emergency that people first selected political leaders. Afterwards, they began to use this new institution, government, to administer and enforce justice.

In showing the need for government in a large, rich society, Hume uses the same explanation he gave for the unjust acts that brought on moral judgment. When we put objects at a distance from ourselves, when we consider them abstractly, we see them in something like their proper proportions, and "give the preference to whatever is in itself preferable" (*T.*, 536). But in practice, we are under the infirmity of preferring present small goods to greater goods far off (*T.*, 428). Generally we can follow a short means-ends chain; however, when the chain is long and complex, it is almost certain that, failing to see the great value of the end, we will refuse to employ the necessary means. The price to be paid now for goods to be gained some time in the future looks too high. But the truth is that the supply of goods and services to be obtained through economic society is always worth the foregoing of any number of unjust acts. In other words, justice is good as a means for every individual in the long run. However, in a large, rich society we often cannot see that far; enthralled by the goods presently at hand, we break the rules. Nor does our feeling of moral obligation suffice to keep us from committing wrongs in such a situation.

The remedy is a government, a person (or a group of persons) placed outside the game to compel the participants to respect private property and contracts. Governors, like the rest of us, suffer from the infirmity of self-centered perception, but because they have been placed beyond the game, they have an interest in enforcing justice, which interest they will see and follow if they understand their role. A government fosters respect for justice by providing penalties sufficiently great to make the goods we would gain immediately by unjust acts appear smaller than the goods we will get in the long run through society. Hume explains the remedy as follows: "Men are not able radically to cure, either in themselves or others, that narrowness of soul, which makes them prefer the present to the remote. They cannot change their natures. All they can do is to change their situation, and render the observance of justice the immediate interest of some particular persons, and its violation their more remote. These persons, then, are not only induc'd to observe those rules in their own conduct, but also to constrain others to a like regularity, and inforce the dictates of equity thro' the whole society."[5]

It is the sentiment of disapprobation we feel when, as spectators, we see acts in violation of the general rule that the government is to be obeyed that gives rise to the *moral* obligation to obey and support the government. Says Hume, "But when men have observ'd, that tho' the rules of justice be sufficient to maintain any society, yet 'tis impossible for them, of themselves, to observe those rules, in large and polish'd societies; they establish government, as a new invention to attain their ends, and preserve the old, or procure new advantages, by a more strict execution of justice. So far, therefore, our *civil* duties are connected with our *natural*, that the former are invented chiefly for the sake of the latter; and that the principal object of government is to constrain men to observe the laws of nature" (T., 543). Unlike the natural duties related to property and contracts, the civil duty of obedience is "factitious": while society is possible without government, particular governments have to be constituted. Nevertheless, the duty of obedience is at least as compelling as the natural duties (*Essays*, 38–39).

The role of a government, to promote peace and prosperity by requiring respect for private property and contracts, entails considerably more

---

[5] Ibid., p. 537. For an even more enlightening statement of Hume's views, see *Essays*, pp. 38–39.

than may be noticed at first glance. All that we have so far is a set of general rules; these must be elaborated into a body of positive law suited as closely as possible to all the diverse situations and requirements of ownership and commerce; and penalties must be set to deter people from breaking the positive law, and thus the principles of justice. There must be law courts and enforcement officers. A government will provide public works to make trade easier and safer: canals, wharves, breakwaters, navigation aids. It will even intervene in the society to provide certain kinds of services—those related to religion, defence, and public finance, for example—that "though useful and even necessary in a state," cannot safely be left to private enterprise (*H.*, 3:135).

In the essay "Of the First Principles of Government" (1741), Hume undertakes to explain the basis of government power, or, to use his words, "the easiness with which the many are governed by the few." Government power, he contends, is conferred—not necessarily institutionally—by the governed; it rests ultimately on the opinion of the governed, at least on the opinion of the dominant part. Those who obey may do so because they believe the government operates in their *interest* as individuals, that is, the interest they share with all members of the public. "By opinion of interest, I chiefly understand the sense of the general advantage which is reaped from government; together with the persuasion, that the particular government, which is established, is equally advantageous with any other that could easily be settled. When this opinion prevails among the generality of a state, or among those who have the force in their hands, it gives great security to any government" (*Essays*, 33). Here we are down to bedrock. At a less fundamental level, the subjects may obey simply because they believe the particular governors have a *right* to rule, that is, a title somewhat comparable to property. Or, even less fundamental, they may obey because of the economic power of the governors— which is based on the governors' *right* to economic goods, in turn the result of opinion. Hume separates government power from economic power; economic power, emphasized strongly by James Harrington, is an important factor, but it is only one of three. Public-law rights are not simply a result of private-law rights.

There are three other causes of authority, but all these are derivative or dependent. First, particular persons or factions may obey and support a governor out of narrow *self-interest*, but self-interest ties people only to those already in office for some other reason, or who on other grounds have a good prospect of coming to power. Second, people may be compelled to obey by *violence*, but the power to coerce itself arises from opinion; if nobody believed that the "king" is king, he would be only one person and would lack the political power to coerce anybody. For example: "The soldan of EGYPT, or the emperor of ROME, might drive his harmless subjects, like brute beasts, against their sentiments and inclination: But he must, at least, have led his *mamalukes*, or *praetorian bands*, like men, by their opinion"(*Essays*, 32–33). Third, people may obey and support governors from *affection*, but the person or family who attracts affectionate support must already have been singled out by opinion, by opinion of right (title), for example.

Consistent with his emphasis on the need for wise laws, Hume saw the well-contrived republic as the best form of government. Worst of all are republics with bad constitutions, where power is lodged with one or two interest groups, for example, the grandees, thus permitting them to exploit and suppress all the others. Both forms of monarchy are fundamentally defective. An inherited monarchy has the merits that the king is accepted as legitimate and in a position to be "disinterested," but the suitability of the man made king is left largely to chance—Hume hammers home the great folly of relying on Providence to send good kings.[6] In an elective monarchy, the desirability of having a suitable person is recognized, but every election invites rival interests to battle for the throne (*Essays*, 18). A mixed government, such as that of Great Britain, has the advantage that all power is not lodged with one person or one body, but inevitably such a government is unstable. However, despite his firm belief in well-contrived republics, Hume's treatment of legitimacy relates mainly to opinion of right (title) and to kings. After all, monarchy was the prevailing form of government in contemporary Europe; a war had been fought over the Spanish Succession, and another had started in 1740 over the Austrian Succession; in Great Britain the conflict between the claims of the Stuarts and the Hanoverians was still a lively topic.

The fact that government is based on consent does not mean that the only legitimate rulers are those designated by contract. Hume is quite ready to allow that government contracts may have been made in some places. Society precedes government, and contracts are common in society; the members of a society might use that familiar instrument when constituting a government, naming the governor in the contract. But now

[6] When explaining that the distinction between arguments from reason and arguments from experience is often misleading, Hume uses the dangers of absolute monarchy as his example: "Thus, for instance, the limitations and restraints of civil government, and a legal constitution, may be defended, either from *reason*, which reflecting on the great frailty and corruption of human nature, teaches, that no man can safely be trusted with unlimited authority; or from *experience* and history, which inform us of the enormous abuses, that ambition, in every age and country, has been found to make of so imprudent a confidence." *Enquiry concerning Human Understanding*, p. 44n. On the unreliability of kings by succession see *Essays*, pp. 15, 46, 112, 527, 548–49, 614. For a radically different reading of Hume's rating of forms of government, one that attributes to Hume a preference for absolute hereditary monarchies, see Nicholas Phillipson, *Hume* (London: Weidenfeld & Nicolson, 1989), pp. 50, 59–60, 65.

we are far removed from any such situation. Few, if any, modern governments trace their titles to a contract; yet nobody regards them as illegitimate on that ground, except those Whigs who believe that original contract is the only alternative to the Tory doctrine of the divine right of kings. Since our moral obligation to allegiance arises from exactly the same source as our moral obligation to respect contracts—public interest—nothing is gained by basing allegiance on contract. At the same time, the doctrine of the divine right of kings is preposterous: it puts the means, obedience to government, above the end, the public interest.

Given the dangers inherent in trying to elect the best man as king, what principles should a wise person bear in mind when considering the claims of rival pretenders? Each of the points mentioned by Hume is worthy of consideration because it makes for peace. A legalistic approach is to be avoided: a ruler's title cannot be traced back link by link to some kind of original grant; the truth is that almost every dynasty had its origin, not in right, but in violence.[7] Long (and continued) possession is best; here present fact coincides with expectation. After long possession, present possession is most persuasive. "Any one, who finding the impossibility of accounting for the right of the present possessor, by any receiv'd system of ethics, shou'd resolve to deny absolutely that right, and assert, that it is not authoriz'd by morality, wou'd be justly thought to maintain a very extravagant paradox, and to shock the common sense and judgment of mankind" (*T.*, 558). Jacobites, *nota bene*. Next, nobody should refuse allegiance to the *de facto* ruler when a former ruler has been overthrown, for to do so would be simply to renew the strife. Nobody should refuse allegiance to a *de facto* ruler because he has come to power by conquest; indeed, a new government from conquest stands higher in the esteem of many people, by reason of the conqueror's achievement, than a new government from revolution (usurpation). When none of these considerations applies, nobody should refuse allegiance to a son of the late king. And where there are constitutional laws, such as primogeniture in England and the Salic Law in France, nobody should refuse to obey those designated by the laws. What the public interest requires is that there be a ruler to maintain justice; provided the ruler is performing his task, the rules of legitimacy are important only because, by preventing revolts and succession crises, they make for peace.[8]

[7] *Treatise*, p. 556; *Essays*, pp. 471, 473–74; *History of England*, 1:162. See especially *History of Great Britain* (Forbes ed.), p. 225n.

[8] After discussing Hume's five rules on title to political power, David Miller asks, "What part do considerations of interest or utility play in the adoption of these rules?" He contends that Hume's use of imaginative acceptability, rather than substantive considerations, as the proper ordinary basis of title rules is fundamentally conservative. David Miller, *Philosophy and Ideology in Hume's Political Thought* (Oxford: Clarendon Press, 1981), p. 89. I cannot

Obviously, the principles to be borne in mind when deciding whom to support as king are not comparable to the rules of private property. While the property rules distribute goods among *many*, in a monarchy the title rules designate the *one* who is to occupy the throne. Pretenders may base their claims on conflicting principles; in that case, might, not right, will determine the outcome (*T.*, 562). Present possession, which does not give title to a foot-stool, gives title to a throne in a monarchy. At the same time the tenure of a king who comes to a throne with an unblemished title is far more precarious than that of the property owner. Our civil duties are subordinate to our natural-law duties. Given the fact that there is only one king, his performance in his role is important to the whole society; if his performance is seriously defective, he may have to be dethroned.

This brings us to Hume's second criterion, performance. Although nothing requiring great genius or virtue is asked from rulers, it does not follow that kings can be counted on to perform well. They are only human; indeed, princes often are spoiled by having been brought up among courtiers. What distinguishes them is their position: they have been placed outside the game, beyond the combat of self-interested parties.

---

agree. The five rules relate to claims of *right* to power. By definition these rules do not relate directly to interest or utility; rather, they are founded on factual situations, for example, that the claimant is the first-born son of the dead king. Hume is asking what *de facto* situations cause the multitude to attribute the right to power to a claimant. He is discussing causes, not reasons. In the *History of England*, he emphasizes the value of long possession and primogeniture as rules in a monarchy; the more seriously these rules are taken by a nation, the more peaceful will be the succession. *History of England*, 1:407, 464, 486; 3:4–11.

A wise person knows that public interest is far too divisive to be used as the criterion in the selection of each new king. He knows, also, that the quality of a king's title, although often sadly unrelated to the quality of a king's subsequent performance, is relevant to a king's authority with the multitude. Consequently, he is prepared to rely on opinion of right and to hope that only one claimant will have a good claim under the rules. We may say, then, that one reason a wise person pays attention to title (opinion of right to power) is that the people tend to take title seriously. In 1688–1689, says Hume, the Lords and Commons deposed James II, and then, having launched themselves on a course of illegal action for the public good, took the wise step of passing over James's son, who, given the family religion, could not have been a satisfactory king. The multitude, having accepted the first step, were ready to accept the second. The Houses had acted prudently: "As the slightest properties of the imagination have an effect on the judgments of the people, it shews the wisdom of the laws and of the parliament to take advantage of such properties, and to chuse the magistrates either in or out of a line, according as the vulgar will most naturally attribute authority and right to them" (*T.*, 566). The vulgar are captivated by titles. But the wise, concerned with public interest and impatient with interminable disputes over the titles of claimants, are ready to accept any *de facto* ruler who provides good governance. This, according to Adam Smith, is the true Whig position: although the form of the British government may not be the best, as long (but only as long) as it provides reasonably acceptable government (the principle of interest or utility), it should be supported and obeyed. *Lectures on Jurisprudence* (Oxford: Clarendon Press, 1978), pp. 318–21, 402.

This, however, only increases the possibility of good government; it does not make it certain. The king may not see that the administration of justice is his cardinal duty. Misunderstanding his role, he may take up some cause—religious uniformity; a foreign policy based on ambition or jealousy; a domestic policy that can be advanced only by violence—and when he does this, he abdicates his role and may be resisted. "Our general knowledge of human nature, our observation of the past history of mankind, our experience of present times; all these causes must induce us to open the door to exceptions [to allegiance], and must make us conclude, that we may resist the more violent effects of supreme power, without any crime or injustice" (*T.*, 552).

When a government ceases to sustain, or becomes subversive of a viable economic society, opinion of interest, the primary motive of allegiance, is gone. In such a situation, the feeling of moral obligation to obey and support the government is likely to continue for some time; but, bad government continuing, gradually that feeling will melt away, leaving the government's constitutional right an empty shell. Obedience to the ruler(s) is constitutionally right; disobedience is constitutionally wrong. However, what is constitutionally right may cease to be good: the government may turn away from its primary task, the maintenance of justice and provision of security. Or a new constitution may become desirable because of (a) socioeconomic change or (b) a change in public opinion. At some point the old right will become obsolete, and a new right—a better government, perhaps even a better constitution—will be established. Hume counsels strongly against disobedience for trivial reasons; no government is perfect. His main concern is to discredit false claims to power, claims such as historic title, divine right, and preeminent merit. The rule that governors are to be obeyed is not unconditional; this the Tories should recognize. For their part, the Whigs should stop undermining allegiance by harping on the fact that bad rulers may be dismissed.

Individualism Basic to Morality

Toward the end of "Of Morals," where he is drawing together and exposing some of the implications of what has gone before, Hume makes two related points, namely, that moral appraisal is made from an impartial viewpoint, and that the moral rules and standards apply to ourselves and others equally. These points imply—indeed, they almost state—the distinction between a particular person and an individual. This distinction is fundamental to Hume's theory of civil society. He never draws our attention to it explicitly; probably an author who had written so subtly on identity, in "Of the Understanding," would have regarded such an old distinction as obvious. But he does use the terms frequently and with precision.

The problem of maintaining a Humean civil society is to get particular persons to act as individuals. We have seen how he introduces us to the distinction. A child is completely "self-ish," completely particular, in his outlook at birth: his judgments are self-centered. His present is the present, his good the good. However, very early he begins to learn that if he is to live safely in both the physical and the social world he must attain a more general perception of both reality and value. Gradually, he comes to bring an educated imagination to bear on both these worlds; he corrects his views, eliminating the distortions caused by egocentricity and proximity. As he grows older, his relations with his parents and with other children teach him to speak and to act more and more as an individual, as no more than an equal. The various roles, of course, differ from each other, but nobody's rights exceed his role; in that basic fact all are equal.

In essence, individualism is egalitarian. To say "each person" is to say "all persons." Claims made by an individual imply assent to equal claims by all other individuals. The more one assumes the status of an individual, the less one claims, as one's right, more economic goods, more attention, and more consideration than are given to each other individual similarly placed. The individual is a person among persons. One who succeeds in putting on the character of an individual speaks and acts as the equal of all.

The individual is a person of "reason." In explaining the origin of government, Hume tells us that when we view goods objectively, we always give preference to whatever is in itself preferable, and that, "This gives rise to what in an improper sense we call *reason*" (T., 536). When explaining that the moral viewpoint is never our own particular viewpoint, he tells us that we correct our sentiments, or at least our words. Our passions, however, seldom come to conform to the objective view.

> 'Tis seldom men heartily love what lies at a distance from them, and what no way redounds to their particular benefit; as 'tis no less rare to meet with persons, who can pardon another any opposition he makes to their interest, however justifiable that opposition may be by the general rules of morality. Here we are contented with saying, that reason requires such an impartial conduct, but that 'tis seldom we can bring ourselves to it, and that our passions do not readily follow the determination of our judgment. This language will be easily understood, if we consider what we formerly said concerning that *reason*, which is able to oppose our passion; and which we have found to be nothing but a general calm determination of the passions, founded on some distant view or reflexion.[9]

[9] *Treatise*, p. 583; see also *Enquiry* II, p. 239.

People learn to speak and, less often, to act as individuals, but they do not become individuals; the particular person puts on to some extent the character of an individual, he comes to act somewhat as an individual. Always there is a possibility, in some circumstances a probability, that he will forget his objectivity and slip back into particularity (*T.*, 348). We are caught in a continuing struggle between particularity and individuality, between our self-centered passions and "reason," between what is found good from a "self-ish" viewpoint and what is morally good.

Hume states that, economic goods being fairly but not desperately scarce, every rational person has a primary motive to follow the rules of justice. He is quite ready to admit that sometimes particular transactions, although just, will not be in the public interest, as when a "seditious bigot" inherits a vast estate. Similarly, he is quite ready to admit that single acts of justice, as when someone ruins himself and his family to honor a contract ill-advisedly made, will not be in that person's immediate interest. However, a society based on the principles of justice works advantageously for all its members.

> But however single acts of justice may be contrary, either to public or private interest, 'tis certain, that the whole plan or scheme is highly conducive, or indeed absolutely requisite, both to the support of society, and the well-being of every individual. 'Tis impossible to separate the good from the ill. Property must be stable, and must be fix'd by general rules. Tho' in one instance the public be a sufferer, this momentary ill is amply compensated by the steady prosecution of the rule, and by the peace and order, which it establishes in society. And even every individual person must find himself a gainer, on ballancing the account; since, without justice, society must immediately dissolve, and every one must fall into that savage and solitary condition, which is infinitely worse than the worst situation that can possibly be suppos'd in society (*T.*, 497).

Does Hume mean that justice is in the long-term interest of every individual or of every particular person? His response seems clear: those who speak and behave as particular persons simply cannot even converse, let alone live and work together; accordingly, there is a primary motive for most to follow the rules of justice, that is, to behave as individuals.

But let us test his assertion with the extraordinary person, as he himself does not test it in the *Treatise*. Here, let us say, is an old man who has made a disadvantageous contract. When Hume says that justice is in everyone's interest, does he mean that in the long run this old man will be economically better off if he keeps his contract, thereby apparently ruining himself? His future is short; long-run thinking means little to him.

Here is another member of society, a soldier ordered by a good government to undertake a mission from which he will not return. Does the first man have a primary motive to act justly? Does the second man have a primary motive to act obediently? Clearly, no, not from their viewpoints as particular men. Clearly, yes, from the objective viewpoint of individuals. Hume's position, I submit, is that, human nature remaining constant and the economic circumstances remaining about the same, both justice and obedience to a good government always are in the long-term interest of a person as an individual.[10]

But why, one may ask, does Hume not say explicitly, when discussing the convention stage of his philosophical history, that most people, but not all, have a primary motive to act justly? When he answers his own question about the effects of occasional unjust acts, he gives a Hobbesian answer: for the *individual*, the bad effects are better than a warring state of nature. In the *Treatise* he does not raise the question whether a particular person who believes that almost everybody else will be just has a primary motive to be just himself; he does not raise the problem of the free rider, the motorist who can cut in and out of traffic because everybody else obeys the law. Perhaps since he was writing about the archetypal civil society, he thought he had to deal only with the archetypal person, the individual.

In *Enquiry* II, Hume undertakes to show that, contrary to the monkish view that the life of virtue is bleak and austere, the virtuous person is the happy person (*E.*, 279). To prove his point, he examines the effects of each of the four kinds of virtues: those agreeable to self and to others; those useful to self and to others. Only when he comes to the fourth kind, those approved because they are useful to others, of which justice is prince, does Hume have to admit that he has some trouble with his thesis that virtue always is in the true interest of every person. Secret dishonesty, injustice, it may be alleged, is the best policy for a particular person, provided that almost all others are just. Hume's rebuttal, as we shall see, involves recourse from one's interest as an economic being to one's interest as a moral being.

Treating vice with the greatest candour, and making it all possible concessions, we must acknowledge that there is not, in any instance, the smallest pretext for giving it the preference above virtue, with a view to self-interest;

[10] David Gauthier has described Hume as a contractarian. He does not mean that Hume traces the obligation to be just and obedient to a contract; rather, he means that Hume holds that in ordinary circumstances the interests of each individual are advanced by property and obedience. Gauthier concludes, correctly I think, that Hume cannot be described as a utilitarian. The utilitarian bases his argument for conformity, not on the individual's own interest, but on the good of the whole society. David Gauthier, "David Hume, Contractarian," *The Philosophical Review*, 88 (1979): 3–38.

except, perhaps, in the case of justice, where a man, taking things in a certain light, may often seem to be a loser by his integrity. And though it is allowed that, without a regard to property, no society could subsist; yet according to the imperfect way in which human affairs are conducted, a sensible knave, in particular incidents, may think that an act of iniquity or infidelity will make a considerable addition to his fortune, without causing any considerable breach in the social union and confederacy. (E., 282)

Hume has a Hobbesian warning for us if we all propose to be unjust; all the benefits of society will be lost if we turn away from justice. He admits, however, that he cannot hope to sway the social parasite, the free rider, who relies on others to be just while acting unjustly himself, except perhaps by scaring him with the prospect of arrest and punishment.

For his ultimate answer, Hume has resort to a higher level of value. The unjust person, in return for mere profit or pecuniary advantage, foregoes genuine happiness, which is impossible without "Inward peace of mind, consciousness of integrity, [and] a satisfactory review of our own conduct." Cunning rogues think that honest people are the dupes of their own integrity; but, regardless of their worldly successes, inwardly such scoundrels are mean and miserable. Dishonest people sacrifice "the invaluable enjoyment of a character, with themselves at least, for the acquisition of worthless toys and gewgaws." The value of the riches for which avaricious people cheat and steal is grossly exaggerated as a means to happiness.

> How little is requisite to supply the *necessities* of nature? And in a view to *pleasure*, what comparison between the unbought satisfaction of conversation, society, study, even health and the common beauties of nature, but above all the peaceful reflection on one's own conduct; what comparison, I say, between these and the feverish, empty amusements of luxury and expense? These natural pleasures, indeed, are really without price; both because they are below all price in their attainment, and above it in their enjoyment. (E., 283–84)

Government Intervention

In *Enquiry* II, Hume amplifies his insistence on the need to rely ordinarily, not on insight into public interest, but on general rules in the allotment of economic goods. He scoffs at those who would apportion riches according to merit or need; he has no patience with them precisely because it would be the height of presumption for mere mortals, lacking both divine omniscience and benevolence, to attempt to form and reform the distribution of riches by their own dim lights.

In a perfect theocracy, where a being, infinitely intelligent, governs by particular volitions, this rule [that the best should be the richest] would certainly have place, and might serve to the wisest purposes: But were mankind to execute such a law; so great is the uncertainty of merit, both from its natural obscurity, and from the self-conceit of each individual, that no determinate rule of conduct would ever result from it; and the total dissolution of society must be the immediate consequence. Fanatics may suppose, *that dominion is founded on grace*, and *that saints alone inherit the earth*; but the civil magistrate very justly puts these sublime theorists on the same footing with common robbers, and teaches them by the severest discipline, that a rule, which, in speculation, may seem the most advantageous to society, may yet be found, in practice, totally pernicious and destructive. (*E.*, 193)

Arguing in the *Treatise* that justice is an artificial virtue, Hume enters as evidence the fact that, unlike the virtues relevant to the natural relationships, justice is equal and general.

Were men, therefore, to take the liberty of acting with regard to the laws of society, as they do in every other affair, they wou'd conduct themselves, on most occasions, by particular judgments, and wou'd take into consideration the characters and circumstances of the persons, as well as the general nature of the question. But 'tis easy to observe, that this wou'd produce an infinite confusion in human society, and that the avidity and partiality of men wou'd quickly bring disorder into the world, if not restrain'd by some general and inflexible principles. 'Twas, therefore, with a view to this inconvenience, that men have establish'd those principles [of justice], and have agreed to restrain themselves by general rules, which are unchangeable by spite and favour, and by particular views of private or public interest. (*T.*, 532)

In short, general rules concerning property, rules which are to be followed blindly, are necessary; they are necessary because busy, engaged men and women cannot confidently be expected to discern and will what is in the public interest.

The distribution of economic goods will often seem unfair. There is, Hume comments, something to be said in the abstract in favor of a government policy of equality in economic goods. Provided that the economic system continued to function efficiently, if goods were divided equally there would be enough to supply everybody with "all the necessaries, and even most of the comforts of life" (*E.*, 193). Moreover, such equality would increase the sum of human happiness, for, "It must also be confessed, that, wherever we depart from this equality, we rob the poor of more satisfaction than we add to the rich, and that the slight gratification of a frivolous vanity, in one individual, frequently costs more than bread to many families, and even provinces" (*E.*, 194). But, given the human condition, such a policy would be destructive. It would ruin economic society. Property and inheritance harness the power of particularity; they make highly productive each person's natural avidity for goods for himself and those dear to him. Nor would the bad effects be limited to the economy; the government, too, would be destroyed. First, this new function, constant intervention to remedy inequality, would require a vast investigative and enforcement bureaucracy. Second, it would create temptations to partiality so great that soon the government would degenerate into tyranny, favoring some at the expense of others. And, third, to eliminate all subordination from society would be to wipe out much of the basis of political authority itself: "Perfect equality of possessions, destroying all subordination, weakens extremely the authority of magistracy, and must reduce all power nearly to a level, as well as property" (*E.*, 194).

By defining justice in a strictly commutative way, Hume lays the basis for a social theory in which the economic game is played by its own rules, without attention to either benevolence or patriotism.[11] Traditional Christian moral theory did not distinguish between the realm of benevolence and the realm of justice: the Christian always was to deal with strangers charitably, as sisters and brothers; with the lower orders always paternalistically, as with children; and with those set in authority over him always reverently, as with parents. In contrast, for Hume a virtuous person is strictly just in his economic activities—he does not steal or break contracts—but he does not do business on the basis of benevolence. In

[11] David Miller comments that "the improvement of judgement," the attainment of more authentic beliefs, "appears in somewhat atrophied form in his [Hume's] theory of justice." This, he states, is an aspect of Hume's conservatism. Miller, *Philosophy and Ideology*, pp. 76, 191. Is the acceptance of a primary distribution of property not based on substantive considerations strong evidence of conservatism? Specifically, is the rule that children are to inherit their parent's estate a conservative rule? Did not the historical liberal position accept the existing allotment of goods, however it had come about, and then emphasize the desirability of having all economic goods—landed estates and factories, as well as commodities—available for exchange between sellers and buyers in a free market? Adam Smith's denunciation of primogeniture and entailed estates is more fervent than Hume's; but the latter's views are clear enough. The principle of primogeniture makes for the peaceful succession of kings, but it is bad when applied to the inheritance of estates: it is "hurtful by [reason of] producing and maintaining an unequal division of private property." *History of England*, 1:486. Edward III's law giving the barons the right to entail their estates was bad because it worked to preserve the wealth and power of great families; of all Henry VII's laws, the most important was the one that gave the nobility and gentry the right to break old entails and to put their lands on the market. *History of England*, 2:143; 3:77. In short, while Hume opposes intervention to maintain an equal division of property, he also opposes intervention to maintain and perpetuate concentrations of wealth and power.

the economic game, he plays to further his own interests. As a civilized, humane person, he is far from indifferent to the well-being of others, but he sees clearly that ordinarily the players' well-being and happiness are advanced best when every player is his own person and plays competitively within the rules. Economic society is a distinct kind of relationship. Obviously, when someone leaves the market and enters into relations with those whom he loves or the unfortunate whom he pities, he is moved by benevolence to try to help them. This reliance on the market—the market, which both Hume and Smith saw as freeing the lower orders from the dominion of the great—is a hallmark of classic liberalism. A belief in private property, clearly, is not peculiar to liberalism, but both conservatives and socialists relied far less than liberals on the efficacy of the market, and consequently were more interventionist, although for different reasons.

Always a moderate, Hume does not go so far as to deny the need for any government intervention. Defence establishments, common-user facilities, and navigation aids are to be provided. In extreme cases, government may have to expropriate land and commodities for the public good. To enable infant industries to overcome the advantages of established foreign competitors, some customs protection may be desirable. Some measures for the welfare of the poor and the unemployed may be required; referring to laws made during the reign of Henry VIII, he comments that the plight of beggars and vagrants is "one of the circumstances in government, which humanity would most powerfully recommend to a benevolent legislator; which seems, at first sight, the most easily adjusted; and which is yet the most difficult to settle in such a manner, as to attain the end without destroying industry" (*H.*, 3:331). In contrast, laws conferring monopolies in trade, either domestic or international, are intolerable and pernicious (*H.*, 4:344–45). Laws prohibiting usury are "unreasonable and iniquitous" (*H.*, 3:77). The wages of laborers and the price of goods "ought always to be left free, and be entrusted to the common course of business and commerce" (*H.*, 3:78, 330). Laws to make laborers stay on the land are vain and absurd: "If husbandmen understand agriculture, and have a ready vent for their commodities, we need not dread a diminution of the people, employed in the country. All methods of supporting [rural] populousness, except by the interest of the proprietors, are violent and ineffectual" (*H.*, 3:79). Laws that, by establishing or maintaining entails, prevent great landed estates from being broken up are bad; likewise, all laws that allow local corporations to erect barriers within the domestic market (*H.*, 3:77, 79).

But we must bear in mind the status of this private-property, free-market economy. When we make the premarket property distribution by succession, long possession, and the like, we are setting up a relationship quite different from a family. The game analogy is helpful. Hume recommends reliance most of the time on the free operation of the economy, but he does so only for pragmatic reasons: ordinarily this is what produces the best results; usually this is the means most effective in achieving the desired end. However, if the supply of a good by far exceeds the demand, that good ceases to be a market commodity; it drops from the game. At the other extreme, if the just society—private property and the market—is unable to provide enough of the necessary goods, or is not distributing them appropriately, the rules of justice can be suspended. Justice, requiring respect for the rights of persons of property, is not to be practiced if the city starves. "As the obligation to justice is founded entirely on the interests of society, which require mutual abstinence from property, in order to preserve peace among mankind; it is evident, that, when the execution of justice would be attended with very pernicious consequences, that virtue must be suspended, and give place to public utility, in such extraordinary and such pressing emergencies. The maxim, *fiat Justitia & ruat Coelum*, let justice be performed, though the universe be destroyed, is apparently false, and by sacrificing the end to the means, shews a preposterous idea of the subordination of duties" (*Essays*, 489). Similarly, Hume recognizes that at times there are those who cannot find gainful employment, and that the government may have to try to help them. These people are outside the game: there are no places for them on the field, or perhaps they have been sidelined by injuries. Justice is not the cardinal virtue of civil society; in circumstances when either the particular person or the public is truly desperate, the requirements of justice are set aside by those of humanity (*E.*, 186–91). Nor is the market so efficacious that there is no place for charity; indeed, "A rich man lies under a moral obligation to communicate to those in necessity a share of his superfluities" (*T.*, 482).

Hume's belief in the market is far from dogmatic; yet, as he says, it is the general rule, not the exceptions, that moralists should emphasize. Clearly, he thought that if for some reason the economic system breaks down, perhaps during a great war, the government ought to act as it thinks best; but this prospect was not one on which he wished to dwell. Discretionary intervention opens up far too many opportunities for those with political power to gratify both their love of dominion and their avarice. Market society is good because ordinarily it is the most efficient arrangement for the production and distribution of goods and services. It is good, also, because it makes for individual liberty; it frees the ordinary person from the power of the great. Besides, even when the governors are truly public-spirited, they are likely to disagree on both the ends and the means of government intervention. Even when people are sincerely honest, there is a strong probability that they will disagree: "The private interest of every one is different; and tho' the public interest in itself be always one and the same, yet it becomes the source of as great dissentions, by reason of the different opinions of particular persons concerning it" (*T.*, 555).

Within civil society most people do not work deliberately to advance the public interest. True, justice is in the public interest, but, says Hume, that the public benefits from people's industry is only a result. People may not always be oblivious of the fact that all, the public, benefit from their labors; but still it is self-interest that moves them. Economic society puts to work what Smith was to call the "invisible hand." The principles of justice arise from "self-ish" interest: " 'Tis self-love which is their real origin; and as the self-love of one person is naturally contrary to that of another, these several interested passions are oblig'd to adjust themselves after such a manner as to concur in some system of conduct and behaviour. This system, therefore, comprehending the interest of each individual, is of course advantageous to the public; tho' it be not intended for that purpose by the inventors" (*T.*, 529).

When we look at the system from below, focusing on those who work to produce, transport, and sell goods, we find that the public good is not one of their ends; they do not will it; rather, it is an unintended result. The public good is the good that flows to all, to strangers and those near and dear alike, as a result of the participation of self-interested people in a division-of-labor system of production and a wide market. Each makes a contribution to the good of all, but not from benevolence. And when we look at the system from above, starting with the whole, starting with the public, we see that what is good for the public (all individuals) is good for each individual.

It comes as no surprise that the one place in the *Treatise* where "the public interest" (or "the public good") is treated as a matter of direct practical concern for citizens is in the discussion of resistance to a ruler. Resistance becomes relevant, considerable, when the whole system, civil society, is endangered because the king (or the government) has forgotten his (its) proper role and acts otherwise. Although contrary to constitutional law, resistance may then be desirable, even imperative, for the good of society, for "the public good." It is not surprising, too, that Hume does not tell us, except in very general terms, just what is against the public good. He says that "nothing is more essential to public interest, than the preservation of public liberty."[12] Beyond that he gives us guidance only

---

[12] *Treatise*, p. 564. Commenting on the death of Charles I, Hume makes the same point even more clearly. The purpose of a government is to prevent disorder by administering a system of rights. Such a system prevents everybody from doing whatever he thinks best. However, a government may become intolerable, so that it will be desirable to replace it or try to establish a new constitution. *History of England*, 5:544–46.

by expressions such as "enormous tyranny and oppression" and by reference to measures "extremely pernicious to the public." Certainly, we are to be practical; reasonably good rulers are not to be turned out. When deciding whether to resist the government, we are to remember that " 'tis certainly impossible for the laws, or ever for philosophy, to establish any *particular* rules, by which we may know when resistance is lawful" (*T.*, 563). What can be tolerated, and what not, is a matter of opinion.

Thus we come to see what should have been obvious from the beginning. A truly civilized people know and favor what normally is in the public interest. And what is the public interest? Normally it is the achievement and maintenance of an authentic civil society, a society based on the principles of justice, one in which the government confines itself to its proper role. Paradoxically, to try to promote the good of the public by providing occasions when particular persons may make decisions directly for the public interest is contrary to the public interest. In modern times, it is the system—the full realization of the economic system made possible by property, trade, and contract, with a government appointed by an acceptable formal test, with an adequate set of general laws, and with judges who apply those laws without regard to irrelevant differences among litigants—in a word, it is genuine civil society, society operating under a full rule of law, that is in the public interest.

Our very willingness to abide by the results of trivial tests and rules, provided only that they are simple and are applied blindly, as when the deceased owner of an estate or a dead king has to be replaced, shows both how highly we value society and our justified, great fear of partiality.[13] While we expect people to be partial or "self-ish" in playing the game, we want the game itself to be controlled by laws, not by men and women. We want to be able to rely on a structure of rights, not on what powerful, interested people think is good.

Life and Liberty

The chief domestic purpose for establishing a government, according to Hume, is the maintenance of respect for property and contracts.

> No one can doubt, that the convention for the distinction of property, and for the stability of possession, is of all circumstances the most necessary to the establishment of human society, and that after the agreement for the fixing and observing of this rule, there remains little or nothing to be done towards settling a perfect harmony and concord. All the other passions, beside this of interest, are either easily restrain'd, or are not of such pernicious con-

[13] *Treatise*, pp. 515, 531, 556; *Enquiry* II, pp. 199, 309.

sequence, when indulg'd. *Vanity* is rather to be esteem'd a social passion, and a bond of union among men. *Pity* and *love* are to be consider'd in the same light. And as to *envy* and *revenge*, tho' pernicious, they operate only by intervals, and are directed against particular persons, whom we consider as our superiors or enemies. This avidity alone, of acquiring goods and possessions for ourselves and our nearest friends, is insatiable, perpetual, universal, and directly destructive of society. (*T.*, 491–92)

From this emphasis on economic goods, we should not conclude that Hume is indifferent to the value of life and liberty; he is not making light of murder or slavery, for example. Undoubtedly, there were incidents of killing and enslavement in pregovernment times, but the task of suppressing such misconduct could be performed by the natural authorities, the parents and elders. The compelling need of early man was not for the more effective protection of life and liberty, but for the production of more economic goods. Consequently, positive action, not defensive action, was taken: economic society was started, and in economic society, it is the secure possession of external goods, not the security of life and liberty, that needs protection. This follows from the very nature of this form of society. Hume does not say that people will not be taken prisoners or killed, or that this is right. What he does say is that of the three kinds of goods, only external goods, estate—things, animals, fields—can be separated from us by force and then taken up by somebody else without diminution (*T.*, 487–88). Life and liberty are not the goods proper to the economic game.[14] Rules are needed to define property rights; but there is no need to write a rule stating that it is wrong for the players to kill each other. That they are not to do so is presupposed. Similarly, there is no need for a rule that they are not to enslave each other.

Why does Hume not spell this out? We must remember that Hume's great concern in "Of Morals," a book on morality, not jurisprudence, was to show that natural motivation and moral obligation must not be confused. This is why he devotes far more of the book to an analysis of the roundabout way in which "interest" gives rise to moral rules than he devotes to the standards of the natural relationships. He focuses chiefly on the principles of the economic game. He tells us relatively little about

[14] For a critical comment, see Harrison, *Hume's Theory of Justice*, p. 42. See also V. M. Hope, *Virtue by Consensus: The Moral Philosophy of Hutcheson, Hume, and Adam Smith* (Oxford: Clarendon Press, 1989), pp. 70–71. It must be remembered that the negative quality of "justice" had already been explained by Hume's predecessors. The narrow (i.e., economic) meaning of justice in the *Treatise* and *Enquiry* II is consistent with (a) Hume's contention that the evaluation of conduct in terms of morality is always different from the evaluation of conduct from any nonmoral standpoint, and (b) his concern to distinguish economic society, to be analyzed more fully in his later writings, from other forms of society, such as the family or neighborhood.

other rights. If Hume had been challenged on his narrow definition of justice in the *Treatise*, which equates justice with honesty, he might have replied that the right to life and the right to liberty ought not to be bulked in with the right to external goods, that a person is hardly to be praised as just merely because he does not kill or enslave others.

If the rights basic to economic society are "artificial," perhaps we can say that the rights to life and liberty are natural rights. They are rights of man, not rights of the participant in civil society. To be rights they must, according to Hume's theory, arise from rules approved by spectators, and this implies the existence of society; however, this "society" is not economic society. It is more basic. Yet the rights to life and liberty are not similar to the rights that appertain to the natural relationships. Particular benevolence, or, failing that, a sense of duty, moves a person to do good within his circle, but the rights to life and liberty are negative in that they only prohibit him from harming others. Thus we find that there are three layers of rights more fundamental than civil rights: first, the rights to life and liberty; second, the rights appertaining to the natural relationships; and, third, the rights derived from the rules of justice. This, I suggest, is what Hume might have said had he been writing a treatise on natural jurisprudence. If each individual has a moral right to life and a moral right to liberty, society must extend down to include not only the natural relationships, but also another stratum, the simple person-to-person relationship of individuals. This is very similar to what Adam Smith was to teach.

Because we generally use "justice" with a far wider meaning, it is easy to forget that for Hume economic society is only useful, not good in itself. It is an artificial relationship, a kind of elaborate game or play. Its basic rules are not arbitrary, but they are put into operation as means to an end. To regard the rights respected by the just person as ends, rather than as means to ends, would, as Hume said, be preposterous.

One might have expected Hume to deal in the *Treatise* with the morality of slavery, an institution that gives some people property rights to others; yet he says little on this matter in that work. The explanation is that the fundamental individualism of Hume's moral theory, based on what is good for beings of the human kind, makes impossible the inclusion of slavery as an institution of a genuine civil society. Accordingly, as we have seen, when he writes about the seizure of goods, he says that neither the goods of the mind nor of the body can be transferred from one person to another as possessions; the possibility of enslaving both mind and body is not even mentioned. For Hume, slavery was a fact of history, but it was barbarous. A civil society is made up of individuals, all of whom are players; slavery is alien to the idea of civil society. It is true that in explaining how property is acquired by accession he refers to "the fruits of our garden, the offspring of our cattle, and the work of our slaves" (*T.*, 509); however, this perhaps is a thoughtless carryover from his studies in Roman law and is not to be taken as evidence that he found slavery acceptable. Indeed, in later works he attacks slavery as both essentially and economically bad.

Hume's use of the word "justice" with a narrow meaning in the *Treatise* arose from his contentions: first, that economic rights are artificial, and, second, that civil society is primarily economic. Too much can be made of this narrow usage. It is clear that he thought that any government ought to practice "good police," that is, it ought to maintain "justice" as ordinarily understood by protecting the lives and liberties of its subjects, as well as their economic rights. For example, in *Enquiry* II, he writes, "When any man, even in political society, renders himself by his crimes, obnoxious to the public, he is punished by the laws in his goods and person; that is, the ordinary rules of justice are, with regard to him, suspended for a moment, and it becomes equitable to inflict on him, for the *benefit* of society, what otherwise he could not suffer without wrong or injury" (*E.*, 187). Here "justice" requires respect for rights other than those related to economic goods and services. Ordinarily it would be wrong, he implies, to intrude upon the man's person—on his life and liberty—as well as on his economic goods. When Hume writes about "the police of the kingdom," as he does repeatedly in the *History of England*, it is clear that he means the administration of "justice" in the wider sense.[15]

Ranks

We turn now to a topic that will be examined more fully in chapter 6, that is, social (or political) structure, what in Hume's day was called "rank." A genuine society is not simply an economy; nor is it a despotism, with all order and opinion created by the ruler. A society involves common beliefs about facts and causes, and settled moral rules and standards; it involves politics; it involves manners, usage, taste, practices; it involves standards of style in literature, rhetoric, dress, architecture, and equipage. In many of these matters, Hume finds, a society is led by its notables, by "the great." The people follow the great, according them deference, precedence, and preference. What Hume has to say about economic society is relatively simple: he argues that the maxims of modern politics, empha-

[15] One result of the Reformation in England was that the clergy were brought under the ordinary law: "The abolition of the ancient religion much contributed to the regular execution of justice." *History of England*, 3:324. See also 3:74, and 2:69, 75, 109, 133, 189, and 279.

sizing private goals and motivation, are more productive of both wealth and happiness than were the maxims of ancient policy, which sought the public good directly. In contrast, what he has to say about social rank is much more scattered and complex. Here he had to take into account the fact that in contemporary France and most other European countries, the social structure was based on inheritance, while in Holland and England it was based mainly on commerce. Neither situation was ideal.

The advantages of having strong natural leaders, people whose authority comes from below and is not dependent on government office, are numerous, Hume finds, especially if those leaders take their responsibilities seriously. Without them, without natural subordination, the society would lack stability and strength; it would be simply a chaotic mass—unless a ruler intervened to impose his will. By providing common standards, styles, and manners, the natural leaders prevent anxiety, confusion, and conflict. When they perform their roles with ability and dedication, they are ideal political representatives and military officers. They embody the nation's character and values. If kings and ministers remain true to those values, they will be supported by the people of rank, thus making for order and peace; if they diverge from them, the people of rank have sufficient authority to act as restraints, to lead resistance if necessary. Without its natural leaders, the people are a mere mob, an undisciplined mass, susceptible to panic and enthusiasm, vulnerable to exploitation by political and religious demagogues. But there can be disadvantages. A society's leaders may not deserve their high status: they may be indolent, inattentive, incompetent; they may be parasites, more concerned to defend their inherited places, honors, and privileges, to spend their time gambling, fishing, or at the races, than in performing the duties of their stations. This is likely to be the case when a society lacks a middle rank, an intermediate class between the many who are poor and the few who are great, an intermediate class whose members may become rich and consequently great by their own exertions, thus challenging and perhaps displacing those born to greatness.

Whom do the masses take as their leaders? In religious times, they turn to priests; in military times, to valorous warriors; in commercial societies, to the rich. Nowadays, on the continent, writes Hume, those of high rank are mainly the descendents of the old nobility; in England they are the rich. Hume acquiesces in the contemporary situation in England. He knows, as we have seen, that philosophers regard riches as a low kind of goods, but he sees that the values of philosophers are not those of the people. Moreover, while philosophers cannot agree whose wisdom and virtue is preeminent, and, hence, should lead, riches have the advantage of being obvious to even the vulgar in England, as has birth that advantage in France. We accept rules that philosophers regard as silly for the basic distribution of economic goods and for the selection of kings, because those rules are simple and give clear results; here, too, we must settle for what works. It is better that the rich, or those of high birth, should lead than that there should be no leaders; for in Babylon a nation without natural leaders is either chaotic or despotic.

Why do the people exalt the great? Why do riches and power cause pride; poverty and dependence, humility? Ordinarily, love is restricted to a few; yet it is a fact that the multitude have a strong esteem, almost love, for the rich and powerful. The lower orders are moved by a strange kind of benevolence for the great. Hume finds this phenomenon so remarkable as to require analysis. Why, he asks in the *Treatise*, are the many so much in awe, not of the virtuous, but of the rich and powerful? He is not concerned with the obvious consequences of riches and power, that the wealthy can buy services, while the powerful can command them. What he focuses on is the fact that the multitude spontaneously follow the rich and the powerful. They do not have to be tricked, cajoled, or coerced into subordination; they themselves thrust leadership on people of rank. What demands explanation is the solicitude of plain people for the welfare of their betters, the reverence they accord them in company, the zeal of the poor to assist the rich, and the deference of the multitude to the views, fashions, manners, and usage of the great, without regard to intrinsic merit. One might have expected the multitude to be envious, even malicious; the very opposite is the case. Although Hume has something to say about power itself, his chief concern is with property and riches as causes of esteem and power.

He first takes up this question in "Of the Passions," when discussing the causes of pride. Because man is a thoroughly social animal, he feels proud of his goods: when abroad he is proud of his country's heroes, at home he boasts of the wonders he saw abroad; he is proud of the salmon stream in his parish, his rich ancestors, his prize bull. Of all the different kinds of goods, the one that most commonly causes pride is economic goods, things that draw attention because they are useful, beautiful, or surprising (*T.*, 309–11). Conversely, one who has few goods is humble. Those who lose their possessions often depart to live among strangers; if they fare well, they return home to parade their wealth (*T.*, 323–24). Indeed, it is in explaining the esteem gained by owning economic goods that Hume first draws our attention to the importance of sympathetic perception: the esteem caused by such goods often is more valuable to their owner than the goods themselves.

He distinguishes between property, riches, and goods. To have property, that is, rights to goods, is a cause of both pride and esteem. Riches are a link back in the causal chain; they are purchasing power, "the power of acquiring the property of what pleases; and 'tis only in this view they have any influence on the passions. Paper will, on many occasions, be consider'd as riches, and that because it may convey the power of acquiring money: And money is not riches, as it is a metal endow'd with certain qualities of solidity, weight and fusibility; but only as it has a relation to the pleasures and conveniences of life" (*T.*, 311). But the imagination runs quickly along the links, with the result that money, riches, and property have much the same social influence as tangible goods. Power, too, is regarded as good because it is a means to pleasures and conveniences. But, in addition, "the vanity of power"—the vanity of dominion—is increased by the fact that the powerful person asserts his will over others, others who in many respects are just as good as he is, perhaps better. The shame of slavery is increased by the same factor reversed. All human beings are much alike; this makes mastery delightful and slavery abhorrent. Often what Mandeville had called "the love of power"—Augustine's *libido dominandi*—is greater than the desire for the services received.

Nothing, neither wisdom, nor prudence, nor sanctity, nor seniority, has "a greater tendency to give us an esteem for any person, than his power and riches; or a contempt, than his poverty and meanness" (*T.*, 357). The rich are given social eminence. We elevate the rich; we exalt them—not the wise, the virtuous, or the elderly—in an upper rank paramount. We see them as the elite of humankind. Why?

Hume weighs three possible answers. The rich own or can buy many beautiful things, things we admire chiefly because they promise to be useful by reason of their form, shape, or constitution. We regard those things as beautiful, thereby recognizing their usefulness; yet they will never be useful to us. The first answer is that the mere sight or thought of all the beautiful things the rich own, that perception alone, makes us happy. We feel good when what we perceive is beautiful, even if we are only reading a poem or story. Second, it may be that we expect the rich and powerful to use their resources benevolently, as "great engines of virtue," as Hutcheson surmised. Third, it may be that we share sympathetically the joy we believe the owners feel because of all their beautiful things. As one would expect, Hume finds the third answer best; it is at this point that he gives us his second long exposition of sympathy. The hard truth is that there is no basis for a belief, no basis for what Hutcheson called "a general presumption," that the rich and powerful will try to help the rest of us; they rarely do. And upon examination, we find that the first answer is only a truncated version of the third (*T.*, 357–60). By sympathy, the multitude shares the felicity of the rich. What is more, so great is the influence of sympathy that not only do the multitude feel the pleasure, the happiness, they attribute to the rich person, but he in turn feels their adulation. The minds of the many and the minds of the few who are rich reflect each other infinitely, like mirrors set facing one another. So pleasant is the exaltation produced by the esteem attending riches that it, the esteem of others, often is a far greater good than the goods themselves.

Thus we see that "society" is not simply an economic system; nor are people, not even ordinary people living obscurely, far from the public stage, interested in external goods for their inherent value alone. Ambition, hunger for recognition and applause, is the greatest passion: "Where ambition can be so happy as to cover its enterprizes, even to the person himself, under the appearance of principle [such as piety or patriotism], it is the most incurable and inflexible of all human passions" (H., 1:207). Even its infamous twin, avarice, ordinarily is the servant of ambition. Henry VII, comments Hume, was a most unusual man: "Avarice was, on the whole, his ruling passion; and he remains an instance, almost singular, of a man, placed in a high station, and possessed of talents for great affairs, in whom that passion predominated above ambition. Even among private persons, avarice is commonly nothing but a species of ambition, and is chiefly incited by the prospect of that regard, distinction, and consideration, which attend on riches" (H., 3:73). Because of their power and riches, some people, some families, are the natural princes of society. They lead and shape public opinion; they guide the electors; they form a natural magistracy; if they are any good, they prevent kings from becoming tyrants.

The rich often are wretched, and the poor happy; yet it is a convention, a general belief, that the rich are happy, and the poor miserable. Because of this convention, the rich are regarded and treated almost as deities. Hume does not argue for a new criterion. Here, again, as with economic goods and thrones, he is willing to rely on readily applied, imaginatively acceptable rules to prevent the conflicts that would be caused by particular judgments. Nevertheless, Hume, as philosopher, is far from content with the dominion of the rich and the great. Some kinds of wealth and power are inimical to the qualities essential to good social leadership. Clearly, those with great wealth in government bonds are unsuitable; they favor wars and whatever else will drive interest rates higher. Those whose only title to rank is birth, the slack descendants of families great in centuries past, are poor leaders. Although merchants and master manufacturers have ability and industry, they are seldom well educated; nor are they informed or thoughtful except in what pertains directly to their business affairs. The most promising group are the industrious, improving landowners: born into good families, many of them are well educated; not deformed in character by wealth, privilege, or life at court, they strive to improve themselves as well as their estates; free from the press of daily business, they have time to read and think. Here status, sound understanding, and virtue have a chance to meet. It appears then that what is needed is a new social structure, together with a constitution appropriate to that social structure—a social structure that elevates the improving landowner at the expense of noble courtiers, a constitution that reduces the political power concentrated at great capital cities such as London. We shall return to Hume's prescription in chapter 6.

Manners

Good manners, Hume finds, are a kind of lesser morality that makes it possible for us to get along together. We now know that if we are to be vigorous and effective in our undertakings, we need the self-confidence that comes with pride. But, as both Hobbes and Mandeville saw, the proud cannot endure the proud. To prevent clashes, human beings have worked out rules of manners. By good manners in speech and conduct, they bridle their pride; they restrain themselves so as to be good members of polite society. Here "society" has a very general meaning: the rules of good manners do not apply specifically to any particular relationship, although good manners in the family, good manners in business, and good manners at court are not always the same. Good manners are buffers between egos; they are the ways of civilized people.

> We have, all of us, a wonderful partiality for ourselves, and were we always to give vent to our sentiments in this particular, we shou'd mutually cause the greatest indignation in each other, not only by the immediate presence of so disagreeable a subject of comparison, but also by the contrariety of our judgments. In like manner, therefore, as we establish the *laws of nature*, in order to secure property in society, and prevent the opposition of self-interest; we establish the *rules of good-breeding*, in order to prevent the opposition of men's pride, and render conversation agreeable and inoffensive. (*T.*, 597)

Good manners, along with benevolence, justice, and allegiance, enable us to live in peace with others. Raw, natural man is fit only to live alone, or with his immediate family. Through civilization, man becomes a social being—a help, joy, comfort, and inspiration, a blessing to his associates. Hume, unlike Rousseau, does not scorn modern society; rather, he accepts ungrudgingly both individualism and all the rules and institutions required to make it possible for individuals to live and work together.

Hobbes Refuted

Thomas Hobbes had shown that reason propounds certain principles of conduct as the means for "the preservation of men in multitudes." These principles bind a person if there are adequate grounds for believing that most others likewise will follow them. For Hobbes this means that they oblige effectively only when there is a ruler to enforce them. "These dictates of reason, men used to call by the name of laws, but improperly: for they are but conclusions, or theorems concerning what conduceth to the conservation and defence of themselves; whereas law, properly, is the word of him, that by right hath command over others."[16] In contrast, Hume shows how, by prolonged common experience, people come to follow the dictates of reason even without a ruler. He shows, also, how the principles of justice come to oblige people as rules sanctioned by moral judgment, that is, as moral laws. For him there are effective moral laws, defining moral right and wrong—binding not only *in foro interno*, but also *in foro externo*—before there is government. The task of government is executive: to administer those laws, the laws of nature.

Experience and Reflection

In reading Hume on the origin of society, especially the economy, the state, and manners, we must guard against two mistakes. The first is a rationalist error. For Hume the economy was not invented by a smart economist; neither did a political scientist invent the state, nor an authority on etiquette good manners. All these are not the products of philosopher-legislators who by reasoning discovered the principles before society began; rather they are the products of ordinary practitioners confronting particular problems and situations: hunters, mechanics, carpenters, traders, men rowing boats, people working and living together. Adam Smith is wrong in accusing Hume of contending that civil society was devised by somebody who saw the utility of the whole system; Hume's explanation is very close to that given by Mandeville in 1729. But in drawing back from one mistake, we must not tumble into another, namely, that Hume dismisses abstruse thinkers as useless and unimportant. He never says this; indeed he says the very opposite again and again. Now that civil society has been established, reflective people can analyze it to learn its principles, thus providing both standards for the criticism of defective laws, obsolete customs, and bad policies, and guides for reform.

[16] Thomas Hobbes, *Leviathan*, ed. Michael Oakeshott (Oxford: Basil Blackwell, 1955), pp. 104–5.

5

HUME AND REFORM: DISCOVERING

TRUE PRINCIPLES

IS DELIBERATE social and political reform, the reform of the institutions, laws, maxims, and practices of a society possible according to Hume? The answer most scholars give seems to be, "No; given his skepticism about reason and his consequent dependence on experience, Hume has no escape from conservatism; his philosophy requires that men rely on prevailing beliefs and customs."[1] I disagree. Hume finds that people are of many different kinds—landowners and merchants, priests and soldiers, nobles and commoners—but by far his most important distinction is between those who have achieved true principles and all the others. The unreflective multitude, the vulgar, including most noble lords, are bound by the opinions and manners prevalent in their age; in contrast, those who understand human nature and moral subjects, persons of true principles, sound politicians, can show the way to reformation. In short, we must distinguish between the beliefs of the wise and those of the multitude.

Is Hume skeptical about morality? No. That men and women observe moral rules and standards is obvious; it is equally clear that moral rules and standards are prerequisites of society. Hume denies emphatically that

---

[1] Frederick G. Whelan, for example, having found (*Order and Artifice in Hume's Political Philosophy* [Princeton: Princeton University Press, 1985], p. 312) that Hume lacks precise criteria for proper moral artifices, states, "Just as experience is authoritative with regard to all possible knowledge of matters of fact, so experience in the form of history and tradition—the accumulated manifestations of human nature in the relevant respects—is authoritative as a source of moral and political values. Just as mental habits unify experience into orderly cognitive patterns, rendering it a reasonable guide to the future, so also does social custom, embodying collective convictions of right, underlie the artificial rules and other continuities that constitute order in our social experience" (p. 322). Whelan contends that it is Hume's emphasis on "rules and order that constitutes the most fundamental element of conservatism in Hume's political thought" (p. 335). "Artifices," he states, "are contrivances intended to create a provisional order in society, yet their artificiality implies both potential change and the absence of rational standards that might provide a final and conclusive justification for any one of conceivable patterns of order" (p. 362). He concludes that Hume's theory "lacks the common liberal confidence in reason as the source or foundation of the social order" (p. 363). Yet earlier Whelan—correctly, I think—had recognized that "Hume's skepticism in no way leads to a renunciation of reason and the scientific enterprise" (p. 203).

the basic content of morality can be discovered by a priori reasoning. He denies also that the rules and standards were devised arbitrarily by politicians intent on keeping the masses quiet, orderly, and industrious. Having rejected those two errors, he devoted all his work on moral theory to the great task of showing the origins of our moral sentiments (our moral beliefs) and to correcting those sentiments. The rules and standards, he argues, are not arbitrary in content, but are shaped by the nature of people (beings of the human kind) living in society, by the prevailing circumstances, and by human understanding. The principles of justice, for example, are natural to people living in society; yet, these principles are "artificial" in that, like Aristotle's principles of politics, they have to be learned and put into operation (H., 3:74). In the full discovery and realization of the principles of civil society, wise philosophers and politicians have an important role.

It may also be said that because he held that it is ultimately the passions that move us, all morality must be subjective for Hume; in other words, that he denies the objectivity of morality. This, too, would be misleading. As we have seen, morality is made up of rules, which restrict, and standards, which guide, our primitive motivation. Those rules and standards are objective in that the evaluation expressed in them is that of spectators who have the interest of humankind as their criterion, and because they apply to all. Morality is not objective in the sense of being alien and opposed to human nature—as divine commands to an utterly depraved race, or as rational moral theorems imposed upon irrational people—for morality has its basis in natural human passions; but it is objective in that society (through impartial spectators) sets the rules and standards, in the light of what is understood to be good for humankind, by which every member is judged virtuous or vicious. Any notion that Hume is a moral subjectivist must be dismissed. For Hume, one who, although living in society, followed only his private or "self-ish" feelings would be both vicious and miserable. Finally, it may be said that Hume's assertion that reason is the slave of the passions means that for him reason cannot bring about changes in morality. Morality may change because circumstances change, but because our ends or purposes are set by our passions, better reasoning can make no appreciable difference in what we regard as good moral conduct. This brings us to the main question: does Hume's denial of the claims that had been made for reason—for "reason alone"—make him a conservative?[2]

---

[2] One basis for labeling Hume a conservative is the seductive view that equates the Enlightenment with rationalism, and both with liberalism, and then treats conservatism as a reaction against the Enlightenment. With these premises taken for granted, it follows that Hume, the philosopher famous for having sought to dethrone reason, must be a conservative.

He describes himself as a "moderate sceptic." Why is he a skeptic of
any kind? The answer is that he is indeed a skeptic, but his skepticism is
directed at the pretenses of those who, without consulting experience,
proclaim that they know the truth. First, he denies the claims of metaphysicians to reveal truths about reality by mere demonstration. Second, he
denies the claims of those moralists who contend that the requirements
of morality are to be learned by the analysis of abstract ideas. Third, he
insists that many of the beliefs on which we rely, especially in civil society,
should be treated with skepticism.

Some schools of moral philosophy, the Epicurean and Stoic, for example, propose to teach recipes for happiness. They claim to be able to
tell their devotees how to reform themselves, that is, how to reorder their
passions, attitudes, and aspirations so that they may be happy in this
world. Hume, as we have seen, denies the efficacy of such regimes and
cures. One's character is far from being readily malleable under the impact of philosophic precepts; such teachings cannot cause drastic, radical,
almost miraculous changes. But this is not to say that one's character
cannot be formed, even reformed, by other means. Education and the
prevailing laws and manners have a powerful formative effect, especially
in youth. Prolonged involvement in any line of activity—in study, warfare, the pursuit of riches—is likely to influence one's values. Moreover,
a person may even deliberately acquire a new virtue or a higher degree of
an old one; by acting over a long period as if he were virtuous in a particular way, perhaps to gain praise or to avoid censure, gradually he may
come to be genuinely motivated to act in that way.[3] Human nature is
tractable; however, nobody should expect pretentious lectures or even
"the severest injunctions of religion" to work instant conversions.

But, granted that it is difficult to change a person's values, can the *mores* of a people be reformed? Can their moral system be improved by legislators and politicians? Or is their morality, their whole way of life,
strictly a matter of custom? To answer these questions, we must turn
briefly to Hume's epistemology. The first book of the *Treatise* was not
intended as a mere contemplative study. Its main purpose, as Hume
states, is practical: to advance the sciences of logic, morals, criticism, and
politics by improving our knowledge of human nature. His aspiration is
to improve our thinking in practical matters. To do this, he has first to
show the authentic operation of the understanding.

The two basic kinds of perceptions are impressions and ideas. In addition, as we shall see, there are derivative kinds of perceptions, impressive
ideas, which result from the combination of impressiveness with ideas.

[3] See p. 148. This is the view that Hume attributes to those whom he describes in the essay
"The Sceptic"; see also *Essays*, pp. 170–71.

According to Hume, we know (perceive) what we know (our perceptions) in five different ways. First, when we perceive the present, the here and now, we are knowing by *intuition*. This is immediate knowing. There is an impressiveness about intuitive perceptions that commands instant acquiescence. We know what we know in this way as real. Regardless of what skeptical philosophers say about the senses, we accept our intuitive perceptions as perceptions of the real world. Hume calls these perceptions simply impressions. All the other kinds of knowing involve ideas. As a result of having impressions—experience—our minds become stocked with ideas: ideas of colors, shapes, tastes, sounds, relationships. By acts of the imagination, we can combine those ideas fancifully, creating purple cows, streets of gold, perfectly just societies, and so on in the mind's eye. This way, *fancying*, is the second way we come to have objects of perception.

Third, *demonstrative reasoning* gives us knowledge about orders or systems—composed of standardized units and shapes, that is, forms and degrees in geometry, and series of numerical units in mathematics—abstracted from the roughly triangular, roughly round, roughly rectangular things we have seen in the real world. We analyze the implications of such forms and systems, showing, for example, that it is logically necessary that the angles at the base of an isosceles triangle be equal. Because such knowledge is absolute, all too often, Hume contends, efforts are made to achieve demonstrable knowledge of the external world and about moral subjects. However, demonstrative reasoning is only analytic reasoning. The reasoner is simply revealing the implications of his own presuppositions: if this figure is rectangular, it follows that it has four sides. Causal relationships in the physical and moral worlds—what causes can be counted on to produce specific effects—are learned, not by abstract reasoning, but by experience and reflection. Moral necessity, too—the obligation to observe the moral rules and standards—is different from logical necessity.

The fourth way of knowing is *remembering*. Here we revive perceptions of what once was present for us. What we know here are impressive ideas, but because the impressiveness of such perceptions weakens as time elapses, we are wise in being hesitant to act—to give emphatic testimony in a law court, for example—on the basis of old memories. Remembering is a way of knowing reality, in contrast to fancying and demonstrative reasoning, which involve only ideas.

But we also know reality beyond our intuited present and our remembered past. To some extent, we understand antiquity, remote in time and place; to some extent, we understand the political system of contemporary China, remote in place; to some extent, we understand what will happen in the future if certain causes are set in operation. Moreover, we act on the basis of this knowledge. What is the nature of this understanding? Hume's answer is, *belief*. We judge certain perceptions to be perceptions of reality although that reality is beyond our past and present.

> 'Tis this latter principle, which peoples the world, and brings us acquainted with such existences, as by their removal in time and place, lie beyond the reach of the senses and memory. By means of it I paint the universe in my imagination, and fix my attention on any part of it I please. . . . All this, and every thing else, which I believe, are nothing but ideas; tho' by their force and settled order, arising from custom and the relation of cause and effect, they distinguish themselves from the other ideas, which are merely the offspring of the imagination. (*T.*, 108)

As a result of repeated experience, we come to believe that certain "effects" are the results of certain "causes" and that certain causes will produce certain "effects"; indeed, by "the real world" we mean a complex stream of causally related occurrences, which we call "the natural world." In the theater of our minds, our imaginations, we survey this stream—past, present in time but remote in place, and future—but unlike the fancied cows and abstract orders, we take these perceptions as perceptions of reality. We find them impressive; we believe them. A *belief*, says Hume, is "a lively idea." Because our intuitions and memories are impressive, sequences of causes and effects beyond the here and now and similar to those we already have experienced are impressive to us. They convince us. This is the positive, constructive side of Hume's epistemology, the side ignored when he was regarded as a simple skeptic. Far from relying on mere ideas, the true philosopher reflectively observes—fully conscious of how error steals into human thought, he observes—what happens in the physical and the moral realms. He strives to achieve a deeper, sounder knowledge of causes and effects. Such an understanding may result in vast improvements in human practice: in agriculture, medicine, ship construction, politics. The bad philosopher flies away on wings of words. The truth is that good reasoning (thinking) is not an independent activity; it employs, not mere ideas, but impressive ideas. In the physical sciences, it must stay close to nature; in the moral sciences, it must stay close to real life.

Following Hume, we can make four points about reasoning. First, reasoning is concerned with achieving a sounder understanding of reality, not with discovering new ultimate values; it is concerned with truth, not value. It helps shape action by influencing our choice of means, not our choice of ultimate ends. Second, the kind of reasoning (thinking) we do when we combine ideas to produce purple cows or a New Jerusalem is fancying; it does not show that purple cows or New Jerusalems exist or could exist in our world. Third, the kind of reasoning we do when we analyze complex ideas such as rectangles or number systems gives truth, but not necessarily truth about the real world. Fourth, if we are to reason successfully about reality, we must begin and stay with impressive ideas, creditable ideas, that is, ideas directly related to experience; provided we do this, and provided we reason reflectively—that is, in accordance with the rules of reasoning—we will gain a sounder understanding of the physical and moral realms. Better understanding comes about, not from experience alone, but from reflection on experience. This method, the deliberate combination of careful observation and reflection, is what Hume calls "the experimental method of reasoning." The strict rationalist relies exclusively on ideas; he neglects experience. But his endeavors always fail; barren skepticism is the wages of his overweening pride. In eating and procreation, man is not dependent on reason for primary motivation. Similarly, we find that nature was far too wise to make man dependent on "reason alone" for the acquisition of knowledge. In a key passage, reminiscent of Hutcheson and Butler, Hume states,

> I shall add, for a further confirmation of the foregoing theory, that, as this operation of the mind, by which we infer like effects from like causes, and *vice versa*, is so essential to the subsistence of all human creatures, it is not probable, that it could be trusted to the fallacious deductions of our reason, which is slow in its operations; appears not, in any degree, during the first years of infancy; and at best is, in every age and period of human life, extremely liable to error and mistake. It is more conformable to the ordinary wisdom of nature to secure so necessary an act of the mind, by some instinct or mechanical tendency, which may be infallible in its operations, may discover itself at the first appearance of life and thought, and may be independent of all the laboured deductions of the understanding.[4]

The real world, not the world of ideas, is primary; unless based on impressions (of the real world), our complex ideas, no matter how cleverly composed, are either fantasies or abstractions. Belief, not abstract reason, is the primary basis of our knowledge of the world beyond our present and past; indeed, reason alone, despite the boast that it can explain nature, cannot even explain the idea of self. This, the rejection of reason's pretensions and the acceptance of what wise nature has provided, is fundamental to what Hume calls moderate skepticism. The true philosopher is not a Platonist; he does not try to supplant belief as at best only an inferior, shadowy kind of knowledge; rather, having accepted

---

[4] *An Enquiry concerning Human Understanding*, p. 55. Hume says also, "Nature must have provided some other principle, of more ready, and more general use and application; nor can an operation of such immense consequence in life, as that of inferring effects from causes, be trusted to the uncertain process of reasoning and argumentation." Ibid., p. 106. See also *Treatise*, pp. 176–79.

belief as our only kind of knowledge about the real world, apart from intuition and memory, he strives to detect and discredit false beliefs and to bring about new authentic beliefs by the experimental method. Again and again Hume returns to his fundamental point that the wise person does not scorn what nature has provided. Instead, the wise person uses the natural operation of the imagination as the basis of the property system; he relies on natural motivation to get people to work industriously. Similarly, the epistemologist accepts believing, a natural way of understanding, as the primary way to general knowledge.

Everybody who acts relies on his beliefs about the prevailing facts and about the consequences of proposed actions. This is true when we scratch matches, walk on ice, and board ships; it is true when we try to help our friends; it is true when we write constitutions for new states, enact statutes, or formulate public policy. Obviously, the validity of our beliefs is of great importance; they are "the governing principles of all our actions."[5] Achieving our ends or purposes depends largely on the reliability of our beliefs. We acquire many of our beliefs through simple experience. The child who has fallen against a hot stove is afraid of hot stoves; he believes that the cause of his past pain will cause pain in the future. The illiterate sailor quickly gets the feel of the helm and discovers how to trim the sails. The woodsman learns the knack of felling a tree just where he wants it, as does the beaver. The village mediciner comes to know what simples to give for common maladies. Often beliefs are acquired subconsciously and remain unstated and unexamined. For example, a child learns very early not to slap down his feet when walking on ice; he learns to creep, especially if the temperature is just below freezing; he does this from experience without profound reflection, and without any notion of the scientific reason why this is the correct technique. Nor is reflection an arcane art. A very young child may believe that the window is bigger than the oak he sees through it, or that it is the shore, not the boat, which moves; very soon, however, reflection leads him to correct these beliefs.

While the beliefs (or opinions) people form about the physical world at

[5] Hume considered improving his discussion of belief in a second edition of the *Treatise*. Commenting on the quality that distinguishes a belief from a mere idea, he proposed to say, "[That quality] is something *felt* by the mind, which distinguishes the ideas of the judgment from the fictions of the imagination. It gives them more force and influence; makes them appear of greater importance; infixes them in the mind; and renders them the governing principles of all our actions." Appendix to the *Treatise*, p. 629. Beliefs are of two kinds: proofs and probabilities. "Mr. Locke divides all arguments into demonstrative and probable. In this view, we must say, that it is only probable all men must die, or that the sun will rise to-morrow. But to conform our language more to common use, we ought to divide arguments into *demonstrations*, *proofs*, and *probabilities*. By proofs meaning such arguments from experience as leave no room for doubt or opposition." *An Enquiry concerning Human Understanding*, p. 56n.

the level of practical experience tend to be reliable, often they are very wrong about the movement of the planets and the composition of matter. Again, some arts are learned quickly: how to hunt and fish, how to build a hut or a canoe. But other productive activities, such as agriculture, involve long, complex causal chains; in them even many ages of experience—experience without much reflection—will achieve only a crude art. Similarly, our beliefs about the moral world are reliable in different degrees. We soon come to know what to expect from a few persons, those whom we know. But our beliefs about classes of people—an Englishman's beliefs about Irishmen or Frenchmen, for example—may be wildly mistaken. And our beliefs about social causation—how to manage trade, how to deal with heretics and tyrants, whether to rule by people or laws, and so on—may be primitive or distorted, with serious detrimental effects on policies, laws, and constitutions.

The second major source of beliefs is education. We receive beliefs through education of various kinds—sermons, lessons, examples, concealed presuppositions in conversation, loaded words, books—thereby gaining knowledge from experience vicariously. The validity of the beliefs thus acquired depends on the knowledge of our teachers and associates and on their good faith. The imprint is almost indelible: "All those opinions and notions of things, to which we have been accustom'd from our infancy, take such deep root, that 'tis impossible for us, by all the powers of reason and experience, to eradicate them; and this habit not only approaches in its influence, but even on many occasions prevails over that which arises from the constant and inseparable union of causes and effects" (T., 116). A few lines later Hume says,

> I am persuaded, that upon examination we shall find more than one half of those opinions, that prevail among mankind, to be owing to education, and that the principles, which are thus implicitely embrac'd, over-ballance those, which are owing either to abstract reasoning or experience. As liars, by the frequent repetition of their lies, come at last to remember them; so the judgment, or rather the imagination, by the like means, may have ideas so strongly imprinted on it, and conceive them in so full a light, that they may operate upon the mind in the same manner with those, which the senses, memory or reason present to us. (T., 117)

The better we understand the nature of the various relationships in which we participate, the higher will be our morality. Indeed, the whole historical process of civilization—the realization of the principles of civil society—together with all the moral advance civilization entails, is attributable to better knowledge. As people's beliefs improved, their perception of physical nature changed; as their beliefs improved, they realized a vastly improved moral world. Improvements in morals arise mainly from improvements in knowledge; both come about as results of "the experimental method of reasoning." Great advances in knowledge and morals "can only be the result of reflection and experience, and must grow to perfection during several ages of settled and established government."[6]

Believing is natural, but not all beliefs are authentic beliefs. This, as we saw, is obvious in the case of beliefs acquired through education, which often inculcates beliefs "contrary to reason, and even to themselves in different times and places" (*T.*, 117). It is also true in the case of beliefs acquired through our own experience. Hume tells us in the *Treatise*, under the title "Of unphilosophical probability," how we acquire false beliefs. Then he gives us the rules to be followed if we are to escape the tyranny of false beliefs (*T.*, 149). For example, one of the most important ways we go wrong is by making unfounded generalizations.

> A fourth unphilosophical species of probability is that deriv'd from *general rules*, which we rashly form to ourselves, and which are the source of what we properly call PREJUDICE. An *Irishman* cannot have wit, and a *Frenchman* cannot have solidity; for which reason, tho' the conversation of the former in any instance be visibly very agreeable, and of the latter very judicious, we have entertain'd such a prejudice against them, that they must be dunces or fops in spite of sense and reason. Human nature is very subject to errors of this kind; and perhaps this nation as much as any other. (*T.*, 146–47)

The unreflective mind is far from reliable. The generalizations to which it is prone often come in conflict with the general rules by which we ought to govern our beliefs.

> When an object appears, that resembles any cause in very considerable circumstances, the imagination naturally carries us to a lively conception of the usual effect, tho' the object be different in the most material and most efficacious circumstances from that cause. Here is the first influence of general rules. But when we take a review of this act of the mind, and compare it with the more general and authentic operations of the understanding, we find it to be of an irregular nature, and destructive of all the most establish'd principles of reasonings; which is the cause of our rejecting it. This is a second influence of general rules, and implies the condemnation of the former. Sometimes the one, sometimes the other prevails, according to the disposition and character of the person. The vulgar are commonly guided by the first, and wise men by the second. (*T.*, 149–50)

The moral and political opinions of the multitude are largely the products of unmonitored experience and of education. Here we must remember the difference between the beliefs laid down by everyday experience

---

[6] *History of England*, 1:254, 79; also *Enquiry* II, pp. 180–81.

in the immediate physical world, on the one hand, and beliefs about economics, constitutions, and international politics, on the other. The former, as mentioned above, tend to be accurate because adequate experience is unavoidable. In contrast, the latter are often wildly inaccurate. They may be the result of partiality: our country's enemies are evil. They may be distorted by prejudice: the French are frivolous, the Scots rapacious, the English dumb. They may rest on a false analogy: a trading nation must at least balance the books; otherwise it will go broke. They may result from the vulgar proclivity to violence: the sure way to quash dissent is to kill the leading heretics. They may rest on false presuppositions: things were far better in olden times. They may be the fruit of fraudulent education and propaganda by those with "self-ish" interests: party representatives, journalists, monks, merchants, demagogues. They may be sustained by cultural inertia, by a sincere but indolent acquiescence in received opinion. No politician should ever take conventional wisdom and old customs lightly. He should remember that "Each century has its peculiar mode in conducting business; and men, guided more by custom than by reason, follow, without enquiry, the manners, which are prevalent in their own time" (*H.*, 2:86). Henry VIII, for example, in seeking separation from Catherine, his brother's widow, had "custom and precedent on his side, the principle by which men are almost wholly governed in their actions and opinions." As a result, he was supported by the people of England, even against both reason and religious authority (*H.*, 3:192).

The vulgar are content to base their lives on a shallow understanding; indeed, they are capable of achieving nothing more profound. However, those philosophers who use the experimental method can provide a far sounder basis. Aware of how errors creep into thought, they monitor themselves as they form conclusions from experience. They bring reflective minds to bear on experience. Hume's purpose is to show us how to rectify and improve our beliefs by assiduous use of the experimental method of reasoning. The view, now in vogue, that Hume was a conservative in his moral and political philosophy results from the opinion, inculcated by generations of professors, that Hume's chief concern was to dethrone reason; that opinion, however, ignores the purpose for which he advocated the experimental method. Moreover, it cannot be pleaded that he was either reticent or obscure about his reformist intentions. He begins three of his works—the *Treatise*, *An Enquiry concerning Human Understanding*, and the *Political Discourses*—by insisting on the relevance of sound knowledge to the reformation of moral subjects, and consequently to the reformation of society: " 'Tis impossible to tell what changes and improvements we might make in these [nonmoral] sciences were we thoroughly acquainted with the extent and force of human understanding, and cou'd explain the nature of the ideas we employ, and of the operations we perform in our reasonings" (*T.*, xv). The prospect for improvement, he submits, is even greater in the moral sciences, which depend far more on human nature. In the very first sentence of *An Enquiry concerning Human Understanding*, he reverts to his analogy of the painter and the anatomist: "Moral philosophy, or the science of human nature, may be treated after two different manners; each of which has its peculiar merit, and may contribute to the entertainment, instruction, and reformation of mankind" (p. 5). The remainder of the section explains how accurate and abstruse philosophers make a contribution to society at least as important as that of those who merely recommend morality. Indeed, although, as Mandeville had said, those who inquire into the reason of things seldom are people of business and action, because they make discoveries and improve our beliefs, they contribute more to the advancement of humankind than those who simply teach old truths and values, even sound old truths and values. Again, in the first paragraphs of the *Political Discourses*—in the essay "Of Commerce"—Hume tells us that the chief business of philosophers, as it ought to be of politicians, is to achieve an understanding of the principles of society, thus providing a foundation for good laws and policies.[7]

Hume wrote against not one but two errors in moral philosophy. The first of these is that since the feelings, both passions and sensations, are inferior to reason, perhaps even evil, reason alone ought to direct and govern all aspects of human conduct. Hume's attack on that error is famous, but, as we have seen, both Hutcheson and Butler had preceded him. The other error, which he found perhaps even more stultifying, is that since the pretenses of the rationalists are hollow, we have no choice but to rely on unexamined beliefs, on beliefs produced perhaps by inadequate experience, faulty education, or false analogy, and on customs, laws, and policies based on those beliefs. It is a grave mistake to focus so intensely on his refutation of the claims made for "reason alone" that his profound distrust of untested belief is ignored. We are not limited to a choice between reason and prevailing opinion; indeed, the declared purpose of the *Treatise* is practical: to explain the need for the deliberate application of the experimental method of reasoning to moral subjects, and to attempt to use that method. What is required is not abstract reasoning and not mere experience, but "reflection and experience." The experimental method is not new; indeed it is wise nature's way to scientific

---

[7] *Essays*, pp. 253–55. Hume did not accept the view that contemplative persons can only *explain* the world. When, after publishing the *Treatise*, he turned to the writing of essays, he presented himself as an ambassador from the "learned" to the "conversible"; these two kingdoms had been too long isolated from each other, to the disadvantage of both. One cause of this was that the learned had come to rely on reason alone. *Essays*, pp. 533–37.

knowledge.[8] The person of experience needs reason, just as the person of reason needs experience. It is by relying on "reason alone"—Mandeville's "lofty self-sufficient Reason"—that scholars have earned their reputation as squabbling "metaphysicians."

It has been argued that Hume's rejection of the rationalist method in moral subjects made him diffident both in advocating and in defending particular institutions; he lacked, it is said, a rational basis for moral distinctions.[9] His reply would be that while pure rationalists provide no ba-

[8] There is nothing extraordinary, Hume says, about examining our beliefs on moral and physical subjects skeptically; indeed, such an approach is a requisite of improvement. For example, it is by employing the experimental method that we put anthropomorphic beliefs behind us: "We find human faces in the moon, armies in the clouds; and by a natural propensity, if not corrected by experience and reflection, ascribe malice and good-will to every thing, that hurts or pleases us." *The Natural History of Religion*, pp. 33–34. The most abstruse speculator and the youngest learner alike test their beliefs by the experimental method. The speculator considers "that every one, even in common Life, is constrain'd to have more or less of this [skeptical] Philosophy; that from our earliest Infancy we make continual Advances in forming more general Principles of Conduct and Reasoning; that the larger Experience we acquire, and the stronger Reason we are endow'd with, we always render our Principles the more general and comprehensive; and that what we call *Philosophy* is nothing but a more regular and methodical Operation of the same kind. To philosophize on such Subjects is nothing essentially different from reasoning on common Life; and we may only expect greater Stability, if not greater Truth, from our Philosophy, on account of its exacter and more scrupulous Method of proceeding." *Dialogues Concerning Natural Religion*, p. 151.

[9] One of the main reasons why Hume's moral and political philosophy is interpreted as conservative is the view that all genuine natural law is inevitably based on demonstrative reason. Hume showed how small and weak the realm of demonstrative reason is; therefore, the destruction of natural law can be attributed to him—as it was by G. H. Sabine in *A History of Political Theory* (New York: Henry Holt and Company, 1937). Much the same approach was taken by Sheldon S. Wolin, who, in an influential article first published in 1954, wrote, "The net effect of this argument [that reason is the slave of the passions] was, of course, to undermine the whole theory of natural law with its immutable values discoverable by rational inquiry." See his "Hume and Conservatism," in *Hume: A Re-evaluation*, eds. D. W. Livingston and J. T. King (New York: Fordham University Press, 1976), pp. 239–56, specifically, p. 242. But is the choice limited to these alternatives: either, on the one hand, natural law discovered by demonstration or, on the other, customary arrangements that work because, like a language, they are generally accepted and practiced? Duncan Forbes, in sharp contrast to Sabine and Wolin, contends that Hume's goal was to achieve a system of natural law that is strictly natural (that is, independent of religious foundations), discovered, not by demonstration, but by the experimental method. See his *Hume's Philosophical Politics* (Cambridge: Cambridge University Press, 1975), pp. 59–90. See also his essay "Natural Law and the Scottish Enlightenment," in *The Origins and Nature of the Scottish Enlightenment*, eds. R. H. Campbell and A. S. Skinner (Edinburgh: John Donald Publishers Ltd., 1982), pp. 186–204. Of course, even if Forbes is correct, as I think he is, this does not mean that Wolin is wrong when he contends that Hume was representative of a change in temper that took place as the achievements of seventeenth-century liberalism became "conservatized" in the Augustan era. Ibid., p. 254. My view is that while it is true that Hume wished to see those achievements fully established, he also had hopes, related (a)

sis whatsoever for moral distinctions, in fact such distinctions are made all the time; they are made by spectators concerned for the good of humankind. Moreover, it is not true that the morals of one era or country are just as good as those of another. What spectators approve depends directly on their knowledge (understanding); for example, the doctrine of tyrannicide, once taught even by the Church, has been nullified by better knowledge. This is why strict adherence to the authentic operation of the understanding, which combines experience and reason, is basic to the improvement of morals. It is true that barbarians are not likely to admire the morals of a civilized society; they know no better. This does not mean that a civilized person should not deplore barbarism.

So far is Hume from complacently accepting the laws, institutions, customs, maxims, and policies of any historical period that when he writes, not as an epistemologist, but as a politician trying to convey the findings of abstruse philosophy to the people of action, he is quite ready to abandon the language appropriate to his theory of knowledge and to revert to ordinary usage. In both the *History of England* and the essays, he uses the words "reason" and "rational" in the familiar way, enlisting himself on the side of reason. As David Miller says, the *History* "is replete with references to the victory of passion over reason, or, less often, the converse."[10] For example, writing about the way Normans treated the people of England, Hume comments that "they pushed the rights of conquest (very extensive in the eyes of avarice and ambition, however narrow in those of reason) to the utmost extremity against them" (*H.*, 1:226). Likewise, there are many critical comments on old beliefs and customs. The history of civilization, Hume holds, is an account of the assault of reason upon false suppositions, misleading prejudices, inveterate customs, and barbarous manners. Most people cling complacently to old opinions and practices: "All advances towards reason and good sense are slow and gradual" (*H.*, 1:359). Dr. Harvey made a capital discovery in medicine; yet it has been noted that "no physician in Europe, who had reached forty years of age, ever, to the end of his life, adopted Harvey's doctrine of the circulation of the blood, and that his practice in London diminished ex-

---

to the need for social progress in Scotland and (b) to aspirations for new advances based on sound political science, that is, sound natural jurisprudence. The wide scope of natural jurisprudence in contemporary Scottish thought is shown by Francis Hutcheson's *A System of Moral Philosophy* (1755). (Republished as vols. 5 and 6 in *The Collected Works of Francis Hutcheson* [Hildesheim: Georg Olms Verlagsbuchhandlung, 1971].) Also by Adam Smith's *Lectures on Jurisprudence* (Oxford: Clarendon Press, 1978). For Smith, natural jurisprudence embraces not only "what concerns justice, but . . . what concerns police, revenue, and arms, and whatever else is the object of law." *The Theory of Moral Sentiments* (Oxford: Clarendon Press, 1976), p. 342.

[10] David Miller, *Philosophy and Ideology in Hume's Political Thought* (Oxford: Clarendon Press, 1981), p. 48.

tremely, from the reproach drawn upon him, by that great and signal discovery. So slow is the progress of truth in every science, even when not opposed by factious or superstitious prejudices!" (*H.*, 6:154). Acceptance of the maxims of dueling, the principal manifestation of the fact that the aristocracy thinks itself above the rules of both state and church, "shed much of the best blood in Christendom during more than two centuries; and notwithstanding the severity of law and authority of reason, such is the prevailing force of custom, they are far from being as yet entirely exploded" (*H.*, 3:169). The notion that duplicity is a vice of civilization, that primitive people are candid and truthful, is totally wrong: "Virtue, which is nothing but a more enlarged and more cultivated reason, never flourishes to any degree, nor is founded on steady principles of honour, except where a good education becomes general; and where men are taught the pernicious consequences of vice, treachery, and immorality" (*H.*, 1:179–80).

The notion of a unique, superior common-law culture in England is foolish: the reception of Roman law, openly in western Europe, covertly in England, wrought a great improvement, for it was a vastly better system, far more rational and conducive to individual liberty than the absurd customary jurisprudence (*H.*, 2:520–23). In 1603 the inhabitants of both the Highlands and Lowlands of Scotland were politically primitive: "Both these races of men, however different in other respects, lived, at that time, in a manner somewhat disorderly; governed by antient customs more than by laws, and attached to their own families more than to their prince or country."[11] James I brought about a great advance in Ireland, hitherto neglected by the English, but first it was necessary "to abolish the Irish customs, which supplied the place of laws, and which were calculated to keep that people for ever in a state of barbarism and disorder" (*H.*, 5:47). The House of Commons, swayed by custom, was deplorably unrealistic in its responses to Charles I's requests for money: "Habits, more than reason, we find, in every thing, to be the governing principle of mankind" (*H.*, 5:159). Apologizing at the end of the pre-Tudor history for having carried his readers "through a series of many barbarous ages," Hume submits that the study of human manners is both profitable and agreeable: even if "the aspect in some periods seems horrid and deformed, we may thence learn to cherish with the greater anxiety that science and civility, which has so close a connexion with virtue and humanity, and which, as it is a sovereign antidote against superstition, is also the most effectual remedy against vice and disorders of every kind." Old beliefs and customs, we may safely conclude, far from being a precious heritage,

---

[11] *The History of Great Britain*; 1st ed., ed. Duncan Forbes (Harmondsworth: Penguin Books, 1970), p. 141.

worthy of reverent conservation, are to be tested rigorously. Again and again Hume deplores the human tendency to praise and magnify the past, to the detriment of true history and reliable political thought.[12] Nor should we forget how fundamental errors about the nature of moral virtue are perpetuated from one generation to another; the persistence of absurd moral beliefs is almost enough to reduce a philosopher to "diffidence and scepticism" (*E.*, 278).

Those who interpret Hume's moral and political philosophy as conservative fail to give sufficient emphasis to the role he assigned to those who discover true principles: sound philosophers and wise politicians. They fail to do so because of one or the other of two mistakes. The first mistake is the extreme view that for Hume the political order observed by a law-abiding person is artificial in the sense that civil society has no essential principles, with the result that a genuine civil society can be changed radically in any direction, provided only that the change takes place gradually, always retaining close continuity between the old and the new. The second is the view that, while he recognizes that there are essential principles, Hume holds that whatever is customary in a country must be regarded as good, as a realization of the principles, and that while improvement, a higher realization, is possible, it must take place incrementally in response to specific cases and problems, that is, unscientifically, much as unreflective mechanics perfect their craft. These mistakes result from confusing what Hume himself keeps separate, namely, the right and the good. The laws established in an age define what is right according to law in that age; however, those laws may not be good, perhaps not even tolerable, in which case the laws will come to be regarded as morally wrong.

The prevailing law may permit entails and require primogeniture in the inheritance of land. If so, that is what is right according to law, but we know that it is not good. Likewise, the constitution may prescribe that the king be elected and that once in office he is absolute. Conformity to this rule would be right according to constitutional law; we know, however, that such a rule is bad. What is right according to law? That is a legal question. What is good? That is a philosophical question. For example, it was right that the people of England should be abject in their obedience to Elizabeth, an absolute monarch; the established constitution of her age required such conduct. Yet in retrospect the English have no reason to hold absolute monarchy in high repute or to form magnificent ideas of the prosperity and liberty of former days; the truth is that in olden times England was a barbarous nation, and that "even *When good*

---

[12] *History of England*, 2:518–19. To glorify the past at the expense of the present is a standard cause of erroneous opinion. See *Essays*, pp. 278, 423, 464; also the *History of England*, 3:329; 5:142. Hume's scorn for the belief that Scotland's past had been glorious had strong anti-Jacobite implications; see chapter 6, note 9.

Queen Elizabeth sat on the Throne, there was very little good Roast Beef in it, and no Liberty at all."[13]

The basic rule of any political order is this: obey the laws made by the government. Hume makes it abundantly clear, however, that some political orders are better than others. In other words, the idea of a better order may challenge an established order. This happened in England during the seventeenth century: James I and Charles I, who had the preponderance of constitutional right on their side, were confronted by a few men who envisioned a better constitution; the latter triumphed in the end—not, lamentably, because of the strength of reason, but because of the power of religious fanaticism. Far from being a constitutional positivist, Hume never says that major reforms should not be promoted, or that a really bad government should not be turned out, by force if necessary. While he has only bitter scorn for "religious puritans," he praises the advocates of the new and better constitution, the ancestors of the "political Whigs." The picture of Hume as a timorous conservative clinging to a raft of artifice because, poor skeptic, he knows nothing better, is belied fully by his *History of England*, which abounds in outspoken denunciations of certain prevalent opinions and established laws and institutions as bad, iniquitous, disgusting, irrational, violent, barbarous. Does Hume ever say that whatever is customary in society is always good? Clearly, it may be "the right," as in the case of the Salic laws, but this is mere tautology! The main value of surveying the manners of past ages is that, freed from the seductive presupposition that the old and the good are the same, we may come to value the new if it is good. This is the lesson Hume sought to teach both those for whom "the ancient constitution" was the good constitution, and those who rejected the post-1689 constitution because it was new.

A favorite text of those who interpret Hume as a conservative comes from *An Enquiry concerning Human Understanding*, where he says: "Custom, then, is the great guide of human life."[14] However, Hume is explaining here not specifically the moral and political order, but the origin of all beliefs, false as well as authentic. The decisive question asks how we can distinguish between false and authentic beliefs. As Hume says in the *Treatise*, "It may . . . be concluded, that our judgment and imagination can never be contrary, and that custom cannot operate on the latter faculty after such a manner, as to render it opposite to the former. This difficulty we can remove after no other manner, than by supposing the influence of general rules. We shall afterwards [in section 15] take notice of some general rules, by which we ought to regulate our judgment concerning causes and effects" (*T.*, 149). In *An Enquiry concerning Human Understanding*, he asks: "Since all reasonings concerning facts or causes is derived merely from custom . . . [how does it happen] that men so much surpass animals in reasoning, and one man so much surpasses another? Has not the same custom the same influence on all?" He then proceeds to list the causes of the great differences in levels of human understanding.[15]

As stated, the key to Hume's position is the distinction between the unreflective multitude and persons of sound understanding. The former tend to equate what is right by law or custom with what is good. They live by received opinion. They build ships and houses in the old ways. They regard all aspects of scientific agriculture—the mechanical profession that requires the most reflection and experience if it is to advance—with indifference or suspicion. They live by prejudice and tradition. Rarely do they examine the established rules of the economic-political order; instead, they take titles seriously, questioning them only when they clash. For them a valid title is sufficient to establish legitimacy; the fact that James I was the great-great-grandson of Henry VII was sufficient to make the people of England accept him, a foreigner, as their king without a murmur (*H.*, 5:3–4). When claims to an estate conflict, the judges do not divide the estate; rather, they pretend to detect the one true owner, often on the basis of "the most frivolous reasons in the world." To do otherwise would reveal the dangerous truth that sometimes there are goods to which nobody has a right (*T.*, 531). In contrast, the wise know the difference between "right" and "good." They also understand how the unreflective mind works.

Up to this point, our question has been this: having recognized that "reason alone" cannot rule the world, are we driven to conclude that mankind is entirely dependent on custom, or on custom as modified by only incremental change? Hume's answer, I have argued, is, no, by experience and reflection we can improve our understanding, thus perhaps discovering the scientific desirability of specific reforms, perhaps radical reforms, in our laws, policies, and constitutional arrangements. The next question relates to means or methods: how should the wise go about achieving desirable reforms?

Popular beliefs about morality differ from popular beliefs about physical nature in one very important way. The physical world exists independent of human opinion, but fundamental laws, manners, customs, rights, and practices, all the forms and functions of a political society, are but outward and visible effects of prevalent beliefs. A constitution, for ex-

---

[15] Ibid., p. 107n. See T. K. Hearn, Jr., " 'General Rules' in Hume's *Treatise*," in *Journal of the History of Philosophy* 8 (1970): 405–22.

ample, works only because the multitude thinks that the rules must be followed. The *form* of old beliefs and customs deserves a wise person's respect, for it is mainly as unexamined belief and custom that civilized rules govern the multitude in their economic and political activities. But a wise person ought to evaluate the *content* of received belief and custom; if they produce bad results, they cry out for reform. Custom may be "the standing wisdom of the country," as Burke was to say; as such it may cause a philosopher either comfort or frustration.

The standards that define obligation in the natural relationships simply establish norms: any divergence between what one does naturally and what duty requires is only a matter of degree; for example, in the case of a parent, the standard requires an appropriate measure of benevolence. Consequently, these standards are stable and secure; their realization is not historical. In contrast, the basic rules of civility—respect property, keep contracts, obey the laws—often require conduct directly contrary to what one would do in the absence of understanding or moral obligation. Like bitter medicines, they are recommended by their long-term effects. While the wise see those good effects, the unreflective multitude behave as good members of civil society chiefly because of habit and education. Accordingly, whenever a major improvement is attempted, there is danger that a fall, not the intended advance, will result. The raft analogy is helpful, but it is the unreflective who can neither fly nor swim; they need the support and guidance of rules, rules to be followed without question. This is shown clearly in the case of the *grundnorm* that a government's laws always are to be obeyed. That rule is false; yet to teach that every person may pass upon every law would be to plunge him into the water on his own or under the power of demagogues. Therefore, unlike the Whig ideologists, the wise leave the presumption in favor of obedience undisturbed.

They see also that if the right as defined by positive law becomes sufficiently bad, it will be challenged. For the same reason, the wise politician always prefers careful reform to sudden, radical change. In careful reformation, enough of the structure of established right is preserved intact to retain the frame of legitimacy; to resort to violent change is to rely on one's might and good fortune for the realization of the projected better order: "Some innovations must necessarily have place in every human institution, and it is happy where the enlightened genius of the age give these a direction to the side of reason, liberty, and justice: but violent innovations no individual is entitled to make: they are even dangerous to be attempted by the legislature."[16] One effect of violent change may be

[16] *Essays*, p. 477. Christopher J. Berry, too, finds that Hume's social and political thought is conservative. However, it is important to notice both what he says and the grounds for

the shattering of the very structure of the society; when this happens, when all habitual social patterns and laws lose their influence, predictably the outcome will be the concentration of power in the hands of one person. This was seen in England in 1653: "By recent, as well as all ancient example, it was become evident, that illegal violence, with whatever pretences it may be covered, and whatever object it may pursue, must inevitably end at last in the arbitrary and despotic government of a single person" (*H.*, 6:54).

The wise politician scrutinizes his beliefs carefully, while the multitude simply accept the beliefs—whatever they are—that have set in or have been taught. In both cases, the fact that our beliefs arise from experience either directly or vicariously through education, a more dubious source, inevitably means that how we behave into the future is causally connected with the past. We cannot fly away to New Jerusalem on the wings of "reason"; for reason here can mean only fanciful flights of the imagination. This position, Hume's position, will be denounced as conservative only by those who deny his epistemology. For Hume, as for Mandeville, the time had come when fancying, the speculation of people remote from experience, had to be distinguished from reason; otherwise, in the future, as in the past, the sciences would remain highly imperfect, with the victories going to those who made the most noise. "Nothing is more dangerous to reason than the flights of the imagination, and nothing has been the occasion of more mistakes among philosophers. Men of bright fancies may in this respect be compar'd to those angels, whom the scripture represents as covering their eyes with their wings" (*T.*, 267).

Provided they keep their eyes open and obey the rules, true philosophers can make progress. The wise, having freed themselves from the notion that whatever is old is good, and having turned away from old beliefs, not to "reason and reflection"—that is, fancying—but to "reflection and experience," can make advances in political science. Hume saw that the good is the genuine, but that the "real" (what exists as established law in any age) may be somewhat false, perhaps even "horrid and deformed."

---

his conclusion: "Society coheres then, for Hume, because of the presence of uniformities or regularities, of expectations deriving either directly from human nature, as we shall see in the case of familial affection and sympathetic association, or indirectly, as in the case of justice. To have expectations capable of supporting actions depends on their having been constantly experienced, which is to say on them being habitual. . . . This, above all, is why Hume's social and political thought is conservative. If society depends on constancy, on habitually sanctioned expectations, then any 'break' or flexibility undermines the cumulatively acquired cohesiveness" (p. 79). Obviously, if this were all that scholars mean when they say that Hume's moral and political thought is conservative, one would agree in substance, while entering a caveat on the use of the term "conservative." See especially Berry's chapter entitled "Social Cohesiveness," in his *Hume, Hegel and Human Nature* (The Hague: Martinus Nijhoff Publishers, 1982), pp. 69–95.

Because a political society is based on the opinions of the people, the wild radicalism of religious fanatics is dangerous. Such people are idiotic; like very young children, they regard their own good as the good; worse, they are possessed idiots, for they take their own will as God's will. "No character in human society is more dangerous than that of the fanatic; because, if attended with weak judgment, he is exposed to the suggestions of others; if supported by more discernment, he is entirely governed by his own illusions, which sanctify his most selfish views and passions" (H., 6:113). It is true that religious enthusiasm sometimes may promote beneficial political change, as in seventeenth-century England, but this is accidental; enthusiasm is far more likely to be destructive. Who knows what its effects will be in any instance, or when it will run amok! Similarly, "political projectors"; those who would reform the state according to their own fanciful systems, are to be scorned: "Of all mankind there are none so pernicious as political projectors, if they have power; nor so ridiculous, if they want it" (Essays, 647).

David Miller states that for Hume the political theorist "had to accept human judgement at face value, as non-rational and corrigible only to a small degree." He comments: "A position of this kind must in a diffuse sense be conservative, not because it is yet committed to any particular set of institutions or social arrangements, but because it must remain closely tied to conventionally-accepted judgements."[17] In opposition, I submit that Hume's contention that human goals are set by the passions and that the understanding cannot achieve demonstrable knowledge about the real world does not make him a conservative. Indeed, the purpose of improving our beliefs is to liberate politicians from merely customary opinions and values. My submission, argued above, is that under Hume's tutelage, moralists and politicians can be progressive, although generally they proceed only in a careful, Fabian way. Hume began the essay "Of the Idea of a perfect Commonwealth" by warning against political projectors, armed or unarmed; he went on to say that "a wise politician is the most beneficial character in nature, if accompanied with authority; and the most innocent, and not altogether useless, even if deprived of it" (Essays, 647).

We have seen that Hume has little confidence in philosophies that pre-

[17] *Philosophy and Ideology*, p. 191. Miller seems to follow closely the interpretation of Book I of the *Treatise* given by Norman Kemp Smith. That interpretation held that the earlier view of Hume as nihilistically skeptical was wrong, that while Hume took demonstrative reason away, he supplanted it with belief. Smith, however, did not emphasize that Hume's main practical purpose was to have us test our beliefs rigorously. My interpretation is far closer to that of David Fate Norton. See his *David Hume: Common-Sense Moralist, Sceptical Metaphysician* (Princeton: Princeton University Press, 1982), pp. 3–20 and 208–38.

tend to make particular people happy. He has far more confidence in the ability of the wise to show how those important moral causes that help determine a nation's character—its laws, constitution, property system, military and religious institutions—can be improved. For example, he begins "Of Parties in General" by disagreeing with Bacon on the proper rating of those who have advanced the arts and sciences and those who have advanced morals.

> Speculative sciences do, indeed, improve the mind; but this advantage reaches only to a few persons, who have leisure to apply themselves to them. And as to practical arts, which encrease the commodities and enjoyments of life, it is well known, that men's happiness consists not so much in an abundance of these, as in the peace and security with which they possess them; and those blessings can only be derived from good government. Not to mention, that general virtue and good morals in a state, which are so requisite to happiness, can never arise from the most refined precepts of philosophy, or even the severest injunctions of religion; but must proceed entirely from the virtuous education of youth, the effect of wise laws and institutions. (*Essays*, 54–55)

This is why he contends that "Of all men, that distinguish themselves by memorable atchievements, the first place of honour seems due to LEGISLATORS and founders of states, who transmit a system of laws and institutions to secure the peace, happiness, and liberty of future generations" (*Essays*, 54). He relies for "general virtue and good morals in a state" not on either philosophical homilies or unexamined beliefs, but on "the virtuous education of youth, the effect of wise laws and institutions." Hume is far from content with untutored public opinion; it tends to be primitive and, therefore, dangerous. It is shallow and prejudiced. It is susceptible to fanaticism. It is nationalistic and bellicose. It exalts the past above the present. But Hume is not resigned: a wise politician, having achieved true principles, may be able to change public opinion. Hume hoped to make his readers realize that, by showing that true principles cannot be achieved by demonstration, he was not implying that such principles cannot be found. In the anonymous apology, *A Letter from a Gentleman*, Hume stated the intention of the author of the *Treatise*:

> All he means by these Scruples is to abate the Pride of *mere human Reasoners*, by showing them, that even with regard to Principles which seem the clearest, and which they are necessitated from the strongest Instincts of Nature to embrace, they are not able to attain a full Consistence and absolute Certainty. *Modesty* then, and *Humility*, with regard to the Operation of our natural Faculties, is the Result of *Scepticism*; not an universal Doubt, which

it is impossible for any Man to support, and which the first and most trivial
Accident in Life must immediately disconcert and destroy.[18]

In *An Enquiry concerning Human Understanding*, he already had explained the function of his kind of skepticism. It is to convince us that in
the natural and moral sciences we cannot rely on either abstract reason
or conventional wisdom. The only way to truth is the experimental
method of reasoning. Moderate skepticism "is a necessary preparative to
the study of philosophy, by preserving a proper impartiality in our judgements, and weaning our mind from all those prejudices, which we may
have imbibed from education or rash opinion. To begin with clear and
self-evident principles, to advance by timorous and sure steps, to review
frequently our conclusions, and examine accurately all their consequences; though by these means we shall make both a slow and a short
progress in our systems; are the only methods, by which we can ever hope
to reach truth, and attain a proper stability and certainty in our determinations."[19]

Justice Not Factitious

The view that Hume regards an established political order as beyond radical criticism arises in large part from a persistent misunderstanding of
why he describes justice, loyalty, and so on as artificial virtues. Mandeville had distinguished between the natural and the artificial: "Every thing
therefore that our Industry can produce or compass, is originally owing
to the Author of our Being. But when we speak of the Works of Nature,
to distinguish them from those of Art, we mean such, as were brought
forth without our Concurrence. So Nature in due Season produces Peas;
but in *England* you cannot have them green in *January*, without Art and
uncommon Industry. What Nature designs, she executes herself."[20] This,
as we have seen, is the distinction Hume employs in the *Treatise*: "Mankind is an inventive species; and where an invention is obvious and absolutely necessary, it may as properly be said to be natural as any thing
that proceeds immediately from original principles, without the intervention of thought or reflexion. Tho' the rules of justice be *artificial*, they are
not *arbitrary*. Nor is the expression improper to call them *Laws of Nature*; if by natural we understand what is common to any species, or even

[18] *A Letter From a Gentleman to his friend in Edinburgh*, eds. E. C. Mossner and J. V.
Price (Edinburgh: The University Press, 1967), p. 19.
[19] *An Enquiry concerning Human Understanding*, p. 150.
[20] *The Fable of the Bees*, ed. F. B. Kay, 2 vols. (London: Oxford University Press, 1924),
2:186.

if we confine it to mean what is inseparable from the species" (*T.*, 484).
To observe "the three fundamental laws of nature" is right according to
natural law; it is a *natural* duty, while obedience to the government's laws
is a *civil* duty (*T.*, 543).

Some social relationships are natural; they result directly from human
feelings for some others. Other relationships are artificial; they are of human institution. The latter, those from institution, are of two kinds: some
are instituted by *convention*, others by *constitution*. In the case of convention, what works best comes about, like a language, by evolution. In
the *Dialogues concerning Natural Religion*, where the infallibility of the
Author of the world is being debated, we find Hume, perhaps following
Mandeville, employing the example of the gradual improvement of ships.

> But were this World ever so perfect a Production, it must still remain uncer-
> tain, whether all the Excellencies of the Work can justly be ascrib'd to the
> Workman. If we survey a Ship, what an exalted Idea must we form of the
> Ingenuity of the Carpenter, who fram'd so complicated useful and beautiful
> a Machine? And what Surprize must we entertain, when we find him a stupid
> Mechanic, who imitated others, and copy'd an Art, which, thro' a long Suc-
> cession of Ages, after multiply'd Tryals, Mistakes, Corrections, Delibera-
> tions, and Controversies, had been gradually improving? Many Worlds
> might have been botch'd and bungled, throughout an Eternity, 'ere this Sys-
> tem was struck out: Much Labour lost: Many fruitless Tryals made: And a
> slow, but continu'd Improvment carry'd on during infinite Ages in the Art of
> World-making.[21]

What now seems a good social and political order may have come about
by evolution, by the retention at each stage of what had worked best.
Alternatively, some institution takes place by constitution, for once the
principles have become a science they can be used prescriptively by the
wise to form and reform at propitious times. In either case, social and
political institutions are not simply arbitrary; they may be badly twisted
and flawed by selfish interest, bad custom, and violence, but the principles
must find some measure of expression and realization. To be seaworthy,
ships, whether shaped by illiterate artisans or by naval architects, must

---

[21] *The Natural History of Religion and Dialogues concerning Natural Religion*, eds.
A. W. Colver and J. V. Price (Oxford: Clarendon Press, 1976), pp. 191. The idea of spontaneous order runs through Scottish Enlightenment thought; see Ronald Hamowy, *The
Scottish Enlightenment and the Theory of Spontaneous Order* (Carbondale: Southern Illi-
nois University Press for the Journal of the History of Philosophy, Inc., 1987). This theory
was Mandeville's alternative to attributing order to "lofty self-sufficient Reason." However,
as we have seen, Hume is not content to rely on spontaneity alone; the discovery of the
principles of justice and governance makes it possible to correct policies and improve institutions.

conform to certain requirements. It is true that in the past justice has been instituted largely by convention; this does not mean that it has no essential principles. The same is true of governance.

Very early Hume saw that his use of the words "artificial" and "artifice" in the *Treatise* had been a mistake: he was accused of treating justice, allegiance, and the like as comparable to the morality Mandeville's crafty politicians had imposed for their own knavish ends. In *A Letter from a Gentleman,* he dealt with the accusation that he had sapped "the Foundations of Morality, by denying the natural and essential Difference betwixt Right and Wrong, Good and Evil, Justice and Injustice; making the Difference only artificial, and to arise from human Conventions and Compacts." He explained:

> When the Author asserts that Justice is an *artificial* not a *natural Virtue,* he seems sensible that he employed Words that admit of an invidious Construction; and therefore makes use of all proper Expedients, by *Definitions* and *Explanations,* to prevent it. . . . By the *natural Virtues* he plainly understands *Compassion* and *Generosity,* and such as we are immediately carried to by a *natural Instinct;* and by the *artificial Virtues* he means *Justice, Loyalty,* and such as require, along with a *natural Instinct,* a certain Reflection on the general Interests of Human Society, and a Combination with others. In the same Sense, Sucking is an Action natural to Man, and Speech is artificial. But what is there in this Doctrine that can be supposed in the least pernicious? Has he not expresly asserted, That Justice, in another Sense of the Word, is so natural to Man, that no Society of Men, and even no individual Member of any Society, was ever entirely devoid of all Sense of it? Some Persons (tho' without any Reason, in my Opinion) are displeased with Mr. *Hutchison's* Philosophy, in founding all the Virtues so much on *Instinct,* and admitting so little of *Reason* and *Reflection.* Those should be pleased to find that so considerable a Branch of the Moral Duties are founded on that Principle.[22]

In 1748, in "Of the Original Contract," he restated his distinction without employing the misleading words.

> All *moral* duties may be divided into two kinds. The *first* are those, to which men are impelled by a natural instinct or immediate propensity, which operates on them, independent of all ideas of obligation, and of all views, either to public or private utility. . . .
>
> The *second* kind of moral duties are such as are not supported by any original instinct of nature, but are performed entirely from a sense of obligation, when we consider the necessities of human society, and the impossibility of supporting it, if these duties were neglected. It is thus *justice* or a regard to the property of others, *fidelity* or the observance of promises, be-

[22] *A Letter from a Gentleman,* pp. 18, 30–31.

come obligatory, and acquire an authority over mankind. For as it is evident, that every man loves himself better than any other person, he is naturally impelled to extend his acquisitions as much as possible; and nothing can restrain him in this propensity, but reflection and experience, by which he learns the pernicious effects of that licence, and the total dissolution of society which must ensue from it. His original inclination, therefore, or instinct, is here checked and restrained by a subsequent judgment or observation.

The case is precisely the same with the political or civil duty of *allegiance*, as with the natural duties of justice and fidelity. Our primary instincts lead us, either to indulge ourselves in unlimited freedom, or to seek dominion over others: And it is reflection only, which engages us to sacrifice such strong passions to the interests of peace and public order. (*Essays*, 479–80)

Hume let this account stand in all subsequent editions of his essays. In *Enquiry* II, he retains the Aristotelian distinction between family and society: since the former is based on instinct and the latter on "understanding and experience," perhaps it is not surprising, he comments, that the principles of society are said to be artificial. However, understanding is natural to human beings: "In so sagacious an animal, what necessarily arises from the exertion of his intellectual faculties may justly be esteemed natural."[23] Given Hume's own recognition that the words "artificial" and "artifice" may mislead readers, and his care to explain those words, in reading the *Treatise*, whether as admirers or critics, we should give them the meaning Hume says he intended them to bear. There is nothing arbitrary about justice and fidelity; they are fundamental to society.

Hume's contention is that although genuine civil societies, like ships, do not exist by nature but have to be built, there are certain basic principles that must be followed, for example, private property is not merely an option. In the past, these principles have been learned by experience; however, the time has now come when people of cultivated understanding can undertake to settle the disputes and formulate the principles. Those who improve our understanding of ship building and statecraft create no new principles, but by discovering the principles implicit in our practice they enable us to improve both construction and navigation. Moreover, while nature insists that the unreflective practitioner cannot go completely wrong for long in building ships, walking on ice, and administering simple medicine, once we turn to subjects where the effects of

[23] *Enquiry* II, p. 307. Because Hume bases his "laws of nature" directly on human nature, the permanence and uniformity, or the opposite, of human nature is a question of fundamental importance. If human nature is unstable, "laws" based on it will lack the constancy usually attributed to laws of nature. Christopher J. Berry argues, with an impressive exhibit of evidence, that for Hume human nature is constant, that it is neither unpredictable nor developing. See his *Hume, Hegel and Human Nature*, pp. 57–68.

causes are far from obvious, we find that unreflective practitioners, be they kings, ministers, husbandmen, or merchants, commonly follow bad maxims and practices. Never does Hume renounce reflection; never does he, with Burke, recommend a policy of simply following inherited tradition, a policy that is "the happy effect of following nature, which is wisdom without reflection, and above it." There is a key role for the person of cultivated understanding. Hume states his position candidly in "Of the Idea of a perfect Commonwealth."

> The mathematicians in EUROPE have been much divided concerning that figure of a ship, which is the most commodious for sailing; and HUYGENS, who at last determined the controversy, is justly thought to have obliged the learned, as well as commercial world; though COLUMBUS had sailed to AMERICA, and Sir FRANCIS DRAKE made the tour of the world, without any such discovery. As one form of government must be allowed more perfect than another, independent of the manners and humours of particular men; why may we not enquire what is the most perfect of all, though the common botched and inaccurate governments seem to serve the purposes of society, and though it be not so easy to establish a new system of government, as to build a vessel upon a new construction? The subject is surely the most worthy curiosity of any the wit of man can possibly devise. And who knows, if this controversy were fixed by the universal consent of the wise and learned, but, in some future age, an opportunity might be afforded of reducing the theory to practice, either by a dissolution of some old government, or by the combination of men to form a new one, in some distant part of the world? In all cases, it must be advantageous to know what is most perfect in the kind, that we may be able to bring any real constitution or form of government as near it as possible, by such gentle alterations and innovations as may not give too great disturbance to society. (*Essays*, 513–14)

At a certain point, enough knowledge had been gained through experience to enable mathematicians—Reneau for Mandeville, Huygens for Hume—to state scientifically the principles of ship construction. Similarly, reflective people, people of cultivated understanding, can show how public institutions and policy ought to be reformed. The bulk of humankind, the unreflective practitioners, engrossed in the habitual and inherited, may do fairly well in daily life, but they can never be scientists.

> Their eye is confounded with such an extensive prospect; and the conclusions, derived from it, even though clearly expressed, seem intricate and obscure. But however intricate they may seem, it is certain, that general principles, if just and sound, must always prevail in the general course of things, though they may fail in particular cases; and it is the chief business of philosophers to regard the general course of things. I may add, that it is also the

chief business of politicians; especially in the domestic government of the state, where the public good, which is, or ought to be their object, depends on the concurrence of a multitude of causes; not, as in foreign politics, on accidents and chances, and the caprices of a few persons. (*Essays*, 254–55)

A second question refers to the methods to be used in reforming a defective civil society. Clearly, since all political power rests ultimately on opinion—for people, unlike brute beasts, are led by opinion—what has to be done is to correct the opinions of those who count. Hume himself set out to do this, to change radically the minds of Britons about knowledge, about religion, about politics, about economics. But what about the use of force? Hume dismisses as absurd all theories that absolutely forbid resort to violence against a very bad regime—who seriously would denounce rebellion against Nero?—but his declared preference is for reform by peaceful means. However, he does not prescribe for the situation where there is no legal process by which reformers can work to bring the status quo closer to the principles. Yet there can be no doubt about his views. No regime has an indefeasible right. The primary motive for allegiance is public interest. Consequently, where there is no legal process by which to reform a bad government, the questions to be asked are not legalistic; rather, they are philosophic and practical. First, how much better would the new order be? Second, what are the chances of success? Third, how great would be the costs? These are questions not to be started lightly among the vulgar.

Hume and the French Revolution

I have argued that Hume's strong attacks on false beliefs, whatever their provenance, show that he was not simply a defender of the status quo on the ground that "reason" is unable to show how improvements may be made. But it still is possible that he had commitments that, on balance, made him more a conservative than a reformer. David Miller advances an argument related to ideology for calling Hume a conservative. He says, first, that some of Hume's beliefs were ideological, for example, his belief that human beings are predominantly motivated by ambition and avarice; and second, that his ideological beliefs were those of the eighteenth-century English aristocracy. Miller makes the point that it is a mistake to think that eighteenth-century writers can be neatly labeled either liberal or conservative, that in the eighteenth century someone like Hume could hold both liberal and conservative views without obvious inconsistency. He finds that although Hume did have liberal commitments, these were secondary to his conservative commitments, so that, confronted by the need to choose, he would have jettisoned his liberal values to save his conservative values. He contends that if Hume had been tested by the French Revolution, his conservative ideological commitments would have prevailed; he would have come out as a genuine conservative. Do Hume's writings on British politics support the charge that at heart he was potentially another Edmund Burke, another zealous protagonist of the old regime?[24] I think not. I adduce the evidence for my view in chapter 6.

Miller criticizes Hume for conservatism; another scholar, Donald W. Livingston, praises him for it. Having shown, first, that Hume destroys the claim of reason to autonomy, and, second, that false philosophy, the product of autonomous reason, fails to respect the sacred character of common life, Livingston concludes that, not Burke, but "Hume should be thought of as the first conservative philosopher."[25] For it was Hume

[24] Miller treats both conservatism and liberalism as ideologies. He argues that in eighteenth-century Britain, the relationship between the landowners and the growing commercial and manufacturing sector was relatively harmonious; this meant that it was possible (a) to be a defender of the existing social hierarchy and (b) to argue for those economic freedoms that encourage the growth of commerce. "The parting of the ways," he says, "comes only when a rising capitalist class is seen as a threat to the stability of the existing order, or, conversely, when the traditional order is seen as a barrier to the full flowering of the economy. At that point we may expect the appearance of an anti-capitalist conservative ideology and an anti-establishment liberal ideology. But in Britain, at least, that moment did not arrive until after 1800, say in the persons of Coleridge and James Mill. Burke was one of the last theorists who could comfortably argue for social hierarchy and for economic freedom in the same breath." "The Macpherson Version" *Political Studies*, 30 (1982): 127. See also Miller's article "Hume and Possessive Individualism," wherein he criticizes C. B. Macpherson for attributing the wrong ideology to Hume: it is proper, he says, to see Hume as the bearer of an ideology, but Macpherson "has misidentified the ideology in question." *History of Political Thought* 1 (1980): 261–78.

[25] Donald W. Livingston, *Hume's Philosophy of Common Life* (Chicago: The University of Chicago Press, 1984), p. 310. Livingston's interpretation of Hume as a conservative has been endorsed by Antony Flew. See his *David Hume: Philosopher of Moral Science* (Oxford: Basil Blackwell Ltd, 1986), pp. 172–75. Flew's commentary, which equates eighteenth-century liberalism with late-twentieth-century British neoliberalism, serves to remind us that, given the way politicians put up their new wines in attractive old bottles, party labels are not to be taken at face value. Alasdair MacIntyre, too, agrees (*Whose Justice? Which Rationality?* [Notre Dame: University of Notre Dame Press, 1988], p. 320) that Hume's philosophy is what Livingston calls "conservative"—and this MacIntyre deplores. According to him, Hume imported into Scotland the morality of an alien, unphilosophical culture, that of the order dominant in England after 1688; in that culture, what Livingston describes as the narrative view of law and morals prevailed. As evidence of Hume's conversion to what Livingston calls conservatism, specifically to English conservatism, MacIntyre quotes from Hume's reference (*Treatise*, p. 272) to honest but unphilosophical gentlemen in England. Hume, says MacIntyre, "constituted himself the philosophical champion of an essentially unphilosophical culture" (p. 324). It should be noted, however, that in the honest-gentlemen passage, Hume is not extolling earthy thoughtlessness; rather, he is simply summing up his attack on "men of bright fancies" and reasserting his confidence in the experimental method as the way to new scientific knowledge. Isaac Newton, a man committed to neither unexamined custom nor specious hypotheses, was his ideal: "Cautious in

who first showed, especially in Book I of the *Treatise* and in his *History of England*, the colossal error of projects for the total restructuring of societies. Although Hume, unlike Burke, did not experience the French Revolution, he did pronounce emphatically against a similar revolution, the Puritan Revolution; his strictures against one set of revolutionaries are applicable to all others. Conservatism, according to Livingston, is the rejection of a certain way of thinking; it is the rejection of the clamor of all those who seek to reform the world radically in the name of standards discovered by autonomous reason. Conservatives know the enemy: "the violent intrusion of rationalistic metaphysics into politics." Basically, there are only two positions: advocacy of reforms recommended by autonomous reason and its opponent, conservatism. For Livingston, the latter is the correct position, because the moral world is a narrative unity of ancestors, contemporaries, and posterity. At the same time, precisely because the moral world is a narrative unity, Hume is not opposed to reforms. These, Livingston says, might go even so far as to bring about changes in the basic property rules: "Grievances are settled by the established rules, and by virtue of retrospective narrative associations the settlement changes the interpretation of the rules. Such changes may lead to a gradual evolution of new rules and eventually to an entirely different narrative order. Evolutionary reform, then, is not only possible in Hume's system, it is internal to the narrative imagination and, consequently, to the moral world which the imagination weaves into existence."[26]

Livingston is correct in saying that Hume abhors reform projects devised by reason alone, as well as reforms inspired by fantasies. But Livingston goes too far. Is it not true that for Hume "the rules of justice are stedfast and immutable; at least, as immutable as human nature?" Is it not true that the principles of civil society are not arbitrary, so that, human nature and the circumstances remaining as we now know them, we can pronounce regimes good or bad, civilized or barbarous, by reason of the extent to which they realize those principles?

Quite apart from the fact that Miller and Livingston fail to give adequate recognition to the advance in moral subjects that Hume hoped

---

admitting no principles but such as were founded on experiment; but resolute to adopt every such principle, however new or unusual." *History of England*, 6:542.

[26] Livingston, *Hume's Philosophy of Common Life*, pp. 308, 340. A major strength of Livingston's work is that it recognizes Hume's emphasis on the historical nature of constitutions and popular beliefs and values. See also his essay "Time and Value in Hume's Social and Political Philosophy," in *McGill Hume Studies*, eds. D. F. Norton, Nicholas Capaldi, and W. L. Robison (San Diego: Austin Hill Press, Inc., 1979), pp. 181–201. Livingston classifies Hume as a conservative because Hume rejects the claims of both "autonomous reason" and false religion to prescribe the right society. This definition of conservatism includes too many: most liberals and some socialists, although not the utopians. And then, having made Hume dependent on a narrative order of right, he says that in Hume's theory even private property is not essential to a genuine civil society.

would be made by the experimental method of reasoning, they make the mistake of assuming that Hume, confronted by the French Revolution, would have chosen one of the extremes, either violent revolution or the new conservatism. When British politics settled down after the post-1815 troubles, various reform proposals were revived from pre-war times: the repeal of the Test and Corporation acts, the emancipation of Roman Catholics, and reform of the representation of the people. A favorite argument against these reforms was that they were in the French Revolution tradition. This was appealing rhetoric, for as the wars (1793–1815) had dragged on, most Britons, including many who in 1789 and 1790 had applauded what was happening in Paris, had rallied to the patriotic cause of beating the French. The opponents of the reforms, the Tories—to be called Conservatives after 1832—denounced them fervently as lethal threats to Anglican society in England. Nor was this mere rhetoric: many Conservatives believed it. In contrast, the liberal Whigs advocated the reforms; they did not see themselves as restricted to choosing between Tory conservatism and political chaos. Indeed, the foundations of what later was to be called the Liberal party had been laid by Charles James Fox in the early 1790s, when, despite all Burke's maneuvers and arguments "he and a handful of whigs resisted the emotionalism of the Terror and the French wars on the one side and the emotionalism of republicanism and Jacobinism on the other side."[27] These liberal Whigs saw a moderate option. They saw a reform road running between and avoiding both conservative Toryism on the right and revolutionary republicanism on the left. My submission is that Hume's views on the matters that were to come to the fore in British politics in the 1820s—religious toleration, economic policy, the representation of the people—would have drawn him to that moderate road. Indeed, we shall see some evidence in chapter 6 that David Hume and his friend Adam Smith helped blaze the trail followed by the liberal reformers of the nineteenth century. While Hume despised fanaticism, he saw unreflective conservatism as preserving false opinion, botched institutions, and barbarous policies.

[27] Sir Ivor Jennings, *Party Politics* (Cambridge: Cambridge University Press, 1961), 2:77–78. Jennings quotes George Tierney's comment on the effect on British politics of what was happening in France in the early 1790s: "The late events in France . . . have made one party here desperate and the other drunk. Many are become wild republicans who a few months back were moderate Reformers, and numbers who six weeks ago were contented with plain, old-fashioned Toryism, have now worked themselves up to such apprehensions for the fate of Royalty as to be incapable of distinguishing between Reform and treason and to threaten death and destruction to all who differ from them." For an enlightening account of Fox's efforts and success in preserving the liberal aspect of Whiggism see L. G. Mitchell, *Charles James Fox and the Disintegration of the Whig Party, 1782–1794* (London: Oxford University Press, 1971), pp. 153–269.

6

CHANGING THE BRITISH MIND

ONCE THE *Treatise* had been completed, Hume began writing as a "politician"; he changed his focus, narrowing it down from general moral philosophy to a different set of questions, to those economic and political questions most relevant to himself as a Scot living in eighteenth-century Britain.[1] Civil society has its principles and dynamics, but because just and lawful conduct is artificial, civil society is realized only through advances in knowledge. This means that "politicians," who can do little or nothing to improve the family, the friendship, and the like, may be able to improve the polity and economy. They can, first, work to achieve a sound understanding of the principles and dynamics of civil society by diligent use of the experimental method of reasoning.[2] Second, they can strive to correct prevailing false beliefs and thus reform existing institutions, laws, maxims, and policies. Hume regarded himself as a pioneer in modern political science. For the most part, politics in the past had been unscientific: the natural principles and dynamics had operated, but because they were poorly understood, the results were distorted, often very badly, by kings and ministers, by unrestrained parties, by vulgar opinion, by unproven "systems" propagated by authorities. This was true

---

[1] We should notice two related terms used by Hume. First, there are "politicians." These persons are not necessarily active in politics; they study and write with the intention of being influential. (In a similar way, we sometimes refer to students of parliamentary procedure as "parliamentarians.") Hume first uses the word "politician" when he rejects the view, often attributed to Mandeville, that the rules of justice were invented by "politicians." *Treatise*, pp. 500, 533–34, 578. See also *Essays*, pp. 254 and 280. In the essays he refers to Polybius, Machiavelli, and Harrington as "politicians." The politician's calling is highly constructive: "Those who employ their pens on political subjects, free from party-rage, and party-prejudices, cultivate a science, which, of all others, contributes most to public utility." *Essays*, pp. 87, 254, 304. Second, there are "legislators," those who found or constitute "peoples" by giving them the laws and institutions that set the character of their culture, as did Moses. *History*, 5:94; *Essays*, p. 54. Legislators, Hume states, "ought to provide a system of laws to regulate the administration of public affairs to the latest posterity." *Essays*, p. 24. By "laws" Hume generally means the basic or constitutional laws; "legislators" are the "fathers of constitutions."

[2] Histories, Hume tells us, "are so many collections of experiments, by which the politician or moral philosopher fixes the principles of his science, in the same manner as the physician or natural philosopher becomes acquainted with the nature of plants, minerals, and other external objects, by the experiments which he forms concerning them." *An Enquiry concerning Human Understanding*, pp. 83–84.

in the maintenance of peace and justice; it was even truer of laws and policies related to the economy, where causation is more complex and selfish interests strive to control public policy. Henry VII made statutes "with regard to [both] the police of the kingdom, and its commerce." It is a fact, says Hume, that "the former are generally contrived with much better judgment than the latter. The more simple ideas of order and equity are sufficient to guide a legislator in every thing that regards the internal administration of justice: But the principles of commerce are much more complicated, and require long experience and deep reflection to be well understood in any state. The real consequence of a law or practice is there often contrary to first appearances" (*H.*, 3:74).

Now, however, a beginning could be made in bringing the principles and dynamics of civil society up to the level of consciousness—in setting them forth as a science—and, thus, a beginning in realizing better constitutions, better laws, and better policies. Experience alone is not enough; nor is "reason and reflection" the answer. What is required is "long experience and deep reflection." But this is only a beginning; since civil society, an artificial order, is highly variable, prolonged investigation will be required before its potentialities can be fully appreciated. Given the brevity of our experience, we must not jump to conclusions: we cannot know "what degree of refinement, either in virtue or vice, human nature is susceptible of; nor what may be expected of mankind from any great revolution in their education, customs, or principles" (*Essays*, 87–88).

Hume's aspirations as a "politician" or "political scientist" were high; yet he was keenly aware of four restricting factors. First, since any working political system is largely a structure of opinion, sudden, radical innovation may jeopardize the entire system. Aggressive reformation may cause not progress, but regress, perhaps collapse into chaos, with tyranny the ultimate result. Minds must first be changed. Second, the politician must remember that his descriptions and prescriptions are given in words—in words which inevitably tend to present polarized views and positions, while the truth always lies somewhere in between; in words, which have elusive meanings; in words which when used in constitutions, laws, and orders often prove too rigid and restrictive to permit what would be best—so that, like a football coach, the "politician" has to hope for something from the practitioners on the field. Third, the law of the constitution cannot be the last word for the political scientist. The law of the constitution as known by lawyers is a set of established rules, defining constitutional right and wrong, but these rules never tell the whole truth. Underlying the lawyers' constitution is the opinion of the populace as to what is good, and thus "right." This, says Hume, is the origin of the notion of fundamental laws; such laws "are suppos'd to be inalterable by the will of the sovereign." If, for example, an absolute government were to change the constitution very radically, the change, although legally right, would not be found morally right or binding by most of the people (*T.*, 561). Lawyers tend to look no deeper than the law of the constitution, but the political philosopher must see constitutional law as a tentative set of rules for the changing body politic. Fourth, political power rests not with the learned, but with the great; even if the political science expounded by the learned is eminently sound, those in power may ignore it.

In 1741, just when Hume was publishing the first volume of his *Essays, Moral and Political*, Great Britain was completing a crucial phase of its constitutional development, the phase when Responsible Government (of a kind) was first established. One result of the constitutional conflicts of the seventeenth century was the conclusive rejection of independent monarchy; the political power of the House of Commons had been made effective by the need for annual supply and an annual Army Act. Yet the constitution remained a strange hybrid: the king continued as chief of the executive government, with vast prerogative powers in foreign and colonial affairs, precisely the matters where the central government was most active, but the king's government could not operate without the regular cooperation of Parliament. The key to the survival of the system was for the king to choose a minister who could get the government's supply and other bills past the House of Commons. If the Tories had been the government party from 1689 to 1742, politics might have been simpler and less interesting; in fact, it was the Whigs who were ascendant, constantly after 1715. Could a politician (Walpole) remain true to revolution principles while serving as "the minister"? Nor was the Country versus Court debate simply a disagreement about constitutional principles: the socioeconomic order was changing, expensive wars were being fought, new institutions were being established. Eventually, in February 1742, Walpole was brought down by the combined efforts of Tories, Country Whigs, and former ministerial colleagues; his successors, however, immediately vindicated his system by perpetuating it. When, about 1739, Hume shifted his focus to contemporary politics, he was joining a fierce debate between Country and Court, a debate in which the language and ideas of the civic tradition were being used both to attack and to defend what was happening to the British economy, social order, and government—in a word, what was happening to British public morality—in the early-eighteenth century.[3] This, too, was moral philosophy, but it was

[3] The idea of a commonwealth did not die at the Restoration (1660); rather, it continued, not as a goal to be achieved, but as an ideal against which Real Whigs could assess the state of England and the performance of ministers, especially Whig ministers. Commonwealth thought drew strength from both Christian and classical roots: on the one hand, dissentient Protestants did not accept divine-right authority in either church or state; on the other, a learned minority looked back to ancient Greece and Rome; the result was the idea of a

moral philosophy quite different from that of the great jurisprudential
tomes. Many of Hume's essays are in or engage the civic tradition: they
are highly sociological; they employ civic-tradition language; they deal
either specifically or incidentally with civic-tradition topics; and they examine the causes of the rise and fall of cities or nations. For the most part,
however, Hume rejected that tradition.[4]

Consistent with the jurisprudential principles he had learned from his
law books, he remained an individualist; for him the chief public virtues
are justice and allegiance, both negative virtues, not public spirit—benevolence—expressed in good works for one's city or nation. He regarded
sweeping denunciations of luxury (private good) as misconceived. He saw
public good largely as a result of private good, not as an alternative. He
saw governments as only means to good governance; accordingly, for
him the right to participate in governing was not essential to the good life.
He denied the pretense of any city or nation to be that public whose interest defines morality. Consistent with his moral theory, built on what is
good or bad for the individual, generally Hume's political theory treats
public good as the effect, not the cause, of the good of individuals. He
traverses civic-tradition terrain, but usually moves from the private to the
public, not from the public to the private.

Hume sprang from the landed gentry of Lowland Scotland, who con-

republic (commonwealth) in which neither kings nor priests had independent authority.

J.G.A. Pocock has explored the commonwealth idea (a) to show its classical philosophic
content; (b) to show how it was revived by Machiavelli and carried into England in Harrington's *Oceana*; and (c) to show how, modified by neo-Harringtonians, it was used in the
century after 1675 to condemn the corruption of England by the new commercial and monied interests and their ministerial friends. There was, he contends, a strong civic humanist
tradition. For Pocock the basic explanation of antiministerial denunciation of places and
pensions, the standing army, expanding commerce, the credit system, the national debt, and
high taxes on landed property is that all these were seen as elements in a process of corruption. See J.G.A. Pocock, "Civic Humanism and its Role in Anglo-American Thought" and
"Machiavelli, Harrington and English Political Ideologies in the Eighteenth Century," in his
Politics, Language and Time (London: Methuen & Co. Ltd, 1972), pp. 80–147. Also *The
Machiavellian Moment: Florentine Political Thought and the Atlantic Republican Tradition*
(Princeton: Princeton University Press, 1975).

It is important to notice that in the civic tradition patriotism ("public spirit")—specifically
zeal for "the liberties of Englishmen" and for their constitution, which preserved them by
preventing "slavery"—was a leading virtue. Bolingbroke advocated Patriotism: thus he (a)
justified a formed opposition to the king's government; (b) enlisted Country Whigs as allies;
and (c) put Walpole in the invidious position of having to repel Patriotic attacks on the
standing army and on Court influence in Parliament. As the years passed, and more Whigs
defected from Walpole, the early Patriotic leaders, Pulteney and Charteret, gained a considerable following. The test of Patriotic sincerity came in 1742 after Walpole's resignation.

[4] For the pioneer statement of this conclusion, see James Moore, "Hume's Political Science and the Classical Republican Tradition," *Canadian Journal of Political Science*, 10
(1977): 809–39.

tinued to make Edinburgh their social and cultural capital throughout the eighteenth century, in contrast to the greater nobles; after 1603 the latter increasingly had yielded to the magnetism of London, and after 1707 had little occasion to spend time in Edinburgh on public business. He shared many of the concerns of that Edinburgh circle of gentry, and of the literati who associated with them.[5] Nor is the nature of those concerns surprising. They had much to do with the fact that Scotland, despite a long, turbulent history in which defense of national independence against England had been a central strand, finally, in 1707, had united with England—accepting the sovereignty of a Parliament in which Scotland's representatives would be only a small minority (45 of 558 in the House of Commons; 16 out of some 230 in the House of Lords); accepting the prospective Hanoverian succession; accepting English taxes and trade laws—in the hope that, as a result of full legislative union, it would cease to be what it had been since 1603, the other kingdom, the poor and neglected kingdom—and come to share the increasing prosperity England had enjoyed for generations. Those concerns had much to do with the fact that after a quarter century in which the dire prophesies of the opponents of the Union seemed to be coming true, about 1730 much of Lowland society began to undergo rapid change.

Inevitably, the Union prompted many questions in Scotland about the nature of the English political system, about the moral and cultural implications of modernization, and about the proper goals of economic endeavors. What had been the effect on Scotland's development of the fact that from 1603 until 1707 she had been her kings' second and minor kingdom? Had the Stuart kings violated the English constitution, so that the political troubles of the seventeenth century could be blamed in large part on the Scottish line? Were conscientious Scots patriotically, even legally, obliged to try to restore the Stuarts as Scotland's royal family? What was the cause of the fierce rivalry between those two great alliances, the Whigs and the Tories, dividing the English political nation, and which, if either, should a Scot support? Was the English constitution the

---

[5] A brief account of Scotland's plight as a "royal province"—tied to the king at London, but not represented in the Parliament at Westminster—is given in P.W.J. Riley, *The English Ministers and Scotland, 1707–1727* (London: The Athlone Press, 1964), pp. 1–23. For a discussion of the Edinburgh gentry-literati, see N. T. Phillipson, "Culture and Society in the 18th Century Province: The Case of Edinburgh and the Scottish Enlightenment," in *The University in Society*, ed. Lawrence Stone, 2 vols. (Princeton: Princeton University Press, 1974), 2:407–48. A succinct analysis of the influence of the events of 1688 and 1707 on Scottish thought in the eighteenth century is given by G. E. Davie in *The Scottish Enlightenment* (London: The Historical Association, 1981). For a discussion of the psychosocial factors that help explain Hume's break with Calvinist culture, see Charles Camic, *Experience and Enlightenment: Socialization for Cultural Change in Eighteenth-Century Scotland* (Chicago: The University of Chicago Press, 1983).

best of all constitutions? What strategy should a government follow in dealing with popular religion? Was it inevitable that Scotland would remain poor despite the establishment of a common market with England? Which was the more promising pattern of economic development for Scotland, a pattern that stressed agriculture (and thus landowners, farmers, and husbandmen), or one that stressed commerce (and thus merchants, master manufacturers, financiers, and the like)? What was the role or place of foreign trade in development? What is the true wealth of a nation? What effect would successful commerce and manufacturing, and consequent luxury, have on the morals and character of the nation? Was the corruption of the people a danger; if so, could it be prevented?

Hume, like Adam Smith after him, was driven to be a sociologist—a student of economic, political, and social development—not by the industrial revolution, then still in the future, but by Scotland's union with an advanced, rich partner, and by the rapid modernization Scotland was undergoing. He dealt with topics of the kind raised by Andrew Fletcher of Saltoun at the time of the Union, topics that continued to draw keen attention in the Edinburgh circle; yet in some respects these were only Scottish versions of questions first examined by Aristotle in the *Politics*. Unlike Edmund Burke, Hume continued to live in the land of his birth and remained an objective observer of the English: given the fact that the two nations occupied a single landmass of moderate size, the decision to unite with England had been correct; the Union, which should have been made a century earlier, could succeed, despite the fact that the English were a very peculiar people.[6] His own contribution would be to help liberate Britons, both north and south of the border, from certain erroneous beliefs that were seriously impeding the progress of society in the United Kingdom.[7] He would be a moral reformer. Specifically, he sought

---

[6] Hume recognized that there were strong geopolitical reasons for the union. See *History of England*, 2:141; 3:145–46.

[7] John Robertson has shown how Andrew Fletcher of Saltoun, writing before the union, diagnosed Scotland's ills and prescribed for them, as a civil-tradition practitioner. "David Hume," says Robertson, "was almost certainly familiar with the issues and arguments of the Union debate; and it may well be supposed that he held in particular respect the contribution of one he once described as 'a man of signal probity and fine genius.'" However, it is not Robertson's contention that Hume drew directly on Fletcher. Hume, he writes (p. 151), "derived the terms of his inquiry [into the progress of society] from a comprehensive knowledge of the civic tradition, its classical antecedents and jurisprudential affiliates." John Robertson, "The Scottish Enlightenment at the Limits of the Civic Tradition," in *Wealth and Virtue: The Shaping of Political Economy in the Scottish Enlightenment*, ed. Istvan Hont and Michael Ignatieff (Cambridge: Cambridge University Press, 1983), pp. 137–78. A somewhat longer analysis of Fletcher, with emphasis on the role of an armed citizenry, is given by Robertson in *The Scottish Enlightenment and the Militia Issue* (Edinburgh: John Donald Publishers Ltd., 1985).

1. to enable Scots, and Englishmen too, to decide, without ideological distortion, to whom they owed allegiance, the Stuarts or the Hanoverians;

2. to have Englishmen reflect upon the origin and nature of their constitution, thus reducing the danger that contention between the two parties, the natural products of that constitution, once again would escalate to civil war;

3. to show that the constitution needed radical reform;

4. to have the danger posed to society by religious enthusiasm and superstition fully appreciated;

5. to expunge the old belief, preached by many Country moralists and politicians, godly and republican alike, that manufacturing and commerce and consequent prosperity (or luxury) would erode the morals, industry, and military strength of the populace;

6. to convince Scottish landowners that the growth of manufacturing and commerce, far from threatening them with ruin, was opening up the prospect of rural prosperity;

7. to obliterate the prevalent belief, exploited by powerful merchants in bending public policy to their selfish ends, that the wealth of a nation is to be measured by the share of the world's precious metals it has managed to engross; and

8. to show that economic cooperation among nations, in the form of free trade, is beneficial for all humankind.

The Matchless Constitution: Moderation versus Patriotic Zeal

Hume found that Englishmen, both the opponents and the supporters of the ministers, were enthralled by the mythology of their constitution: that it was the best, the matchless constitution, was for them an established verity. Absorbed and possessed by party conflict, they failed to stand back to analyze the nature of governance in general, the nature of constitutions, and the history of government in England; as a result, they were deeply divided by the rivalry fostered by a constitution in which each of the two main elements, the king and the House of Commons, reasonably could claim dominance. Some Country politicians attacked Walpole and the other Whig ministers vituperatively as self-serving (unpatriotic), corruptive of the constitution, and disloyal to England's glorious past. Others, Tories, added to this the charge that the ministers, lukewarm Christians at best, were out to destroy the Church. The ministers and their scribes had two lines of rebuttal. The first was civic: those Whigs who had broken with Walpole, far from being genuine representatives of the country, were simply a power-hungry faction striving to replace ministers who had the support of the truly public-spirited gentry. The other line was historical: the bulk of the opposition were really Tories, probably in many cases Jacobites, and as such were disloyal to the new state achieved in 1688 and made secure in 1714.[8] Over half the essays published by Hume in 1741—just when the great Patriotic surge, in which Country Whigs and Tories cooperated in an effort to free Britain from Walpole's grip, was moving into its final and successful phase—were written to allay the divisive antagonism of the parties. His *History of England*—published in four tranches, in 1754, 1757, 1759, and 1761—was intended to have the same pacifying effect. His purpose was three-fold. The English political mind was to be liberated from the sway of two extremist ideologies: the Divine Right of Kings, supporting royal absolutism, and the Contract theory, proclaiming a right of revolution. Those theories were deceptive: the first put all the measures of a *de jure* king beyond challenge except by passive resistance; the second gave all the people, severally as well as collectively, the right to disobey a law whenever they thought it was wrong. Next, the English were to be set free from the deceptive belief that the old is the good by being shown that it was the contemporary constitution, inaugurated in 1688–1689, that for the very first time—contrary to the myth of an ancient constitution—had given them established liberty. Finally, their attention was to be focused on the realities of the contemporary constitution so that they would understand its strengths and weaknesses and then, having recognized that the constitution fosters both a Court and a Country interest, work together to preserve and improve that constitution.

Hume's discussion of the English constitution is based on clearly formulated principles. He analyzes governance mainly in terms of authority and liberty; both are essential to good governance. Politics "considers men as united in society, and dependent on each other"; it has nothing to do with a state of natural liberty. Once civil society has been realized, the era of natural liberty has been left behind, or rather, thereafter any outburst of natural liberty in violation of justice is wrong. Civil society abolishes mere natural liberty; it introduces a higher form of liberty, civil liberty, under which the individual can live and act in security behind the protective walls of his rights.

> The same creature, in his farther progress, is engaged to establish political society, in order to administer justice; without which there can be no peace among them, nor safety, nor mutual intercourse. We are, therefore, to look upon all the vast apparatus of our government, as having ultimately no other object or purpose but the distribution of justice, or, in other words, the support of the twelve judges. Kings and parliaments, fleets and armies, officers

---

[8] See P. S. Fritz, *The English Ministers and Jacobitism between the Rebellions of 1715 and 1745* (Toronto: University of Toronto Press, 1975).

of the court and revenue, ambassadors, ministers, and privy-counsellors, are all subordinate in their end to this part of administration. (*Essays*, 37)

To follow Hume's argument, we must remember his terms and distinctions. Civil liberty entails a rule of law; it requires established rights with respect to economic activity, speech, religion, and so forth. These rights provide the predictability without which liberty is impossible in society. The rights may be narrow or wide. They may, for example, permit criticism of the government within only narrow limits or with virtually no limits. In short, we must distinguish between the presence of civil liberty (a rule of law) and the nature and extent of the liberties established by the law. Then, a "free state" is an independent state, a republic; that is, the state does not belong to a king or any other body external to the citizenry. Free states provide civil liberties for their citizens, but so do some absolute monarchies; indeed, the established liberties sometimes are narrower in republics than in absolute monarchies. Again, civil liberty does not imply political liberty, the right to participate in the government, either directly or by representatives. This is obvious in an absolute monarchy with a rule of law. Even in republics, where all the citizens enjoy the same civil liberties, citizenship alone rarely confers the right to participate in politics at all levels: some citizens are excluded from participation in elections, from the assembly, or from certain offices by reason of age, sex, or economic status. Hume, as we shall see, regards extensive civil liberty as incomparably more important than rights of political participation; this follows from his emphasis on the importance of private (generally economic) interest.

Although Hume distinguishes clearly between economic power and political authority, he sees economic and political progress as closely interrelated. The nature of the prevailing governance has socioeconomic effects; similarly, it is almost certain that major economic changes will produce changes in governance. He ties the rise of genuine governance to a three-phase socioeconomic development. In the hunting and fishing stage of civilization, there was little in the way of private property to defend; nations then were really only extended families or tribes. Such governance as was required was provided by chiefs or elders. Then, gradually, people learned to produce goods by agriculture, and their investment of labor in particular pieces of land and products led them to introduce rights to goods, that is, to begin to follow the five rules of property. Soon a government became necessary to defend property, first, against alien invaders, later, against theft and robbery. In this, the second stage, government frequently took the form of absolute monarchy. The early kings undertook the basic tasks (a) of establishing political power, the right to govern distinct from the right to economic goods, and (b) of creating states by extending their rule to all quarters of their own countries. The great defect of their regimes was that they were governments of persons, not of laws. The king himself had absolute power, but instead of making general laws as a legislator, laws to be administered by his agents, in each province he set up a vicegerent, who in his absolute power was the image of the king himself. The vicegerents were under no restraint other than the king's own commands. Such a regime was "barbarous"; it was a form of government, but only a primitive form (*Essays*, 116).

In the third stage, agriculture is supplemented by commerce, initially by commerce with foreign places, later by manufacturing and commerce within the country. This complicates the social structure by introducing merchants and traders, capitalists and the laborers ("manufacturers") whom they employ, and then a monied interest. These new groups live, not scattered throughout the countryside, but gathered in towns. In dealing with this stage, Hume refers to two different historical situations: first, to the city-states of antiquity; second, to the city-states in the middle ages. In the former case, small primitive kingdoms were converted into republics. In the latter, the one Hume emphasizes, initially the cities acquired by charter the right to govern themselves in the republican manner, as enclaves within empire or kingdom. Given the fact that in these republics, both those of ancient times and those of the late medieval period, political power was vested in various social groups, a great deal of jealous attention was given to the constitution, that is, to the division of power between or among the groups (*Essays*, 117–18). As a result of this assiduous constitutionalism, these republics were the laboratories in which the principles of civilized or genuine governance were first discovered.

The essential difference between an absolute monarchy and a republic (or "free state") is not that the legal power of the government is greater in the former—it may be less in fact, although the same in theory—but that power is divided between or among different bodies, generally with all the important socioeconomic interests participating either directly or by representatives in one or more of the branches, but almost always in the legislative branch. Because the powers of each branch are defined precisely, the people are governed by general rules, by laws, not by the decisions of any one person or body. Only what the law prohibits or requires is in fact prohibited or required. The discretion (power) of judges and administrators is not eliminated; rather it is strictly defined. It is confined within stated limits; otherwise, the judges and administrators would usurp the power of the legislature. Accordingly, we see that republican government is not only structurally different, but that it is carried out in a different way; a republic relies on the rule of laws.

A well-contrived republican government is far better than a barbaric monarchy. Under it the people enjoy the advantages of having a government, but also those of having a rule of law. They are secure from foreign and domestic enemies of the peace, as they would be under an effective barbarous monarch; they are secure from the governors also, that is, from the judges, the ministers, and the several members of the legislature. They enjoy a high degree of civil liberty; secure in the knowledge that if they do not break the law, they cannot be molested legally, they can act freely. In the essay "Of the Rise and Progress of the Arts and Sciences," Hume insists that the technique of governing by a complex body of law could never have been learned in a barbarous monarchy; it could be discovered only where competing interests had distinct roles and powers.

> To balance a large state or society, whether monarchical or republican, on general laws, is a work of so great difficulty, that no human genius, however comprehensive, is able, by the mere dint of reason and reflection, to effect it. The judgments of many must unite in this work: Experience must guide their labour: Time must bring it to perfection: And the feeling of inconveniencies must correct the mistakes, which they inevitably fall into, in their first trials and experiments. Hence appears the impossibility, that this undertaking should be begun and carried on in any monarchy; since such a form of government, ere civilized, knows no other secret or policy, than that of entrusting unlimited powers to every governor or magistrate, and subdividing the people into so many classes and orders of slavery. (*Essays*, 124)

Moreover, just as commerce and manufacturing foster republican governments, the republican form of government fosters economic development. The security provided by a rule of law promotes industry and enterprise, for the person who invests his time and labor has reason to believe that whatever he accomplishes will benefit himself; besides, the ethos of a republic is more candidly "materialistic." In republics those who seek preferment must look to the people; in monarchies they must court the great. The people value the useful virtues most; the great, with their own material needs already amply met, tend to emphasize the agreeable virtues (*Essays*, 125–26). Industry and riches are the great goods in republics; what is held in high esteem in monarchies is birth, title, and station (*Essays*, 93). In a monarchy those who have succeeded in business are likely to leave the wharf, factory, and exchange and take up the idle life of consumers, living off rents and pensions.

Far from being the antithesis of civil liberty, authority is its absolute prerequisite; let any doubter consider the sorry plight of the Scottish people before 1707.[9] Provided the king pays some attention to the adminis-

[9] *Essays*, pp. 40–41, 94, 124–25. Again and again Hume makes the point that the Scots had not been a civil society before the union with England. They had been "the rudest,

tration of justice, even a barbarous monarchy is far better than a Hobbesian state of nature. The mere introduction of authority produces a degree of governance; then, as the government comes to rely more and more on general laws based on the principles of justice, the regime becomes better and better. When all laws are made by an established legislative process and due process is followed meticulously in administering the laws, the absolute of civil liberty has been attained.

Civil liberty, freedom under law, is the perfection of governance. However, there will be emergencies—certainly in foreign affairs, probably in domestic—requiring action more urgent and drastic than the ordinary processes permit. In short, reliance on the rule of law cannot be complete. The government must be able to cope with such emergencies; it must have power to do whatever is necessary to defend the state and protect the people. In ordinary times, the power of those in public office can be restricted narrowly, but in times of crisis they need greater power, power to do whatever the emergency requires.

As we saw in chapter 4, when Hume compares absolute monarchies and republics, he finds that each form has strengths and weaknesses. The essential features of true absolute monarchy are that the king comes to power, not by election, but by inheritance (unless he is a conqueror or usurper), and that his right to rule is unlimited. He has no constitutional dependence on his people. This means that the various interest groups are

perhaps, of all European Nations; the most necessitous, the most turbulent, and the most unsettled." *Letters*, 2:310. Despite centuries of trying, Scotland's kings had never succeeded in bringing the country under their control. They never succeeded in subordinating the great nobles; this increased the reliance of the common people in both the Highlands and the Lowlands on tribal leaders. In the eleventh century, "Duncan, king of Scotland, was a prince of a gentle disposition, but possessed not the genius requisite for governing a country so turbulent, and so much infested by the intrigues and animosities of the great." *History of England*, 1:137–38. At the end of the fifteenth century, Scotland "had not yet attained that state, which distinguishes a civilized monarchy, and which enables the government, by the force of its laws and institutions alone, without any extraordinary capacity in the sovereign, to maintain itself in order and tranquillity." Ibid., 3:24. Over a century later, when the Duke of Albany, regent during the minority of King James V (1513–1542), arrived in Scotland from France, no progress had been made: "That turbulent kingdom, he found, was rather to be considered as a confederacy, and that not a close one, of petty princes, than a regular system of civil polity; and even the king, much more a regent, possessed an authority very uncertain and precarious. Arms, more than laws, prevailed; and courage, preferably to equity or justice, was the virtue most valued and respected." Ibid., p. 117. Then, after 1555, the Reformation struck Scotland; the result was that it became the duty of the multitude to resist any governor who deviated from the will of the Lord. In the first version of his account of the reign of James I (1603–1625), Hume comments on the state of Scotland at that time: "The weak authority of the laws thro'out every part of Scotland, made all the inhabitants seek for security by a close adherence to their own tribe, which alone was able to protect them: And this devoted attachment loosening the ties to their country, served still farther to weaken the authority of the laws." *History of Great Britain*, p. 142.

not aroused to compete for influence whenever the throne becomes vacant, as they would be if there were elections, and that the king has no reason derived from the constitution to favor one interest group above others. On the other hand, history shows that absolute monarchy leaves far too much to chance: the men who become kings often are irrational in their means, vicious in their ends, or altogether arbitrary and inconstant, often all three at once (*Essays*, 614). In contrast, as we have seen, republics govern by means of general laws, which makes for predictability and thus for greater civil liberty. But republics always involve elections to fill some of their offices, and when great issues are at stake, the election campaigns easily can escalate to bloody strife. Absolute monarchy makes for unity in the state, because the monarch is independent, set high above all the internal interests and conflicts; but the monarch may be irrational, wicked, lazy, or capricious. Ordinarily, a republic makes for far more orderly government, and thus for greater liberty; yet there is the danger of violent shocks or revolutions caused by antagonism among the interests. However, it is possible to provide a republic with a well-contrived constitution, a constitution that harnesses the different interests and makes them serve the public. Hume's political science, sounding a strong antimonarchial note, insists on the importance of a scientifically sound constitution: "Legislators, therefore, ought not to trust the future government of a state entirely to chance, but ought to provide a system of laws to regulate the administration of public affairs to the latest posterity" (*Essays*, 24). The less the future is left to chance the better.

While there is no comparison between a barbarous monarchy and a good republic, not every absolute monarchy is barbarous—a point the English should recognize and admit. Once the principles of true governance, discovered in republics, became known throughout the West, the absolute monarchs of Europe, moved by public opinion, upgraded their regimes by imitating the republics; from them they learned how to rule by wise laws carried into effect by law-abiding judges and administrators. Although they retained their own absolute power, they made their regimes civilized and acceptable. Thus, there is no incompatibility between a modern absolute monarchy and civil liberty. Indeed, a modern absolute monarchy has something to recommend it: the monarch serves as a unifying force over and above the various interests; yet his government is a rule of law. Hume's prime example is France; contrary to the ranting of many Englishmen, the people of France are not abject slaves. France's constitution is still absolutist in form—as was England's in the vaunted age of Elizabeth—but, thanks to the power of public opinion, France is governed in a civilized way (*Essays*, 125). This, of course, does not mean that modern absolute monarchies have no defects (*Essays*, 94).

As we have seen, Hume is deeply concerned by the threat posed to impartial government and domestic tranquility by selfish domestic groups. There is no point in pretending that the nation, the public, is, or ought to be, a homogeneous whole, one body united by constant devotion to a common will, cause, or purpose. Inevitably, there are wheels within the great wheel. Some of these are economic; for example, the landed interest, the trading interest, the monied interest. Other groups are less strictly economic; they have recognized status—"rank"—and perhaps also legal definition, for example, the nobles and the commons in England. Other groups are occupational: soldiers, lawyers, priests, merchants, scholars. Others are regional, for example, the great central city versus the remote provinces; Hume mentions Rome and its provinces, London and York-shire, London and Ireland.[10] Some of these groups are beneficial; through specialization—by the different ranks, trades, vocations, by the inhabitants of regions with different natural resources—the general interest of all is advanced. However, the relations between and among even fully legitimate interests will be antagonistic if each fails to recognize the contribution made by the others and seeks myopically to advance its own interest excessively. Some groups may even be parasitic; Hume's favorite example is those "priests"—some Protestant ministers as well as some Anglican and Roman Catholic priests—who exploit the natural religiosity of the multitude so as to gain dominion, respect, and easy living for themselves; such priests often start religious factions. Toward all legitimate interests a government ought to be even-handed. At the same time, a government ought to do whatever it can to prevent the growth of parasitic interests and, failing that, to neutralize them, especially if they endanger public order, civil and religious liberty, or prosperity.

Big interests often find expression as political parties in republics and mixed governments. Such parties—parties of *interest*—are far more reasonable and excusable than those based on either of the other causes of parties: *principles* (extremist theories such as Divine Right and Original Contract) and *affection* (e.g., love of a particular royal family, such as the Stuarts). Indeed, parties of interest may be desirable in that they may help prevent legitimate interests from being exploited. With reference to governments without a popular basis, Hume writes, "In despotic governments, indeed, factions often do not appear; but they are not the less real; or rather, they are more real and more pernicious, upon that very ac-

---

[10] One of the characteristic differences between absolute monarchies and free states is that the latter, unlike the former, exploit their subordinate provinces for the benefit of the homeland. In a free state, the "conquerors . . . are all legislators, and will be sure to contrive matters, by restrictions on trade, and by taxes, so as to draw some private, as well as public, advantage from their conquests." Compare, says Hume, how well France treats its *pais conquis* with England's oppression of Ireland. *Essays*, pp. 18–21.

count. The distinct orders of men, nobles and people, soldiers and merchants, have all a distinct interest; but the more powerful oppresses the weaker with impunity, and without resistance; which begets a seeming tranquillity in such governments" (*Essays*, 59–60).

The dangers associated with parties are decisive in determining Hume's views on forms of government. He is staunchly opposed to elective monarchy, especially if the monarch has real power; hereditary monarchy is far better because, although the merits of the heir are unpredictable, the power of the government is not put up as a prize to be sought, perhaps bought in the Polish manner, by competing factions. He condemns any form of representative government that does not make adequate provision to prevent one or more of the partial interests from gaining control. Consequently, he opposes any move in Great Britain toward government by the House of Commons alone; by reason of its seven-year term, the power of grandees in many constituencies and the irresponsibility of the members to the electors, the House is so independent that, if unchecked by the Crown, it would become a distinct interest, a distinct oligarchic faction, ruling the country mainly for its own benefit.

His own ideal form was a republic, and not just any kind of republic, but one scientifically contrived to make the powerful interests check each other.

> All absolute governments must very much depend on the administration; and this is one of the great inconveniences attending that form of government. But a republican and free government would be an obvious absurdity, if the particular checks and controuls, provided by the constitution, had really no influence, and made it not the interest, even of bad men, to act for the public good. Such is the intention of these forms of government, and such is their real effect, where they are wisely constituted: As on the other hand, they are the source of all disorder, and of the blackest crimes, where either skill or honesty has been wanting in their original frame and institution. (*Essays*, 15–16)

What is required is a constitution in which the power of the government is skillfully divided between and among several parts to the end that no part can govern in its own narrow interest, but all must work for the public interest.

> When there offers, therefore, to our censure and examination, any plan of government, real or imaginary, where the power is distributed among several courts, and several orders of men, we should always consider the separate interest of each court, and each order; and, if we find that, by the skilful division of power, this interest must necessarily, in its operation, concur with public, we may pronounce that government to be wise and happy. If, on the

contrary, separate interest be not checked, and be not directed to the public, we ought to look for nothing but faction, disorder, and tyranny from such a government. (*Essays*, 43)

These, then, were the basic views on governance with which Hume approached the contemporary British political scene. He saw his mission as one of pacification and reform. He did not participate in the current adoration of the English constitution. It was a unique hybrid. All the other great European states, all predominantly agricultural, had become absolute monarchies as feudalism declined. In contrast, in every major state where commerce had transformed society the government became republican. England, however, had gone both ways. After a strong beginning under the Tudors, absolutism failed to mature; yet although the republican element had become powerful, the monarchy had not been abolished. The result was that after 1688–1689 the English constitution was contradictory: one part, the Crown, embodied the monarchic principle; the other, the House of Commons, embodied the republican principle. Such a constitution has serious defects. True, ostensibly it is a mixed (or balanced) constitution, with a monarchic, an aristocratic, and a democratic element, as prescribed by Polybius. But are all three elements genuine? And is a mixed constitution best? Hume's reply to both those questions is negative. Having surveyed the evidence, he concludes that elective kingship, feudal aristocracy, and participatory democracy all are bad: "It may therefore be pronounced as an universal axiom in politics, *That an hereditary prince, a nobility without vassals, and a people voting by their representatives, form the best* MONARCHY, ARISTOCRACY, *and* DEMOCRACY" (*Essays*, 18). The English constitution conforms to sound political science in that the kingship is hereditary. But although the democratic element appears correct, participatory democracy being avoided, in fact the laws regulating the representation of the people are sadly in need of correction. The aristocratic element, too, at first glance appears correct; in fact, the hereditary House of Lords is only a relic from gothic times. Given the obsolete representation of the people and the weakness of the House of Lords, the English government really consists of only two parts—a powerful monarchic element, the Crown, and a powerful House of Commons controlled by grandees—two elements locked in a perpetual tug-of-war.

This arrangement is commendable in that it affords a great deal of liberty: first, a strict rule of law; second, extensive freedom. Consequently, industry is fostered, the arts and sciences are encouraged, and the inhabitants are quite free and happy; all this flows from the nervous suspicion with which the Crown is regarded by the House of Commons. The Crown is the executive government, but because it is dependent on the cooperation of the House for both new revenue and new statute law, the

House is able to insist that it act only with the greatest legality. There is a higher degree of civil liberty in England than in the republics, for in a republic the legislature regards the executive government as a subordinate body, not as a rival to be given little discretionary power (*Essays*, 12).

The vigilant attitude of the House of Commons toward the Crown explains the great freedom of the English press, and also the incessant, clamorous denunciation of the ministry. The House sees the press as an ally in keeping the ministers under surveillance and as the best means for arousing the people against the Court; as a result, it will tolerate few restrictions on political invective and distortion by the press. Given the absence of legal limits and the frenzy of the government's opponents, the chief business of many journalists is condemnation, calumny, and derision directed against the ministers. Yet, commented Hume in 1741, although much of what is published against the ministers is founded only on the presupposition that whatever they do must be either stupid or wicked, no real harm results; the people are not as easily misled as once was thought.[11]

Contrary to the Country view propounded by dissident Whigs and adopted by many Tories, the idea of an ancient English constitution, a constitution that expressed the superlative political genius of the English people and their noble love of liberty, was mere illusion. In the Middle Ages, all the major European countries, including England, had Gothic constitutions, mixtures, not of authority and liberty, but of authority and anarchy. But while the others had become absolute monarchies, England developed a hybrid system. Why? Not because the English are the chosen people of liberty, but chiefly because of unusual circumstances and accidents. England shared the British isles with no expansionist enemies and was able to annex Wales and suppress Ireland; consequently, no need was felt to replace the feudal militia with a standing army until the beginning of major continental involvements after 1688. The Tudors, although fully as absolutist as any rulers west of Moscovy, were so popular and powerful that they did not feel threatened by Parliament; indeed, they used Parliament as an instrument of their own arbitrary rule. Thus Parliament was preserved and strengthened. Then the gradual growth of commerce created a rich, powerful middle rank in society, and this rank gained control of the House of Commons. In the seventeenth century, the "religious puritans," fanatics, wild enthusiasts with no thought of improving the constitution, found the House of Commons an ideal vehicle for their assault upon the established order in religion. Soon they became enemies of the kings, who supported the Church. The eventual result was that after

[11] See pp. 306–7.

1688–1689, England had a truly new constitution, a constitution unique in Europe, a constitution half monarchical, half republican.

The revolution was made, not chiefly by those opposed to royal authority in the state, although there were such people, but by the religious puritans, enemies of the established church. The writers of those times recognized this fully: "[A]ll historians, who lived near that age, or what perhaps is more decisive, all authors, who have casually made mention of those public transactions, still represent the civil disorders and convulsions, as proceeding from religious controversy, and consider the political disputes about power and liberty as entirely subordinate to the other" (*H.*, 5:303). The established church, of course, saw the kings' cause as its own.

> On the other hand, opposition to the church, and the persecutions under which they labored, were sufficient to throw the puritans into the country party, and to engender political principles little favorable to the high pretensions of the sovereign. The spirit too of enthusiasm; bold, daring, and uncontroled; strongly disposed their minds to adopt republican tenets; and inclined them to arrogate, in their actions and conduct, the same liberty, which they assumed, in their rapturous flights and extasies. Ever since the first origin of that sect, thro' the whole reign of Elizabeth as well as of James, *puritanical* principles had been understood in a double sense, and expressed the opinions favorable both to political and to ecclesiastical liberty. And as the court, in order to discredit all parliamentary opposition, affixed the denomination of puritans to its antagonists; the religious puritans willingly adopted this idea, which was so advantageous to them; and confounded their cause with that of the patriots or country party. Thus were the civil and ecclesiastical factions regularly formed; and the humor of the nation, during that age, running strongly toward fanatical extravagancies, the spirit of civil liberty gradually revived from its lethargy, and by means of its religious associate, from which it reaped so much advantage and so little honor, it secretly enlarged its dominion, over the greatest part of the kingdom.[12]

Throughout most of the seventeenth century, the opponents of Anglican episcopacy were strong while the proponents of civil liberty were weak. Here we have the ancestors of the "religious Whigs" and the "political Whigs," to whom Hume, as we shall see, referred in 1747 in his defense of Archibald Stewart.

[12] *History of Great Britain*, pp. 172–73. There were, Hume says, those who, inspired by the classics, worked for the achievement of a better and freer constitution; however, we are not to attribute too much to them. Paradoxically, it was the religious puritans, fanatics devoid of any idea of civil or religious liberty, who provided the energy to break the old order; their zeal helped produce a result they never sought. *History of England*, 4:145–46; 5:18–19, 42, 80.

In his accounts of the reigns of James I and Charles I, Hume generally sides with the Crown on constitutional questions. Almost all the practices of the Tudor period—the precedents that, taken together, made up the constitution in the early-seventeenth century—were on the Crown's side. Moreover, most of the members of the House of Commons were childishly unrealistic; while insisting that they did not wish to make England a republic, they stubbornly asserted the rights of the House in legislation, especially in taxation, without admitting that those rights, unless exercised responsibly and cooperatively, with an open eye to the requirements of the Crown, were incompatible with the successful conduct of government. They acted as if the king could continue to provide all the services of government without adequate revenues. Hume's conclusion is that while James I and Charles I undoubtedly were often maladroit in their dealings with the House, as kings probably they were above average. Certainly, they were not the main cause of the English constitutional struggles. In terms of constitutional law, they were in the right; the times, however, required far greater political genius and flexibility than they possessed. Contrary to Whig history, the main causes of the turmoils were these: the clash between the increasing prosperity of the commons and the continuing strength of monarchy; the lack of an effective method of assuring cooperation between the Crown and the House of Commons; the fanatical hostility of the religious puritans to the Church establishment.

In contrast, Hume shows no interest in defending James II. By 1685 the shape of the new constitution was almost settled. Moreover, by then it was evident that England was going to move toward the greater religious and civil liberty suitable to a commercial society. James was hopelessly miscast as England's king: by ostentatiously turning his back on the Church of England, and by hasty moves to advance Roman Catholics, he destroyed his legitimacy. Far more interesting for Hume, as for his contemporaries, was the question of the wisdom of passing over James's son in favor of William and Mary in 1689, and of bringing in the Hanoverians in 1714. Persuasive arguments were in conflict. Wise politicians saw that the Stuarts, entitled to the throne by inheritance, had a strong claim on the loyalty of the populace, a factor making for obedience and peace; however, they saw also that a professed Roman Catholic could not be the head of a Protestant church and state. Hume reveals no affection for either line. The decisive consideration is practicality: James's departure from England blemished his son's title, not legally, but in the mind of the public; the parliamentary leaders were wise to take advantage of this fact; given English attitudes, the Stuarts, as ardent Roman Catholics, could never be successful kings of England. They were incompatible with English public opinion; even the rabid High Church faction, who saw the

Whig ministers as enemies of the Church, would never accept a Roman Catholic as head of the Church.[13]

The struggle between monarchical and republican forces did not end in 1688–1689; indeed the modern constitution is simply a formalization of the struggle. A tug-of-war has been established, but neither side is supposed to pull too hard. As we saw, both authority and liberty are essential to good governance under any constitution. In England the cause of authority is championed by the Crown: it favors strong government; it is impatient when the House of Commons fails to vote supply quickly; it emphasizes the need for prerogative power so as to be able to conduct foreign policy and wage wars successfully, to resist subversion, and so on. In contrast, many members of the House of Commons, in typical republican manner, insist on the danger of such powers, on the need for an elaborate due process in legislation, and on strict attention to legality in the law courts and administration. As a result, the Crown and the House of Commons, the two main institutions of this strange constitution, stand as separate interests vying for the support of the political nation. They divide the people of England into two parties, primarily parties of principle. Pressed hard enough, each party will admit that the other principle, authority or liberty, is essential to good governance; yet normally each champions only its own darling. Each gives a partial, unbalanced, untrue view of the constitution.

Were the BRITISH government proposed as a subject of speculation, one would immediately perceive in it a source of division and party, which it would be almost impossible for it, under any administration, to avoid. The just balance between the republican and monarchical part of our constitution is really, in itself, so extremely delicate and uncertain, that, when joined to men's passions and prejudices, it is impossible but different opinions must arise concerning it, even among persons of the best understanding. Those of mild tempers, who love peace and order, and detest sedition and civil wars, will always entertain more favourable sentiments of monarchy, than men of

[13] The publication of the essay "Of the Protestant Succession," in which Hume examines the arguments germane before 1714 for a Stuart restoration, was held up until 1752. Hume had intended to publish it in 1748, along with two others, "Of the Original Contract" and "Of Passive Obedience," showing the absurdity of the parties' high theories. The arguments for a Stuart restoration had been strong: first, many people in England, Scotland, and Ireland saw the Stuarts as the legitimate royal family; second, turning from the Stuarts to the Hanoverians made for greater involvement in continental balance-of-power politics. But now, more than thirty years later, there was no going back. Hume's conclusion was clear; yet he was admitting that the Jacobites had had a strong case in 1714. Although Hume was ready to publish "Of the Protestant Succession" in 1748, his friend, Charles Erskine, Lord Tinwald, decided that this would not be prudent so soon after the Rebellion of 1745. *Letters*, 1:112. It was published in 1752 in *Political Discourses*. See E. C. Mossner, *The Life of David Hume*, 2d ed. (Oxford: Clarendon Press, 1980), p. 180.

bold and generous spirits, who are passionate lovers of liberty, and think no evil comparable to subjection and slavery. And though all reasonable men agree in general to preserve our mixed government; yet, when they come to particulars, some will incline to trust greater powers to the crown, to bestow on it more influence, and to guard against its encroachments with less caution, than others who are terrified at the most distant approaches of tyranny and despotic power. Thus are there parties of PRINCIPLE involved in the very nature of our constitution, which may properly enough be denominated those of COURT and COUNTRY. (*Essays*, 64–65)

This basic difference of principle gives rise to a second cause of conflict, a difference of selfish interest between the leading figures of the two parties. The king selects some of the notables as his ministers. Deprived and angry, those excluded from office embrace the Country position. The party leaders, the opposition heads as well as the ministers, are carried to extremes of partiality by their own selfish interest, now engaged on behalf of the Country and the Court respectively.

Hume found that a simple Country-versus-Court analysis, such as that given by Bolingbroke in 1739, in "Of the State of Parties at the Accession of George the First," a pamphlet written to help sustain the Tory-Country alliance against Walpole, concealed the complexity of the contemporary struggle between the Whigs and the Tories; it failed to reveal the main causes of rancor and intransigence, namely, disputes over religion and over the dynasty. Those differences had originated in the Country-versus-Court struggle of the previous century; anachronistic though they were, they continued to bedevil the political scene. Hume's summary description of the two English parties as they stood about 1740, haunted by the past, was as follows: "A TORY, therefore, since the *revolution*, may be defined in a few words, to be *a lover of monarchy, though without abandoning liberty; and a partizan of the family of* STUART. As a WHIG may be defined to be *a lover of liberty though without renouncing monarchy; and a friend to the settlement in the* PROTESTANT *line*" (*Essays*, 71). The central difference is dynastic: the Stuarts, who probably would continue to be Roman Catholics, versus the Hanoverians, unquestionably Protestant. The politics of the present is distorted by the past. The claim of opposition politicians that they are simply a Country or Patriot party united by abhorrence of the corruption of England by Walpole, and free from old Toryism with its strong Jacobite tendencies, simply is not true. Nor are the Court Whigs simply a government party. Each is mixed in its membership, attitudes, and policies. For years the Whigs have played the role of the Court party, while the Tories, out of power, have adopted the Country stance. Roles, principles, histories, and rhetoric have been swapped: now in office, the Whigs stress the need for strong, efficient government; now out, the Tories are keen for liberty, for weaker, less active government, for lower taxes. Yet neither party can free itself from its past, and each draws support from interests naturally inclined to the other. The Tories, even while adopting republican poses, lapse into laments for Charles the Martyr and love sermons on the divine right of kings. The Whigs, now the Court party, still preach the right of resistance. The politics of the clergy provide proof positive that neither the Court nor the Country is a simple, pure party. The priests of an established episcopal church are natural allies of a Court, while nonconformist clergy naturally side with the opposition; yet in England the lower clergy—not the bishops, loyal to their maker, a Whig—are solidly Country, while the nonconformists support the Court. Moreover, the Whigs favor Protestant, republican, commercial Holland, while the Tories favor France— hardly what one would expect of a royalist Court party or a republican Country party (*Essays,* 612)!

Hume saw roles in Britain for both a true Court and a true Country party, each defending an essential part of the constitution. But neither of the parties could perform its role well until it had cleared its mind by jettisoning its false, partisan account of past conflicts and its extremist political theory. Obviously, Hume was demanding far more of the Tories than of the Court Whigs; yet the latter, too, especially some of their scribblers and historians, had much to learn.[14]

When, about 1740, Hume surveyed party politics in Scotland, he found a far simpler scene. First there were the Jacobites. However congenial some of them might be personally, their case was fatally ill founded. They argued for a return to the past, when Scotland was an independent kingdom ruled by its rightful kings. They failed to see that it was only with the Union that Scotland had gained the benefits of true civil society. In the first and second editions of his essays (published in 1741 and 1742)

---

[14] The context of Hume's essays on government and politics (1741) is the Country versus Court controversy (1726–1742) about the nature and history of the English constitution; see Isaac Kramnick, *Bolingbroke and His Circle: The Politics of Nostalgia in the Age of Walpole* (Cambridge: Harvard University Press, 1968), esp. pp. 17–38, 111–36. The nature of English politics after 1714 remains in dispute; for the view that Toryism, although prevented by the unreformed election laws from winning a majority in the House of Commons, remained strong throughout England, see Linda Colley, *In Defiance of Oligarchy: The Tory Party 1714–60* (Cambridge: Cambridge University Press, 1982); and J.C.D. Clark, *English Society 1688–1832* (Cambridge: Cambridge University Press, 1985). Also, William Speck, "Whigs and Tories dim their glories: English political parties under the first two Georges," in *The Whig Ascendancy*, ed. John Cannon (London: Edward Arnold [Publishers] Ltd., 1981), pp. 51–70. On the continuing strength of divine-right theory after 1714, see J.A.W. Gunn, "The Spectre at the Feast: The Persistence of High-Tory Ideas," in his *Beyond Liberty and Property* (Kingston and Montreal: McGill-Queen's University Press, 1983), pp. 120–93.

Hume comments that in Scotland there never had been any true Tories, with their special intermediate position—emphasizing authority, but not to the extent of suppressing liberty—but only Whigs and Jacobites. Accordingly, he reports rather proudly, given the insignificance of the Jacobites, the relevant distinction in Scotland, the distinction in terms of which party politics now are discussed, is simply the entirely defensible distinction between Court and Country. This admirable state of affairs he attributes to Scotland's separate constitutional development before 1707 and to the religious settlement in Scotland: in 1690 the established church, the Church of Scotland, had been cast in the presbyterian mold, and the episcopalians were turned out of the state churches; consequently, the presbyterian clergy support the Whig ministers while the episcopalian clergy oppose them. The former are "in" in both church and state; the latter are "out" in both. In addition, to some extent the contrast between the party situation in Scotland and England arises from different social structure of the two countries.

> There are only two Ranks of Men among us; Gentlemen, who have some Fortune and Education, and the meanest slaving Poor; without any considerable Number of that middling Rank of Men, which abounds more in EN-GLAND, both in Cities and in the Country, than in any other Part of the World. The slaving Poor are incapable of any Principles: Gentlemen may be converted to true Principles, by Time and Experience. The middling Rank of Men have Curiosity and Knowledge enough to form Principles, but not enough to form true ones, or correct any Prejudices that they may have imbib'd: And 'tis among the middling Rank, that TORY Principles do at present prevail most in ENGLAND. (*Essays*, 616)

This paragraph was dropped in all the editions published after 1745. Hume may have found the view of the middling rank expressed therein at least superficially inconsistent with the highly laudatory comment on that rank to be published in 1752 in his apology for commerce. A more immediate reason was that the '45 and its aftermath had revealed that the Scottish political scene was more complex than Hume had thought. First, Jacobitism had not vanished in Scotland. Second, it had become evident that the Whigs were divided, not only by Court and Country inclinations, but by a far more profound difference. Some were motivated primarily by an admirable commitment to good government, others by odious religious prejudices.

In a postscript, dated November 4, 1747, to his defence of Archibald Stewart, Lord Provost of Edinburgh in 1744–1746, charged with failure to defend the city against the Jacobite army, Hume explains the different reactions to Stewart's acquittal. There are, he reports, two kinds of Whigs, political and religious Whigs. "The Idea I form of a political *Whig* is, that of a Man of Sense and Moderation, a Lover of Laws and Liberty, whose chief Regard to particular Princes and Families, is founded on a Regard to the publick Good." The leaders of this group are "Men of great Worth": Duncan Forbes of Culloden (the Lord President) and Lord Milton (the Lord Justice Clerk). In contrast, the other group is utterly despicable: "The religious *Whigs* are a very different Set of Mortals, and in my Opinion, are much worse than the religious *Tories*; as the political *Tories* are inferior to the political *Whigs*." And why are the religious Tories better than the religious Whigs? "I know not how it happens, but it seems to me, that a Zeal for Bishops, and for the Book of Common-Prayer, tho' equally groundless, has never been able, when mixt up with Party Notions, to form so virulent and exalted a Poison in human Breasts, as the opposite Principles. Dissimulation, Hyprocrisy Violence, Calumny, Selfishness are, generally speaking, the true and legitimate Offspring of this kind of Zeal." Hume concludes by tying this analysis to the reactions to Stewart's acquittal. The religious Whigs are seething with righteous indignation. In contrast, "The political *Whigs* are, many of them, his personal Friends; and all of them, are extremely pleased with his Acquital, because they believe, what is, indeed, undeniable, that it was founded on his Innocence. I am charitable enough to suppose, that the Joy of many of the *Tories* flowed from the same Motive."[15] As we have seen, Hume

[15] The pamphlet "A True ACCOUNT Of The *Behaviour* and *Conduct* Of Archibald Stewart, *Esq*; Late Lord Provost of *Edinburgh*" has been reprinted by J. V. Price in *The Ironic Hume* (Austin: University of Texas Press, 1965). The postscript appears at pp. 170–72. Stewart was imprisoned in the Tower from December 13, 1745, until January 23, 1747. On November 2, 1747, he was found not guilty of neglect of duty and misbehavior in the execution of his office.

Hume's denunciation of religious Whiggery seems the result of his increasing antagonism to Country views and sentiments. From the early years of the century, there had been two rival Whig interests in Scotland: the *Squadrone Volante*, a group of intermarried Lowland magnates, and the Argathelians, the interest headed by the second and third Dukes of Argyll, leaders of one of the greatest Highland clans, the Campbells. From 1725 to 1740, the second duke, John Campbell, was the leading Scot supporting Walpole's ministry; his brother, Archibald, Earl of Islay, managed Scotland. In other words, the Argathelians were Court. Out of power, the *Squadrone* inclined to Patriotism. In 1733–1734 the Patriots made a major gain in Scotland: in 1733 Alexander Hume, second Earl of Marchmont and a leading member of the *Squadrone*, became active against Walpole; in the election of 1734, Marchmont's able sons, Lord Polwarth and Alexander Hume-Campbell, were elected to the House of Commons as Patriots. (These two, along with "the cousinhood," Richard Grenville [later Earl Temple] and his brother, George Grenville; George Lyttelton; and William Pitt, brother-in-law of the Grenvilles—the "Boy Patriots," as Walpole called them—were coached by a prominent Patriot peer, Richard Temple, Viscount Cobham, uncle of the Grenvilles.) Hume's relations with Polwarth (Marchmont, after his father's death in 1740)—they were close neighbors in the Merse—seem to have become distant after 1740; see *Letters* 1:28, 103, 110, 162; 2:124, 163.

Although for years an opponent of the Patriots, John Campbell, second Duke of Argyll,

was to use this distinction between political and religious Whigs in the *History of England*; indeed, his attitude to the Puritan Revolution cannot be understood unless the distinction between political and religious puritans is kept in mind. Although Hume found either a genuine Court position (untainted by Toryism) or a genuine Country position (free from Pa-

---

finally broke with Walpole in 1739–1740; he had found irresistible the opposition's attack, in which Pitt was prominent, on Walpole's "pusillanimous" attempt to settle differences with Spain over trade with the West Indies by treaty rather than war. Archibald Stewart was elected to the House of Commons in 1741 as a member of "the Duke of Argyll's Gang." After Walpole's resignation, in 1742, Argyll demanded the creation of a "broad-bottomed" ministry, which would include Tories; he was not prepared to accept the continuation of the old order, altered only by the removal of Walpole and the addition of a few Patriots such as Charteret and Pulteney. When it became clear that he could not prevail, he retired from public life, leaving the way open for the *Squadrone*. Stewart and two other friends of Hume, James Oswald and William Mure, voted as independents during the period of *Squadrone* ascendancy. After 1746, when the Argathelians, then led by Archibald Campbell (Islay), who had become Duke of Argyll at his brother's death in 1743, were back in influence, both Oswald and Mure cooperated with the ministry, but as independents. Stewart, who had moved his business to London, did not seek reelection in 1747.

The second Duke of Argyll flirted with Jacobitism after his break with Walpole. Romney Sedgwick, *The History of Parliament. The House of Commons 1715–1754*, 2 vols. (HMSO, 1970) 1:71–72, 114. Whether and how far Hume's friends in "Argyll's Gang" supported the Duke in this flirtation is hard to say, but it is to be noted that Alexander Carlyle believed that Archibald Stewart had assisted the Prince in taking over Edinburgh in 1745. *The Autobiography of Dr. Alexander Carlyle of Inveresk 1722–1805* (London and Edinburgh: T. N. Foulis, 1910), pp. 122, 132. In 1741 Hume had written, "[T]he *Jacobite* Party is almost entirely vanish'd from us [in Scotland]" *Essays*, pp. 615–16). It is to be remembered, first, that several of Hume's closest friends were Jacobites, some for reasons Hume understood, such as the heavy-handed treatment accorded Scotland in the decades after 1707, and, second, that Jacobites had good reason not to proclaim their political sentiments. According to one Jacobite, William Macgregor of Balhaldy, "The many sanguinary penal laws since the Revolution, whereby the crime of Jacobitism is rendered more horribly dreadful in its consequences than murder, witchcraft or even open deism or atheism . . . has brought such a habit and spirit of dissimulation on them, that a Jacobite can never be discovered by his words. It must be his actions that decypher him." Eveline Cruickshanks, *Political Untouchables: The Tories and the '45* (London: Gerald Duckworth & Co. Ltd., 1979), p. 45.

The cynicism of the Patriotic Whigs, revealed in 1742, is examined by M. M. Goldsmith, "Faction Detected: Ideological Consequences of Robert Walpole's Decline and Fall," *History* 64 (1979): 1–19. Probably Hume was not greatly surprised by the transactions of 1742. In the first volume of his *Essays*, published in Edinburgh in June/July, 1741, he had dismissed the Patriots' wild charge that Walpole was corrupting Britain's constitution: if the constitution was all that wonderful, how could someone as bad as the "zealous patriots" said Walpole was possibly have remained in office so long? And how could the hybrid constitution work without places and pensions? *Essays*, pp. 30, 45, 608–9. In the autumn of 1742, Hume speculated in jest that Mure was a Patriot. *Letters*, 1:45. In "Of Public Credit" (1752), Hume wrote, "Mankind are, in all ages, caught by the same baits: The same tricks, played over and over again, still trepan them. The heights of popularity and patriotism are still the beaten road to power and tyranny; flattery to treachery; standing armies to arbitrary government; and the glory of God to the temporal interest of the clergy." *Essays*, p. 363. In

triotic zeal and cant) compatible with true political principles, for religious Whiggery he had only contempt.

Hume saw English politics at the middle of the eighteenth century as very much a continuation of the struggles of the previous century. The main difference, aside from dynastic loyalties, was that, although the power of the House of Commons was now fully established, the susceptibility of members of the House to Crown influence meant that constitutional deadlocks and civil strife could be avoided. For well over a hundred years, the mixed constitution had brought forth rival parties, parties that battled each other year after year, sometimes with words, sometimes with swords, and all quite irrationally given the fact that what divided them, aside from religion and their leaders' ambition, was mainly a quite understandable difference of emphasis on liberty and authority. Presumably, they would continue fighting in the same way in the future, certainly with words, perhaps with swords, unless they could be made aware of their symbiotic relationship. The English, he proposes, forgetting both extremist theories and biased histories, should acknowledge that the basic position of neither party is entirely right or wrong, and admit candidly that their matchless constitution is bad in at least one important respect: by setting one essential requirement, authority, in systematic conflict with

---

his later years he regularly dismissed Patriots as knaves.

Aside from the Duke of Argyll (Islay) himself—"a Man of Sense & Learning" (*Letters*, 1:113)—Duncan Forbes and Andrew Fletcher (nephew of the famous writer) were the most prominent Argathelians of the 1745–1747 period. The vehemence of Hume's denunciation of religious Whiggery probably arose in part from personal experience. The *Squadrone* had contributed greatly to the failure of his candidacy in 1744–1745 for appointment as professor of ethics and pneumatic philosophy at Edinburgh. E. C. Mossner and J. V. Price, in introducing *A Letter from a Gentleman to his friend in Edinburgh*, attribute the controversy over Hume's candidacy to the rivalry of the Argathelian and *Squadrone* interests; however, one must ask why Hume was acceptable to many (although not all) Argathelians and unacceptable to many (althought not all) of the *Squadrone*. The answer may be that his moral philosophy was found somewhat lacking in "warmth in the cause of virtue"—with virtue standing for revolution principles as understood by immoderate Whigs. And, of course, it is true that he did not believe that the Revolution had been clearly legal, nor that Jacobites were enemies of true religion and freedom, nor that presbyterianism was divinely ordained. See R. B. Sher's "Professors of Virtue: The Social History of the Edinburgh Moral Philosophy Chair in the Eighteenth Century," in *Studies in the Philosophy of the Scottish Enlightenment*, ed. M. A. Stewart (Oxford: Clarendon Press, 1990), pp. 87–126, esp. 104–6.

In 1751 Hume commented in *Enquiry* II (p. 242) that the contrast between the patriotic (public-spirited) rhetoric of those in public life and their actions, combined with the contrast beween the prominence of benevolence in philosophers' theories and the lack of it in their performance, had produced in Great Britain an incredulity so great that it was difficult for an enemy of moral skepticism such as himself to persuade readers that qualities such as patriotism, benevolence, and humanity actually do exist. In 1744 Hume, writing to Mure (*Letters*, 1:58), had complained about the apparent failure of Hutcheson, "that celebrated & benevolent Moralist," to support his candidacy at Edinburgh.

the other, liberty, it causes the political nation to divide into parties of principle.

In their diatribes against Walpole, the Country politicians rage against the minister's use of honors, appointments, and pensions to win elections in the country and votes in Parliament. But how else, Hume asks, can the Crown preserve its role, and thus the mixed nature of the constitution, against erosion by the House of Commons? The old superstitious reverence for kings has been extinguished: "The mere name of *king* commands little respect; and to talk of a king as GOD's vicegerent on earth, or to give him any of those magnificent titles, which formerly dazzled mankind, would but excite laughter in every one" (*Essays*, 51). What then, Hume inquires, enables Walpole and his colleagues to get the Crown's business done in Parliament, and to keep the House of Commons from transforming the country into a republic? Mainly the power of appointment: by adroit use of places, the ministers are able to create a majority. The Crown uses its own economic power to check the economic power of the grandees, who otherwise would control the House of Commons. Although the Crown's economic leverage is small relative to that of the commons as a whole, it is concentrated and can be deployed in a concerted way (*Essays*, 48–49). To assert that the most sublime constitution the world ever has known depends for its success, even survival, on bribery and corruption may seem blasphemous; nevertheless, that is the plain truth (*Essays*, 45).

Yet another defect of the constitution is its instability. Either side, the Crown or the House, may begin imperceptibly to pull the other, with either absolute monarchy or oligarchy the final result. The influence of shifting economic power, the power of the armed forces, and the key role of the king, who may be competent or incompetent, all make for instability (*Essays*, 46). In the essay "Whether the British Government inclines more to Absolute Monarchy, or to a Republic" (1741), Hume surveys the situation and prospects. His conclusion is that constitutional change, which since 1603 had been strengthening the House of Commons, had just begun to move the other way. True, kings no longer are held in religious awe, but the increasing revenues and expenditures of the Crown—more than one-thirtieth of "the whole income and labour of the kingdom"—were bringing in a new era of executive strength. Of the alternatives, this seemed the better. Obviously, a well-designed republic would be preferable to an absolute monarchy, but a system in which the House of Commons as then constituted was virtually absolute would be far inferior to a civilized monarchy. Such a monarchy would provide a high degree of liberty, but the former would give unlimited power to one small body of interested men, the great men in the House of Commons (*Essays*, 52–53).

In 1758, with the Stuarts gone, the Hanoverians thoroughly settled in, and the Walpole-Pelham monopoly finally broken, Hume sounded a hopeful note in the essay "Of the Coalition of Parties." At long last the animosities inherited from the past seemed forgotten. The fears and hatreds which for six or seven generations had bedeviled Great Britain had died away, at least temporarily. A new beginning was now possible.

Hume, the Scotch politician, had advice for the English, especially the shrill Patriotic extremists. Instead of misleading themselves by equating the good and the right, and the right and the old, they should correct and clarify their beliefs about their constitution. They should see it, not as the product of primordial Anglo-Saxon wisdom and love of liberty, but as largely the result, the fragile result, of circumstances, accidents, and compromises. It allows a great deal of civil liberty, far more than either a simple monarchy or a republic ever would tolerate. This is all very good, provided the press does not corrupt public opinion, thus destroying the foundation of the system. Logically, the constitution is inconsistent: the members of the House of Commons have no legal responsibility to govern the country; yet legally they can cut off the money that is indispensible to the Crown. But this inconsistency need not be fatal. Practical people, those who see the wisdom of refusing to press *de jure* rights to the extreme, can make even the English constitution work. In addition, they can strengthen the constitution greatly by making certain major reforms.

In the essay "Of the Idea of a perfect Commonwealth," first published in *Political Discourses* (1752), Hume outlines the constitution best suited to an ideal civil society. The essay, he insists, is not to be taken as a call for constitutional revolution in Great Britain; yet therein he argues that Britain's limited monarchy needs major reforms. Two changes should be made. First, the representation of the people should be reformed (a) by making the constituencies equal in terms of population, and (b) by standardizing the property qualification for electors throughout the country at a fairly high level (*Essays*, 526–27). These electoral reforms would have had the effect of eliminating the English "rotten boroughs"—but Hume does not spell this out. Also, they would have increased the number of Scottish electors, while reducing the number of electors in the English counties. Second, the atrophied third element in the constitution, the upper house, should be modernized. The obsolete House of Lords has no power to check either the House of Commons or the ministers. The standing army and the weakness of the House of Lords, Hume was to comment in the *History of England*, had produced a situation in which the people "are totally naked, defenceless, and disarmed, and besides, are not secured by any middle power, or independant powerful nobility, interposed between them and the monarch" (*H*, 4:370). This fundamental defect could be remedied by dropping the two special kinds of lords, the bishops and the Scotch representative peers, and by changing the basis of membership from inherited rank to merit. All Lords of Parliament should be life peers, selected by cooption, with no commoner allowed to decline a summons to the House of Lords. Moreover, the number of peers should be increased. The result would be that the House of Lords would consist "entirely of the men of chief credit, abilities, and interest in the nation; and every turbulent leader in the house of Commons might be taken off, and connected by interest with the house of Peers." Hume is proposing that the traditional nobility be supplanted by something much closer to a genuine aristocracy. He sees a strong upper house as a desirable restraint on the lower house, as well as on the king. The members of the House of Commons persistently press for more power—not for an increase in the power of the people—and now are held back only by the king and his ministers. This means that "At present the balance of our government depends in some measure on the abilities and behaviour of the sovereign; which are variable and uncertain circumstances" (*Essays*, 527).

But even after these two radical reforms, the British constitution still would have three major defects. In all the early versions of this essay, 1752 to 1768, Hume sums up his criticism as follows:

> This plan of limited monarchy, however corrected, seems still liable to three great inconveniencies. *First*, It removes not entirely, though it may soften, the parties of *court* and *country*. *Secondly*, The king's personal character must still have great influence on the government. *Thirdly*, The sword is in the hands of a single person, who will always neglect to discipline the militia, in order to have a pretence for keeping up a standing army. It is evident, that this is a mortal distemper in the BRITISH government, of which it must at last inevitably perish. I must, however, confess, that SWEDEN seems, in some measure, to have remedied this inconvenience, and to have a militia, with its limited monarchy, as well as a standing army, which is less dangerous than the BRITISH.

The last two sentences were dropped from the editions of 1770, 1772, and 1777, the last editions prepared by Hume himself.[16]

As we have seen, for Hume civil society is primarily an economic relationship: a government's main task is to promote the independence and prosperity of its subjects, ordinarily chiefly by enforcing justice. Accordingly, the private-law rules by which economic goods are assigned to owners are more fundamental than the public-law rules relating to thrones and ministries; indeed, Hume counsels us to take the claims of royal pretenders very lightly. He favors the established Hanoverian regime, but for liberal, not conservative, reasons. David Miller quotes

[16] *Essays*, pp. 527 and 647.

Hume's criticism of the accounts given by Whig historians of early-seventeenth-century constitutional struggles: "[F]orgetting that a regard to liberty, though a laudable passion, ought commonly to be subordinate to a reverence for established government, the prevailing faction has celebrated only the partizans of the former, who pursued as their object the perfection of civil society, and has extolled them at the expence of their antagonists, who maintained those maxims, that are essential to its very existence."[17] Miller argues that Hume, confronted with a choice, would have put security ahead of liberty, and concludes that this reveals an ultimate conservatism. How valid is this conclusion?

As we have seen, the relations among civil liberty, good governance, and the right to govern are fundamental to Hume's political philosophy. He develops his position with clarity and candor in six essays; the entire *History of England* is informed by it. A court party, he finds, emphasizes the need for the government to be able to act quickly and effectively, while a country party stresses the importance of liberty. Each is blind in one eye. Nor is this surprising given the different roles played by the two parties; in the two-party dialogue, each has its own viewpoint and stock lines. Hume stands back as a spectator; he sees strength and weakness in each position: the truth lies somewhere between the extremes. He recognizes that what is required is a balance, an adjustable balance, with government power waxing in times of public need and waning when the circumstances permit an increase in individual liberty. No wise politician will attempt, by either law or philosophy, to fix the balance permanently: if the power of the government is fixed low, the public may suffer in times of emergency; if it is fixed high in anticipation of great emergencies, the liberty of the citizens will be restricted unnecessarily most of the time. The balance appropriate to a particular time must remain a matter of discretion. What would be good in every circumstance cannot be defined precisely in a constitution.

For Hume government power is not the enemy of liberty; rather, properly used, it is a basic means to liberty. Natural liberty, with everybody doing whatever he pleased without government restriction, was possible only in primitive times. Even then there were moral restraints; in addition, the clan or tribal chiefs exerted patriarchal power. At the other extreme, the only theory of unquestionable power, the divine-right theory, is absurd. Hume opts for a middle position, for liberties defined and protected by positive laws, laws made and changed only by due process. By "civil liberty" Hume means individual liberty of choice, choice that is meaningful only if the consequences of one's acts are predictable to a

[17] David Miller, *Philosophy and Ideology in Hume's Political Thought* (Oxford: Clarendon Press, 1981), p. 195; *History of England*, 6:533.

considerable degree. For this reason the order a government produces is a prerequisite of liberty.

In the very late (1777) essay "Of the Origin of Government," Hume makes the very point on which his criticism of both the House of Commons in the early-seventeenth century and the Whig historians is based. After noting that, even though a government may be absolute in constitutional law, authority in fact is never absolute, he proceeds to tell us that we are not to think that "free government" means weak, strictly limited government; indeed, "free governments" (republican governments) often are far less limited, more restrictive, than monarchial governments.

> The government, which, in common appellation, receives the appellation of free, is that which admits of a partition of power among several members, whose united authority is no less, or is commonly greater than that of any monarch; but who, in the usual course of administration, must act by general and equal laws, that are previously known to all the members and to all their subjects. In this sense, it must be owned, that liberty is the perfection of civil society; but still authority must be acknowledged essential to its very existence: and in those contests, which so often take place between the one and the other, the latter may, on that account, challenge the preference. Unless perhaps one may say (and it may be said with some reason) that a circumstance, which is essential to the existence of civil society, must always support itself, and needs be guarded with less jealousy, than one that contributes only to its perfection, which the indolence of men is so apt to neglect, or their ignorance to overlook. (*Essays*, 40–41)

It may be thought that when Hume says that authority should be given preference above liberty, he is saying that the right to govern is more important than good governance. But here again he is perfectly clear. He agrees flatly with Locke against the advocates of unquestionable authority, either divine right or Hobbesian. A right to govern is justified only by good results: authority is justified only if the public interest is served. This requires both liberty (i.e., a set of laws establishing rights) and good laws (i.e., the laws must at least be reasonably good). This the wise politician knows. The multitude, of course, are moved to obedience mainly by opinion of right and by the power of property; but even their sense of obligation to obey will dwindle away if the government fails to serve the public interest for a long period. And this is highly advantageous, for the right is only a means to the good. As we know, the maxim, *fiat justitia, ruat cœlum* is false, and "by sacrificing the end to the means, shews a preposterous idea of the subordination of duties." Hume continues, "The case is the same with the duty of allegiance; and common sense teaches us, that, as government binds us to obedience only on account of its tendency to public utility, that duty must always, in extraordinary cases, when public ruin would evidently attend obedience, yield to the primary and original obligation. *Salus populi suprema Lex*, the safety of the people is the supreme law."[18] He makes the same point emphatically in describing Magna Carta. Certain of its articles "involve all the chief outlines of a legal government, and provide for the equal distribution of justice, and free enjoyment of property; the great objects for which political society was at first founded by men, which the people have a perpetual and unalienable right to recal, and which no time, nor precedent, nor statute, nor positive institution, ought to deter them from keeping ever uppermost in their thoughts and attention" (*H.*, 1:445).

For Hume the basic reason behind the obligation to be just and obedient is precisely that such conduct is useful. We saw above that "government binds us to obedience only on account of its tendency to public utility." Here Hume releases us, presumably after we have made some kind of calculative appraisal, from our normal obligation to obey; to sacrifice public utility to blind obedience would be madness.

Hume's rejection of constitutional positivism must be borne in mind if his views on constitutional questions are to be understood. What is lawful in an era will be found right in the courts, but what is right according to law may not be good; if it is to be criticized, the charge should be, not that it is constitutionally wrong, but that it is bad. It was this rejection of positivism, this insistence on distinguishing between what is required by constitutional law and what is good, and his consequent criticism of Whig historians who contended that James I and Charles I acted illegally, that gave rise to Hume's early reputation as a Tory historian; this reputation, in turn, now contributes to the mistaken view that his theory of understanding leads to conservatism. His distinction between the right and the good led him to reject the vulgar Whig interpretation of the constitutional conflicts of the seventeenth century, and consequently their Manichaean view of the two parties. In the *History of England* he shows, that there had never been an ancient constitution in which the good was the right; that Good Queen Bess by right was a tyrant; that James I and Charles I were mainly in the right; and that the exclusion of James II's son was unconstitutional. It is easy to understand why many Whigs denounced Hume as a Tory. Yet Hume was quite ready to assert that "many constitutions, and none more than the British, have been improved even by violent innovations" (*H.*, 4:355). Here speaks the "political Whig," the defender of the post-1714 settlement as a far better order, the "political Whig," who in his essays justifies resistance without resort to the contract theory, who challenges all Jacobite or Tory dissidents to shift their loyalties from the past to the present, and their hopes to the future. Even dis-

[18] *Essays*, p. 489. Also *Enquiry* II, p. 186.

counted for gallantry, his letter to Catherine Macaulay reveals his rejection of constitutional positivism. On the one hand, "the mixed monarchy of England, such as it was left by Queen Elizabeth, was a lawful form of government, and carried obligations to obedience and allegiance." On the other, the cause of liberty is "noble and generous"; if the principles of civil liberty had been advanced, not by those who disgraced them by cant, hypocrisy, and bigotry, but "in the amiable light which they receive both from your person and writings, it would have been impossible to resist them; and however much inclined to indulgence towards the first James and Charles, I should have been the first to condemn those monarchs for not yielding to them."[19] Unfortunately, Hume's distinction between the right and the good (and between both these and the ancient) was too subtle for many Whigs, who knew that what their forebears had fought for was the ancient, the right, and the good, all one and the same.

When Hume described the English constitution as "singular and happy," he was referring to its contemporary merits, not its conformity to an ancient constitution. The Craftsman in the 1730s, in true neo-Harringtonian style, exhorted the people of England to rise to the Patriotic challenge of recovering liberty by restoring the ancient constitution. The rebuttal made on Walpole's behalf was that there never had been a primordial constitution of liberty, that in fact liberty had been attained only after 1688 and was sustained by the contemporary constitution. Hume found this defence of Walpole substantially correct—as he would undertake to prove in the History of England.[20] In addition, he saw that the

[19] New Hume Letters, pp. 81–82. Hume's rejection of constitutional positivism is expressed most clearly in appendix 3 at the end of his account of the reign of Queen Elizabeth. History of England, 4:354–56, 370. Originally Hume distinguished between "what is best" and "what is usual," but in his final revision he replaced "what is usual" with "what is established." Duncan Forbes, Hume's Philosophical Politics (Cambridge: Cambridge University Press, 1975), p. 271.

Hume's political essays found favor with James Madison and Thomas Jefferson; by 1807, however, the latter had come to see how Hume's History had sapped the foundation of the idea of an ancient popular constitution. See the essay by Douglass Adair, " 'That Politics May be Reduced to a Science': David Hume, James Madison, and the Tenth Federalist," and the essay by Craig Walton, "Hume and Jefferson on the Uses of History," both in Hume: A Re-evaluation, eds. D. W. Livingston and J. T. King (New York: Fordham University Press, 1976), pp. 404–17 and 389–403. Hume's contention that the Whigs were making a serious mistake by constantly preaching that obedience to an established government is conditional made an understandable appeal to the supporters of the old order in France. See L. L. Bongie, David Hume: Prophet of the Counter-Revolution (Oxford: Clarendon Press, 1965).

[20] The view that Hume wrote a "Tory history" is refuted by Duncan Forbes in his introduction to The History of Great Britain, pp. 18–43. See also his Hume's Philosophical Politics, pp. 240–60. For a discussion that shows the difficulty confronted by later Whig historians in distinguishing between Tory history and Hume's Walpolian history, see J. W.

propagandists of Patriotism, with their emphasis on a Machiavellian restoration, showed no appreciation of commerce as a prerequisite of liberty.

False Beliefs on Policy Refuted

The Benefits of Manufactures and Commerce

From the *Treatise* we know that, according to Hume, the five rules of property, the primary institution of economic society, arise from human nature: those rules conform to the operation of the imagination and are recommended by their utility. We know, also, why they have the status of moral rules. Moreover, we know the role of trade and contracts. So far, however, we have only the foundations of Hume's economic theory. For that theory we must turn to his essays. Two of the twenty-seven essays published in 1741 and 1742 deal directly with economic matters. Those two essays—"Of Liberty and Despotism" (renamed "Of Civil Liberty" in 1758) and "Of the Rise and Progress of the Arts and Sciences"—contain the primary elements of Hume's political economy; as their titles suggest, they show the effects of economic change on politics, and *vice versa*. Most of the essays in *Political Discourses*, published in 1752, are succinct analyses of specific economic topics: money, interest, taxes, and so forth. Taken together these essays explain and recommend a socioeconomic order based on private property and the extensive production, exchange, and enjoyment of economic goods. This is civil society realizing its purpose and potential, civil society making possible "the good life." In it we strive to benefit ourselves by producing goods—by agriculture as well as manufacturing—for a market. We produce and trade under the restraint of justice—avoiding wrongs, but not officiously doing good works for the public. The locus of exchange of economic goods and services is the market, with money serving as the general medium of exchange, thus making the whole country one integrated society.

As we have seen, while Hume thought that the principles of governance can be learned to some extent even when the practitioners are unreflective, he was convinced that improvements can be made by philosophers. They can establish the principles as a practical science. The same is even truer in the case of political economy. In the essay "Of Interest," we are told, "Besides that the speculation is curious, it may frequently be of use in the conduct of public affairs. At least, it must be owned, that nothing can be of more use than to improve, by practice, the method of reasoning

Burrow, *A Liberal Descent: Victorian Historians and the English Past* (Cambridge: Cambridge University Press, 1981), pp. 21–35.

on these [economic] subjects, which of all others are the most important; though they are commonly treated in the loosest and most careless manner" (*Essays*, 304). The unreflective practitioners, the adepts of the old ways, often are sadly mistaken, and the nation suffers the consequences.

In these essays Hume draws together private property, commerce, and republicanism as mutually supporting causes of improvement: improvement in governance, in the useful and the liberal arts, in the prosperity of the common people, in the good (full) life, and in civility. Commerce showed its revolutionary power in the late Middle Ages by producing small city-states within the Holy Roman Empire, most notably Florence and Venice, but the only large commercial states to appear so far are Holland and England, both necessitous maritime countries in which Protestantism helped to shatter the old royal-chivalrous-priestly culture. England, of course, has a king, but English manners are almost entirely republican. France, a large Catholic monarchy, seems an exception; we must remember, however, that commerce is not indigenous to France, but was introduced there—late, and as only a minor sector—chiefly because the French saw how commerce had increased the prosperity of their two neighbors.

> [I]n all history, we find only three instances of large and fertile countries, which have possessed much trade; the NETHERLANDS, ENGLAND, and FRANCE. The two former seem to have been allured by the advantages of their maritime situation, and the necessity they lay under of frequenting foreign ports, in order to procure what their own climate refused them. And as to FRANCE, trade has come late into that kingdom, and seems to have been the effect of reflection and observation in an ingenious and enterprizing people, who remarked the riches acquired by such of the neighbouring nations as cultivated navigation and commerce. (*Essays*, 343–44)

Like Mandeville, Hume saw nothing improper in the desire of common people "to better their condition" (*Essays*, 266). He believed that they could best do this—and, as a result live fuller, happier lives—in a commercial society. He was quite prepared to defend their aspiration against "men of severe morals [who] blame even the most innocent luxury, and represent it as the source of all the corruptions, disorders, and factions, incident to civil government" (*Essays*, 269). By clear implication, he was rejecting the charge that by allowing, nay promoting, the transformation of England's economy, the ministers were revealing themselves friends of corruption. Moreover, he realized fully that by defending luxury against those who would have Britons return to the plain ways of olden times, he was rejecting one of the basic strands of Western moral and political thought.[21]

---

[21] *Essays*, p. 275. For a valuable discussion of both the origins of hostility to luxury and

British writers, he complains, tend to accept without question the views of the ancients. The Greek and Roman politicians observed the relationship between forms of government and the rise and decline of the arts and sciences; nowadays their conclusions are received uncritically. Similarly, the explanation given by Roman historians for the fall of the republic— that the fall was due to "oriental luxury," rather than Rome's bad constitution and failure to resist excessive expansion—has become axiomatic, a truth drilled into every schoolchild. Likewise, the ancients' omissions are misleading. They never appreciated the implications of commerce. They never saw how commerce can change, improve, economic circumstances. Xenophon does mention trade, but "with a doubt if it be of any advantage to a state." Plato, in *The Laws*, "totally excludes [trade] from his imaginary republic." Until very recent times, all political writers ignored commerce: "Trade was never esteemed an affair of state till the last century; and there scarcely is any ancient writer on politics, who has made mention of it. Even the ITALIANS have kept a profound silence with regard to it, though it has now engaged the chief attention, as well of ministers of state, as of speculative reasoners. The great opulence, grandeur, and military atchievements of the two maritime powers seem first to have instructed mankind in the importance of an extensive commerce" (*Essays*, 88–89). But perhaps the omission is understandable. The commerce of ancient times was confined to those agricultural commodities in which certain states had a natural advantage; because there was no specialization by cities in particular manufactures, trade in manufactured goods was of no importance (*Essays*, 418).

Hume proposed to show how commerce and manufacturing had already changed the human condition, and how they could, if properly understood and managed, change it even more—and all for the benefit of humankind.[22] He regarded these essays as a new beginning in moral and

---

the debate on the topic in early eighteenth-century Britain, see John Sekora, *Luxury: The Concept in Western Thought, Eden to Smollett* (Baltimore: The Johns Hopkins University Press, 1977). Hume blamed chiefly monks for distorting the moral values of Christendom. First, by comparing human beings with God, they convinced themselves that human nature is utterly mean and contemptible; this was the origin of the "monkish virtues." *The Natural History of Religion*, p. 62. Second, they then sought to gain control of the Church by insisting that they were far holier than the secular clergy. It is hard, Hume says, to believe that the secular clergy were as dissolute as the monks said: "It is more probable, that the monks paid court to the populace by an affected austerity of life; and, representing the most innocent liberties, taken by the other clergy, as great and unpardonable enormities, thereby prepared the way for the encrease of their own power and influence." *History of England*, 1:99. Indeed, history shows that the political disadvantages of Roman Catholicism were almost entirely due to monks, who managed to extend their sway throughout the Church. *History of England*, 3:227. Nor are the monkish virtues peculiar to Roman Catholicism; Puritan fanatics understand all too well that ostentatious austerity gains them adulation and power. *History of England*, 5:11.

[22] An indispensible account of British foreign policy, the national debt, and taxation dur-

political thought; they took into account what the ancients had ignored; they explored the value of manufacturing and trade. Accordingly, it was proper, he submitted, to explain at the beginning of the work why, instead of simply leaving these subjects to the practitioners, it is both possible and desirable to write scientifically about trade, manufacturing, money, interest, and the like, and about their influence on the social order, the form of the government, and the quality of life.

In making his case for manufacturing and commerce, Hume relies on his three-stage schema of socioeconomic development. His basic contention is that the higher the development, the more genuine the society, and the more virtuous and happy the people. In the primitive stage, when people simply harvest goods by hunting and fishing, they possess little— a few bows, arrows, spears—in the way of property; consequently, they can rely on elders to maintain peace within the tribe. In the second stage, when they engage in agriculture, they establish titles to land. Soon they are divided into the rich, who own the land, and the poor, who, since they must have access to land, are dependent on the rich. Property is necessary if goods are to be produced, but property entails economic, social, and political dominance and dependence. The rich are "the landed interest"; the poor do all the work on the land (*Essays*, 297–98). The landed interest make provision for the defence of their property against both invaders and internal disorder; and these arrangements, although rudimentary, are sufficiently distinct from family authority and economic power to be called "government." In the third stage, both manufacturing and commerce flourish alongside increasingly scientific agriculture. The importation of exotic products is a catalyst for economic development, for the consumers of these luxuries are moved to produce a saleable surplus, for example, wool, to be exported in exchange. The eventual results are, first, a great deal of manufacturing for domestic consumption as well as for export, and, second, the spread of scientific agriculture. The social structure has been changed: instead of a society made up of a few landowners and many serfs, we now have landowners, farmers, and husbandmen in the agricultural sector, capitalists and their hired hands in manufacturing, traders in domestic commerce, merchants in foreign commerce, and ultimately a monied interest. In such a developed and differentiated society, the principles of both justice and governance are realized to a high degree. Hume is writing to advocate modern society, with its manufacturing and commerce, against the reactionary proponents of the old order, headed

---

ing Hume's life is given by John Brewer in *The Sinews of Power: War, Money, and the English State 1688–1783* (London: Unwin Hyman Ltd., 1989). The debate between the friends and foes of the new economic order is surveyed in part 2 of J.G.A. Pocock's essay "The Varieties of Whiggism from Exclusion to Reform," in *Virtue, Commerce, and History* (Cambridge: Cambridge University Press, 1985), pp. 230–53.

by an old-fashioned landowning aristocracy. He is recommending to fellow Scots the kind of society he saw already well developed in England; integration with such a society was one of the benefits of the Union. In addition, he is writing to refute certain major errors in government policy.

It will be helpful to notice that by "the arts" Hume means the coarse or mechanical arts—manufacturing—the usefully good arts, as distinct from the intrinsically good (or liberal) arts. Moreover, we should remember that whatever he calls *violent* is very bad, and whatever he calls *natural* is good.

A market society is a genuine society. The essential characteristic of a market is that the individual gives his goods and services in return for what he finds an acceptable price. Value is exchanged for value. The transaction is voluntary: neither buyer nor seller is constrained by forces other than economic considerations. The buyer addresses neither the benevolence nor the fear of the seller, but rather his self-interest. The participants are free and independent. Such a society is vastly superior, Hume argues, to a second-stage society, where those who do all the agricultural work are subservient to lords. In comparing modern with ancient society, Hume focuses on slavery as the greatest difference: "According to ancient practice, all checks were on the inferior, to restrain him to the duty of submission; none on the superior, to engage him to the reciprocal duties of gentleness and humanity. In modern times, a bad servant finds not easily a good master, nor a bad master a good servant; and the checks are mutual, suitably to the inviolable and eternal laws of reason and equity" (*Essays*, 384).

It is through the market that individuals are integrated into economic society in civilized countries. The demand for private good drives the whole system. It is far better for the government to raise revenue by taxation and then hire people to work for the public than to conscript them, and far better for it to buy goods than to confiscate them. When the governments of antiquity took goods and services directly, rather than by appeal to self-interest, they acted violently. The only exception was where the citizens were strongly motivated by public spirit, as they sometimes were—the early Romans, for example, above all else wanted to serve their city—but such civic zeal is extraordinary and nowadays cannot be assumed. Sound policy ought to address the citizen's self-interest by offering price for goods and pay for service; to extort either goods or services by appealing to patriotism tends to violence. Moreover, it gives excessive power to those who define the public good. "It is natural on this occasion to ask, whether sovereigns may not return to the maxims of ancient policy, and consult their own interest in this respect, more than the happiness of their subjects? I answer, that it appears to me, almost impossible; and that because ancient policy was violent, and contrary to the more natural and usual course of things" (*Essays*, 258–59).

Governments should rely on the natural motivation of their people—in economic matters, on that great spur of industry, the ordinary person's desire to better his condition—and eschew systems and policies that presuppose great civic virtue. Value systems can be changed—undoubtedly the ancient Greeks and Romans were earnestly patriotic—but many causes must concur, and over a very long period, to bring about attitudes such as theirs. What is contrary to normal values should be rejected; it is best for a government "to comply with the common bent of mankind, and give it all the improvements of which it is susceptible. Now, according to the most natural course of things, industry and arts and trade encrease the power of the sovereign as well as the happiness of the subjects; and that policy is violent, which aggrandizes the public by the poverty of individuals" (*Essays*, 260).

Not only is reliance on the market the natural way to motivate people to work, but a society with both manufacturing and commerce enjoys also the progressive development of governance; indeed, it is only in such a society that true governance is achieved. In a simple agricultural society, the bulk of the people are treated as both economic and political inferiors by the great landlords, who, loving dominion, rule them capriciously. In contrast, in a flourishing market society, not only are those engaged in manufacturing and commerce independent, but "the husbandmen," the heads of families tilling the land, become increasingly prosperous and less and less subservient to the lords. A new rank, the commons, emerges between the lords and the laborers; those of this rank, "the middling rank," refuse to tolerate the constant disruption of peace and order by unruly grandees; they demand a rule of law. Either they bring about a republican regime or they force the monarch, whose legal power is challenged by the commons' economic power, to modernize his regime. They force him to give it moral legitimacy. In the essay "Of Refinement in the Arts," Hume ties increased civil liberty to the stages of development.

> In rude unpolished nations, where the arts are neglected, all labour is bestowed on the cultivation of the ground; and the whole society is divided into two classes, proprietors of land, and their vassals or tenants. The latter are necessarily dependent, and fitted for slavery and subjection; especially where they possess no riches, and are not valued for their knowledge in agriculture; as must always be the case where the arts are neglected. The former naturally erect themselves into petty tyrants; and must either submit to an absolute master, for the sake of peace and order; or if they will preserve their independency, like the ancient barons, they must fall into feuds and contests among themselves, and throw the whole society into such confusion, as is perhaps

worse than the most despotic government. But where luxury nourishes commerce and industry, the peasants, by a proper cultivation of the land, become rich and independent; while the tradesmen and merchants acquire a share of the property, and draw authority and consideration to that middling rank of men, who are the best and firmest basis of public liberty. These submit not to slavery, like the peasants, from poverty and meanness of spirit; and having no hopes of tyrannizing over others, like the barons, they are not tempted, for the sake of that gratification, to submit to the tyranny of their sovereign. They covet equal laws, which may secure their property, and preserve them from monarchical, as well as aristocratical tyranny. (*Essays*, 277–78)

Another good effect of commerce and manufacturing is an improvement in the standard of living of most of the people. This in itself is good; in addition, the greater social equality makes for a stronger state and for fairer taxation.

It will not, I hope, be considered as a superfluous digression, if I here observe, that, as the multitude of mechanical arts is advantageous, so is the great number of persons to whose share the productions of these arts fall. A too great disproportion among the citizens weakens any state. Every person, if possible, ought to enjoy the fruits of his labour, in a full possession of all the necessaries, and many of the conveniencies of life. No one can doubt, but such an equality is most suitable to human nature, and diminishes much less from the *happiness* of the rich than it adds to that of the poor. It also augments the *power of the state*, and makes any extraordinary taxes or impositions be paid with more chearfulness. Where the riches are engrossed by a few, these must contribute very largely to the supplying of the public necessities. But when the riches are dispersed among multitudes, the burthen feels light on every shoulder, and the taxes make not a very sensible difference on any one's way of living.

Add to this, that, where the riches are in few hands, these must enjoy all the power, and will readily conspire to lay the whole burthen on the poor, and oppress them still farther, to the discouragement of all industry. (*Essays*, 265)

While Hume defends luxury against monkish moralists, he criticizes Mandeville for arguing that private vice, in the form of *excessive* luxury, is necessary for public prosperity. The same good effects on economic activity would be produced if the rich person, instead of living in selfish luxury, fulfilled his moral obligations to help others. "Suppose, that he correct the vice [of excessive luxury], and employ part of his expence in the education of his children, in the support of his friends, and in relieving the poor; would any prejudice result to society? On the contrary, the same consumption would arise; and that labour, which, at present, is employed only in producing a slender gratification to one man, would relieve the necessitous, and bestow satisfaction on hundreds. The same care and toil that raise a dish of peas at CHRISTMAS, would give bread to a whole family during six months" (*Essays*, 279). Yet it is true that if the rich cannot be made benevolent, it is better—if Mandeville had said only this, he would have been correct—that they should live luxuriously than that they should hoard their wealth: "Luxury, when excessive, is the source of many ills; but is in general preferable to sloth and idleness, which would commonly succeed in its place, and are more hurtful both to private persons and to the public" (*Essays*, 280).

In addition to giving a general defense of modern society, Hume undertook to refute several specific charges.[23] To begin with, it is an error to believe that the growth of manufacturing is inevitably detrimental to those who own, those who rent, and those who work the land.[24] Contrary to Country propaganda that the Whig ministers are the enemies of rural Britain, the truth is that the prosperity of the countryside depends on a rural-urban division of labor, with busy towns as buyers of food and raw materials and suppliers of manufactured goods. With the progress of commerce, the old socioeconomic order disappears, but the new order is a vast improvement. The great landlord must change his ways if he is to buy the new commodities: either he must sell his lands or make them productive. The manufacturers create new goods; these in turn make agriculture profitable. True, agriculture may flourish in countries without a manufacturing sector, but this is due to special advantages of soil and climate. Ordinarily, the progress of agriculture requires the progress of manufacturing: "The most natural way, surely, of encouraging husbandry, is, first, to excite other kinds of industry, and thereby afford the labourer a ready market for his commodities, and a return of such goods as may contribute to his pleasure and enjoyment. This method is infallible and universal" (*Essays*, 419–20).

It is an error to believe, with the foes of commerce, that advances in the arts of production make a people value only economic goods. Progress in these arts brings on advances in the liberal arts. "The spirit of the age affects all the arts; and the minds of men, being once roused from their

[23] A thorough analysis of the theories set forth in Hume's economic essays has been provided by Eugene Rotwein in his introduction to *David Hume: Writings on Economics* (Edinburgh: Thomas Nelson and Sons Ltd., 1955). On the question whether the *Political Discourses* (1752) should be read as a reaction to Montesquieu's *The Spirit of the Laws* (1748), Rotwein's conclusion (p. lvi) is that there are only a few strands of direct connection between the two works. For a comparison between the general position taken by Hume on economic questions and his comments on particular historical transactions, see C. N. Stockton's valuable article "Economics and the Mechanism of Historical Progress in Hume's History" in *Hume: A Re-evaluation*, pp. 296–320.

[24] *Essays*, pp. 261, 277–78.

lethargy, and put into a fermentation, turn themselves on all sides, and carry improvements into every art and science. Profound ignorance is totally banished, and men enjoy the privilege of rational creatures, to think as well as to act, to cultivate the pleasures of the mind as well as those of the body" (*Essays*, 271). Moreover, they are far less susceptible to enthusiasm and superstition.

It is an error to believe that a nation with a high standard of living is likely to be morally corrupt. Those who storm at commerce and opulence as the root of evil are simply ignorant of how morality advances. In a second-stage economy, the masses are dependent, poor, mean-spirited, and servile, while the lords are brutish and uncouth, seeking relief from boredom in gluttony and drunkenness. In contrast, a developed people lives a far better life. Abandoning the sterile solitude of the countryside, they congregate in cities, where admiration and emulation spur them to do their very best in thought, conversation, and the liberal arts. They become civilized. Their humanity flowers. Independent and gainfully employed, they have neither time nor inclination for vice and crime; the true scenes of sloth, extravagant luxury, and depravity are royal and noble courts crowded with vain, obsequious, idle courtiers.

It is an error to believe that a nation with a high standard of living is less happy than a primitive society. Action and pleasure, not indolence, makes for happiness. The notion that the old days, with few wants and plenty of time to kill, were superior is plain nonsense.

> Indolence or repose, indeed, seems not of itself to contribute much to our enjoyment; but, like sleep, is requisite as an indulgence to the weakness of human nature, which cannot support an uninterrupted course of business or pleasure. That quick march of the spirits, which takes a man from himself, and chiefly gives satisfaction, does in the end exhaust the mind, and requires some intervals of repose, which, though agreeable for a moment, yet, if prolonged, beget a languor and lethargy, that destroys all enjoyment. Education, custom, and example, have a mighty influence in turning the mind to any of these pursuits; and it must be owned, that, where they promote a relish for action and pleasure, they are so far favourable to human happiness. In times when industry and the arts flourish, men are kept in perpetual occupation, and enjoy, as their reward, the occupation itself, as well as those pleasures which are the fruit of their labour. The mind acquires new vigour; enlarges its powers and faculties; and by an assiduity in honest industry, both satisfies its natural appetites, and prevents the growth of unnatural ones, which commonly spring up, when nourished by ease and idleness. (*Essays*, 270)

It is an error to assert, citing the Italians as evidence, that a high standard of living erodes a nation's ability to defend itself. The exertions of industry make a people vigorous in mind and body. They may be less ferocious, but their higher sense of honor makes them readier to do their duty; besides, they are capable of greater skill and discipline (*Essays*, 275).

It is an error to think that modern institutions and practices are inferior to those of olden times. The truth is quite the opposite. Hume takes it for granted that modern public morality—the economy, society, and government of a modern state—is vastly superior to that of dark, Gothic ages; the real test is comparison with ancient Greece and Rome. In the essay "Of the Populousness of Ancient Nations," he uses population figures as an index in comparing modern and ancient morality. There is far more in this essay, or rather in the first part, than one might gather from either the title or the exhaustive survey of population estimates and sources. It goes a long way in revealing Hume's attitude to the adulation of antiquity characteristic of the civic tradition. Slavery, he states, is the chief difference between ancient and modern economies. Slavery is deplorable because it is inhumane. Besides, it makes for a smaller population: "All I pretend to infer from these reasonings is, that slavery is in general disadvantageous both to the happiness and populousness of mankind, and that its place is much better supplied by the practice of hired servants" (*Essays*, 396). The modern practice of relying on the labor market is incomparably better.

At the same time, the small size of the ancient states, before the expansion of Rome, made for equality in social structure and for better political institutions, with greater liberty than exists in the large monarchies of modern Europe, some of which center upon vast cities. The ancient nations had also the advantage, for those times, of being *small republics*. They were city-states, with few very poor and few very rich citizens. This relative equality among the citizens is highly commendable (*Essays*, 401). But the ancient polities were inferior in several important ways. War was total in effort and results; it was far more destructive of life and property than modern war because the ancient armies, made up of committed citizens, were given to slaughter and pillage, while modern armies, made up of the lowest sort of men, must be restrained from plundering the vanquished because of perils to discipline. In addition, the hatred between domestic factions, chiefly between the nobles and the people, was intense; as a result, revolutions were frequent and bloody. In modern times comparable blind inhumanity is found only in strife between religious factions (*Essays*, 407).

A leading cause of political disorder in ancient times was the lack of a generally accepted social (or political) structure, and since what was most valuable in an era when one could not rely on established law for protection was the right to participate in the making of all judicial and policy decisions, all citizens were determined to take part. The legitimacy of any qualification test always was challenged: any citizen excluded from the assembly or from public office because of a qualification requirement saw himself the victim of an intolerable injustice; he felt honor-bound to put matters aright (*Essays*, 415).

Moreover, ancient times were inferior to modern in economic development: extensive manufacturing and commerce, the complements of good agriculture, were lacking. Agriculture, "the species of industry chiefly requisite to the subsistence of multitudes," flourished at some places at some times in antiquity; yet ancient agriculture depended for productivity more on favorable natural conditions than on the knowledge and enterprise of those who worked the land. Hume sums up the first part of the essay as follows:

> Thus, upon comparing the whole, it seems impossible to assign any just reason, why the world should have been more populous in ancient than in modern times. The equality of property among the ancients, liberty, and the small divisions of their states, were indeed circumstances favourable to the propagation of mankind: But their wars were more bloody and destructive, their governments more factious and unsettled, commerce and manufactures more feeble and languishing, and the general police more loose and irregular. These latter disadvantages seem to form a sufficient counterbalance to the former advantages; and rather favour the opposite opinion to that which commonly prevails with regard to this subject. (*Essays*, 420–21)

His conclusion is that although certain aspects of ancient institutions and practice are commendable—and, presumably, should be emulated, if separable from concomitant disadvantages—on the whole there is no basis for preferring the small, participatory structures of antiquity to truly modern civil societies, with their reliance on private motivation, rights under law, and governments that take the enforcement of justice as their principal duty.

The Ends of Policy Correctly Understood

In the arguments we have just examined, Hume is addressing those who deplore the new emphasis on manufacturing and commerce. His contention is that, far from causing corruption, the pursuit of a higher standard of living is beneficial, at least when confined within the bounds of "innocent luxury." So far, he is defending the Union and the Whig ministers. But it is not only the enemies of modernization who are in error. Those Scots who at the turn of the century had hoped to make Scotland strong and wealthy by producing most of her requirements domestically had misunderstood the basic purpose and function of commerce. Increasingly now (1752) those same mercantilist views, based on a misunderstanding of what makes a nation prosperous, are shaping British trade and foreign policy, thus causing colonial wars and raising the national debt, and all for the benefit of certain ports and merchants and those who live off wars and colonies.

It is an error to believe that a strong, wealthy nation is one with great stocks of precious metals. True strength and wealth are the results of a vigorous domestic economy, that is, of a skilled, industrious people, extensive internal trade, and natural resources. Always it is to be remembered that domestic industry is "much more valuable than foreign trade" (H., 4:374). The real importance of foreign trade is not that the nation thereby earns money, but that such trade serves as a catalyst to domestic economic development.

It is an error to believe that the actual amount of money in a country makes much difference. Money in circulation is important because it helps make a country one great market and enables the government to draw on the strength of the country by taxation, but, provided that adequate liquidity is maintained, the specific amount of money does not matter. If the supply of goods and services remains constant, doubling the amount of money in the country will serve simply to double rents, wages, and prices; halving the money will simply halve rents, wages, and prices. A person who suddenly finds himself with twice as much money as before will be able to buy only the same quantity of commodities if prices have doubled. However, a gradual increase in the quantum of money relative to the supply of goods and services produces a boom, while a gradual decrease causes economic depression (Essays, 288).

It is an error to believe that the quantum of money in a country at any one time is the cause of high or low interest rates, for, as we have seen, a sudden doubling of the money would bring on a compensating increase of rents, wages, and prices. Interest rates are determined by three factors: the availability of accumulations of riches—in the hands of a monied interest—the natural result of successful commercial activity; the size of the profit the monied interest can make by plowing their profits back into their businesses; and the demand for borrowed money. The old-fashioned gentry, rather than fulminating against commerce for driving up interest rates, should busy themselves learning and practicing scientific agriculture; indeed, without commerce there would be little or no money for them, or anybody else, to borrow.

It is an error to believe that amassing money through the maintenance of a favorable balance of trade with foreign countries will enhance the wealth and power of a nation. As we already know, what constitutes the wealth of a nation is, not money, but a large, industrious labor force combined with resources and facilities. Moreover, even if money were genuine wealth, such policies are self-defeating: an increase in the money in a country without a similar increase in goods only drives up prices in that country, thus decreasing exports and increasing imports. A shopkeeper trades to make money; in contrast, a government should foster trade because the people may thereby enjoy better, cheaper goods and become industrious, civilized, and happy. The real benefits of international trade are obvious. First, as we have noticed, the availability of exotic imports often serves to start the economic, social, governmental, and cultural advance from a second-stage to a third-stage society. Second, by exploiting each other's natural advantages, trading nations can produce and consume more and better goods than if each depends on itself alone. Third, the increased competition brought on by the wider market makes for a better allocation of resources and for greater industriousness. Hume found that the notion that England's interest had been well served over the years by the priority given to the production of woolen cloth for export, "to make money" for England, was wrong. The development of the nation's entire agricultural economy had been distorted by this policy, and by bad tillage, with the people driven from the land to make room for sheep (H., 3:369–70).

Legal and tax barriers at national borders, erected to give effect to the belief that making money is the great purpose of international trade, are about as defensible as similar restraints on commerce would have been within England itself if the heptarchy had continued (Essays, 314). The removal of such barriers between England and France would be highly advantageous to both nations; as a result, the English would drink better wines at lower costs, while the French would buy high-quality English wheat and barley.

> From these principles we may learn what judgment we ought to form of those numberless bars, obstructions, and imposts, which all nations of EUROPE, and none more than ENGLAND, have put upon trade; from an exorbitant desire of amassing money, which never will heap up beyond its level, while it circulates; or from an ill-grounded apprehension of losing their specie, which never will sink below it. Could any thing scatter our riches, it would be such impolitic contrivances. But this general ill effect, however, results from them, that they deprive neighbouring nations of that free communication and exchange which the Author of the world has intended, by giving them soils, climates, and geniuses, so different from each other.[25]

In 1759 (or 1760) Hume inserted an essay, "Of the Jealousy of Trade," between two of the original ones: "Of the Balance of Trade" and "Of the Balance of Power." In that new essay, he argues that it is an error to be-

[25] Essays, p. 324; also ibid., p. 329.

lieve that the prospering of one nation will hurt its neighbors.[26] New prosperity only makes a nation a supplier of better goods and a better market for exports. Provided a country has some advantage—in soil, climate, or established competence in a line of manufacturing—it will be able to participate successfully in the international market. The English have been led to believe that their strength in the wool trade will decline if others enter that trade; but if the wool trade is a staple, if indeed the English do have "peculiar and natural advantages" in it, they have nothing to fear. Besides, even if their exports of woolens were to diminish, the results would not be serious.

> If the spirit of industry be preserved, it may easily be diverted from one branch to another; and the manufacturers of wool, for instance, be employed in linen, silk, iron, or any other commodities, for which there appears to be a demand. We need not apprehend, that all the objects of industry will be exhausted, or that our manufacturers, while they remain on a equal footing with those of our neighbours, will be in danger of wanting employment. The emulation among rival nations serves rather to keep industry alive in all of them: And any people is happier who possess a variety of manufactures, than if they enjoyed one single great manufacture, in which they are all employed. Their situation is less precarious; and they will feel less sensibly those revolutions and uncertainties, to which every particular branch of commerce will always be exposed.[27]

Only a nation that relies exclusively on providing commercial services—perhaps because of a shortage of land and resources, as in the case of Holland—is threatened by the progress of its neighbors. Scots should not think that England's great wealth dooms Scotland to perpetual poverty.[28]

[26] In "Of the Balance of Trade," published in 1752, Hume contends that since from the public viewpoint the purpose of international trade is not to make money, anxious concern for a favorable balance is pointless, indeed futile. The important essay "Of the Jealousy of Trade" was inserted in copies (published in late 1759 or early 1760) of the 1758 edition; it is discussed in Eugene Rotwein, *David Hume: Writings on Economics*, pp. lxxii–lxxviii. Hume's advocacy of free trade, in *Political Discourses*, relates to international trade; however, as Rotwein states (pp. lxxviii–lxxxi), his views on government intervention in the domestic market are made clear in *History of England*.

[27] *Essays*, p. 330. Writing to Lord Kames in 1758, Hume explained that the principle of the discourse "Of the Jealousy of Trade" is "levelled against the narrow malignity and envy of nations, which can never bear to see their neighbours thriving, but continually repine at any new efforts towards industry made by any other nation." *Letters*, 1:272.

[28] Hume's friend, James Oswald of Dunnikier, M.P., an independent Whig, served as a member of the Board of Trade from 1751 to 1759, and on the Treasury Board from 1759 to 1763. Although his "vast knowledge and great experience brought him great reputation and many friends," he never attained high office because he had been born on the wrong side of the Tweed. Hume showed "Of the Balance of Trade" in manuscript to Oswald. In a letter, dated October 10, 1750, the latter commented that a country with the balance of

The essay "Of the Balance of Power" deals specifically with a topic of great concern to Hume, the hostility of England to France. Given the publication date, 1752, the essay can be read as commentary on three wars with France—1689–1697, 1702–1713, 1744–1748—and as anticipating Hume's attitude to the Seven Years' War (1756–1763). Hume finds the English so blinded by rage against the French that, under the cloak of maintaining the balance of power in Europe—a valid maxim, but one that, having become conventional wisdom, inhibits thought—they protract every war with France, they let England's allies extort subsidies from her, and they recklessly increase the national debt. This obsessive hatred of the French arose originally from a geopolitical factor: with no formidable enemies within the British Isles, the English focused their hostility on their only major continental neighbor. An "ancient and inveterate animosity to France," set aside only by temporary outbursts of hostility toward Spain and the Netherlands, became fundamental to English foreign policy. For their part, the French never reciprocated fully; for them England was only one of several powerful neighbors.[29] The time is long past

---

trade strongly in its favor—a rich country—would have many advantages relative to its poorer trading partners: cheap imports, a growing population, cheap labor. "The advantages of a rich countrey in this respect, compared with the disadvantages of a poor one, are almost infinite, and all infallibly take place, after a free communication of the necessarys of life and materials of manufacture, and an easy settlement of new inhabitants, are established. A countrey in this situation would, in some measure, be the capital of the world, while all neighbour countreys would, in respect of its advantages, tho' not of their own, be as its provinces." *Caldwell Papers*, 2:i, 104–5. Hume replied, on November 1, 1750, that eventually the concentration of production in the rich country would be arrested, because its poorer trading partners would take over the production of all the simpler and more laborious manufactures. *Letters*, 1:143–44. Some years later (1758), he was still of the same opinion. Having read some papers by Josiah Tucker, he wrote to Lord Kames that poor countries have certain advantages that eventually will redress the balance: "I am pleased when I find the author insist on the advantages of England, and prognosticate thence the continuance and even further progress of the opulence of that country; but I still indulge myself in the hopes that we in Scotland possess also some advantages, which may enable us to share with them in wealth and industry. It is certain that the simpler kind of industry ought first to be attempted in a country like ours. . . . It was never surely the intention of Providence, that any one nation should be a monopolizer of wealth: and the growth of all bodies, artificial as well as natural, is stopped by internal causes, derived from their enormous size and greatness. Great empires, great cities, great commerce, all of them receive a check, not from accidental events, but necessary principles." *Letters*, 1:271–72. That Hume had the future of Scotland's economy especially in mind in the *Political Discourses* is made evident by Istvan Hont's analysis of the continuing debate over how a poor country would fare in a common market with a rich country. See "The 'Rich Country-Poor Country' Debate in Scottish Classical Political Economy," in *Wealth and Virtue*, pp. 271–315.

[29] *History of England*, 2:203; 3:32; 6:217. It is interesting to compare Hume's own attitudes to England and France. He found revulsive the English sense of their manifest superiority over all other nations, the religiosity of puritanism, and the "democratical frenzy" of Londoners; yet he liked the prosperity, social mobility, and religious liberty of contempo-

for England to put her foreign policy on a more rational basis: any French effort to rule all Europe should be resisted, but bigotry and hysteria, fanned by those whose interests are advanced by war with France, should cease to influence policy. Hume's attitude may seem Tory, for it was the foreign kings, first William of Orange, then the Hanoverians, who had put the balance of power on the continent to the fore in English policy; but, remembering "the Old Alliance," it is probably simply the attitude of a Scot, a Francophile, a foe of "religious Whiggery," an advocate of free trade, an opponent of (expensive) wars. Hume did not accept Edward Young's pronouncement, in *Night Thoughts*, that France as "a land of levity, is a land of guilt."

The next essay in *Political Discourses* is "Of Taxes." It is an error to believe that the imposition of a new tax creates the ability to pay it by increasing proportionately the industry of the people. Moreover, not all taxes are of equal merit: taxes on tangible possessions, although easy to collect, and arbitrary taxes, poll taxes, for example, are bad. Specifically, the theory that the only tax should be a land tax, because ultimately all taxes are paid by the landowners—the theory advanced by Country politicians in 1733 against Walpole's contention that an excise on wines and tobacco would make possible a reduction of the land tax—is false. Taxes on consumption, especially of luxuries, although awkward to levy, are the best taxes. Such taxes are self-limiting, fall chiefly on the rich, and distort the economy far less than taxes on necessities.[30]

This essay leads directly into "Of Public Credit," wherein Hume shows the dangerous economic, social, and political consequences of paying for unnecessary wars with borrowed money. It is true that the purchase of government bonds is a more convenient way than the purchase of land for the trading interest to invest its savings, and bonds, by serving as a ready and profitable form of liquidity, do stimulate economic activity; yet heavy reliance on bonded debt has many disadvantages. First, bonds damage the economy in that, (a) as near-money, they can be inflationary; (b) the taxes necessary to pay the interest on the bonds are likely either to impose a burden on the laboring poor or to bring about an increase in their wages; and (c) bonds make it unnecessary for rich bondholders to

---

rary England. At the same time, he was a Francophile. As a young man, he had retired to La Flèche, traditionally a favorite resort of Scottish students, to compose the *Treatise*. Forbes, *Hume's Philosophical Politics*, pp. 140–41, 150; also Mossner, *The Life of David Hume*, pp. 92–105. In his retirement years, after 1769, he revived the prospect of making his home in France. Mossner, op. cit., pp. 92, 187, 344, 390; *Letters*, 2:295.

[30] Hume stated, in a letter to Turgot, that in England and France the income of those who invest in commerce and manufacturing is much greater than that of the landed interest; the former, therefore, should be obliged to help support the government by paying taxes on their consumption. *Letters*, 2:94.

engage in productive activity. Second, the sale of bonds makes unnecessary wars politically feasible by shifting the incidence of their costs. Third, a large debt threatens the social and political order. When, trying to cope with the debt, a government has exhausted all the good taxes, it will turn to bad taxes, that is, to sales taxes on necessities, which bear heavily on the poorer sort, and to very high property taxes, which devastate the landowners. In the end, with all the taxes screwed up to the limit, the great majority will toil simply to maintain the idle bondholders. An unnatural, polarized social structure, with a few very rich creditors at one extreme and all the rest of the populace an impoverished proletariat, will be created, with many attendant evils. What is more, the greater the debt the more difficult it is for the government to raise money to pay for any genuinely necessary war.[31] In a crisis the government might simply disown its bonds, thus sacrificing the thousands to save the millions; this would be "the *natural death* of public credit." Alternatively, if relief was not sought in that way, perhaps because of the bondholders' influence with the government, the country would simply become supine before its enemies; this would be "the *violent death* of our public credit." Thus the millions would be sacrificed in a vain attempt to save the thousands. Hume's preference is obvious.

Hume was out to refute all aspects of the argument that the rise of commerce and manufacturing was ruining Britain—its true proprietors, the moral fiber of the lower orders, the matchless constitution, the na-

---

[31] Eugene F. Miller comments that the passage, in "Of Public Credit" (1752), ridiculing arguments that public debt is advantageous was directed specifically at Walpole and the Whigs. Notice, however, that Hume said that Walpole himself was too able to believe such arguments. *Essays*, 352n, 636. Hume's attitude to Walpole changed dramatically. One of the essays, "Whether the British Government inclines more to Absolute Monarchy, or to a Republic," in the first volume of *Essays, Moral and Political*, published in Edinburgh in June/July, 1741, was reprinted in *The Craftsman* that autumn. In December, 1741, James Oswald, who, along with Archibald Stewart, had been elected to the House of Commons earlier that year as an opponent of Walpole, thought that Hume's piece" A Character of Sir Robert Walpole"—pronouncing Walpole's private character far better than his public, and advocating his defeat—was to come out at a most opportune time. However, when the "Character" appeared, Hume informed his readers, in the advertisement to the volume, that the "Character" had been written some months earlier. He went on to confess that "at present, when he seems to be upon the Decline, I am inclin'd to think more favourably of him, and to suspect, that the Antipathy, which every true born *Briton* naturally bears to Ministers of State, inspir'd me with some Prejudice against him." Later, Hume backed off even more; in a footnote added to the editions from 1748 to 1768, he commented that he [Hume] "cannot forbear observing, that the not paying more of our publick debts was, as hinted in this character, a great, and the only great, error in that long administration." *Essays*, pp. 574–75; see also Mossner, *The Life of David Hume*, pp. 143–44. Perhaps it is only coincidental that the second Duke of Argyll and his "gang," with whom Oswald was cooperating, had broken with Walpole in 1739 and that after 1746 the Argathelians, headed by the third Duke, were back in power as allies of the Pelhams.

tion's military prowess. Admittedly, the increase of general prosperity—defensible luxury—made possible by industrious labor, scientific agriculture, brisk commerce, and ingenious manufacturing was changing the socioeconomic order; but that change was vastly for the better. The cause of virtue in England and Scotland did not require that the old order remain unaltered, that those who worked the land should remain poor and stunted, that the multitude should be kept submissive and diligent by Church and Kirk. At the same time, Hume was out to refute beliefs that were distorting public policy: that making money by foreign trade should be a cardinal goal of public policy; that a far-flung colonial empire is desirable; that prosperous neighboring countries are dangerous rivals, rivals to be beggared by tariffs or, better still, trounced in war.

Religion in Politics

In the eighteenth century, religion was under attack in England and France: the world as understood and explained throughout the centuries by Christians was being supplanted by the machine paradigm of the natural scientists; the mechanical view of understanding—concentrating on describing natural causation—was challenging the religious view with its emphasis on design and purpose; vital fields such as governance and education in which clerics had once been prominent, had been or were being taken over by laity; two hundred years of war—wars of religion—had eroded patience and credulity. Against its enemies religion was defended as central to the life of a people. The dogmas, it was said, express and the rites dramatize the people's fundamental beliefs and values. The spirit of a people's laws, their *mores*, are rooted in and sustained by their religion. The clergy, charged with the tasks of guiding and supporting, perhaps directing, the civil authorities; procuring the cooperation of the supernatural; and shepherding the laity through all the joys and sorrows of life, were defended as an essential estate of society. While it is the consolation of the poor, the unfortunate, and the victim of injustice, religion serves also, it was said, to humble the victorious and the great. In his *Reflections on the Revolution in France*, Edmund Burke eloquently enunciated a traditional attitude to the civic function of religion: the national religion strengthens and deepens the cohesion of the nation. Machiavelli had stated a more cynical view. He had depicted the great early legislators such as Moses and Numa Pompilius, the founders of peoples, as crafty men who had put their own laws in the mouths of the gods; they had used religion to create and form peoples. Subsequently, except when diverted to their own ends by priests, the power of religious obligation helped to keep the people obedient to their governors and formidable in war.

Hume's attitude is far removed from that of either Burke or Machiavelli. For him, popular religion, at least in modern times, is not a positive force in politics, but must be viewed as a threat to peace, order, and good morals; accordingly, he recommends a prophylactic strategy.

Hume was a true agnostic. By reasoning, he argued, we strive to understand nature: we try to discover what effects follow what causes, and *vice versa*. But reason has its limits. Even when dealing with nature, it is a mistake to think we can do more than describe what happens. Certainly, to try to apply "the mechanical philosophy" outside nature is absurd: "While Newton seemed to draw off the veil from some of the mysteries of nature, he shewed at the same time the imperfections of the mechanical philosophy; and thereby restored her ultimate secrets to that obscurity, in which they ever did and ever will remain."[32] The dogmatic atheist and the dogmatic theist make exactly the same mistake: each claims to have natural knowledge (as distinct from revealed knowledge) about the ineffable. In the last part of the *Dialogues concerning Natural Religion*, Philo makes the point that what divides the theist and the atheist is largely a dispute of words.

> The Theist allows, that the original Intelligence is very different from human reason: The Atheist allows, that the original Principle of Order bears some remote Analogy to it. Will you quarrel, Gentlemen, about the degrees, and enter into a controversy, which admits not of any precise meaning, nor consequently of any determination. If you shou'd be so obstinate, I shou'd not be surpriz'd to find you insensibly change sides; while the Theist on the one hand exaggerates the Dissimilarity between the supreme Being, and frail, imperfect, variable, fleeting, and mortal Creatures; and the Atheist on the other magnifies the Analogy among all the operations of Nature, in every period, every situation, and every position.[33]

[32] *History of England*, 6:542. Hume says that human reason tries to resolve the complexity of natural phenomena into a few general causes; but "as to the causes of these general causes, we should in vain attempt their discovery; nor shall we ever be able to satisfy ourselves, by any particular explication of them. These ultimate springs and principles are totally shut up from human curiosity and enquiry." *An Enquiry concerning Human Understanding*, p. 30. For a discussion of Hume on religion, see Terence Penelhum, *Hume* (London: The Macmillan Press Ltd., 1975), pp. 163–96. On the many faces of skepticism, see David Fate Norton, *David Hume: Common-Sense Moralist, Sceptical Metaphysician* (Princeton: Princeton University Press, 1982), pp. 239–310.

[33] *Dialogues Concerning Natural Religion*, pp. 249–50. Lamentably, all too many people fail, Hume finds, to achieve anything like a truly religious attitude: betrayed by pride, they become stubbornly dogmatic. Thomas Hobbes, for example, although he started out with a skeptical attitude toward religious dogma, ended up at the other extreme and no better off, in dogmatic atheism. *History of England*, 6:153. To be positive and dogmatic, says Hume, is more destructive of reasoning than even excessive skepticism would be if it could be maintained. *Enquiry* II, p. 278.

This said, Philo and Cleanthes proceed to debate the consequences of *popular* religion: regardless of how vital their own interminable disputes may seem to a few speculators, the truly significant topic is the moral and political consequences of popular religion. Beliefs, Hume saw, play a vast part in shaping human behavior; consequently, he sought to show how beliefs originate. Moreover, religious beliefs are one of the most powerful factors in morals and politics, as the history of both recent and remote times shows. Has religion's influence been good or bad? What policy should a government adopt regarding religion?

In *The Natural History of Religion*, published in 1757, Hume deals with the origins and results of polytheism and theism. What gives rise to polytheism, and what to theism? Does history show that polytheism and theism have different moral and political consequences? Early religion was, and remains, polytheistic. Startled, astounded by the effects of unknown causes, the people of those times attribute those effects to gods and goddesses. Then, seeking help and comfort as they confront the uncertainties of life, they turn to those gods and goddesses. Thus polytheism arises. Theism, defined by Hume in *The Natural History of Religion* (p. 49) as "the doctrine of one supreme deity, the author of nature," comes later; it is the natural result of praise and magnification. Over time one of the gods is promoted as greatest and best; all the others fade and ultimately disappear. Like polytheism, theism is anthropomorphic; yet it can slide over into the indeterminacy of mysticism.

Theism is far more sophisticated than polytheism. But consider the moral and political consequences of popular theism! The gods and goddesses of early polytheism were all too human: they could be induced to exercise their powers by bribes, flattery, even threats; besides, their morals often were barbarous. But, although they went out to do battle beside their peoples, they themselves did not cause wars; they were not jealous gods, for each had his own place and role. In contrast, theism entails a far higher personal morality—the god is morally perfect—but has serious political effects. First, the believer may feel compelled to obliterate all different or deviant beliefs: "One God, One Truth," is his cry. The result, as the histories of Spain, England, and Ireland show, is inquisition, persecution, revolution, and sectarian strife. Second, betrayed by aspiring pride, the believer may compare himself obsessively with the Perfect; as a result, he may come to extol and teach false (monkish) virtues. Third, philosophy, which speculates on the ultimate cause of nature, can readily be taken over by theism, but not by polytheism; when this happens the result is a new variety of belief, theology. Various theological schools spring up, each with its orthodoxy; these schools war against each other far more bitterly than the priests of the early polytheistic cults ever did.

Principle confronts principle; hence the infamous *odium theologicum* (hatred generated by theological controversy).

Christianity is both theistic and polytheistic. Its theology is fundamentally theistic; consequently Christendom has experienced all the bad results theism entails. But because it was unthinkable to expect the Absolute to perform the works of patronage (particular providence) the multitude require daily, the gods and goddesses of polytheism were revived; they were enlisted as God's aides and assistants. Both a functional and a geographical division of labor was established; each god and goddess was made the patron of a role or place. As lieutenants of God, their morals are infinitely better than those of the ancient gods and goddesses; however, they too respond to offerings, praise, and so on.

While theistic Christians are in danger of becoming enthusiastic, superstition travels with polytheism. These two kinds of religious corruption are analyzed by Hume in the early (1741) essay "Of Superstition and Enthusiasm," and again and again in his later works he draws attention to their moral and political effects. While theism and polytheism express different conceptions of the supernatural, enthusiasm and superstition relate to the believer's psychological condition; they arise from different states of mind, and in turn work to produce different states. Both are widespread among Christians, but some denominations incline more to superstition, others more to enthusiasm. Superstition, based on fear, adds priests as a distinct interest group to the social structure. The priest is thought to have supernatural powers, powers that enable him to make peace with the angry god (or gods) by sacrifices, incantations, and gestures, thus quieting the anxieties of the faithful. The term "priests" as used by Hume refers to an order of men with special powers; those powers make them sacred and give them authority over the laity. In contrast, enthusiasm springs from exuberance "arising from prosperous success, from luxuriant health, from strong spirits, or from a bold and confident disposition." In the exalted state, the enthusiast experiences great raptures, soaring highs; these he attributes to the immediate presence with him of his god. Soon he finds himself a peculiar favorite of the divinity. At that point "every whimsy is consecrated: Human reason, and even morality are rejected as fallacious guides: And the fanatic madman delivers himself over, blindly, and without reserve, to the supposed illapses of the spirit, and to inspiration from above" (*Essays*, 74). The enthusiast has no need for professional clerics; the true "man of God" has naught but scorn for the formation, education, and ordination of priests and ministers.

Enthusiasm is politically volatile. The fanatic is free from all constraints and ordinances; moreover, his fancy, not content to pave the floors of Heaven with gold, is likely to take all society, the whole moral order, for its empire. When this happens, the enthusiast becomes a wild social deformer, a menace to property and government; guided from above, he has only contempt for rules and standards derived from mere experience and reflection. But fortunately the fires of enthusiasm burn out quickly; the devotee soon becomes cool and sedate. Hume's favorite example of the natural progress of enthusiasm as a political force is the Quakers; indeed, as we have seen, he attributes the success of the revolutionaries in the English civil war, not to a widespread aspiration for a better constitution, but to enthusiasm; strong in the knowledge that they were fighting God's war, the religious Puritans never hesitated to attack the established order in church and state. In contrast, the immediate effect of superstition is the pacification of the laity. This is salutary; yet superstition entails two political dangers. First, if untended, priests are likely to become a powerful interest group, striving either to insinuate themselves into the civil government or to set up as an independent authority. Second, the national church may break up into rival churches, thus creating the danger of religious civil war.

Hume found that during the Middle Ages the influence of the Church, despite much superstition, had been progressive. The humanity of many priests led them to promote learning and morality. The power of tyrannical grandees and kings was restrained. A tradition of literacy, artistic endeavor, and peace was maintained as a rival to the crude militarism of the lay elite (*H.*, 2:14). Indeed, before the Church fell under the bad influence of monks, otherworldly monks ambitious for worldly power, it was a very reasonable religious establishment. In contrast, virtually nothing good flows from enthusiasm except by accident. Fear, revulsion, and derision are Hume's reactions to fundamentalist fanaticism. Mob madness and bigotry had blighted England, Scotland, and Ireland for over 150 years. This was barbarism, not the simple barbarism of savages, but barbarism made odious by fraudulent religiosity, and destructive by impetuous arrogance.[34] Nor had the danger to civility posed by enthusiasm been left behind. After describing the beginning of the religious wars in Scotland, Hume comments, "With these outrageous symptoms, commenced in Scotland that cant, hypocrisy, and fanaticism, which long infested that kingdom, and which, though now mollified by the lenity of the civil power, is still ready to break out on all occasions." Even worse, indeed worst of all, was the plight of Ireland.[35]

[34] Hume's break with his Calvinist family background has been examined convincingly by Shirley Robin Letwin, *The Pursuit of Certainty* (Cambridge: Cambridge University Press, 1965), pp. 18–28. See also Norman Kemp Smith's introduction to *Hume's Dialogues concerning Natural Religion*, 2d ed. (Edinburgh: Thomas Nelson and Sons Ltd., 1947), pp. 1–8.

[35] *History of England*, 4:24–25. In the discourse "Of the Populousness of Ancient

Superstition and enthusiasm influence politics in yet another way. When church and state are allies, superstition favors strong political authority. Eager to maintain their sway, priests are no friends of religious liberty; it follows that they are wary of civil liberty. In contrast, religious enthusiasts are all for liberty; at the extreme they are anarchists. It is no accident, Hume comments, that in contemporary England the Tories tend to be devout members of the Church of England. The Whig leaders, being deists and latitudinarians, favor religious toleration; accordingly, the various dissenting Protestant denominations, whose origins were enthusiastic, support the Whigs. As for the Roman Catholics, "The resemblance in their superstitions long united the high-church *tories*, and the *Roman catholics*, in support of prerogative and kingly power; though experience of the tolerating spirit of the *whigs* seems of late to have reconciled the *catholics* to that party" (*Essays*, 79).

Hume had clear views on the correct strategy to be followed by a government. He saw the dangers of popular religion as inevitable; yet there was a good chance that by careful management popular religion could be made relatively harmless to civil society. His views were expressed, not as direct recommendations, a mode Hume generally avoided, but as observations, chiefly in the *History of England*. There should be an established church with a structure compatible with the constitution of the civil government: if the constitution is monarchical, the church should be episcopal, and the king must be of the established faith; a republican (presbyterian) church structure would be best for a commonwealth. The main purpose of establishment is not to fan, but to damp the industry of the clergy. If left on their own, they will compete for followers; they will carry them from soft religion up to hard religion, and then to harder and harder, as competition increases. Put the clergy on the government payroll, and their interest in popular religious fervor wanes. In addition, with an established church, the government can intervene to foster seemly forms of worship—impressive liturgies, costumes, settings, music—to occupy the minds of worshipers, leaving no room for religious fantasies. It can also discourage theological sermons of the Presbyterian type; these arouse religious passions and make the people disputatious and sour.[36]

When the essay "Of Superstition and Enthusiasm" was first published, Hume, in a footnote, distinguished between priests and members of the

---

Nations" Hume comments, "The country in EUROPE in which I have observed the factions to be most violent, and party-hatred the strongest, is IRELAND. This goes so far as to cut off even the most common intercourse of civilities between the Protestants and Catholics. Their cruel insurrections and the severe revenges which they have taken of each other, are the causes of this mutual ill will, which is the chief source of the disorder, poverty, and depopulation of that country." *Essays*, p. 640.

[36] *History of England*, 3:135–36; 5:68, 240–41, 459–60.

clergy. From 1748 to 1768, that footnote read as follows: "By *Priests*, I here mean only the pretenders to power and dominion, and to a superior sanctity of character, distinct from virtue and good morals. These are very different from *clergymen*, who are set apart *by the laws*, to the care of sacred matters, and to the conducting our public devotions with greater decency and order. There is no rank of men more to be respected than the latter" (*Essays*, 619). In all the early editions, the Church of England was graded as highly superstitious, but in 1770 it was dropped from the list of dangerous denominations. In the Tudor part of the *History of England*, published in 1759, Hume had praised the Church of England: it was a reformed church—that was a merit—and happily its reformation had been moderate. After detailing its many good qualities, he concludes, "And the new religion, by mitigating the genius of the ancient superstition, and rendering it more compatible with the peace and interests of society, had preserved itself in that happy medium, which wise men have always sought, and which the people have so seldom been able to maintain" (*H*, 4:120). The religious settlement in England is entirely commendable. The rites and services of the Church of England express and satisfy the religious emotions of the people; yet the clergy, kept in their place by politicians, cannot establish theocracy.

Hume's other recommendation was that the government should be quite indifferent to dissent from the established church. The old opinion that religious pluralism is incompatible with civil order had been disproved; indeed, there is much to be said for toleration. In the *History of England*, he reports with approval the arguments for toleration put forward by Cardinal Pole during the reign of Mary Tudor. First, if religious unity were to be sought, all curiosity would have to be quashed, and all the good results of curiosity foregone. Second, a society from which all divergent views have been purged will produce stunted, immature people. And, third, history had demonstrated that persecution is counterproductive; it makes troublesome sects flourish. Hume makes much of Pole's last argument (*H*, 3:431–34). The old belief, the one to which "vulgar politicians" cling, is that the peace can best be promoted by suppressing sectarianism. Experience, however, counsels a different policy. "An unlimited *toleration*, after sects have diffused themselves and are strongly rooted, is the only expedient, which can allay their fervour, and make the civil union acquire a superiority above religious distinctions."[37]

[37] Ibid., 6:322–23; 5:130. Resistance against High Church aspiration to theocracy is central to the history of Whiggism from 1688 to 1715. (In sharp contrast, the triumph of the Presbyterians in Scotland in 1690 opened the way for "religious Whiggism" in that country, as Hume was well aware.) Locke, Shaftesbury, Molesworth, and Toland were prominent opponents of Anglican theocracy; this helps explain both their hostility to priests and their strong advocacy of toleration. See Mark Goldie, "John Locke and Anglican Royalism" *Po-*

Hume's prescriptions are consistent with his disapproval of "religious Whigs" and his approval of "political Whigs." In the essay "Of Parties in General" (1741), he attributes religious strife mainly to theology, the off-spring of religion and philosophy; as Shaftesbury had said, pretences of religious knowledge bring on conflict, bigotry, and intolerance. By a state establishment for worship, Hume intends to keep many, perhaps most, of the priests contented and controlled; this is to be no Anglican or Presbyterian theocracy. At the same time he hopes that any dissentient sects, deprived of the spur of grievance, will not be militant.

For Hume the body politic is not an organism, a single body of which the established church is the spiritual aspect; accordingly, he sees dissent as no threat to civil society unless rendered explosive by suppression. Moreover, western civilization is not the product of religion. The rules and standards of morality have natural origins: while learned and humane clergy have been, and are, prominent as teachers of morality, and as moderators of enthusiasm, popular religion as such has been, and remains, a threat to civilization. Nor does Hume propose that the religious credulity of the multitude be exploited to enhance the authority of the government. But beyond these points, what is notable is Hume's agreement with Shaftesbury that the civil authorities must take care, by an appropriate establishment, to prevent both priests and fanatics from subverting peace, order, and good morals.

A Commonwealth Aspiration

As we have seen, Hume, the politician, was keenly interested in the relationship between the various forms of government and the socioeconomic order. Many things influence the character of a nation: soil, climate, religion, the stage of economic development, and so on, but it is to forms of government, constitutions, that he gives most attention. Good governance is necessary for the general prosperity and happiness of a people; although far from enough, it is essential. And the quality of governance depends greatly on the form of the government; for example, inherited monarchy, as we have seen, leaves far too much to chance.

In "Of the Idea of a perfect Commonwealth," published in 1752, Hume sets down the main features of the ideal constitution. Up to the

litical Studies 31 (1983): 61–85. Toland was especially vigorous in attacking "priestcraft" and the corruption of morals by religion; see Stephen H. Daniel, *John Toland: His Methods, Manners, and Mind* (Kingston and Montreal: McGill-Queen's University Press, 1984). Franco Venturi emphasizes the influence of Shaftesbury, Toland, and the other English deists in the eighteenth-century revolt against the old order in Europe. *Utopia and Reform in the Enlightenment* (Cambridge: Cambridge University Press, 1971), especially pp. 47–73.

present, he reports, little science has gone into the making of constitutions; most constitutions are "botched and inaccurate." Products, not of science, but of circumstance and accident, the clash of interests, and ad hoc amendment, to the extent that they prevent the abuse of power, they do so fortuitously. However, it is possible to state the ideal of good governance: chiefly, the careful administration of justice through a rule of law, the furtherance of international commerce, and adequate defence against foreign aggression. It is also possible to recognize the kinds of interests legitimate in a society, all of which are to be protected, and also those interests that are not to be fostered. Starting from this, it is possible to prescribe the main features of a good system of government. But Hume is no revolutionary. Although defective, the English constitution is workable. Moreover, it has the inestimable advantage of being the established constitution; no mere blueprint, it exists as a working constitution, accepted, revered, by the people. But, as we have seen, it requires major reforms.

Hume's perfect commonwealth has been described as a *jeu d'esprit*, a kind of playful fancy.[38] Is that correct, or should it be taken seriously?

[38] Shirley Robin Letwin dismisses "Of the Idea of a perfect Commonwealth" as an amusement containing "merely some innocuous observations on an administrative machine, representative and republican in form." *The Pursuit of Certainty*, p. 89. Frederick G. Whelan describes this discourse as "almost a *jeu d'esprit*." He finds it ironic that such an uncharacteristic "speculative exercise" may have influenced the thought of James Madison and consequently the Constitution of the United States of America. *Order and Artifice in Hume's Political Philosophy* (Princeton: Princeton University Press, 1985), p. 342. David Miller, too, doubts that Hume meant his plan of a perfect commonwealth to be taken seriously. *Philosophy and Ideology*, p. 158. As evidence that "Of the Idea of a perfect Commonwealth" is not to be regarded as a major piece, Miller quotes Hume's comment on Harrington, that the idea of "a perfect and immortal commonwealth will always be found as chimerical as that of a perfect and immortal man." *History of England*, 6:153. Hume's comment, however, is not to be read as retracting either his criticisms of monarchy or his praise of well-contrived republics. The essay was written primarily to show that the perils of republicanism can be overcome in a constitution based on the aphorisms of sound political science. Hume never claimed that such a commonwealth might aspire to *immortality*; indeed, he says exactly the opposite in the essay. *Essays*, pp. 528–29. Similarly, Hume's letter (December 8, 1775) to his nephew, who had come under the influence of John Millar, an advocate of a republican constitution for Great Britain, does not show a change of mind. Therein Hume writes,

> I cannot but agree with Mr. Millar, that the Republican Form of [Government] is by far the best. The antient Republics were somewhat ferocious, and torn [internally] by bloody Factions; but they were still much preferable to the Monarchies or [Aristocracies] which seem to have been quite intolerable. Modern Manners have corrected this Abuse; and all the Republics in Europe, without Exception, are so well governd, that one is at a Loss to which we shoud give the Preference. But what is this general Subject of Speculation to our Purpose? For besides, that an establishd Government [cannot] without the most criminal Imputation, be disjointed from any Speculation; [Republi-

There is a passage in the *History of England* that helps explain his view of constitutions. After having shown that Queen Elizabeth was a true divine-right absolute monarch, Hume springs to her defence. She spoke and acted, he says, in strict conformity with the constitution as established in the minds of the people of her age. It was right that she should follow that constitution.

> In the particular exertions of power, the question ought never to be forgotten, *What is best?* But in the general distribution of power among the several members of a constitution, there can seldom be admitted any other question, than *What is established?* . . . If any other rule than established practice be followed, factions and dissentions must multiply without end: And though many constitutions, and none more than the British, have been improved even by violent innovations, the praise, bestowed on those patriots, to whom the nation has been indebted for its privileges, ought to be given with some reserve, and surely without the least rancour against those who adhered to the ancient constitution. (*H.*, 4:354–55)

In other words, we must distinguish between playing the game well according to the established rules and introducing new, better rules. Elizabeth is not to be denounced because she played according to the absolutist rules she found established. But we must recognize also that constitutions are in "continual fluctuation." Sometimes they change without formal amendment, in response to changes in public opinion and circumstances. Sometimes wise politicians see defects and the remedies for them. Such politicians, when they have a choice, always prefer gradual reform to wholesale new construction. King Alfred, praised by Hume as "the model of that perfect character, which, under the denomination of a sage or wise man, philosophers have been fond of delineating," was a true politician. While it is possible that the excellent institutions attributed to him were the result of radical innovation, it is more probable that "he contented himself with reforming, extending, and executing the institu-

---

canism] is only fitted for a small State: And any Attempt towards it can in our [Country], produce only Anarchy, which is the immediate Forerunner of Despotism. [Will he] tell us, what is that form of a Republic which we must aspire to? Or will [the Constit]ution be afterward decided by the Sword? *Letters*, 2:306. (The manuscript is defective; where I have "[the Constit]ution," Greig has "[the Revol]ution.")

This is simply a reiteration of Hume's view on British constitutional questions: abide by the established British constitution, preferably with major amendments; certainly, do not renounce it in favor of a republic without knowing both the design of the projected new order and how it is to be achieved. In contrast to Letwin, Whelan, and Miller, John Robertson takes the discourse seriously; he sees it as drawing together the two main lines in Hume's political essays, that is, his analysis of socioeconomic development and his analysis of forms of government. See "The Scottish Enlightenment at the Limits of the Civic Tradition," in *Wealth and Virtue*, pp. 169–74. I agree with Robertson.

tions, which he found previously established" (*H*, 1:74–79). Where the established rules are reasonably good, the wise reformer always opts for cautious reform. But where there are no rules, or where they are hopelessly rudimentary, he may have to strike out boldly as a "legislator." Violence is often the means by which "the good" is established as "the right." In the *History of Great Britain*, Hume dismisses the patriarchal and contract theories of the origin of government as obfuscations: "Into how many shapes have political reasonings been turned, in order to avoid an obvious, but, it seems, too homely a truth? . . . Men are unwilling to confess, that all government is derived from violence, usurpation or injustice, sanctified by time, and sometimes by a seeming imperfect consent."[39] In the reign of James I, says Hume in an important revision of his *History*, there were some in the House of Commons who looked beyond the established constitution to a far better one: "The leading members, men of an independent genius and large views, began to regulate their opinions, more by the future consequences which they foresaw, than by the former precedents which were set before them; and they less aspired at maintaining the ancient constitution, than at establishing a new one, and a freer, and a better."[40] In such cases an important decision, not a legal, but a practical decision, is required. An existing constitution has the great advantage of stability; yet it may be ill suited to new circumstances or valid new aspirations. "Of the Idea of a perfect Commonwealth" gives us Hume's views on the best constitution for the best possible society. He recommends a republican constitution for a commercial society. Contrary to the opinion of many, the large size of modern states does not mean that they must be monarchies. Properly designed, the republican form can be realized successfully even in large states; indeed, a large republic can be far better than a small one. Specifically, a well-contrived republican constitution would be highly suitable for the United Kingdom.

What particular constitutional arrangement does Hume recommend and why? All the eligible freeholders and householders—all who meet the prescribed property qualification—in each of the hundred parishes in each of the hundred counties into which a country the size of Great Britain and Ireland is to be divided are *annually* to elect one representative. These hundred parish representatives, in turn, are to serve as a county electoral college. Each college is to elect *by ballot*, from their own body, ten magistrates for the county and one senator to represent the county in the national senate. Hume's constitution is based on the principle of ascending power: power comes from below. "The lower sort of people and small proprietors," he says, "are good judges enough of one not very dis-

[39] *History of Great Britain*, p. 225n.
[40] *History of England*, 5:42. This passage appears in the 1763 and subsequent editions.

tant from them in rank or habitation; and therefore, in their parochial meetings, will probably chuse the best, or nearly the best representative: But they are wholly unfit for county-meetings, and for electing into the higher offices of the republic. Their ignorance gives the grandees an opportunity of deceiving them" (*Essays*, 522). Hume does not estimate either the number of electors or the percentage of the population who, under his plan, would be eligible to vote in Great Britain and Ireland. The first fully visible element of the constitutional structure is the ten thousand county representatives; that number, he comments, is "a basis large enough for any free government."[41]

[41] In the first two editions of the *Discourses*, both published in 1752, all freeholders in the county parishes and all who pay "scot and lot"—taxes for local or national purposes—in the town parishes are to be eligible to vote. In the editions published in 1753–1754, 1758, 1760, 1764, and 1768, Hume limited the franchise to freeholders worth ten pounds a year, and householders worth two hundred pounds in the towns. Finally, in 1770, he raised the property qualification to a twenty-pound freehold in the counties, and five-hundred-pound households in the towns. In the *History of England*, he mentions with approval the fixing in 1430 of the county qualification as a freehold worth forty shillings a year; he comments, "This sum was equivalent to near twenty pounds a-year of our present money; and it were to be wished, that the spirit, as well as letter of this law, had been maintained." *History of England*, 2:452–53. The term "grandees" is used with scorn in the *History of England*; see 2:18, 173, 324. Hume may have adopted it from William Drummond of Hawthornden, whom he follows closely when depicting (n. 9) the chaotic state of Scotland in the sixteenth century. *The History of the Lives and Reigns of The Five James's, Kings of Scotland*, in *The Works of William Drummond, of Hawthornden* (Edinburgh: James Watson, in Craig's-Close, 1711), p. 82. Also, probably Hume was referring slyly to "overmighty subjects" far nearer his own day; between 1688 and 1707 the desirability of reducing the power of "the boisterous pretending grandees" had been made abundantly clear. See P.W.J. Riley, "The Structure of Scottish politics and the Union of 1707," in *The Union of 1707: Its Impact on Scotland*, ed. T. I. Rae (Glasgow: Blackie & Son Limited, 1974), pp. 1–29.

Applied to the eighteenth-century English franchise, Hume's recommendations would have cancelled the effects of inflation on the county property qualification and standardized the borough qualifications. In Scotland it would have introduced genuine representation. There the sixty-five royal burghs, with the exception of Edinburgh, were divided into fourteen groups. The town councillors of each burgh elected one delegate; these delegates then met as an electoral college for their group. Thus fourteen Members of Parliament were elected. The town council of Edinburgh elected one Member directly. A survey made in 1831, just before the Reform Act, showed that only 1,303 persons had a formal part in the selection of the fifteen burgh Members. In the counties, which elected a total of thirty Members, the basic qualification was "a forty shilling land of old extent" held from the Crown, or land held from the Crown valued at four hundred pounds annual rent. Although titles often were created simply to create voters, the numbers remained small. According to a survey made in 1788, only 2,662 persons had a right to vote in county elections; another survey, in 1820, put the number at 2,889. The small total, about 4,000 for burghs and counties together, meant that "viceroys" such as Argyll and Dundas, with the cooperation of a small number of landlords, generally could send a solid contingent to the House of Commons. "In Scotland," commented Charles James Fox in 1795, "there is no shadow even of representation. There is neither a representation of property for the counties, nor of pop-

The national executive power is to be lodged in the senate. This body is to select annually, from within its membership, a protector (head of state), two secretaries of state, and various departmental councils. It is to appoint the higher judges. Provision is made for a kind of emergency council, to have high prerogative power, for six-month periods, in cases of "extraordinary emergencies."

The process of legislation may be started by the senators or on the initiative of either the magistrates or the representatives in any county, but all bills are to be debated by the senate before being submitted for decision by the county assemblies (or, if uncontentious, by the county magistrates). To be enacted a bill must have the support of a majority of the hundred assemblies. This arrangement provides for good debate (in the senate); a large assembly is simply a mob, liable to be swayed by emotion and demagogues. At the same time, it limits the influence of the senate in legislation. Hume explains, "All free governments must consist of two councils, a lesser and greater; or, in other words, of a senate and people. The people, as HARRINGTON observes, would want wisdom, without the senate: The senate, without the people, would want honesty." But how are "the people"—the ten thousand county representatives, not the electorate—to be given a role without risking demagoguery and tumult? Hume's solution is simple: "Divide the people into many separate bodies; and then they may debate with safety, and every inconvenience seems to be prevented" (*Essays*, 522). In the early essay "Of the first Principles of Government" (1741), he had anticipated this solution to the problem of participation by the people: "For though the people, collected in a body like the ROMAN tribes, be quite unfit for government, yet when dispersed in small bodies, they are more susceptible both of reason and order; the force of popular currents and tides is, in a great measure, broken; and the public interest may be pursued with some method and constancy" (*Essays*, 36).

One reason why the ancient republics were turbulent was their small

ulation for the towns." Edward Porritt, *The Unreformed House of Commons*, 2 vols. (Cambridge: Cambridge University Press, 1903), 2:5, 128, 157. Hume's recommendation would have broken the monopoly of both the great landowners and the burgh councillors.

By the Reform Act, 1832, the franchise requirements were standardized throughout the United Kingdom, as Hume had recommended, but the property qualifications were set far lower than he had proposed. Basically, in the counties the vote was given to owners of property worth ten pounds annually, with additional provisions for tenants, and in the burghs to householders with premises worth ten pounds a year. As a result of the Reform Act, the Scottish electorate increased by 1,400 percent, while the English electorate increased by only about 80 percent. I.G.C. Hutchison, *A Political History of Scotland 1832–1924* (Edinburgh: John Donald Publishers Ltd., 1986), p. 1. See the analysis of the Scottish constituencies in Sir Lewis Namier and John Brooke, *The History of Parliament. The House of Commons, 1754–1790*, 3 vols. (HMSO, 1964), 1:469–512.

size. They could choose to be democracies, with all citizens participating, or at least trying to participate, in all decisions, whether judicial, executive, or legislative. The principle of such a constitution—the people will decide—made a strict rule of law impossible. The assemblies were numerous; in such large bodies infectious passion commonly prevailed over arguments based on prudence and humanity. With such a constitution, the elite, however defined, tended to be discontented and rebellious. Alternatively, they could choose to be aristocracies, with power restricted to those few ranked as great. This exposed the people to exploitation. Moreover, quite aside from the real grievances provoked by the greed and arrogance of the great, all those excluded from power, the major part of the citizenry, felt that the aristocratic constitution was unjust, for they too were citizens. In contrast, Hume's perfect commonwealth is to have a rule of law; the senate is only to propose and debate, not to decide; and while the ten thousand county representatives are to enact the laws, they themselves, "the people," are elected, and they debate and vote in one hundred assemblies spread throughout the country.

Hume provides an organized opposition. Every unsuccessful candidate for the senate who received more than one-third of the votes cast in his county college is to be a member of a "court of competitors." This body has no power to govern, but may examine the public accounts and present indictments to the senate, with an appeal from senate acquittals to the county assemblies. The danger that the senate will become a distinct interest exploiting the country for its own advantage—as would the House of Commons if it became the ruling body of Great Britain—is prevented by (a) the annual elections, (b) the fact that the senators are chosen "not by an undistinguishing rabble, like the ENGLISH electors, but by men of fortune and education," who will be independent of the grandees, (c) the senate's advisory role in legislation, and (d) the critical scrutiny of the court of competitors. As we have seen, the expression, "Gentlemen, who have some Fortune and Education," had been used in 1741, in "Of the Parties of Great Britain," to describe the upper rank in Scotland.

One of the foremost advantages of this plan is that it will not produce parties of principle. "The chief support of the BRITISH government," argues Hume, "is the opposition of interests; but that, though in the main serviceable, breeds endless factions. In the foregoing plan, it does all the good without any of the harm. The *competitors* have no power of controlling the senate: They have only the power of accusing, and appealing to the people"(*Essays*, 525).

Each county is a petty republic; its assembly is to be able to enact bylaws, subject to repeal by the senate or any other county assembly. "Every county-law may be annulled either by the senate or another county; because that shows an opposition of interest: In which case no part ought to decide for itself. The matter must be referred to the whole, which will best determine what agrees with general interest" (*Essays*, 525).

Most of the work of executive government is to be done at the county level by the popularly elected magistrates, but under the supervision of various national councils—for trade, laws, religion, and the like—appointed by the senate. The magistrates will administer justice; in addition, they will make provision for the collection of taxes. They are to appoint a minister of religion in each parish. Although there is to be a presbytery in each county, the magistrates are to have power to depose any presbyter and to remove ecclesiastical cases from the church courts to the civil courts. In short, although each county is to have an ecclesiastical structure distinct from the magistracy, the civil authorities will be able to prevent the rise of a strong, independent religious estate or party, a church interest.

Although Hume never discusses military organization as a distinct topic and in a systematic way, his scattered comments show that he had given careful thought to this important topic.[42] He recognizes that provision must be made for defense: to repel invaders and to prevent hegemony on the continent. Both a standing army and a militia have merits: the former can provide professional efficiency and do the job without disrupting domestic society; the latter puts power to resist the central government in the hands of local authorities—which, depending on the circumstances, may or may not be desirable. Perhaps, then, provision should be made for both. But this solution is defective: to choose it is really to opt for a standing army, for if the government is allowed to have a stand-

[42] For a review of Hume's comments on the militia versus standing army debate, see Robertson, *The Scottish Enlightenment and the Militia Issue*, pp. 60–74. This debate was a staple of the Court-Country controversy. The veto of the Scottish Militia Bill in 1708 left the Scottish militia on its pre-union basis. Both the English and Scottish services, established in the 1660s, very early had suffered atrophy; if an attempt to revive them was to be made in the eighteenth century, new legislation would be required. In 1757 the English militia was reconstituted by Act of Parliament. This gave keenly loyal North Britons a noble cause; Scotland's status and honor were at stake. In 1760 a bill to reconstitute the Scottish militia was defeated at second reading in the House of Commons by 194 to 84; George II, Newcastle, and Hardwicke did not want arms in the hands of Scottish civilians, especially Highlanders. As Robertson says, it is impossible to show exactly where Hume stood; although many of his friends took up the cause, he would have been concerned about the social and political implications of such a force. The only Scot who spoke in the House of Commons against the Scottish Militia Bill was Robert Dundas, younger, of the *Squadrone*. Dundas thereby won the favor of Newcastle and Hardwicke, and immortality as Bumbo in *Sister Peg*. Note Hume's contemptuous reference to Bumbo in 1763 (*New Hume Letters*, pp. 75–76). The anonymous pamphlet "The History of the Proceedings in the Case of Margaret, Commonly called Peg, only lawful Sister to John Bull, Esq.," first published in 1761, has been edited (and attributed to David Hume) by David R. Raynor. See *Sister Peg: A Pamphlet Hitherto Unknown by David Hume* (Cambridge: Cambridge University Press, 1982).

ing army, it will neglect the training and equipping of the militia. This brings us to the grave dangers that may be posed by a standing army. When an army becomes large and powerful, it becomes also a domestic threat. If a country's constitution depends on a precarious balance of forces, as does the British, the presence of a standing army commanded by the king, while the militia is either badly neglected (as in England) or virtually nonexistent (as in Scotland), means that the Crown has a card that could be decisive in its favor. Nevertheless, Hume does not propose abolishing the British standing army. Why? His reasons relate to the political and constitutional situation. The fact that the Hanoverian settlement still (1742, 1748) is questioned rules out reliance on a militia.[43] Moreover, given the absence of republican government structures in the counties, to supplant the standing army with a strong militia would be Gothic; it would increase the sway of the grandees at the expense of the national government. In contrast to the British situation, for which he had no happy solution, in a properly constituted commonwealth, particularly one surrounded by enlightened neighbors, who also had seen the madness of religious, commercial, and imperialist wars, a militia would be the ideal defense force.

For his perfect commonwealth, Hume proposes a militia in each county. Normally, each county force would be commanded by a colonel appointed by the magistrates. In wartime, however, the national general, commissioned by the senate, would appoint the colonels, but all such appointments would require confirmation after one year by the county authorities. A total of twenty thousand men, selected by rotation, would undergo camp training each summer. In military as in ecclesiastical matters, the ideal arrangement is the avoidance of any interest independent of the popularly elected local authorities. This is essential in a republic: "Without the dependence of the clergy on the civil magistrates, and without a militia, it is in vain to think that any free government will ever have security or stability" (*Essays*, 525).

As we have seen, given the nature of their economies, the small, surveyable republics of antiquity had some advantages; but they had serious disadvantages also, chiefly related to participatory democracy. Hume concludes the essay by arguing that well-designed large republics, such as either France or Great Britain and Ireland could become, would have many of the merits of the republican form without the defects (*Essays*, 528). Large republics can have the advantages of a republican constitu-

---

[43] In 1742 Hume favored the retention of a standing army. *Letters*, 1:44. In "Of the Protestant Succession," published in 1752, when listing the arguments against disturbing a hereditary royal title, he commented, "A prince, who fills the throne with a disputed title, dares not arm his subjects; the only method of securing a people fully, both against domestic oppression and foreign conquest." *Essays*, p. 509.

tion—reliance on institutional arrangements rather than on particular people, the balancing of legitimate interests, and the rule of law—while retaining the strength and stability possible only in large states. Europe, like ancient Greece, is divided into many states: this makes for variety and emulation; it checks military power and prevents monolithic authority in culture, religion, and philosophy. But the European nations are monarchies, and even a civilized monarchy is inferior to a good republic. Hume's ideal prospect is a Europe divided into large well-contrived republics.

Montesquieu, in *The Spirit of the Laws* (1748), found *la virtu* essential to a democracy, and *la modération* to an aristocratic republic. Hume, too, saw a close connection between the political culture of a nation and the character of its government—witness his comment on modern absolute monarchies. But, consistent with what he had written over ten years earlier in "That Politics may be reduced to a Science" and "Of Parties in General," his concern in "Of the Idea of a perfect Commonwealth" is with constitutional laws. Good laws are causes of "general virtue and good morals in a state" (*Essays*, p. 55); consequently, legislators can be moral reformers. But they should be realistic, taking into account both the nature of civil society and the prevailing manners. They should remember that justice and obedience, both negative virtues, are the great virtues of public life. In forming or reforming a constitution, the modern legislator should not assume much in the way of public spirit among the people; indeed, he should assume that men, parties, and ranks are "self-ish." He should try to frame a constitution that will make even "self-ish" interests serve the public (*Essays*, pp. 15–16). Hume insisted on the importance of good laws, that is, correct franchise provisions, checks and controls in the legislative process, limits on executive power, the institutionalization of opposition, and the like; this is why "Of the Idea of a perfect Commonwealth" is both precise and detailed.

Rank in Society

Outside society, according to Hume, human beings are distinguished only by their natural differences. But since the natural state entails scarcity, people turn from it to economic society, a system of production and distribution based on private property. As we have seen, Hume recognized that the property rules result in economic inequality, an artificial inequality inherent in the property system. In addition, he held that, quite apart from the division of labor, there are a number of different roles to be performed in a society. This causes social ranking: some roles and places are higher than others. Some people are the elite of their society; they lead while others follow. Should the elite be rich? More pertinently, should the very rich be the elite? David Miller contends that Hume was committed to economic, social, and political principles that would have kept the old aristocracy in power. This is a central element in his argument that Hume was basically a conservative.

For Hume the primary question is not whether a leadership structure is desirable, but on what criteria it ought to be based. Even in an absolute monarchy, this question remains pertinent, for the *de jure* constitution does not tell the whole story: although it confers absolute legal power on the king, nonlegal factors such as sanctity, high birth, wealth, ability, valor, and integrity will give authority to some others, regardless of whether or not they hold office under the king. Seeing all such independent authority as a threat, tyrants seek to level society; they try to destroy all leadership not based on their own appointment or commission. Hume holds that without the inspiration and guidance of its natural leaders, the populace is ineffectual, a mere mob lacking either specific goals or considered tactics, fated to fail in any rising, justified or not, against its rulers.

A society needs leaders; otherwise, it will be shapeless, simply an atomized mass. Unfortunately, those of high rank often betray their trust. Forgetting that their power and privileges are justified only by service to the country, they exploit the populace in every imaginable way: economically, by exemption from certain taxes; socially, by special privileges (such as exclusive hunting and fishing rights); religiously, by requiring their tenants to adopt their beliefs; politically, by using public power for their own ends (e.g., promoting wars for their diversion, profit, and glorification); and psychologically, by dominion over the people. Enured to the arrogance of the great, the people rarely complain or revolt: they pay the taxes, fight the wars, obeying and deferring meekly. "To be sacrificed to the interest, policy, and ambition of the great, is so much the common lot of the people, that they may appear unreasonable, who would pretend to complain of it" (*H.*, 5:186–87). And when, the oppression of the great having become unbearable, the people revolt, reviving "the ideas of primitive equality, which are engraven in the hearts of all men," invariably they fail—unless headed by leaders drawn from among the elite (*H*, 2:290–93).

We have seen that while Hume insists that we must rely on "wise nature" to provide us with both basic knowledge and basic moral standards, he assigns the task of improving both our knowledge and our morality to the understanding. What happens naturally where the structure of society is concerned? Can improvement be made? There is ample evidence, albeit scattered, that the question of social rank concerned Hume greatly. When we draw together what he says in various places, his views, as we might expect, are far more philosophical than ideological. He accepts Aristotle's basic categories: high rank, middle rank, low rank. These do not necessarily imply a pyramidical social structure: the middle may be small, almost nonexistent, as in an hourglass, or it may be large, as in a lozenge.

Hume found three main sociopolitical structures in contemporary Western Europe. There were the great monarchies, and also clusters of petty ones trying ridiculously to imitate them. Here kings had succeeded in making themselves absolute with the help of standing armies. At the other extreme were the republics. These had their origins in commerce; in them present riches were the basis of distinction. And then there was England. Although England was a monarchy, English society was primarily commercial. In the European monarchies, the descendants of the old nobility claimed most of the higher offices in the civil and military services, and much was made of the relics of bygone family status: titles, decorations, stands of antique weapons, trophies of the chase, old castles, courtly manners. In contrast, in countries such as England, where commerce had exerted a major influence, the evidence of one's worth was far simpler, and styles and manners were plainer. There the prime consideration was present riches: the social and political standing of ancestors mattered but little. Hume concludes one section of *Enquiry* II, by relating the rank structure to the monarchical and republican forms of government.

> In most countries of Europe, family, that is, hereditary riches, marked with titles and symbols from the sovereign, is the chief source of distinction. In England, more regard is paid to present opulence and plenty. Each practice has its advantages and disadvantages. Where birth is respected, unactive, spiritless minds remain in haughty indolence, and dream of nothing but pedigrees and genealogies: the generous and ambitious seek honour and authority, and reputation and favour. Where riches are the chief idol, corruption, venality, rapine prevail: arts, manufactures, commerce, agriculture flourish. The former prejudice, being favourable to military virtue, is more suited to monarchies. The latter, being the chief spur to industry, agrees better with a republican government.[44]

This contrast between the structure of commercial and precommercial societies—between Holland and England, on the one hand, and France

---

[44] *Enquiry* II, pp. 248–49. As between old-fashioned pride of family and the new emphasis on riches, not all the advantages are on one side. In writing to Alexander Home of Whitfield in 1758 about their family, Hume commented, "I am not of the opinion of some, that these matters are altogether to be slighted. Though we should pretend to be wiser than our ancestors, yet it is arrogant to pretend that we are wiser than the other nations of Europe, who, all of them, except perhaps the English, make great account of their family descent. I doubt that our morals have not much improved since we began to think riches the sole thing worth regarding." *Letters*, 1:276.

and most other European countries, on the other—was of recent origin. Well into the seventeenth century, England, for example, was still a traditional society, one in which the great, aware that their status was not justified by ability, hid their incompetence behind elaborate formality.

> High pride of family then prevailed; and it was by a dignity and stateliness of behaviour, that the gentry and nobility distinguished themselves from the common people. Great riches, acquired by commerce, were more rare, and had not, as yet been able to confound all ranks of men, and render money the chief foundation of distinction. Much ceremony took place in the common intercourse of life, and little familiarity was indulged by the great. The advantages, which result from opulence, are so solid and real, that those who are possessed of them need not dread the near approaches of their inferiors. The distinctions of birth and title, being more empty and imaginary, soon vanish upon familiar access and acquaintance. (H, 5:132)

Hume, as we know, had no contempt for economic goods, but this does not mean that he shared the multitude's fascination with and respect for great wealth, old or new. He declares his admiration for Socrates' "resolute contempt for riches" and, like Adam Smith after him, regards many of the things that captivate the multitude as of little or no value other than to feed vanity: "worthless toys and gewgaws" is Hume's description; "baubles and trinkets" is Smith's.[45] Indeed, as we have seen, Hume found the people's choice of the rich and the great as the modern elite sufficiently remarkable to require careful analysis. The explanation he gives in the *Treatise* is that the populace sympathizes with the rich: because the rich possess the whole apparatus of conspicuous opulence, all the outward and visible signs of felicity, the people regard them as the great; only their mortality, as Smith was to say, prevents their adoration as gods. The vulgar live by whatever opinions they happen to have acquired; the philosophic live self-consciously, skeptically, scrutinizing their beliefs and values. One may wish that the wise and virtuous were the elite, but that cannot be. Although the values of the people are distorted, their test has the advantage of causing few disagreements. If it were possible to convert the multitude to a higher criterion, who would have the capacity to apply it? Unlike wisdom and virtue, opulence is a simple test.

Hume's view of the character traits of the very rich is clearly revealed in his piece "Of Impudence and Modesty."[46] Therein he explains how Confidence, intended by Jupiter to be the companion of Virtue and Wis-

---

[45] *Enquiry* II, pp., 256, 283; Adam Smith, *The Theory of Moral Sentiments* (Oxford: Clarendon Press, 1976), p. 184. See also "Of Avarice," in *Essays*, pp. 569–73.

[46] The essay "Of Impudence and Modesty" appeared in the first edition of the essays and in all subsequent editions before 1764, when it was dropped; perhaps Hume had decided that his brush was too wide. *Essays*, 552–56.

dom, having become impatient with the caution of Wisdom, withdrew in order to team up with Vice and Folly; while Diffidence, intended as the companion of Vice and Folly, but driven out by Vice, joined up with Virtue and Wisdom. Subsequently, Vice, Folly, and Confidence accepted the hospitality of Wealth, a great landlord, while Virtue, Wisdom, and Diffidence settled in with Poverty, one of his tenants. In these new alliances, Confidence became Impudence, and Diffidence became Modesty. Thus it was, according to Hume, that Vice, Folly, and Impudence came to reside with Wealth, while Virtue, Wisdom, and Modesty live with Poverty. Unfortunately, we tend to ignore these shifts: when we see someone pushing himself to the fore with great assurance, we expect him to be virtuous and wise; similarly when we see that someone is reluctant to be a leader, we assume that he is vicious and foolish. The meaning and importance of this essay as social criticism becomes obvious when we remember, from chapter 3, that pride (confidence) is essential to achievement, while humility impedes both endeavor and success: the world is ruled by the rich, who tend to be both foolish and vicious.

In another essay, "Of the Middle Station of Life," Hume gives a highly Aristotelian account of the defects of those who inherit greatness, compared with the virtues fostered by medium status. The great are people of "indolent understanding"; they are deaf to philosophy—not just abstruse thought, but even the basic principles of good government—because they are far too busy, not with making a living (as are the laboring poor), but with gambling, fishing, hunting, and horse racing. Conforming to their circumstances, they tend to be generous and affable, but lack industry and integrity. Nor are they challenged, as are those of middling rank, to improve their natural talents: "[M]ore Capacity [is] requisite to perform the Duties of that Station [the middle station], than is requisite to act in the higher Spheres of Life" (*Essays*, 548). Even army officers drawn from the nobility, whose claim to command was the military prowess of their rank, often have proven inferior to commoners.[47] Edmund Burke was to write, "There is no qualification for government but virtue and wisdom, actual or presumptive." Actual virtue and wisdom—ability—is "the passport of heaven to human place and honour." Yet, says Burke, the presumption that the heads of great landed families are wise and virtuous is valid; accordingly, such people ought to have power in society. Moreover, since property is "sluggish, inert, and timid," it is to be "out of all proportion predominant in the representation." In France the middle classes, possessed by the spirit of ambition, had undertaken "to reverse the order of Providence"; no longer were they willing to allow the moral and political world "to be controlled by the force and influence of the grandees." As a

---

[47] *History*, 2:99; 5:429; 6:41.

result, "the chain of subordination, even in cabal and sedition, was broken in its most important links. It was no longer the great and the populace."[48] Hutcheson had speculated that the vulgar look up to and follow
the great because of a presumption that "the great engines of virtue,"
which the great possess, will be used benevolently by them. Hume, as we
have seen, found such a presumption ill founded; it is true that the grandees are exalted, but that is the result, not of their good works, but of
sympathy. If people were ranked by their genius and capacity, philosophers, followed by poets, would be at the top. And what is more, contrary
to vulgar opinion, "the middle Station of Life is more favourable to *Happiness*, as well as to *Virtue* and *Wisdom*" (*Essays*, 551).

Although both Hume and Smith at times sigh a little for Jerusalem, they
pitch their tents by the waters of Babylon. It is far better that the multitude should follow the opulent and the great than that they should engage
in endless disputes, perhaps battles, about true merit. Place according to
merit is too sublime a maxim for Babylon. In *Enquiry* II, Hume explains
how the two standards of value, those of the vulgar and those of the
philosophic, are to be reconciled.

> A man who has cured himself of all ridiculous prepossessions, and is fully,
> sincerely, and steadily convinced, from experience as well as philosophy, that
> the difference of fortune makes less difference in happiness than is vulgarly
> imagined; such a one does not measure out degrees of esteem according to
> the rent-rolls of his acquaintance. He may, indeed, externally pay a superior
> deference to the great lord above the vassal; because riches are the most con-
> venient, being the most fixed and determinate, source of distinction. But his
> internal sentiments are more regulated by the personal characters of men,
> than by the accidental and capricious favours of fortune. (*E.*, 248)

If the values of Jerusalem are too high, if this world must remain Babylon, what is the best social structure for Babylon? As we have seen,
Hume has three different situations in mind: the absolute monarchies, the
republics, England. Clearly, in those continental countries where commerce has not produced republican forces strong enough to challenge the

---

[48] Edmund Burke, "Reflections on the Revolution in France," in *The Works and Correspondence of the Right Honourable Edmund Burke* (Francis & John Rivington: London,
1852), 4:191–92; also "Letters on a Regicide Peace," in *Works and Correspondence*, 3:343.
To help us gain insight into Hume's thought and attitudes, Miller mentions (*Philosophy and
Ideology*, pp. 202–3) an addition made by Adam Smith in 1789–1790 to *The Theory of
Moral Sentiments* on the dangers of political reforms undertaken by "men of system" and
suggests that Smith may have been condemning the revolution in France. We ought to look
also at the new chapter, added by Smith in that edition, wherein he deplores "the corruption
of our moral sentiments, which is occasioned by this disposition to admire the rich and the
great, and to despise or neglect persons of poor and mean condition." Smith, *The Theory of
Moral Sentiments*, pp. 61–66.

kings, there is a need for strong and able intermediate powers—persons of rank—to prevent despotism. Hume, with Aristotle, recognizes that although absolute monarchy is the best form of government in abstract theory—because the king stands above, detached from all the competing interests—in reality those who become monarchs rarely are worthy of such transcendent power. Accordingly, he finds desirable in a monarchy the presence, not of mere courtiers, but of strong natural leaders, people of authority, who attract the support of the populace, even when they hold no offices in the royal government; this was one of the valuable functions of the clergy in the Middle Ages. On the one hand, such natural leaders are far too influential to be ignored by a king and his ministers; thus the natural leaders have a moderating effect on the government. On the other hand, because the people follow their lead, they can increase the authority of a good government by setting an example of respectful obedience and by leaving no place for demagogues.

We must remember, however, that although Hume insisted that Englishmen showed bigotry in deriding France and other civilized monarchies as slave states, he had a strong preference for commercial republics, for "free states" or commonwealths, among which, for certain purposes, he included England. In practice, a monarchy, even one with a rule of law, is inferior to a well-designed commonwealth; in monarchies the nobles and their retainers are likely to live as idle, privileged parasites, puffed up by "false ideas of rank and superiority," while those who do the work are poor.[49] But for a commonwealth to be clearly superior, it must not be oligarchic, with the riches and power concentrated in a few; otherwise, as in monarchy, the few will exploit the many. A commonwealth has the advantage of being free from people ranked high merely because of birth. A commonwealth with wide equality among its citizens avoids the evils of oligarchy.

Again and again, Hume emphasizes the importance of motivation: if we are to make the most of our potential, we must have demanding circumstances and challenging prospects. Those born to high rank suffer the disadvantage of rarely having occasion to bestir themselves. Living contented, unreflective lives, they do not cultivate their understandings; in addition, they tend to be haughty and violent, regarding themselves as above the law. At the other extreme, the hopeless poor seldom see beyond the drab routines of bare existence. In contrast, those neither too high nor too low will be industrious, concerned to better themselves and their condition. Moreover, they know both how to lead and how to be led. What is needed, then, is a society whose values put a premium on all the great natural and artificial virtues—on generosity and charity (wise benevo-

---

[49] *Essays*, pp. 265–66, 448.

lence) within their proper sphere, on justice and fidelity, on industry and frugality, on allegiance and respect for the law, and so on. Although philosophic lectures have little effect on people's characters, moral causes are powerfully effective in shaping the values, attitudes, and manners of nations, and some of those causes can be deliberately improved. Hume rejoices in the impact of manufacturing and commerce on the lives of the multitude. In "Of Commerce," as we have seen, he argues that the effect of the new economic activity is to raise more and more of the populace out of poverty. That it has this effect, of improving the condition of the laboring poor, is one of the chief advantages of economic progress: "[P]overty and hard labour debase the minds of the common people" (*Essays*, 198). It is true, as some complain, that the high wages commanded by the workers in an industrialized economy may make a nation's exports more expensive. But what of that! Such a consideration "is not to be put in competition with the happiness of so many millions" (*Essays*, 265).

A modern commercial society, a society with productive agriculture, busy manufacturing, swarming trades, and all the admirable features of the good life such a society fosters and sustains, would be a vast improvement. Such a society is inherently republican in both structure and ethos. Those in business, Hume found, make good citizens for republics, but not for monarchies: resenting the frivolity, indolence, deceit, and extravagance of royal courts, they bring to public life the diligence and honesty required for success in private economic affairs. Independent landowners, too, those who have integrated their agricultural operations into the market, are good citizens for a republic. Indeed, the gentry have the special merit that, unlike their city cousins, they are free from the daily, hourly, demands of business; consequently, they can achieve a sound understanding of the principles of economics and government. Both Aristotle and Hume recommend republics: they differ in that while Aristotle praises small, plain-living, agricultural republics, Hume opts for large, commercial republics, with the citizens engaged in manufacturing, scientific agriculture, and trade. A commercial republic is superior in that all citizens, not just a small, closed class of considerable landowners, but also the many small freeholders and industrious tradesmen and mechanics, can hope to attain the kind of economic independence prerequisite for personal freedom.

When we revisit the institutions of Hume's perfect commonwealth to see what they reveal about its social structure, we find no evidence of partiality for the old ruling class: indeed, we find ourselves far removed from the scene familiar to the eighteenth-century English aristocracy, far away in another world, a world shaped by what Hume had learned from republicanism, both ancient and medieval. In the constitution of the perfect commonwealth—his optimum agenda—Hume ties the right to vote to a property qualification set high enough to exclude those susceptible to grandee control. All those who pass this one test may participate in politics, electing and seeking election, ruling and being ruled in turn, although it is assumed that the "lower sort of people and small proprietors" will be confined to the basic parts of the system. Moreover, contrary to Harrington's proposal, the ultimate legislative power is to belong to "the people."[50] Applied to contemporary Britain, the result would have been to increase the power of those in the middle station at the expense of the aristocracy. Differences in wealth among the citizens are assumed, but no provision is made for constitutionally recognized ranks. Hume's ideal society is not one ruled by a small aristocracy, but one in which many citizens, ideally most citizens, are in the middle station. It is these people—thoughtful, competent, balanced, moderate people—not monarchs and nobles, who are to have political power in his ideal commonwealth. Moreover, neither war nor religion is to be the basis for a rank or status superior to the ordinary citizenry, a point Aristotle would have applauded.

Hume has little time for either religion or chivalry. Indeed, so restrained is his praise for the past performance of the first and second estates that some conservatives might regard him as a forerunner of that materialistic age of calculators and economists deplored by Burke. Hume

---

[50] Hume states three criticisms of Harrington's constitution: first, any attempt to limit the size of landed estates by an agrarian law is bound to fail; second, the provision that, after having served each three-year term, a legislator be ineligible for reelection during the next three years, would be "inconvenient"; third, Harrington's legislative process, which requires that all bills pass the senate before being presented to the lower house, would enable the senate to prevent the other house from even debating reform proposals. Hume gives greatest emphasis to the third criticism. "The OCEANA provides not a sufficient security for liberty, or the redress of grievances. . . . It appears then, that in the OCEANA, the whole legislature may be said to rest in the senate; which HARRINGTON would own to be an inconvenient form of government, especially after the *Agrarian* is abolished." *Essays*, pp. 515–16; *Letters*, 2:306–7. While David Robertson recognizes that Hume regards civil liberty as more important than the right to participate in politics, he finds that Hume retains the civic ideal of participation as an attribute of true citizenship and suggests that, in Hume's view, "commerce will in the long run make it possible for every individual to satisfy the material and moral requirements of citizenship." See John Robertson, "The Scottish Enlightenment at the Limits of the Civic Tradition," in *Wealth and Virtue*, p. 159. My interpretation, which locates Hume mainly in the jurisprudential tradition, is that Hume, although hopeful that commerce will do much to improve the lot of the poor, sees no need for general political participation. While a "people" is a necessary component of a good republican constitution, the "people" need not be a very large body; consequently, he is able to recommend a high property qualification for electors so as to reduce grandee influence. Similarly, although Hume advocates a militia for his commonwealth, he does so, not to provide a school of civic virtue, but to give the citizenry an effective force with which to restrain those in the higher bodies of the government.

regarded the old order as Gothic; he limned the shape of a new order based on the economic, legal, and religious independence of free citizens, a new order worthy to be called civil society.

Hume's powerful attack, in "Of Public Credit," on borrowing to cover cumulative war debt is sometimes cited as evidence that he saw the landed aristocracy as the proper leaders and rulers of Britain. In contrast, I have depicted him as recommending, especially to fellow Scots, a society in which manufacturing and commerce draw upon an active rural economy for food and raw materials, sending back "luxuries" in return, thus producing both rural and urban prosperity. This is not late-nineteenth-century Britain relying heavily on exported manufactures to pay for imported food. Yet market forces are powerfully at work in his model: the estates of the nobility are being broken up into productive units owned by improving landlords; science is being applied to the most beneficial of all the arts, agriculture; the rural laborer is being paid an increasing real wage. In Hume's model, we have the rural and urban basis for a republican government. However, in fact Britain was a monarchy; indeed, according to Hume, there were reasons—the growing influence of the Crown and the strength of the standing army—why it might soon become an absolute monarchy like most of its neighbors. It was contemporary British society, not Hume's model, that was threatened by excessive government borrowing; obviously, if Hume's polemics against war, debt, and high taxes were to have any effect, he had to convince those with power or influence that contemporary British society was endangered.

Why is constant government borrowing bad? It enables the government covertly to revert to the maxims of ancient policy, elevating public good, specifically offensive war, above the private good of individuals and families. It diverts money away from productive investment in land and trade. It robs those on whom taxes on land and necessities fall heavily, and benefits the idle rich. It swells the ranks of those who live in residential cities. To show the economic, social, and political implications of the national debt, in 1764, at the end of the great colonial war with France, Hume added six paragraphs to the essay; therein he takes up the most extreme case, where almost the entire annual national product goes to pay the interest on the debt.

> In this unnatural state of society, the only persons, who possess any revenue beyond the immediate effects of their industry, are the stock-holders, who draw almost all the rent of the land and houses, besides the produce of all the customs and excises. These are men, who have no connexions with the state, who can enjoy their revenue in any part of the globe in which they chuse to reside, who will naturally bury themselves in the capital or in great cities, and who will sink into the lethargy of a stupid and pampered luxury,

without spirit, ambition, or enjoyment. Adieu to all ideas of nobility, gentry, and family. The stocks can be transferred in an instant, and being in such a fluctuating state, will seldom be transmitted during three generations from father to son. Or were they to remain ever so long in one family, they convey no hereditary authority or credit to the possessor; and by this means, the several ranks of men, which form a kind of independent magistracy in a state, instituted by the hand of nature, are entirely lost; and every man in authority derives his influence from the commission alone of the sovereign. No expedient remains for preventing or suppressing insurrections, but mercenary armies: No expedient at all remains for resisting tyranny: Elections are swayed by bribery and corruption alone: And the middle power between king and people being totally removed, a grievous despotism must infallibly prevail. The landholders, despised for their poverty, and hated for their oppressions, will be utterly unable to make any opposition to it. (*Essays*, 357–58)

Hume's concern with the mounting public debt went back to his earliest days. Borrowing permits useless wars, wars waged for the benefit of ambitious politicians, military careerists, some merchants, some ports, London, while the rest of the country foots the bill. This was Hume's constant complaint. The essay "Of Public Credit" gives one of his arguments for international peace and trade. By his 1764 addition, depicting the plight of a nation polarized into the rich and the poor, like ancient Rome, he hoped to alarm even the feckless leaders of Britain. Therein he addresses himself, not to the learned, but to the powerful. Given the fact that Britain has an increasingly strong monarchic executive government and may become absolutist, intermediate ranks are essential in Britain. By wiping these out, excessive taxation will open the way to despotism. Hume's purpose in "Of Public Credit" was not to endorse the social structure of Britain as best, but to convince Britain's leaders that offensive wars financed by borrowing were dangerous to contemporary British society, indeed, to any society.[51]

[51] Hume's attitude to war was much like Walpole's. In his early works, Hume treated continental involvement as an inevitable consequence of bringing in foreign kings. But, like Walpole, he favored a restrained foreign policy; for one thing, such a policy would not cause taxes and the debt to soar. In the *Political Discourses* (1752), Hume laid the theoretical basis for the denunciation of an imperialist foreign policy. Walpole's opponents had always advocated a "blue water" policy, which entailed the avoidance of both continental entanglements and a large army. In 1739 his Patriotic critics forced Walpole into the War of Jenkins's Ear with Spain. During the Seven Years' War, the foreign-policy aspect of Patriotism, distinct from the domestic and constitutional aspect preeminent from 1726 to 1742, came to the fore: Pitt was still a Patriot; now, however, his Patriotism put its emphasis on mercantile imperialism in North America, the West Indies, India, and Africa; the kind of war he believed in was, in the words of George (Bubb) Dodington, "a Marine, Commercial, Colony War." In 1752 Hume, as we have seen, revealed the errors of mercantilism; thus his denunciation of anti-French prejudices was placed on the solid foundation of free-trade

From the jurisprudential tradition, on which he drew heavily when describing civil society in the *Treatise*, Hume adopted the concept of "the person." The right fundamental to each member of civil society is the right to own, produce, and trade goods freely, a right for which every man is eligible in a genuine society. Economic independence is essential if any relationship beyond the range of particular benevolence is to be free from corruption. Moreover, he develops the universalism of his individualism: economic activity ought not to be restricted by corporate, national, religious, or racial barriers. Given his application of the concept of "personality" to all individuals, he objects to slavery, which had been basic to the economies of the ancient republics. Slavery is philosophically indefensible; in addition, it polarizes the social order, because those few citizens who are very rich, having slave labor at their command, have no need to employ the many who are poor. Personality was violated in a second way in ancient times in that the labor and materials required for public enterprises often were taken directly, without passing through the nexus of the market. This excluded personal choice; it was violent, except when heavily glazed with patriotic sugar. Third, excessive emphasis on public good, in the form of military greatness, meant that offensive wars were common; making war, not living well, was the great enterprise, with the result that relations among states were characterized by hostility and strife, not by bustling commerce. Personal individualism, by subordinating what is trumpeted by ambitious politicians and selfish interests as "the public good"—the conquest of colonies, beating the French, a favorable balance of both trade and power—gives priority to the welfare and happiness of the citizenry, as chosen by themselves. Fortunately, Hume found, when individuals strive to better their own condition, in normal circumstances they enhance also the true wealth and strength of the public.

In summary, we must say, first, that Hume had no illusions about enlightened despotism, for history showed that monarchs, born in high places, are more likely to be bad than good; second, that he, like Montesquieu, believed that intermediate powers are essential in a monarchy; third, that he had no great respect for either the Scottish or the English aristocracy—some, no doubt, were admirable, but all too many were incapable of anything more serious than trouting, chasing foxes, horse racing, and gambling; fourth, that his ideal society comprises few who are very rich and few who are very poor, with many in the middle; fifth, that

principles. On the close connection between Pitt, Patriotism, popularity, and the radical Tory populism of the middling rank in London, see Marie Peters, *Pitt and Popularity: The Patriot Minister and London Opinion during the Seven Years' War* (Oxford: Clarendon Press, 1980), esp. pp. 5–14, 24–27, 261–76. Also George Rudé, *Wilkes and Liberty: A Social Study of 1763 to 1774* (Oxford: Clarendon Press, 1962), pp. 20–21.

he thought that the "senate," either the national assembly in a perfect commonwealth or the reformed House of Lords, should be composed of those distinguished by their own accomplishments, not some ancestor's good fortune or ability; sixth, that he thought that wisdom and virtue, qualities found most among those of the middle rank, can be more influential in the councils of well-contrived republics than at the courts of kings. Indeed, Hume's attack on the old order, especially on royal courts, is so vehement, his picture of commercial society so glowing, that he might be thought to be sounding a call to arms against *l'ancien régime*.[52]

The Frustrations of a Reformer

During the last period of his life, extending from 1761, when he published the last tranche of the *History of England*, to 1776, when he died, Hume undertook no major new philosophical or historical work. During some of those years, he held government office: with the embassy at Paris for over two years (1763 through 1765) and as under secretary of state (northern department) for eleven months (February 1767 to January 1768). As a result, he became deeply interested in the politics of the first years of George III's reign. Although he had descended into politics primarily as an amusement and because the pay was good, his letters suggest that he was willing to stay on for some time; however, this was not to be, and his last years were spent in Edinburgh. Some of his writings of this period, 1763 to 1776—letters and certain revisions in the *History* and the essays—have been seen as evidence that his life ended with a "pessimistic Tory period."[53]

Although the old party division, Tory versus Whig, which had worried

[52] Miller points out (*Philosophy and Ideology*, pp. 196–201) that Burke agreed with Hume and Adam Smith on economic theory; from this he concludes that they would have agreed with him on the French Revolution. Perhaps it is true that Burke, by reason of great perspicacity, saw that the French Revolution was likely to spread ideas highly dangerous to capitalist economies, as C. B. Macpherson argues in *Burke* (Oxford: Oxford University Press, 1980), pp. 51–70. If so, Burke failed to convince the Foxites that they must choose between conservatism and the revolution; but then many of them were myopic because of "Scotch knowledge," that is, "political economy." The fact that Hume had many friends among the Scottish gentry is not decisive, for Charles James Fox, Charles Grey, and other Whig aristocrats opposed the war against France as black reaction, drawing its strength from patriotic Francophobia, religion ("fear of the godless republic"), persistent Tory zeal for divine-right kings, and Tory opposition to liberty (the rule of law). Was Hume more likely to defend the old order than Fox and Grey were?

[53] Kramnick, *Bolingbroke and His Circle*, p. 82. Kramnick draws upon Giuseppe Giarrizzo's *David Hume politico e storico* (Turin: Einaudi, 1962). See Forbes, *Hume's Philosophical Politics*, p. 174, and also Forbes's review of Giarrizzo's book in *The Historical Journal* 6 (1963): 280–95.

Hume before 1760, had lost its intensity now that the Stuarts were finally gone and the new king was refusing to let the Old Whigs (Newcastle, Rockingham, etc.) enjoy a monopoly of power, all was far from well at London. A vicious circle or syndrome, comprising many of the things Hume deplored, had set it. Many of the notables prominent in politics were incompetent by reason of ignorance, stupidity, or irresponsibility. The old prejudice against Scots, fanned to new heights by the frustrated ambitions of William Pitt and his brother-in-law, Richard Grenville (Earl Temple), and by hostility to Bute, was disrupting the normal process of assimilation. Mercantilist imperialism and popular bellicosity, the winds that filled Pitt's sails, were blowing storm force after the heady successes of the Seven Years' War. The middling rank in London was being enflamed against the Scots. By bungling, the American colonies were being lost. The high costs of war and empire were driving the national debt ever higher. The letters written by Hume in the 1763–1776 period, especially those written to intimate friends who knew his game, are full of subtleties, elaborate rhetoric, and exaggeration, as their author, deliberately maintaining the character of the great historian, pontificates on contemporary affairs; consequently, although their meaning is always clear, the letters cannot be taken at full face value. For the most part, the English ministers, he found, had only the shallowest understanding of policy; yet any Scot, no matter how clearheaded and diligent, would be driven from office by the barbarians on the Thames.[54] The letters reveal both pessimism and frustration. But was it "Tory" to deplore the bungling incompetence of the ministers and the chauvinistic demagoguery of Pitt?

"Anti-Scottish feeling in England was the eighteenth-century equivalent of anti-Semitism."[55] The resignation of Pitt and Temple in the fall of 1761—because the majority of the ministers were opposed to going to war with Spain and were ready to make a peace settlement far too easy on France for the merchants of Liverpool, Bristol, and London—together with the power of Bute, real or imagined, set the scene for The North Briton, in which Wilkes and Churchill denounced the Scots for depriving Englishmen of power and places. The Scots were aliens: "A Scot hath no more right to preferment in England than a Hanoverian or a Hottentot" (The North Briton, no. 34). They were pestiferous: "The restless and turbulent disposition of the Scottish nation before the Union, with their constant attachment to France and declared enmity to England, their re-

---

[54] In letters to friends, Hume frequently mentions the barbarians on the Thames. He is referring, not to the mob, but to the better sort. They were insular, arrogant, and poorly educated; they were too factious to appreciate impartial history; they were all too willing to foster and exploit the rage against the Scots. Letters, 1:384–85, 415, 417, 436, 492, 497–98; 2:209, 216, 269.

[55] Namier and Brooke, History of Parliament. The House of Commons, 1:168.

peated perfidies and rebellions since that period, with their servile behaviour in times of need and overbearing insolence [when] in power, have justly rendered the very name *Scot* hateful to every true Englishman" (*The North Briton,* no. 44).[56] Hume never forgave Wilkes: he had raised doubts about the Union; besides, anti-Scottish racism had blighted Hume's own career and those of several of his best friends.[57] Nor did he forgive Pitt: a man of genius, a demagogue, a "Patriot," a megalomaniac lusting for glory at any cost in blood and money.[58]

Some of Hume's friends—William Mure of Caldwell, Sir Gilbert Elliot of Minto, Sir Harry Erskine, James Oswald of Dunnikier—rallied to Bute and remained King's Friends after Bute had left office, but Hume's own forays into public life in the 1760s came about, not through them, but through Lord Hertford and his brother, Henry Seymour Conway, men related to Walpole. In 1763 Hertford was named the first post-war ambassador to France; he wished to have Hume as the secretary of his embassy. However, the post was given to Charles Bunbury, a well-known rake, the Duke of Richmond's brother-in-law, who was unacceptable to

[56] Quoted by G. Birkbeck Hill in *Letters of David Hume to William Strahan* (Oxford: Clarendon Press, 1888), p. 61.

[57] In 1763 Henry Fox proposed James Oswald for Chancellor of the Exchequer: "His abilities are so great . . . that nobody will think he was made because he is a Scotchman." While the king and Bute concurred in Fox's estimate of Oswald, they rejected the proposal because they feared a negative reaction. Namier and Brooke, *History of Parliament,* 1:168. Gilbert Elliot of Minto was held back as a Scot. Earlier, General Sir James St. Clair may have suffered: "[Pitt said] that General St. Clair was undoubtedly the best, the ablest officer, and the fittest person [to be commander in chief] . . . . I declared [Newcastle wrote] my opinion against St. Clair and nothing shall make me alter it. Certainly no great general, certainly a Scotchman who would fill the army with all Scotch, a low Scotchman. . . ." Ibid., 1:169 and 3:398. Although Hume was irked by "the factious Barbarians of London," there is some exaggeration in his ire; he saw the humor of Jonah swallowing the whale. When Gilbert Elliot, perhaps in jest and perhaps paraphrasing "be still a man," wrote that Hume should "above all continue still an Englishman," Hume retorted, "Am I, or are you, an Englishman? Will they allow us to be so? Do they not treat with Derision our Pretensions to that Name, and with Hatred our just Pretensions to surpass & to govern them?" Hill, *Letters of David Hume,* p. 57; *Letters,* 1:470.

[58] Three of the "Boy Patriots"—William Pitt, George Grenville, and Richard Grenville (Earl Temple)—contributed greatly to Hume's frustration with English politicians. Hume was appointed secretary to the embassy at Paris only after the fall of George Grenville's ministry in 1765. *Letters,* 2:502. Temple provided financial support for *The North Briton.* See R. R. Rea, *The English Press in Politics, 1760–1774* (Lincoln: University of Nebraska Press, 1963), pp. 19–41. Hume had an abiding dislike for William Pitt (Chatham)—a cutthroat, a quack, a madman. According to Lord Charlemont, "Nothing ever gave Hume more real vexation than the strictures made upon his *History* in the House of Lords by the great Lord Chatham. Soon after that speech I met Hume, and ironically wished him joy of the high honour that had been done him. 'Zounds, man,' said he, with more peevishness than I had ever seen him express; 'he's a Goth! he's a Vandal!' " Hill, *Letters of David Hume,* p. 195.

Hertford. From October 1763, Hume served as acting secretary; from July 3, 1765, as secretary; and from July 21, 1765, until November 17, 1765, as *chargé d'affaires*. When Hertford was appointed lord lieutenant of Ireland late in 1765, he proposed to take Hume with him as the secretary, but this fell through. According to Hume, "Lord Hertford, on his Arrival in London, found great Difficulty of executing his Intentions in my Favour. The Cry is loud against the Scots, and the present Ministry are unwilling to support any of our Countrymen, lest they bear the Reproach of being connected with Lord Bute."[59] However, in February 1767, when William Burke resigned as under secretary of state (northern department) in sympathy with his "cousin" Edmund Burke, who had gone out with the Rockingham party, Hertford put forward Hume's name, and Conway arranged to have Hume appointed the new under secretary. When Conway resigned as secretary of state (northern department) in January 1768, Hume's political career came to an end. Eighteen months later, at the end of August 1769, he was "back in Edinburgh, having 'done with all Ambition.' "[60] Taking his pensions with his royalties and investment income, no longer was he moved by necessity; besides, he had seen enough of the great.

John Wilkes returned from fugitive exile and began his efforts to get back into the House of Commons late in the winter of 1768, well before Hume left London. What struck Hume was the irresponsibility of the journalists, the gullibility of Londoners, and the weakness of the ministers.[61] This was a period of "Calumny, Faction, Madness and Disorder."[62] Hume was not alone in this opinion. Benjamin Franklin, for example, commented, "It is really an extraordinary event to see an outlaw and exile, of bad personal character, not worth a farthing, come over from France, set himself up as a candidate for the capital of the kingdom, miss his election only by being too late in his application, and immediately carrying it for the principal county. The mob . . . requiring gentlemen and ladies of all ranks, as they passed in their carriages, to shout for Wilkes and liberty."[63] Hume never underestimated Wilkes's ability to play on the mob's prejudices; he feared also that Pitt would exploit the

[59] *Letters*, 1:519.

[60] Mossner, *The Life of David Hume*, p. 556. The Conways were nephews of Robert Walpole's wife. Henry Seymour Conway was the second husband of Caroline, Lady Ailesbury, the daughter of the fourth Duke of Argyll. Although Hume had departed the great life, he and Henry Seymour Conway remained friends to the end; they vacationed together in 1769 and 1771; in 1776 Hume planned to pass some weeks in the autumn with Conway and Lady Ailesbury. *Letters*, 2:207, 246, 249, 320. Conway, according to Hume, was "the most moderate Man of the whole [Grafton ministry]." *Letters*, 2:152.

[61] See Hill, *Letters of David Hume*, pp. 120–24.

[62] *Letters*, 2:212.

[63] Hill, *Letters of David Hume*, p. 122.

situation to regain control over the government: "Think of the Impudence of that Fellow; and his Quackery; and his Cunning; and his Audaciousness; and judge of the Influence he will have over such a deluded Multitude."[64] Hume was somewhat reassured when finally, early in 1770, Grafton was succeeded by a serious politician, Lord North, but still was not fully convinced that the cauldron of popular frenzy could be kept from boiling over.

In 1741, when he published "Of the Liberty of the Press," Hume was convinced that freedom of the press, though certain to be abused, posed no great danger to the public mind; in fact, there was much to be said for this form of liberty. The multitude—Plato's great beast—is neither as gullible nor as dangerous as once was believed, especially if not assembled.

A man reads a book or pamphlet alone and coolly. There is none present from whom he can catch the passion by contagion. He is not hurried away by the force and energy of action. And should he be wrought up to ever so seditious a humour, there is no violent resolution presented to him, by which he can immediately vent his passion. The liberty of the press, therefore, however abused, can scarce ever excite popular tumults or rebellion. And as to those murmurs or secret discontents it may occasion, 'tis better they should get vent in words, that they may come to the knowledge of the magistrate before it be too late, in order to his providing a remedy against them. Mankind, it is true, have always a greater propension to believe what is said to the disadvantage of their governors, than the contrary; but this inclination is inseparable from them, whether they have liberty or not. A whisper may fly as quick, and be as pernicious as a pamphlet. Nay, it will be more pernicious, where men are not accustomed to think freely, or distinguish between truth and falshood.

It has also been found, as the experience of mankind increases, that the *people* are no such dangerous monster as they have been represented, and that it is in every respect better to guide them, like rational creatures, than to lead or drive them, like brute beasts. Before the United Provinces set the example, toleration was deemed incompatible with good government; and it was thought impossible, that a number of religious sects could live together in harmony and peace, and have all of them an equal affection to their common country, and to each other. ENGLAND has set a like example of civil liberty; and though this liberty seems to occasion some small ferment at present, it has not as yet produced any pernicious effects; and it is to be hoped, that men, being every day more accustomed to the free discussion of public affairs, will improve in the judgment of them, and be with greater difficulty seduced by every idle rumour and popular clamour.

[64] *Letters*, 2:197–98.

These paragraphs were withdrawn from the 1770, 1771, and 1777 editions. In the 1777 edition, Hume added one terse sentence: "It must however be allowed, that the unbounded liberty of the press, though it be difficult, perhaps impossible, to propose a suitable remedy for it, is one of the evils, attending those mixt forms of government."[65] Hume had not changed his estimate of journalists; in 1741 he saw them as mercenary and irresponsible, but believed that they would do little real harm. In the final period of his life, having seen the impact of *The North Briton* and then the hysteria attending the "Wilkes and Liberty" crisis, he came to fear deeply the power of a bigoted, racist, chauvinist press. Like Plato, he did not blame the multitude; the culprits were the demagogic politicians and the malevolent journalists, who intoxicate and enrage the people for their own knavish ends.

During the winter of 1771, Hume feared that North's ministry, running before Pitt and Patriotism, would begin a war with Spain over the Falkland Islands: Britain's claim to title was weak; the islands were of little value; the costs would be vast. As the ministry increased the land tax and mobilized for war, Hume reverted to a familiar refrain, the high cost of war. Some aspects of contemporary affairs, he agreed, went well, but not all.

> But when I reflect, that, from 1740 to 1761, during the Course of no more than 21 Years, while a most pacific Monarch sat on the Throne of France, the Nation [Great Britain] ran in Debt about a hundred Millions; that the wise and virtuous Minister, Pitt, could contract more Incumbrances, in six months of an unnecessary War, than we have been able to discharge during eight Years of Peace; and that we persevere in the same frantic Maxims; I can forsee nothing but certain and speedy Ruin either to the Nation or to the public Creditors. The last, tho' a great Calamity, woud be a small one in comparison; but I cannot see how it can be brought about, while these Creditors fill all the chief Offices and are the Men of greatest Authority in the Nation. In other Respects the Kingdom may be thriving: The Improvement of our Agriculture is a good Circumstance; tho' I believe our Manufactures do not advance; and all depends on our Union with America, which, in the Nature of things, cannot long subsist. But all this is nothing in comparison

---

[65] *Essays*, pp. 604, 13. In 1772 Hume wrote to William Strahan that he wished the words "and happy," which he had dropped, restored to his description of the British constitution as "singular and happy." He explained, "I own that I was so disgusted with the Licentiousness of our odious Patriots, that I have struck out the words *and happy*, in this new Edition; but as the English Government is certainly happy, though probably not calculated for Duration, by reason of its excessive Liberty, I believe it will be as well as restore them." *Letters*, 2:261.

of the continual Encrease of our Debts, in every idle War, into which, it seems, the Mob of London are to rush every Minister.[66]

In the last months of his life, Hume's best prose dealt with the misconduct of American affairs. Throughout the decade before 1776, Hume regarded the eventual independence of the colonies as inevitable, even desirable in the nature of things: this was consistent with his well-developed views on extensive empires and the exploitation of provinces by free governments, as well as his confidence in free trade. His ringing summations in 1775 follow on from principles established earlier. They reveal also his contempt for the incompetence of the rulers of Great Britain. Even if it were desirable to suppress by force the American desire for independence—he had no interest in the lawyers' insistence that Parliament had a sovereign right to impose taxes on the colonies—how could this possibly be done by an efficient free government, let alone one whose ministers were blind, lazy, and indecisive? On October 25, 1775, he summed up his stand as follows:

We hear that some of the Ministers have propos'd in Council, that both Fleet and Army be withdrawn from America, and these Colonists be left entirely to themselves. I wish I had been a Member of His Majesty's Cabinet Council, that I might have seconded this Opinion. I shoud have said, that this Measure only anticipates the necessary Course of Events a few Years; that a forced and every day more precarious Monopoly of about 6 or 700,000 Pounds a year of Manufactures, was not worth contending for; that we shoud preserve

---

[66] Ibid., 2:237. In his last revision of his account of Elizabeth's reign, Hume commented, in an appendix, that "the minister [Pitt], in the war began in 1754, was, in some periods, allowed to lavish in two months as great a sum as was granted by parliament to queen Elizabeth in forty-five years. The extreme frivolous object of the late war, and the great importance of hers, set this matter in still a stronger light. . . . But our late delusions have much exceeded any thing known in history, not even excepting those of the crusades. For, I suppose, there is no mathematical, still less an arithemetical demonstration, that the road to the Holy Land was not the road to Paradise, as there is, that the endless encrease of national debts is the direct road to national ruin. But having now compleatly reached that goal, it is needless at present to reflect on the past. It will be found in the present year, 1776, that all the revenues of this island, north of Trent and west of Reading, are mortgaged or anticipated for ever." *History of England*, 4:373n. In 1770 Hume added a paragraph to the essay "Of Public Credit," making the connection between ambition, war, and national debt: "It is very tempting to a minister to employ such an expedient [war and borrowing], as enables him to make a great figure during his administration, without overburthening the people with taxes, or exciting any immediate clamours against himself. The practice, therefore, of contracting debt will almost infallibly be abused, in every government. It would scarcely be more imprudent to give a prodigal son a credit in every banker's shop in London, than to impower a statesman to draw bills, in this manner, upon posterity." *Essays*, p. 352. Hume was convinced that the Seven Years' War had been fomented by "some obscure designing Men, contrary to the Intentions of the two Kings, the two Ministries, even the Generality of the two Nations." *New Hume Letters*, p. 235.

the greater part of this Trade even if the Ports of America were open to all Nations; that it was very likely, in our method of proceeding, that we shoud be disappointed in our Scheme of conquering the Colonies; and that we ought to think beforehand how we were to govern them, after they were conquer'd. Arbitrary Power can extend its oppressive Arm to the Antipodes; but a limited Government can never long be upheld at a distance, even where no Disgusts have interven'd: Much less, where such violent Animosities have taken place. We must, therefore, annul all the Charters; abolish every democratical Power in every Colony; repeal the Habeas Corpus Act with regard to them; invest every Governor with full discretionary or arbitrary Powers; confiscate the Estates of all the chief Planters; and hang three fourths of their Clergy. To execute such Acts of destructive Violence twenty thousand Men will not be sufficient; nor thirty thousand to maintain them, in so wide and disjointed a Territory. And who are to pay so great an Army? The Colonists cannot at any time, much less after reducing them to such a State of Desolation: We ought not, and indeed cannot, in the over-loaded or rather overwhelm'd and totally ruin'd State of our Finances. Let us, therefore, lay aside all Anger; shake hands, and part Friends. Or if we retain any anger, let it only be against ourselves for our past Folly; and against that wicked Madman, Pitt; who has reducd us to our present Condition.[67]

In the spring of 1776, one of Hume's physicians recommended that he go to Bath for his health. At an inn on the way, he came upon the Earl of Sandwich, the First Lord of the Admiralty, and some friends, together with "two or three Ladies of Pleasure," out on a trouting expedition. This ministerial irresponsibility Hume found incredible.

I do not remember in all my little or great Knowlege of History . . . such another Instance; and I am sure such a one does not exist: That the First Lord of the Admiralty, who is absolute and uncontrouled Master in his Department, shou'd, at a time when the Fate of the British Empire is in dependance, and in dependance on him, find so much Leizure, Tranquillity, Presence of Mind and Magnanimity, as to have Amusement in trouting during three Weeks near sixty Miles from the scene of Business, and during the most critical Season of the Year. There needs but this single Fact to decide the Fate of the Nation.[68]

Hume had not changed his politics, but perhaps he had become less hopeful for the realization of true principles. The forces of conservatism had proven strong: old prejudices still shaped public opinion; knavish politicians still played the Patriot game; journalists still lived off alarms, scandals, racism, and bigotry; the nation's foreign policy was still shaped

[67] *Letters*, 2:300–301; also 303.
[68] Ibid., p. 319.

by influential merchants. Moreover, the British constitution had not been reformed.

The Dangers of Civic Virtue

One way conservatives defend an established order is to assert that it has proven both effective and acceptable, and that, given the fact that it is the result of myriads of discrete decisions made over many centuries, no truly legitimate alternative is possible. The laws, manners, and institutions of the nation are a magnificent historical achievement. Future change is not rejected, but it must come, it is insisted, in the same way that change came in the past, incrementally, as the response of the national genius to particular cases and situations. This is the strategy of Burkean conservatism. Hume's theory of social and political change is far different: his moral philosophy is not a philosophy of group subjectivism. He was prepared, as he says repeatedly, to take the risk of being described as "an abstruse thinker." He was prepared to analyze the polity radically—the socioeconomic order and its governmental system—and to evaluate it, ascertaining what, if any, improvements might be made. Subsequently he was prepared, as we have seen, to recommend major changes in both institutions and policies.

His attitude to national states, too, was far from conservative. If one contends that an established order, a customary way of life, or an old constitution is good and ought to be cherished, one is recommending the traditional order of a particular city or nation, for example, the laws of Abdera or the laws of England. And when one contrasts the private good with the public good, the latter is the good of a particular city or nation. On this basic point, early modern conservatism—whether in the form of divine right or Burke's custodial aristocracy—and the civic tradition, inspired by the small republics of antiquity, are alike. Both conservatism and the civic tradition have a specific public in mind and require service and loyalty to that public by all its members. On this point Hume stands remote from both the civic tradition and conservatism. Shaftesbury, "that excellent author," in a passage cited by Hume, had discussed the human tendency to contract loyalty or obligation to smaller and smaller groups: thus humankind is divided into empires and kingdoms, and these into cities and provinces; then these, in turn, into factions or parties. The result is the wheels-within-wheels problem. Hume saw clearly that morality cannot be based on the benevolence that follows love: since we love only those somehow related to ourselves, and the nearest dearest, a system of morality based on love alone would be divisive. It is true, of course, that we expect people to do good works for their families, friends, neighbors, and country, but these are only wheels within the great wheel. Strive as we may to do good for ourselves, our neighbors, our country, we have a moral obligation to respect justice.

Hume recognizes that nations differ greatly in their characters, the result of both moral and physical causes: there are differences brought on by sympathy among those living together, differences brought about by geographic circumstances, differences in cultural experience, differences in religions, economies, and constitutions. These are historical facts; their importance is not questioned. Hume recognizes also the need for distinct governments; he would never advocate one state, one government, for the world. The great task of administering justice must be undertaken in Europe, even if it is neglected between the tropics. Besides, there are important practical reasons why states should not be too large. States of moderate size are best: large enough to prevent participatory tumult, but small enough and numerous enough to check power and authority and to encourage emulation. The truth is that *"nothing is more favourable to the rise of politeness and learning, than a number of neighbouring and independent states, connected together by commerce and policy. The emulation, which naturally arises among those neighbouring states, is an obvious source of improvement: But what I would chiefly insist on is the stop, which such limited territories give both to power and to authority."*[69]

However, the boundaries of states, like the titles of kings, are largely fortuitous. Just where they are drawn often depends on accidental and circumstantial factors like the course of rivers, the outcome of battles, and royal marriages—such as the union, in 1603, of the crowns of Scotland and England because Elizabeth had died without an immediate heir, while James was the great-great-grandson of Henry VII—as well as political decisions, such as the bad one made by the House of Commons in 1606 to reject the union of the kingdoms, and the good one for union in 1705–1707. The idea that a nation is created by a general will expressed in a social contract is false. Nor is there anything substantial—racial, religious, or cultural—that fixes the boundaries of a state; there is no reason why each nation ought to be a distinct state with its own government. In the case of England and Scotland, reason called for a full union a hundred years before 1707: England would have been relieved of the dangers posed by the northern kingdom; Scotland, instead of suffering neglect without independence, would have moved more rapidly away from Gothic turbulence, grim religiosity, and grinding poverty. Unhappily, both sides were blind: the English from prejudice, which represented Scots as contemptible, and the Scots from pride.[70]

[69] *Essays*, p. 119; also pp. 340–41.
[70] *History of England*, 5:34, 66. It is evident that Hume thought that Scots should not

Individualism implies universalism. Hume's moral thought deals, not with Athenians or Romans, French, or English, but with humankind. This part of his work, like the rest, is based on his view of human nature, on the nature of beings of the human kind. Justice for him is blind to racial, religious, or linguistic differences. It ought to be applied to the Chinese, the Jews, the French, the English, and the Scots alike whenever they have economic relations, whether or not there is a common government. The rules of justice apply equally to all involved in the economic game. Moreover, that game is not the same game played separately on many different fields; through commerce, the local games overlap and tend to run together—for Hume, the more, the better. The author of nature, by creating a highly diversified world, made it clear that human beings are to trade extensively; accordingly, neither the city nor the nation can be the ultimate public. The English public, the French public, the Scottish public, the Dutch public, all are but parts of the European public, in turn but a part of the worldwide public.

Hume saw clearly how false patriotism distorts both understanding and morality: the vulgar think of other nations in crude stereotypes; the vanity, ambition, and interest of nations cause politicians to act unjustly; conquering princes, gory from barbarous wars, are acclaimed heroes; the nation's cause is God's cause; the cry, *delenda est Carthago* (Carthage must be destroyed), reveals the patriotic heart, and scholars write their histories according to "national prepossessions and animosities." He saw clearly how pleas of "national interest" are used to exploit the people, how pretense of public good is always the tactic of those who want the government's laws and policies bent their way. Only piety, he finds, rivals patriotism as the virtue of knaves. Almost always the best way to promote true public interest, both domestically and internationally, is to let individuals work for their own interest within the rules of justice.

Rousseau was fully aware of the implications of civic particularism. Contrasting ancient patriotism with Christian universalism, he wrote,

> The patriotic spirit is an exclusive spirit which makes us look on everyone but our fellow citizens as strangers, and almost as enemies. Such was the spirit of Sparta and Rome. The spirit of Christianity on the contrary makes us look on all men as our brothers, as the children of God. Christian charity will not allow of odious differences between the compatriot and the foreigner, it is neither good to make republicans nor warriors, but only Chris-

---

allow romantic ideas about Scotland's past—disturbed by grandees and fanatics—to blind them to the advantages of the union with England. Ambitious young Scots should learn to speak and write the common language in the English manner. *Letters*, 2:154–55. Hume's conviction that the union, finally achieved in 1707, was highly advantageous to both countries helps explain his outrage at the exploitation of anti-Scottish sentiment in London during the last fifteen years of his life.

tians and men; its ardent zeal embraces indifferently the whole human race. Thus it is true that Christianity is in its very sanctity contrary to the particular social spirit.[71]

Hume's individualism, derived in part at least from natural jurisprudence, allies him with Christian universalism, rather than ancient civic particularism. "That neglect," he declared, "almost total, of truth and justice, which sovereign states discover in their transactions with each other, is an evil universal and inveterate; is one great source of the misery to which the human race is continually exposed."[72]

While he rejects the narrow loyalty, the hostility to aliens, of a strong civic commitment, he rejects also the universalism of political empire, Roman or British, and of a universal church: extensive power and authority stifle the human spirit. The primary relationship, beyond the scope of love, is economic; therefore, the universal order is economic, not political or religious. Whether or not the English and the French speak of each other as brothers and sisters in God makes little difference; what is important is that they open their eyes to their mutual interest in trade, and get on with the pursuit of that interest in the most expedient way. Although Hume admits that the universe, with its order and commodious arrangements, bears marks of having been created by a designing creator, ordinarily he refrains from reading this creator's mind. He limits himself to the discovery of the effective causes operating within the creation, and abstains from trying to reveal divine purposes. But when he writes about trade, especially international trade, he invokes divine authority; those who erect barriers against trade act contrary to the will of "the Author of the world."[73] Hostility among nations is destructive; it is contrary to humanity, contrary to the good of the true public, the great society of humankind. In contrast, trade is in the interest of the entire species. Trade is nature's way to individual liberty and general prosperity. Human beings are to love their families, friends, and neighbors; as for all the others, make trade, not war, is nature's great command.

A New Beginning

Again and again Hume returns to human nature as the true basis of morals. Following Shaftesbury, Hutcheson, and Butler, he insists that neither the philosopher nor the politician scorn what "wise nature" has pro-

[71] Letter to Usteri, 1763, quoted by Lucio Colletti, *From Rousseau to Lenin: Studies in Ideology and Society* (New York: Monthly Review Press, 1972), p. 177. See also "First Letter from the Mountain," in *Oeuvres Complètes de Jean-Jacques Rousseau* (Paris: Edition Gallimard, 1964), 3:703–5.

[72] *History of England*, 2:133. See *Treatise*, pp. 567–69.

[73] *Essays*, pp. 324, 329; *Treatise*, pp. 514, 520.

vided. This is true whether they are explaining the acquisition of knowledge or deciding how the primary property distribution should be made, to whom to render allegiance, who should be the social leaders, or what should be the goals of public policy and how to foster industry. Setting aside the dictates of "authorities" prescribing from on high, discover what conforms to human nature; begin there.

Hume joins Shaftesbury and Hutcheson in rejecting the absolutist view that righteousness is obedience to a sovereign legislator, either mortal or immortal. First, that view requires that the legislator's will be done regardless of what is commanded. Second, it explains obligation largely in terms of self-interest. Third, in an age of many civil and ecclesiastical sovereigns, it may result in conflicting accounts of righteousness. Hume rejects also the view that the rules of righteousness can be known by "reason alone." Demonstrative argument is analysis of ideas composed of defined components, for example, angles, lines, and points. Its conclusions are timeless; they never change. In contrast, morality concerns the conduct of men in society in changing circumstances; it relates to a realm in which men act to achieve good and to avoid evil, and in which beliefs—about facts, about causes and effects, and about what is good and what bad—influence their conduct. Reason alone—the reason active in demonstration—can provide neither content nor obligation for morals. Consequently, having rejected both voluntarism and rationalism, Hume turns to human nature and to the judicious spectator for the origin of the standards and rules of society. First, as human beings grow up, they are formed to some extent—as Shaftesbury said, no innate ideas are required—by experience and reflection. From self-centered infants they grow into moral beings; as they advance to "the age of reason," they acquire beliefs about moral good and evil. Second, they acquire beliefs about facts and about causes and effects. Moreover, both the relevant circumstances and the prevailing beliefs about facts and about causation may change over time, thus changing the moral rules, as shown by the Church's reversal of its teachings on the important question of tyrannicide.

For Hume the rules of civil society, like the standards of "family-society," are not arbitrary; as he says again and again in the *Treatise*, they are not the products of artifice. Men live in various kinds of society; the standards and rules prescribe the conduct appropriate to those kinds of society. This is why Hume is hostile to "higher authorities"—divine-right monarchs, prophets, monks, fanatics, projectors—who assert a right to rule because of truths beyond those achieved by experience and reflection. This is why he writes about "fundamental laws," and about a perpetual and inalienable right to good government. This is why he dismisses the contract theory: no breach of contract is required to justify resistance to bad rulers. This is why he finds the desire of the common man to gain "all the necessaries, and many of the conveniences of life" neither sinful nor irrational.

Hume's rehabilitation of the passions does not imply that reasoning cannot be powerful in forming and reforming morals. But here reasoning means, not the demonstrative method of reasoning, but the experimental method of reasoning. Hume does not deny the role of moralists and politicians; on the contrary, he insists on their importance. Provided they accept the goals of human nature as the ends to be sought, they can, by the experimental method of reasoning, first, help to clear away pernicious old beliefs, and second, help to discover the best means to those ends. The value of testing our beliefs about facts and causation is especially great in politics and economics, where error readily becomes conventional wisdom, to be transmitted unchallenged from one generation to another.

Hume regarded many of the verities of the vulgar—Jacobite, Tory and Whig, noble and common—as false, the detritus of inadequate or misunderstood experience, misleading analogies, old prejudices, religious bigotry, national pride, disguised selfish interest, and bad education; what was needed was painstaking use of the experimental method—neither thoughtless, mechanical experience, nor the imposition of an ideology, but experience and reflection. Far from being either complacent or resigned, Hume sought to reform public opinion radically, starting with Britain, by discovering sound political and economic principles.

It is surprising to see how advanced Hume's views were before he was thirty years of age; after 1741 most of his work was elaboration and application. His first undertaking in politics was to convince the Jacobites that the time had come for them to accept the new order: the Union of 1707, the singular English constitution, even the German kings. That new order, he found, had no intellectually respectable argument capable of winning the allegiance of those who, under the spur of present grievances, dreamed and sang of old days and old loyalties. The argument he originated and then put to the wise, after analyzing how the multitude thinks, is that an established order is to be evaluated in terms of general interest; indeed, to refuse to do so, to insist on other tests, is immoral. Any established regime is a rightful regime. In addition, it may also be the best, the most useful regime for the circumstances; that is a matter of judgment, not of title. In all this Hume was justifying the present by comparison with the past; here, as an advocate of the post-revolutionary, Hanoverian settlement, he addressed himself to all those Scots who doubted the legitimacy of the new order. Those who believed that olden times had been glorious were sadly deluded. For many generations, the common people of Scotland had suffered "the ravages of a barbarous nobility" and "the more intolerable insolence of seditious preachers." Finally, in 1707 they had gained civil liberty—a stable regime and the rule of law—the basis for economic and social progress. Paradoxically, as a result of the union "with England, their once hated adversary, they [had] happily attained the experience of a government perfectly regular, and exempt from all violence and injustice."[74]

Next, with the argument for the new allegiance made, he turned a sharp North British eye on the strange world of English politics. He found the English constitution a unique combination of the old (precommercial) and the new (commercial); yet it was a constitution that should be supported and strengthened, especially since, if it failed, the replacement was likely to be either absolute monarchy or absolute oligarchy. And English politicians, he found, were plagued by misconceptions: many denounced the ministers in the name of good old days that had never existed in either old Rome or old England; at the same time the ministers, blind to the full potential of a commercial society, persisted with policies that, although beneficial to some merchants, to the moneyed interest, and those who lived and profited by war, were highly detrimental to the general public, especially those living in provinces remote from London.

Then, again widening his focus, he looked ahead with that keen vision sometimes given to those whose cultures have undergone traumatic change, and in a modest way opened up the prospect of a new republican European order based on the potential of commercial society. The essay "Of the Idea of a perfect Commonwealth" outlines the kind of government appropriate for the new Great Britain, the new France, and so forth.

What influence Hume's proposals—his proposals for the reform of the representation of the people; his proposal for a house of life peers; his advocacy of unlimited religious toleration; his criticism of the English oligarchy's exploitation of Ireland, Scotland, and America; and his hostility to extensive empire—may have had on later thought can only be the subject of speculation. His insistence on the value of well-devised constitutions and the rule of law, a cardinal feature of his liberalism, probably had some influence, especially in America. The socioeconomic model he presented as the means by which the common people may be liberated from the power of the great was largely a prescription for the Scottish

[74] *History of England*, 5:19; 6:223. Adam Smith was to make much the same point: "By the union with England, the middling and inferior ranks of people in Scotland gained a compleat deliverance from the power of an aristocracy which had always before oppressed them." *The Wealth of Nations*, 2 vols. (Oxford: Clarendon Press, 1976), 2:944. Hume observed that it was not until the power of the chiefs had been broken—the heritable jurisdictions were abolished in 1747—that the liberties essential to civil society had come to be enjoyed by the people in the Highlands. "The Highlands of Scotland have long been entitled by law to every privilege of British subjects; but it was not till very lately that the common people could in fact enjoy these privileges." *History of England*, 1:173–74.

situation; yet that model, elaborated and popularized by Adam Smith—
and then distorted by "men of system" so enthralled by the beautiful in-
tricacies of the means that they forgot the end, just as Smith had predicted
they would—was to remain influential long after Hume and his progressive friends were dead. In the nineteenth century, his model of civil society
was to be adopted by many reformers—liberals—throughout Europe, as
they sought to topple the religious and noble elites of *l'ancien régime*.

INDEX

abstruse thought, 105, 148–49, 193, 195, 203–4, 204n, 206, 219, 224–25, 224n, 258, 259–60, 310

Act of Settlement, 13, 60–61

agriculture, 181, 210, 229, 233, 257, 260, 261, 262, 264, 267, 268, 269, 297

Aikenhead, Thomas, 13

Alfred, King, 283–84

allegiance: causes of, 170–71; legalistic theories, 171–72, 231; party theories, 172, 237; reasons for, 172–74

America, 19, 168, 219, 307–9, 316

anger, 128

Anne, Queen, 10n, 60, 61

Árdal, Páll S., 110n

Argathelians, 10, 10n, 247–49n, 273n

Argyll, Archibald Campbell (Earl of Islay), 3rd Duke of, 10, 10n, 247–48n, 273n, 285n

Argyll, John Campbell, 2nd Duke of, 10, 10n, 247–48n, 273n

Aristotle (and Aristotelian), 16, 17, 18, 26, 55, 160, 195, 218, 229, 291–92, 296, 297, 298

"Author of the world, the," 269, 313. See also Providence; wise nature

avarice and ambition, 5, 24, 56, 69, 139, 191, 206

Bacon, Francis, 37, 106n, 107n, 214

Bank of England, 61

Barbeyrac, Jean, 15n, 16n, 27n, 91, 94n, 95n

Bayle, Pierre, 78, 105n

beauty, 78–80, 129–30

belief: defined, 115, 198; proofs and probabilities, 200n; sources of beliefs, 148, 197–98, 199–201. See also "custom and education"

beliefs: of the vulgar, 172, 202–3, 206–8, 214–15, 219–20, 280; of the wise, 210, 212; role of general rules, 202, 209–10, 212; skepticism, 214–15. See also abstruse thought; experimental method of reasoning, the

benevolenc: Hume's predecessors, 41–42, 49, 78, 81–83, 86–88, 90, 99, 103–4, 105n, 107; private benevolence (Hume on), 111, 113–14, 118, 119, 120, 125, 128, 132, 155; general benevolence (Hume on), 136–40

Berry, Christopher J., 211–12n, 218n

Bolingbroke, Henry St. John, Viscount, 11n, 227n, 244

Brewer, John, 11n, 259–60n

Bunbury, Sir Charles, 304–5

Burke, Edmund (and Burkean), 7, 9, 211, 219, 221, 222, 223, 229, 274, 294–95, 298, 302n, 305, 310

Burke, William, 305

Bute, John Stuart, Earl of, 303, 304n

Butler, Rt. Rev. Joseph, 14, 37, 39, 59, 97–105, 107, 110, 111, 111n, 116, 119, 125n, 130, 133, 145, 146, 146n, 151, 199, 204, 313

Calvinism, 11, 13, 23, 25–26, 37, 59, 91n, 228n, 278n

Campbell, Archibald (Prof.), 13

Camic, Charles, 228n

Cant, R. G., 36n

Carlyle, Alexander of Inveresk, 107n, 248n

Carmichael,Gerschom, 14, 35, 35n, 76, 107

Carneades, 16

Charlemont, James Caulfield, Earl of, 304n

Charles I, King, 62, 143n, 183n, 207, 209, 242, 245, 255, 256

Charteret, John (Earl Granville), 227n, 248n

Cicero, 36, 42, 105n, 106n

civil humanism, 5, 62, 226, 227n, 229n, 230

civil society, 123, 159, 168. See also economic society, governance

Clark, J.C.D., 245n

Clarke, Samuel, 4, 37–44, 45, 77, 93–94, 97, 98, 106, 109, 133

clergymen. See religion

Colley, Linda, 245n

commerce. See trade

conjectural history, 161

rules and standards, 124–25, 125n, 140–41

Sabine, G. H., 205n
St. Augustine (and Augustinian), 59, 105, 190
St. Paul, 42–43, 101, 109
St. Thomas Aquinas (and Thomistic), 15, 16, 17, 105
Salic law, 172, 209
Sandwich, John, Earl of, 309
Scotland: Highlands, 316n; political parties, 245–47; pre-union, 207, 208n, 228n, 234–35n, 245, 278, 315–16; economic prospects, 270–71n. See also Jacobites; Union of 1707
Sekora, John, 258–59n
"self-liking" (Mandeville), 66–67, 115
Shaftesbury, Anthony Ashley Cooper, 3rd Earl of, 4, 5, 14, 37, 39n, 43, 47–59, 63n, 69, 74, 76, 77, 78, 82, 84, 87, 89, 97, 105, 116, 130, 133, 138, 145, 149, 280n, 281, 310, 313, 314
Simpson, John (Prof.), 13
Sister Peg, 288n
skepticism, Hume's variety of, 196, 198, 199, 205n, 209, 214–15, 275n
Skinner, Quentin, 11n, 15n
slavery, 185–86, 261, 266, 301
Smith, Adam, 3, 5, 15n, 37, 145n, 173n, 180n, 181, 182, 183, 186, 193, 206n, 223, 229, 293, 295, 295n, 302n, 316n, 317
Smith, Norman Kemp, 213n, 278n
sociability, 16, 28, 29, 51, 53–54, 58, 100, 103, 133, 151
social passions, Hume's four, 112
society, kinds of, 120, 152–53, 162
Socrates, 123, 293
spectator, the, 5, 40, 50, 83, 92, 122, 123, 128, 133–36, 169
Squadrone Volante, 9, 10n, 247–49n, 288n
Stair, James Dalymple, Viscount, 36, 36n
standing army. See militia
St. Clair, General James, 304n
Stewart of Allanbank, Archibald, 9, 10, 241, 246, 247–48n, 273n
Stockton, C. N., 264n
Strahan, William, 307n
Suarez, William, 15n

sympathy, 5, 53, 89, 114, 116, 122, 123, 130–33, 151, 167, 190

Temple, Richard Grenville-Temple, 2nd Earl, 247n, 303, 304n
"the ancient constitution." See English constitution, (Hume on) the
The Craftsman, 256, 273n
The North Briton, 303–4, 304n, 307
theology and conflict, 51–53, 276–77, 281
Tierney, George, 223n
Tinwald, Lord. See Charles Erskine
"to better their condition," 69, 72–73, 258
Toland, John, 39n, 280–81n
toleration, 61, 75, 96, 223, 280, 280n, 306, 316
trade, freedom of, 20, 31, 158, 159, 269–70, 270n, 312, 313
Tuck, Richard, 22n
Tucker, Josiah, 271n
Tully, James, 32n, 63n
Turgot, Anne-Robert-Jacques, 272n
tyrannicide, 143, 143n, 206

Union of 1707, 9, 11, 13, 228, 229n, 245, 248n, 267, 311, 315–16

Venturi, Franco, 281n
Vinnius, 36
virtues, natural and artificial, 117, 118–19, 120–22, 124–25, 125n, 140–41
virtues and abilities, 126, 128–29
Voet, 36

Walpole, Sir Robert (Orford), 10, 10n, 11, 11n, 64, 226, 227n, 230, 244, 247n, 248n, 250, 256, 272, 273n, 300n, 304, 305n
"warmth in the cause of virtue," 149n, 249n
wars, 60, 61, 171, 271, 299, 300n, 300–301, 303, 307
"wheels within wheels," 55, 237, 310
Whelan, Frederick G., 3, 6–7, 194n, 282–83n
Whig history, 252–54
Whigs, political and religious, 9, 10, 11, 13, 209, 241, 241n, 246–47, 249n, 255, 277, 280n, 284
William (of Orange), King, 60, 61, 63, 242, 272

Wilkes, John, 303–4, 305, 307
"wise and virtuous men," 5, 49, 57, 147
wise and the vulgar, the, 203, 210, 211, 212, 219–20
wise nature, 85, 100, 145, 145n, 199n, 199–200, 204–5, 291
"wise politicians," 213–14. *See also* politi-

cal science and reform
Wolin, Sheldon S., 205n
Wollaston, William, 4, 37, 44–45, 77, 106

Xenophon, 259

Young, Edward, 272